PRAISE FOR *MUSIC WITH STANLEY CAVELL IN MIND*

A collection of exciting new essays by philosophers and practitioners of music in the full breadth of its range of art and thought; an exemplary display of versality and insight.

—LYDIA GOEHR, Fred and Fannie Mack
Professor of Humanities, Columbia University, USA

At last, a comprehensive book on the rich and beguiling relationships between philosophy and music in Cavell's work. These essays—which mix biography, philosophy, and critical reflection with a wide array of musical examples—give us deep insights about the ways music is inseparable from the varied forms, passions, and intentionalities of human life.

—MICHAEL GALLOPE, Associate Professor, Cultural Studies &
Comparative Literature, Music, University of Minnesota, USA

In his memoir, Cavell recalls a famous anecdote. During a performance, the jazz saxophonist Ben Webster once stopped improvising on "Blue Skies" and afterwards when someone asked why he stopped playing so abruptly, he replied that he forgot the words. The authors of these essays recall, deeply and imaginatively, the music woven into Stanley Cavell's words and the meanings intimated by a wide range of musickings, some of which he probed with his incomparable acumen, other forms he did not (e.g., punk). The range of referents runs from Schoenberg, Webern, and Cage to Elvis Costello without being strained or contrived. The contributors include a composer along with professors of music, education, art history, and philosophy. Each in a singular way offers a lesson in listening to the music of Cavell's words and the meanings made available by a wide range of musical genres.

—VINCENT COLAPIETRO, Professor Emeritus of Philosophy &
African American Studies, Pennsylvania State University, USA

Also by David LaRocca from Bloomsbury

Praise for *The Thought of Stanley Cavell and Cinema: Turning Anew to the Ontology of Film a Half-Century after* The World Viewed

A brilliant collection of original essays by major figures in the field. The genius of Cavell's writings on film is in sharp focus throughout—likewise the continued provocation of *The World Viewed* and its successor books and essays.

—MICHAEL FRIED, J. R. Herbert Boone Emeritus Professor of Humanities and the History of Art, Johns Hopkins University, USA

Stanley Cavell argued that film exists in a state of philosophy. Part of what he meant by this was that thinking about a film is a way of doing philosophy. That has been his influential and most controversial claim. The authors in this collection explore what he might have meant in ways more variegated, thoughtful, original and illuminating than anything I have seen before. *The Thought of Stanley Cavell and Cinema*, exemplary in its clarity and carefulness, is a watershed both in our understanding of Cavell and of film itself.

—ROBERT PIPPIN, Evelyn Stefansson Nef Distinguished Service Professor, University of Chicago, USA

Praise for *Inheriting Stanley Cavell: Memories, Dreams, Reflections*

Inheriting Stanley Cavell, beautifully edited by David LaRocca, is so much more than a gathering of reminiscences and testimonials. So many of the pieces in the volume prove gripping, and they cumulatively transformed my sense of what Cavell had accomplished. This volume makes a strong case for the revolution that Cavell's extraordinary philosophic sensibility, powerful presence as a teacher, and wide-range of concerns brought about in North American philosophy. For many of the contributors, Cavell not only revived their faith in philosophy, but showed them what it meant to be alive in their feelings and thinking. He demonstrated, not only in *The Claim of Reason* but in his astonishing exploration of films, Shakespearean tragedies, and Wittgenstein, Emerson, and Thoreau, that the road back to ordinary language criticism was open, and our best hope for restoring value to humanistic study. The collection is also impressive for its decision to include dissenting voices.

—GEORGE TOLES, Distinguished Professor of English, Theatre, Film & Media, University of Manitoba, Canada

The voices gathered in this collection, each finding a different balance between the claims of memory, sympathy, and critique, together illuminate the relation between Stanley Cavell's life and his writings, and disclose an unattained but attainable future for philosophy to which we all might be attracted.

—STEPHEN MULHALL, Fellow and Tutor in Philosophy, New College, University of Oxford, UK

Praise for *Movies with Stanley Cavell in Mind*

This volume pushes Cavellian scholarship forward, showing that the value of Cavell's work lies not simply in understanding it but in applying it. By extending the philosopher's methods to an exciting range of international and contemporary films, the chapters compose a timely consideration of what it is to read a film, and to read a film generously.

—KYLE STEVENS, Associate Professor of Film Studies, Appalachian State University, USA

Stanley Cavell is, to my mind, the best thinker for helping us account for the power of the film experience, and the fourteen chapters collected here provide ample reason for understanding the importance of Cavell for the study of film. All of the contributors to this wonderful, collective enterprise—brought together by David LaRocca—have in a similar way encountered him and his work. Whether they are revisiting films Cavell loved or taking up the invitation to explore new films, they reveal the importance of Cavell's writing and method.

—SANDRA LAUGIER, Professor of Philosophy, Université Paris 1 Panthéon-Sorbonne, France

Music with Stanley Cavell in Mind

Edited by

David LaRocca

BLOOMSBURY ACADEMIC

NEW YORK • LONDON • OXFORD • NEW DELHI • SYDNEY

BLOOMSBURY ACADEMIC
Bloomsbury Publishing Inc
1385 Broadway, New York, NY 10018, USA
50 Bedford Square, London, WC1B 3DP, UK
29 Earlsfort Terrace, Dublin 2, Ireland

BLOOMSBURY, BLOOMSBURY ACADEMIC and the Diana logo are
trademarks of Bloomsbury Publishing Plc

First published in the United States of America 2024

Epigraph by Stanley Cavell © Stanley Cavell, "A Matter of Meaning It" (1967), in *Must We
Mean What We Say? A Book of Essays* (Cambridge: Cambridge University Press, 1976),
229. Permission to feature excerpt granted by the Stanley Cavell Trust and literary estate.

The second epigraph, by Ludwig Wittgenstein, is reproduced with permission of the
copyright holder. Maurice O'Connor Drury, "Conversations with Wittgenstein," in
Recollections of Wittgenstein, ed. Rush Rhees (Oxford: Oxford University Press, 1984), 160.

Permission to reprint the photograph on pages TK courtesy of the Stanley Cavell Trust.

For legal purposes the Acknowledgments on pp. 277–279 constitute an
extension of this copyright page.

Cover design: Louise Dugdale
Cover image courtesy of the Stanley Cavell Trust

A catalog record for this book is available from the Library of Congress

ISBN: HB: 979-8-7651-1104-8
         ePDF: 979-8-7651-1106-2
         eBook: 979-8-7651-1105-5

Typeset by Integra Software Service Pvt. Ltd.

To find out more about our authors and books visit www.bloomsbury.com
and sign up for our newsletters.

When Luther said, criticizing one form in which the sacraments had become relics, "All our experience of life should be baptismal in character," he was voicing what would become a guiding ambition of Romanticism—when religious forms could no longer satisfy that ambition. Baudelaire characterizes Romanticism as, among other things, intimacy and spirituality. This suggests why it is not merely the threat of fraudulence and the necessity for trust which has become characteristic of the modern, but equally the reactions of disgust, embarrassment, impatience, partisanship, excitement without release, silence without serenity. I say that such things, if I am right about them, are just facts—facts of life, of art now. But it should also be said that they are grammatical facts: they tell us what kind of object a modern work of art is. It asks of us, not exactly more in the way of response, but one which is more personal. It promises us, not the re-assembly of community, but personal relationship unsponsored by that community; not the overcoming of our isolation, but the sharing of that isolation—not to save the world out of love, but to save love for the world, until it is responsive again.

—STANLEY CAVELL

Who can understand my philosophical work who does not know what music has meant in my life?

—LUDWIG WITTGENSTEIN

CONTENTS

Movement III / Recitatives

Movement IV / Intervals

OVERTURE

In Walked Stanley

CHARLES BERNSTEIN

Dizzy, he was screaming
Next to O.P., who was beaming
Monk was thumping
Suddenly in walked Bud
And then they got into somethin'
—JON HENDRICKS, Lyrics to Thelonious Monk's "In Walked Bud" (1947)[1]

On a human scale, it would seem reasonable to us to accept the idea
that sound is understood as melody in a final sense. Texture, silence,
the ebb/flow of tension, meter, pitch control, etc: the complete range
of all the components finally comes to rest in some kind of melodic
realization.
—JULIUS HEMPHILL[2]

I MET STANLEY CAVELL during my first year at Harvard. He was starring
in the second part of a year-long history of philosophy, staged twice-weekly
on the ground floor of Emerson Hall. In the fall of 1968, I was swept away
by Rogers Albritton's sinewy commentaries on Augustine, Aquinas, and the
Sermon on the Mount (I'd sign up for Albritton's version of Christianity in
two shakes of a sophist's tail).

In walked Stanley: swerving from Rousseau to Marx to Mill to Nietzsche.
And swinging too. God wasn't dead so much as transmogrified (or is it
transubstantiated?) into the possibilities of thought.[3] Cavell wasn't about
theorizing but thinking. Each week he talked us through the history of ideas,

FIGURE 1 *(Opposite) A fifteen-year-old Stanley Cavell leading the band, the*
McClatchey Melodiers, and playing alto saxophone at C. K. McClatchey High
School, Sacramento, California, 1942.

as if the ideas were the standards that Cavell used to bounce off for his improvised riffs. Something closer to bebop than explanation. All performed with the understanding that what we say, how we use verbal language, matters. Language matters, that is, not just as a way of describing things or as a way of adjudicating things, but as a way of bringing the world into consciousness.

Something I wrote the next year, after one of Cavell's *Walden* improvisations, stays with me: We are limited to language but not by language. Cavell showed that consciousness is both individual and shared, because its site is language, which is collective and singular.

Fifty years later, I was back in that same classroom for Cavell's memorial. I paid tribute to Cavell as a writer for whom philosophy was a genre, not a prescribed mode of exposition; a thinker who was aversive to rationality in the pursuit of reason. I stressed that his wide range of topics—Emerson and Thoreau, Wittgenstein and Austin, Hollywood comedies and Shakespeare tragedies—did not take him outside of philosophy but rather put him at philosophy's center. Cavell was never eclectic. The objects of his attention together formed a constellation (in Walter Benjamin's sense).

A central focus for Cavell is how language means. He greatly broadened my ability to recognize the semantic field as something that exists in n-dimensional space. Cavell was at pains not to refute, but to respond to, skepticism—not just to the problem of how we know anything for sure, but also the problem of how we know words mean what they say. His response was that words, as the world, mean by doing, and that we know by responding. Our knowledge of the world is reciprocal: you get what you give, but only if you can acknowledge that.

I am tempted to say that for Cavell, skepticism and analytic logic share an avoidance of music, if by music we mean the performative dimensions of language, the doings, that come to meaning through call and response, testing one thought against another, parry and reprise, variation and extension.[4] In *Must We Mean What We Say?*, Cavell discusses the "temptation" to say something and its reformulation as the Wittgensteinian dialectic that brings "self-knowledge" back in play, after its long exile from philosophy.[5] This is not the music of the metronome but the art of the fugue and the practice of improvisation. Cavell was writing the foreword to his first book just at the time I first heard him perform. He called *Must We Mean What We Say?* "a book of essays": not papers, articles, or arguments: essays in the sense of *tries*, suggesting Montaigne more than Aristotle.

Essays are thought set to music; or are they music set to thought? Music is what animates the words just as words animate music. In *Little Did I Know*, Cavell tells a story about Ben Webster, the saxophonist whose improvisations on Irving Berlin's "Blue Skies" are echoed by Thelonious Monk's "In Walked Bud."[6] Webster, Cavell says, "suddenly stop[ed] playing in the middle of a chorus, seeming bewildered. Asked why later, Webster replied that he had forgotten the words."[7] The words of the song, say "Blue Skies," don't accompany the song but are part of the music, whether sung out loud or not. When you lose the music, you lose the words (and the other way around).

The philosopher stops in the middle of a talk: "I forgot the music." Rationalistic analytics is philosophy without the music. Rationality without fantasy is tyranny.

Robert Musil marvelously illustrates the musical contrast I'm flagging here. Musil's immediate target is the "Dichter des Generals," bloated Idealist poets of the general, those bloviators of the context-free universal sentiment, who Musil compares to Heine, who, like Cavell, is a Jewish master of the ingenious interstitial weave. But might we not also hear, in this passage from Musil, a critique of the Vienna Circle, who were part of Musil's cultural milieu:

His ceremonious idealism echoes the deep, low instruments in the orchestras, which resemble locomotive boilers raised up high spewing unaccountable grunts and bellows. They cover with one sound thousands of possibilities. They blow big balloons full of eternal feelings.[8]

I want to shift the frame from Cavell on music to Cavell as music. What if we read Cavell as poetic or literary writing rather than as philosophical argument, as opening up reason to "thousands of possibilities" in contrast to a narrowing of rationality to one possibility as time? Cavell's work enacts an aversion to rationality in the pursuit of reason as he moves from "the claim to rationality," the title of his dissertation, to "the claim of reason," the title of the book that comes out of it many years later. Of course, it is possible, even common, to argue for multiple possibilities within a rational discursive plain. But Cavell's writing averts that chiasmus.

Rogers Albritton's dissatisfaction with writing, which he shared with Wittgenstein, is related to the kind of flattening of discourse he would have found in much of the professional philosophical writing of his contemporaries: small balloons (not to say ballrooms) of eternal truths. In his improvised, talking philosophy Albritton did give the sense of sounding thousands of possibilities. I remember Rogers telling me that something I wrote didn't have an "ear" for the philosophical terms I used (mine was always sore thumbs). Cavell understood the problem that kept Albritton from writing, but he was not deterred. "At some point in Beethoven's work you can no longer relate what you hear to a process of improvisation. [...] At that point music, such music, must be written."[9] Cavell was able to put the talking/performative—stand-up—philosophy of Albritton, Austin, and Wittgenstein into writing, but not without difficulty. Still, he had practice from early on: as a teenager he reports "spending every night in my room imitating and transcribing for hours the clarinet improvisations from Goodman and Shaw recordings."[10]

During his talks for the 1968 class, Albritton introduced Aristotle's hoary distinction between *energeia* and *kinēsis*. I know that *e* and *k* go together like a horse and buggy or labor and its fruits. Myles Burnyeat calls the Aristotelean source text for this distinction a "freak performance" and would be skeptical of the attention I want to give it; but maybe a "freak performance" is just what I want. Evidently, *e* as "seeing" versus *k* as "building something" is more accurately covered by *e* vs. *dynamus*.[11] In an apparently unrelated article, Burnyeat takes to task Thompson Clarke, Cavell's comrade-in-skepticism, for what Burnyeat characterizes as a kind of freakish Pyrrhonism, where everyday consciousness is insulated from the philosophical exercise (excess) of skepticism.[12] I'm still looking for the tune, something bluesy, but the words might go something like this: ♪ I believe I don't know and better believe me, baby, I know I don't believe ♪. I imagine Burnyeat shaking two fists at latter-day Sirens Clark and Cavell in an homage to G. E. Moore. ("Progress is our most important product," as the GE ad used to say.)—I'd propose that skepticism is a blowback of *k* (which is why I spell *skepticism* with a *k* as the second letter rather than a *c*) that can be resolved by the formula $e = mk^2$, where *m* is music. If you can't hear the music, you lost the meaning of the words: ♪ It don't mean a thing if it ain't got that swing ♪.[13]

As it socked me in '68, *k* is a means to an end, something for the sake of something else; while *e* is something that needs no justification, evoked for me that year by John Coltrane's *Ascension*. In my 1968 freakish pata-Aristotelianism, the analogy to *k* vs *e* would be mescaline vs. amphetamine. War was our demonic *kinēsis*. We were in the streets protesting a means to a bad end: "US out of Vietnam, Harvard out of Gulf." In 1968, *energeia* attracted me, like Emerson's moral perfectionism, as Cavell later echoed it; or maybe something else out of Aristotle's era, the *Bhagavad Gita*.

As 1969 dawned, but before the Harvard Strike, I was sitting in another lecture room in Emerson Hall, trying to hear what Willard Van Orman Quine was explaining in Symbolic Logic 101. Unlike the delightful, lucid wit of his essays, Quine mumbled through his lectures, rarely turning toward the students, never engaging us directly. Symbolic Logic, I gathered, jumping the gun, was *kinēsis*, not a pure mathematics but a means to an end (or maybe artificial intelligence *avant la lettre*).

In *Must We Mean What We Say?*, Cavell makes the distinction between positivists and "post-positivists."[14] He treated the history of philosophy the way Coltrane treated "My Favorite Things"—motifs to spin, themes to try on, possibilities to consider. This was *energeia*: music to my ears. It wasn't just Quine, whose identification with the political right made him an even easier target for the likes of me. The altogether liberal John Rawls was another *kinēsis* guy, though the ends of his argument were admirable. Quine and Rawls—and Aristotle too—were acrobatics of deductive, rather than inductive, reasoning. Cavell was dance.

E = outside the bounds of logic but inside the limits of reason alone. In other words: do not make an argument to prove what you think but rather write an essay to find what you think.

In his essays, Cavell is not making an argument, he's finding arguments. His sentences are not in the service of a foregone conclusion but a tool for actively inconclusive thinking, even when he comes to conclusions. His writing is difficult or obscure if you expect deductive rationalization. For those who prefer improvisation, the work is a musical delight, where music marks the embodiment of language in the act of composition. Cavell plays the scales of reason, sounding each note in different pitches, so we may find our way through the traps and allures. Syncopation, echo, reverse, recapitulation, extension: arguments become tunes that are sounded, sometimes till where you almost think it's lost and then it comes back again, only now you hear it not as linear but in multidimensional space. Recombinant, recursive, inferential, associative—what I call echopoetics. Hemphill writes of exploring "the possibilities of a redistribution of usual rhythmic functions so that the role of rhythm is more diffuse."[15] I want to say that Cavell redistributes (constellates, arrays) the argument, logic, themes, motifs, *topoi*, topics, subjects.

Imagine for a moment that the standards Cavell improvises on, through impromptus, themes, and variations, are keynote motifs: sometimes tonal and sometimes *outside* the tune, sometimes syncopated and sometimes dissonant. In *Must We Mean What We Say?*, Cavell provides a stunning "thematic index," itself a kind of list poem:

Acceptance, acknowledgment (and its refusal), alienation, America, answer, audience, belief, bring words (or the mind) back, comedy, confession, convention, conviction, criticism, dialectic, difficult, dogmatism, dreaming, epistemology, everyday language, fashion, forgetting forms of life, fraudulence, freedom, God, grammar, heightened meaning, history, intention, interpretation, intolerance, knowing, language and fact, learning, listening and hearing, literal and figurative, logic, medium, modern, modernism, morality, natural and unnatural, necessity (and need), new criticism, normative obscurity, obviousness, ordinary and extraordinary, ordinary language philosophy, Oxford philosophy, particular case or occasion, performance, perspective, phenomenological facts, philosophy (and art, audience, common "belief," distraction, ideology, impotence, madness, memory, paralysis, impatience, poetry, irrelevance, science, theology, tragedy, wonder, world brought to consciousness), picture, post-positivist, presentness, prophesy, psychology, questioning, revelation, revolutionary, saying and meaning, self-knowledge, separateness, silence, singleness, sitting quietly in a room, skepticism, speaking, stopping, taste, teaching, terms of criticism, totally in view, tradition, tragedy, transcendental logic, wonder, words, world, writing.[16]

Only Cavell's autobiographical writing on his younger days focuses on jazz. Nonetheless, improvisation is an ongoing motif, sometimes in counterpoint to chance and composition and other times as setting, as with his remark on Beethoven: when improvisation stops, writing begins. Arnold Davidson, in an essay mostly on Sonny Rollins, published in a collection edited by George Lewis, makes a compelling argument that Cavell's Emersonian approach to Moral Perfectionism offers a valuable approach to critical improvisation studies.[17] In any case, it is of fundamental value to bring these too often competing discussions of music together, much the way Cavell brought Emerson and Thoreau into philosophical play, over and against those who discounted them as "merely" literary writers.

Doing things with words (*do* is an instrument): in *Little Did I Know*, Cavell writes about his purgatorial year as a UCLA philosophy student:

I would occasionally pause for an hour improvising on show tunes, perhaps to keep in touch with the somehow reassuring remnants of an old talent, perhaps for the sheer pleasure of invoking the exuberant and so often perfect, if from a certain perspective limited, American accomplishments in popular words and music, effortlessly including the unfathomable inspiration of its grateful and resourceful immigrants.[18]

Dial back a few years. Cavell's father gives him an alto saxophone as a belated Bar Mitzvah present.[19] You don't have to be a Jacques Lacan to see the symbolic power of this gift: *the Word is music*. Traditional Bar Mitzvah presents, in addition to money, include pens and dictionaries (Cavell's immediate contemporary, poet Larry Eigner, got a typewriter). The Bar Mitzvah is the moment a young person presents himself to the congregation as a full member through cantillation (chanting) of the Torah. The saxophone, often heard as speaking or singing, giving melody to sound, marks, as in *The Jazz Singer*, the reframing of the congregation as American as much as Jewish, inspired by "resourceful immigrants," such as Irving Berlin. This moment also anticipates, not so many years later, Cavell's reclaiming a version of his family's surname from Goldstein, the ethnically marked one given at Ellis Island; a move that is, in the end, Americanizing on the surface only.[20] There is a similar echoic consciousness in Cavell's transformation of the rabbinic into the secular vocation of the jazz singer as philosopher.

So perhaps it's time—with an illocutionary flourish, perhaps the shofar's *teruah*—to enroll Cavell in the ranks of what Isaac Deutscher, in 1958, called the "non-Jewish Jew," Spinoza and Marx being Deutscher's paradigmatic examples.[21] My 1972 college thesis (advised by Cavell with Albritton and G. E. L. Owen as readers) was on Wittgenstein and Stein.[22] To make an explicit context for $L=A=N=G=U=A=G=E$, I'll add, as a quick graph, Krauss, Celan,

Derrida, Bergson, Antin, and Jabès.[23] But in terms of the style of Cavell's composition, as it relates to music, I want to single out Benjamin.

From 1999 to 2004, Brian Ferneyhough and I wrote a "thought opera" in and around the work and life of Benjamin. With Brian on music and me on words, we wanted to bring Benjamin's philosophy into music.[24] Ferneyhough, who synthesizes aspects of Cage and Schoenberg, Feldman and Stockhausen, shows the limits of Cavell's insistence on intention in "Music Discomposed," a compelling essay for anyone interested in these composers, irregardless (!) of whether, like me, you disagree with Cavell on Cage (or Michael Fried[25]). I like to think of Ferneyhough, George Lewis, and Antin when they were together in the 1990s at the University of California, San Diego.

Why do we say "poetic license" but not "philosophic license"?

[BLACKOUT]

Was it 1971 that Cavell briefly stopped by my pad at Adams House? As I recall, perhaps it's a fantasy, Monk's *Misterioso* was on the stereo.

—Dug bebop when I heard it, Reb said, but realized I'd never get to where Monk or Miles or Bird already were.

—I had to find another way.

Notes

1   Calling out Dizzy Gillespie, Oscar Pettiford, Bud Powell, and Thelonious Monk.

2   Liner notes by Julius Hemphill for the Janus Company recording, December 10, 1977. Included in the booklet, ed. Marty Ehrlich, accompanying *The Boyé Multi-National Crusade for Harmony* (Brooklyn: New World Records, 2020), 18.

3   Cavell finished the foreword to his first book, *Must We Mean What We Say?*, in December 1968.

4   See Stanley Cavell, "The Avoidance of Love: A Reading of *King Lear*," in *Must We Mean What We Say?* (New York: Charles Scribner's Sons, 1969; Cambridge: Cambridge University Press, 1976).

5   See Stanley Cavell, "The Availability of Wittgenstein's Later Philosophy," in *Must We Mean What We Say?*, 68 and 71.

6   "In Walked Bud," itself a standard, echoes the chord progression in Irving Berlin's "Blue Skies" (1923). Webster's "Blue Skies" (1944) features Pettiford on bass (Savoy Records, no. 553).

7   Stanley Cavell, *Little Did I Know: Excerpts from Memory* (Stanford: Stanford University Press, 2010), 269. Saxophonist Marty Ehrlich first told me this story. After I showed him Cavell's account, he replied, "Now a poet could stop in the middle of a reading and say, 'I forgot the music!'"

8   "Sein feierlicher Idealismus entsprachjenen großen tiefen Blasinstrumenten in den Orchestern, welche in die Höhe gestellten Lokomotivkesseln gleichen und ein ungefüges Grunzen und Schollern hervorbringen. Sie decken mit einem Ton tausend Möglichkeiten zu. Sie pusten große Pakete voll der ewigen Gefühle aus." Robert Musil, *Der Mann ohne Eigenschaften*, Book 1 (Hamburg: Rowohlt, 2013), 405–406; my translation. The comment about the Vienna Circle needs to be leavened by Musil's engagement in the scientific thinking of his time; he was especially taken by Ernst Mach.

9   Stanley Cavell, The *Claim of Reason: Wittgenstein, Skepticism, Morality, and Tragedy* (New York: Oxford University Press, 1979), 5.

10   Cavell, *Little Did I Know*, 71.

11   Aristotle, *Metaphysics*, ch. 9, 1048b18–35. See Myles Burnyeat, "Kinēsis vs. energeia: a much-read passage in (but not of) Aristotle's Metaphysics," in *Explorations in Ancient and Modern Philosophy*, vol. 4, pt. I, ch. 4 (Cambridge: Cambridge University Press, 2022).

12   See Myles Burnyeat, "The Sceptic in His Place and Time," *Explorations in Ancient and Modern Philosophy*, vol. 1, pt. II, ch. 12 and Thompson Clarke, "The Legacy of Skepticism," *The Journal of Philosophy*, vol. 69, no. 20 (1972).

13   Irving Mills lyric to Duke Ellington's melody (1931); the line may have already been circulating.

14   "Post-positivists (the later Wittgenstein; 'ordinary language philosophy') rallied to the insistence that ordinary language—being *speech*, and speech being more than the making of statements—contains implications necessary to communication, perfectly comprehensible to anyone who can speak, but not recordable in logical systems." Stanley Cavell, "Ending the Waiting Game: A Reading of Beckett's *Endgame*," *Must We Mean What We Say?*, 123.

15   See Hemphill, op. cit.

16   See Cavell, *Must We Mean What We Say?*, 357–360.

17   Arnold Davidson, "Spiritual Exercises, Improvisation, and Moral Perfectionism: With Special Reference to Sonny Rollins," in *The Oxford Handbook of Critical Improvisation Studies*, ed. George Lewis and Benjamin Piekut (New York: Oxford University Press, 2016), vol. 1.

18   Cavell, *Little Did I Know*, 268.

19   Ibid., 71.

20   Ibid., 200–202.

21   Isaac Deutscher, *Non-Jewish Jew and Other Essays* (London: Oxford University Press, 1968).

22   *Three Compositions on Philosophy and Literature* (1972; Asylum's Press Digital Edition, 2012), pdf: writing.upenn.edu/epc/3-Steins.php/.

23   In *L=A=N=G=U=A=G=E* (1978–81), we published a preview of *The Claim of Reason: Wittgenstein, Skepticism, Morality, and Tragedy* as well as excerpted my first essay on Cavell. See *L=A=N=G=U=A=G=E: The Complete Facsimile*, ed. Matt Hofer and Michael Golston (Albuquerque: University of New

Mexico Press, 2020). My early essay, "The Objects of Meaning: Reading Cavell, Reading Wittgenstein," put forward Cavell against Derrida on meaning. First published in *boundary 2*, vol. IX, no. 2 (1981), it was collected in *Content's Dream*: *Essays 1975–1984* (Evanston: Northwestern University Press, 2001).

24 See writing.upenn.edu/epc/authors/bernstein/shadowtime/.

25 See my "Artifice of Absorption," in *A Poetics* (Cambridge, MA: Harvard University Press, 1992).

PRELUDE

Sounds of Philosophy

DAVID LAROCCA

WHAT HAPPENS WHEN A MUSICIAN BECOMES A PHILOSOPHER? In this volume of newly commissioned essays, illustrious contributors with a range of interdisciplinary interests and manifold talents—in music theory, improvisation studies, the philosophy of music, language philosophy, poetics, aesthetics, and musical performance—pursue substantive, durable, and orienting replies to our chosen exemplar, Stanley Cavell. Fittingly, ours is the first book dedicated entirely to music in its pervasive, resonant, and varied roles in Cavell's life, how music, for him, evolved from literal act (through instrumentation and composition) to metaphorical inscription (on the subject of sound and in the audibility of written texts). Once his days as a public musician had elapsed, his time as a musically minded philosopher commenced, eventually permeating nearly every aspect of his major contributions to consecutive thought, including what he deemed, in a valedictory mood, "my quest for a sound of a philosophical prose that I could place conviction in."[1] Music—and sounds, more generally: speech, song, and so on, as well as silence—can, at times seem to structure his remarks, at others become their content, and even, on many occasions, illuminate a transcendental feature. Here we listen for those moments when music is *in* Cavell's prose (as topic, as trope) as well as perk up our ears to the music *of* his writing. Befitting his own contest to discover a language for his thought (would it be music or philosophy or inhabit some other vernacular?), Cavell's relationship with music as a phenomenon, once and ongoing, is not uncomplicated. Continuing the complex and involving conversation about music's evocative presence in Cavell's life calls us to respond now, and, as his enduring work is wont to do, it surely will again.

"On our beginnings seems somehow our self possession to depend a good deal," wrote Ralph Waldo Emerson to Margaret Fuller, "as happens so often in music."[2] The observation holds true for Cavell, whose beginnings did incontestably shape his self-possession and his prospects. Depending on the selected topic—movie-going, psychoanalysis, the work of J. L. Austin, the discovery of Emerson, to name but a few—readers will find themselves emplaced in a different spot in the spectrum of Cavell's biography. Music as a subject brings us back to his origins, starting with his musically adept mother (who possessed perfect pitch) and his adolescent performances in Sacramento and later, Berkeley. But music also reaches into his maturity—all the way to a season of crossover—when, haunting the halls of Juilliard, he traded his alto saxophone, clarinet, piano, and composition notebooks for Freud, the silver screen, and soon enough, the study and practice of philosophy (if still playing, one day down the line, at the grand piano centrally situated in his Brookline living room). Thus, even as Cavell trained and later became a philosopher himself, he remained a music man, a person who approached writing philosophy like jazz performance—attuned, as was his way, to the sounds, scales, rhythms, intervals, pitches, phrases, motifs, and measures of his prose, and the ideas they conveyed. Here we note a crux in the crossover: where some have said "music is language without meaning," philosophers presume that linguistic expression should surely convey sense.[3] Cavell opts for a "redemptive" account in which music would supply "understanding without meaning."[4] Whether we must mean what we say remains a question he will make his own. It turns out, then, that Cavell didn't have to become (and remain) a musician, or composer, or even to write explicitly "about music" (as a philosopher) in order to honor his beginnings. The domain suffuses all that followed—from ordinary language philosophy to the study of cinema, opera, Shakespeare, American philosophy, and philosophy-written-in-the-key-of-autobiography (and vice versa)—often indirectly, often with a background of first-hand experience in music worn lightly. But, of course, famously, if not always influentially, he did directly address music in his life "out of" music, as a philosopher.[5] These works—written most intensively early in his career and returned to in late dispensations—draw our collective and individual attention in what follows, that is, in the dilating, innumerable pathways betokened by Charles Bernstein's welcoming overture. As genre conventions insist, we cannot help but seek "the end in the beginning," the way the first stirrings and observable talents wend their way along strange, unpredictable paths to sublime expressions, notions worthy of our sustained attention. How did the son of an immigrant pawnbroker who spoke broken English end up an enviably articulate, globally celebrated, and distinctively endowed chair of philosophy at Harvard? Sounds like the beginning of a song.

* * * *

IN THE YEARS LEADING UP TO the Second World War, a teenage Jewish boy born in 1926 in Atlanta, Georgia, but now living in Sacramento, California, played alto saxophone in an all-Black jazz band. He was very good. And when the draft came, he wasn't able to enlist in the army because, of all things (ironic symbolism duly noted), he suffered an ear injury as a six-year-old child. But this stalwart saxophonist, who also played the clarinet (like his beloved Benny Goodman), and also the piano (like his talented mother, Fannie Segal), led his high school band, the McClatchey Melodiers, during the first year of the war and subsequently enlisted instead in rigorous music training at the University of California, Berkeley. There he studied with the likes of famed composers Ernest Bloch and Roger Sessions; at Cal he wrote music and performed it, including for theatrical productions. By this point, the teenager about to leave for college, Stanley Goldstein had changed his name to Stanley Cavell (a stage name? a cognomen fit for the stage? which stage?) and was, in due course, headed to the vaunted Juilliard School in New York City.[6] But a funny thing happened on the way to becoming a professional musician and composer: Stanley started reading Freud in the morning and going to the movies at night—and as needs must, shirking the demands of his elite musical education; one type of difficult curriculum was being overtaken incrementally by new and differently immersive preoccupations, each of them layered upon his wide-ranging experience in music.

Back in California from the fall of 1948 through the summer of 1951, Cavell had begun his apprenticeship in professional philosophy at UCLA. He had carried with him from New York an awareness not just of the roiling evolution of musical culture (think of the ecstatic state of jazz in Greenwich Village and Harlem at this moment), but also its wider tumult in fine art (especially painting), film, and that vague and capacious but still-powerful syntagma "popular culture." First, while roving the cinematic streets of mid-century Manhattan, then on the sunny sidewalks of West Hollywood, Cavell was jealously, breathlessly reading the literary critics and intellectual periodicals of the day: James Agee in *The Nation* as well as Kenneth Burke, who was the music critic there from 1934 to 1936; the *Hudson Review* and *Sewanee Review* featured marquee members of the New Criticism—William Empson, R. P. Blackmur, Allen Tate; *Partisan Review* and *Commentary* called upon Chicago Jewish intellectuals—Saul Bellow, Isaac Rosenfeld—and New York ones too: Clement Greenberg, Lionel Trilling, Paul Goodman—"If Paul Goodman had been born in Paris," Cavell estimates, "his name [...] would be as famous as Foucault's."[7] But it was Robert Warshow, writing in *Commentary*, that proved a mighty distraction and moving inspiration for the nascent philosopher. "The trembling anticipation I note," Cavell recalls in approaching each new issue of these periodicals, "was distinctly, but only partly, directed to the pleasures I knew the reading would afford me. It was equally directed to my daily reminders that these pleasures were not welcome in the profession of philosophy, at any rate, not then and there, when English and continental analytical philosophy were its dominant modes, together with American pragmatism."[8] As he tried to fathom the distance between his life in the philosophy classroom and on the street, holding these critical tidings in hand, Cavell remained immersed in his version of the "crisis of reconstituting one's education."[9] Caught up in, or caught off guard by, the contest of this interstitial space—intellectually, culturally, personally—Cavell pondered his conditions:

> [M]y consciousness was alerted to the fact that philosophy, in any form, was essentially absent from the cultural commitments, literary or political, of any of the quarterlies. I was having too much trouble recognizing the subjects I was being taught as essential to what I had imagined I wanted from the study of philosophy—something, let's say, that spoke to my crisis in giving up music—to welcome having to face the fact that my America was one in which philosophy and the life of literature were forbidden to each other.[10]

At least literature retained its status as high culture and within the privileged precincts of the academy, while it also managed to leak out onto the newsstands (something philosophy hadn't, still hasn't, managed to do). But it was the specter of that left-behind life in music and the immanent presence of movies in his new daily experience (*Adam's Rib* would have appeared on the marquee during this phase of California days) that left Cavell muddled about "coming to terms" with "his relation to our culture"—our wide, wild, American popular culture.[11] Enter Warshow, who, according to Cavell may have been the critic with the most to say to him about these gaps, fissures, and impasses. Though Cavell was learning from these periodicals how to read (and in time) write public-spirited and astute criticism of the fine arts as well as the commercial ones, film and music, Warshow offered a prototype that aligned uncannily with Cavell's intellectual needs at this time of "spiritual crisis," and could be said to have shaped or anticipated directions Cavell would pursue from within Harvard's Emerson Hall for the next half-century.[12] Warshow "expresses his sense of the necessarily personal" in his writing about the life of culture, namely: "a sense of the writer's having to invent his own audience, of the writer's having to invent all the meanings of experience, of the modern intellectual's 'facing the necessity of describing and clarifying an experience which has itself deprived him of the vocabulary he requires to deal with it.'" Cavell asks:

> What experience has caused this devastation? [...] I note the magnitude of the claim. It expresses an isolation (he is without an audience) so extreme as to deprive him not only of meaningful speech (as if he is effectively aphasic) but also of that access to recognizable experience of his own that is the cause of meaningful speech. Something of this sense of inexpressiveness or suffocation is how I would come, two decades later, to characterize a fundamental philosophical motive of Wittgenstein's *Philosophical Investigations*, to teach us to return to ourselves the language that philosophy, in response to modern culture,

would repudiate, the ordinary language in which we can recognize our desire.[13]

Philosophy, as it was being taught, was unfitting Cavell for the pleasures of his experience in and within popular culture—as well as his continuing commitments to literature and psychoanalysis. It denied him a language with which to speak about them and it deranged his own desire to appreciate, understand, and contribute to the conversation of their making and inheritance. When Cavell comes to formalize his class notes in *Cities of Words*, after decades of teaching moral reasoning, the other half of his acknowledgment of desire is his experience of disappointment, no doubt a dyad he will assume we recognize as familiar to our own circumstances.[14] Though the book appeared fifty years after Cavell read Warshow and others with "trembling anticipation," the shuddering remained. But this time, in a more fully matured state, it was delivered with an announcement of the "moral calling of philosophy," something Cavell names "moral perfectionism," or even more specifically, Emersonian perfectionism.[15] Given such results—with Cavell building a realm of thinking by way of Wittgenstein and Emerson—it may be clear by now how we stand with respect to Cavell as he did with regard to Warshow: these are our guides for recognizing and admitting our desires and then for finding words to account for our experience of them, including our disappointments. It is work that appears worth the length of a lifetime to discover.

We can appreciate something distinctive and also familiar about that temporal arc for Cavell when we range from his mid-century enthusiasm for Warshow, et al. to his memoir, *Little Did I Know*, published some sixty years later. The themes appear reliable and recognizable throughout, merely finding their variations of expression as Cavell makes contact with the formation of his character and career (early musical performance, Berkeley, Juilliard, UCLA, Harvard Society of Fellows, Princeton Institute for Advanced Study, Harvard professorship, etc.) and the cultures of his own time that would become his subjects, as if notes on a stave (J. L. Austin, Wittgenstein, Beckett, Henry James, Shakespeare, Plato, *avant-garde* music, opera, cinema, television, Romanticism, Fred Astaire, Thoreau then Emerson, and so on).

Even as a life in music, that is, professional music, was lost to Cavell as he emerged as one of his generation's leading philosophers, music itself became a central part of his intellectual project, including such core notions as the sounds of philosophy (for him, evident at the level of syntax—finding its order and tone by way of thoughtful words placed with the warmth of a human heart); the varied registers of the human voice (on the page, on the movie screen, in opera, and in the therapist's office); and in the measures and pitch of speech that comprise ordinary language ("What it contrasts with [...] is a fixated *philosophical* language which precisely would preempt the extraordinary from disturbing customary experience.")[16] A propitious distinction—and one that will radiate long into his lengthy career—appears in the first few dozen pages of his first book, in the title essay, namely, where he acknowledges that "emphasizing the *functions* and *contexts* of language" are familiar to both Wittgenstein's work and "fundamental to American pragmatism," we ought to avoid rushing to equivalencies, since, after all "we must keep in mind how different their arguments sound, and admit that in philosophy it is the sound which makes all the difference."[17] Such a finding has the confidence and cadence of a syllogism's conclusion and the sonic verve of a final line of verse (different/difference; arguments sound/sound which makes). Cavell exercises, flexes, in fact, his prodigious skills as a reflexive stylist—as someone who can mobilize the tenor and intimacy of autobiographical confession to accompany filigrees of logic.[18] After all, it was he who wondered "why philosophy, of a certain ambition, tends perpetually to intersect the autobiographical."[19] Spoken like a true fan of Warshow.

Cavell is sufficiently sensible, we must believe because of his training in music, to discern the differences between philosophy written at a remove from human concerns (from the sound of the human) and one that makes evident down to the level of the syllables—as Austin and Wittgenstein were in their own ways, and as Emerson, Thoreau, and Nietzsche were in theirs—a gift for those points at which immanent speech touches the eternal, where the fate of embodiment finds liberation through well-wrought sentences. In his study of utterances, for example, Cavell could descry one that is "an offer of participation in the order of law" (the performative) and one that is "an invitation to improvisation in the disorders of desire" (the passionate).[20] After he brushed up against the institutional trends at Juilliard, Michael Gallope notes how Cavell found "total serialism objectionable" and, as if in response, "opted for the nondoctrinaire and humanist name 'improvisation.'"[21] Heed that "improvisation"—a jazz gesture from our man, our jazz man, Stan, imported at a moment of important terminological constitution, a crossover term that blends the necessary virtuosity of talent with the hard-won results of practice.[22]

Philosophical prose should arrive neither in imitation of math nor in envy of physics, but under its own *sound* auspices (the doubleness of the word reverberating to especial effect). Given Cavell's investments in the style (and voice) of philosophical writing, we shouldn't want to appraise the philosophical import of Cavell's project, nor could we, without factoring the extent to which his life *remained* a life in music. As Wittgenstein asked of his own sensibilities, so we can ask on Cavell's behalf: "Who can understand my philosophical work who does not know what music has meant in my life?"[23] For the salience of the connection, arriving from a philosopher dear to his heart, and a fellow clarinetist, Cavell had cause to "wonder the harder why [Wittgenstein] actually says so little about music."[24] Perhaps because, like

Cavell (like Emerson, Nietzsche, and Wittgenstein), music was internalized to the sound of prose.[25] As William H. Gass remarked, "no prose can pretend to greatness if its music is not also great; if it does not, indeed, construct a surround of sound to house its meaning."[26] One no longer has to write "about music" when each line becomes its own ministry of music. After Garrett Stewart, we could anoint such seamless alignment between form and content, such syncopation between inscription and sound, a properly phonemic writing.[27]

In retrospect, a logic flows from happenstance and objectives, technologies and encounters: how music "accompanies" cinema pre-1927; how film becomes a "talkie"—and thus voiced, a medium capable of carrying music with(in) it or beside it (as synchronized); how the human voice is a kind of music all its own; how opera (and other pre-cinematic musical traditions) can be represented *in* cinema—in effect, given a voice of their own on screen; how cinematic technology affords a layering of sounds (human voices, diegetic sounds, voice-over, soundtrack, and score). Cavell's *philosophical* interest in sound and voice (discovered in the 1950s, expressed publicly as early as the mid-1960s), then in emergent centrality to his writing on movies throughout the 1970s and 1980s, is followed by attention to the aural dimensions of Thoreau and then Emerson, opera, skepticism, tragedy, and Wittgenstein—all of them coalescing around Cavell's attunement to the audibility—that is, potential intelligibility—of the world. When the just-invoked Gass was in Wittgenstein's presence in Ithaca in 1949, he noted the "master's" speaking style had its own distinctiveness, "with a kind of deep stammer involving not mere sounds or words, but yards of discourse."[28] From where Gass sat, "what you heard" from Wittgenstein "was something like a great pianist at practice: not a piece of music, but the very acts which went into making that performance."[29] If we press the analogy between these musically-trained-and-music-loving philosophers, we could say that Cavell's writing announced its finishedness, even as it retained the energy of the improviser: at times roving, at other times halting, curious then cautious, pleased with an initial run of notes then rehearsing them recursively to test their merit.

One can easily imagine a counterfactual history in which the title of the book in hand would still suit Cavell but be about a very different life—one in which he had been a professional musician and composer, a conductor and librettist, solo improviser and music critic—instead of a philosopher. In place of this retrospective of a life unlived, we have a book about Cavell's life as he did, in fact, live it: in *and* out of music, taking up his thoughts about music and his contributions to musical sensibility along alternative vectors (counting among them the philosophical, the psychoanalytic, and the literary). Music with Stanley Cavell in mind thus will mean something different as we dip into the various temporal horizons and incarnations of his experience in the 1940s, 1960s, 1980s, and for us, in the 2020s and beyond, i.e., commencing with a pre-philosophical performer, then finding

ˌa stride as a philosophical critic, and at last to what he has become for us: a posthumous resource for our ongoing consideration of music's significance, including its pertinence to the work philosophy claims as its own, or that we claim on its behalf.

On this progression, though, let's dwell a moment more in order to gloss a thought Cavell has shared with us about "what I had imagined I wanted from the study of philosophy—something, let's say, that spoke to my crisis in giving up music."[30] It would be fitting to name Cavell's crisis one of vocation (*vocare*), of finding a voice in one place or another (perhaps by hearing a summoning sound, a call to a calling). We may also look to the way certain fields of human expression share preoccupations. Returning to the notion, Brian Kane finds connections that might have appealed to Cavell, even in those early phases of transition (reading Freud in Manhattan, studying Warshow in Los Angeles, and listening to Austin in Cambridge). What "both philosophy and music share" is:

> a certain pitch, a certain emphasis on the smallest details of enunciation, a certain way of hearing and rehearing our world and our languages, a certain responsibility to which we hold one another for every nuance in the shaping of a phrase, sentence, or idea. In this respect, the figure of the critic, analyst, or teacher is exemplary in Cavell's thinking, for they are the ones who attempt to communicate this way of listening, of tracking such inflections by negotiating with the work and interrogating it down to even its minutest details.[31]

By invoking Freud, Warshow, and Austin, I have aimed to anticipate in order to underwrite Kane's shrewd line-up of figures: critic, analyst, and teacher. Cavell's biography attests to such attractions and is our first evidence. Subsequently, though, there is his work—where he labors eloquently through these effects. As the critic, analyst, and teacher may find their unity in Cavell's writing (and pedagogy), so may we, in our late-stage role as inheritors of Cavell's patrimony, discover and rediscover this powerful trinity reflected and refracted by the astute reports to come.

One of the attributes an education in music affords the philosopher-in-training is a well-developed aesthetic sense. We know from David Hume (who counseled that "reason is, and ought only to be the slave of the passions")[32] and Edmund Burke (who wrote one of the earliest modern books on the sublime and the beautiful) that aesthetics—the discernment and exploration of subtle differences of value—should occupy an elevated role in human life. Management of such judgments, the willingness to be struck before one speaks, or to speak with a sense of awe—is a powerful training for philosophical investigations generally. Cavell's eclecticism as a thinker about myriad topics and texts appears directly beholden to an early life spent with his ears open—including at the movies. Before he had read Hume or Burke or Kant on aesthetic judgment, Cavell was familiar with art—with beauty—with the intelligence of emotion. When he came to read Plato, Austin, Wittgenstein, Emerson, Thoreau, and Nietzsche, he recognized the music of their prose, the sounds of sense they made in this alternative mode of human performance. We could say of Cavell what Peter Yates said of John Cage: he was a "philosopher of [a]esthetic instances."[33] And we could ponder whether what Leslie Chamberlain attributed to Nietzsche could apply to Cavell as well: "What he had [...] was a wonderful musical way with words. In that sense he was a musician. In that sense he did fulfill his desire to make music the fundament of his creative life."[34] In her phrasing, we are preoccupied by the thought—and transfixed by the experience—of "sublime tunefulness" in music and in writing.

Keen ears source findings from the American wilderness—if within earshot of the town center—in Cavell's two-phase composition, *The Senses of Walden*. First published in 1972—with a dedication to one of our authors, John Harbison—Cavell reports from a season of listening in on Thoreau; then, in 1979, he expands the edition by featuring two essays in which he addresses (as it were apologizes for and explains) his belated discovery of Emerson.[35] By virtue of a year's sinecure, Cavell could constitute his own idyll in the Connecticut green world (a gesture familiar to the big city types of remarriage comedies, who flee the asphalt to re-solve their troubles in the woods).[36] The Thoreauvian conditions proved propitious for a reader of *Walden*—at once an American philosopher and a trained musician—who could muse profitably on the tandem chapters "Sounds" and "Solitude" (including the latter's plangent invocation of silence) as well as detect wisdom in Thoreau's disquisitions on the mother tongue and father tongue. We have found our sought after sonic translator of American scripture, of the American pitch in the history of global philosophy. With Cavell on the dais, the chanticleer, owl, and loon join the dawn chorus only to realize we're already awake—and listening attentively.

Also in the early 1970s, in an enviably productive spell as well as retrospective mood, Cavell notes at the beginning of his first book on cinema, *The World Viewed* (1971), that "[m]emories of movies are strand over strand with memories of my life."[37] A decade later, in *Pursuits of Happiness* (1981), Cavell arranges his proposal for a genre of films called the comedy of remarriage by situating the stakes of what is audible between people, especially between intimate others:

What does a happy marriage *sound* like? Since the sound of argument, of wrangling, of verbal battle, is the characteristic sound of these comedies—as if the screen had hardly been able to wait to burst into speech—an essential criterion for membership in that small set of actors who are featured in these films is the ability to bear up under this assault of words, to give as good as you get, where what is good must always, however strong, maintain its good spirits, a test of intellectual as well as of spiritual stamina, of what you might call "ear."[38]

No doubt, by this point in his career, we were all ears—listening to how George Steiner (after first disparaging Cavell's writing) described the "American grain and prodigality" of Cavell's prose: "At its best, his play of thought, his 'wordings of the world' have a music, a stroke of wonder rare in current philosophical argument."[39] Music as a conceptual frame recurred at the turn of the new millennium when Cavell invoked Franz Liszt by anointing his book on Ralph Waldo Emerson, *Emerson's Transcendental Etudes* (2003), studies at that point conducted over three decades, which begin with memories of "[s]pending my childhood in a musical household— seeming to remember reading notes on a stave before I could read words of my speech."[40]

When Cavell shared his memoir, *Little Did I Know* (2010), the overlap of Cavell's life and thought remained prominently associated with music, including sounds and sonic metaphors—playing, listening, voices, pitch, performance, varieties of "reading" (e.g., sight-reading, close reading), and all the relevant rest. Beginning as early as the second paragraph of the book, such themes thereafter charge the entire manuscript, not unlike the threatened heartbeat that pulses as he gets under way (capturing, as he does, the urgency that such a rhythm presents when it is endangered, or worse, stilled). The book, like Cavell himself, lives and dies with its ear tu(r)ned to the audible and affecting thought. Always attuned, that is, to notions of belatedness, postponement, and deferment, Cavell's heart was in need of help and the emergency appears not only to have renewed his awareness of mortality but also to have jump-started anew his effort to present what he calls "excerpts from memory." As Cavell's life was flashing before his mind's ear, it was the sound of music that appeared most saliently as the leitmotif of his life's melody. While the memoir of this philosopher— who conducted his philosophical investigations mainly in the second half of the twentieth century—includes many dispensations on the nature of that discipline, its evolution, Cavell's role in shaping it, and so on, the recurrence of music—as an orienting phenomenon, as a philosophically reverberating fact, indeed, as a persistent, indispensable source of joy—stretches from a scene of reading Vladimir Jankelevitch on Debussy (page two) through re-inscriptions from a notebook on Mahler and Mozart (486f).

The way that a life in (professional) music was lost to Cavell creates a kind of shadow life, "a life unlived in music." Does this dissolution liberate Cavell to philosophy? Or does it animate a double life—in which one (unlived) life haunts the other (lived one)? And thinking of Cavell's training in psychoanalysis, his serious flirtation with abandoning the academy for the therapist's clinic, how it forms yet another (third) path he was tempted to take, almost took, but let go of. Is it important to *not* do something artistically in order to do something *else* artistically? To not paint in order to philosophize? To not perform in music in order to perform in philosophy?[41] Cavell's life makes these questions feel rhetorical; perhaps, in some suitable measure, they are for all of us too.

Or instead, if such questions remain alive and solicit us to mull replies, we could note variations on Cavell's own trajectory—whether self-directed or contingent—not just among historical figures who fathomed music's essential contribution to the meaning of life while pursuing other vocations (Nietzsche, Wittgenstein, and the like), but also among contemporaries. An only child born to Jewish parents a decade after Cavell, Steve Reich also had a father who wasn't sure of his son's prospects. At sixteen, the precocious Reich enrolled at Cornell University where he majored in philosophy. "My father paid my tuition," he writes, "while I earned money for food by playing in jazz and dance bands on the weekends."[42] In those days, the philosophy department was still under the spell of Wittgenstein's visit to Ithaca, and Reich was duly inaugurated into the rarefied cadre of adepts and acolytes, among them Norman Malcolm and Max Black. Reich wrote his thesis on Wittgenstein—"Actually, I wrote a thesis criticizing Gilbert Ryle for criticizing Wittgenstein. When I wasn't drumming or listening to jazz or Stravinsky, I spent my time in college reading Wittgenstein's *Philosophical Investigations*."[43] For those attuned to J. L. Austin's presence and decisive influence on Cavell at Harvard (for instance, that because of Austin, Cavell found a way forward in philosophy), we'll all be amused to read that Reich, who also studied music at Cornell, was mainly under the guidance of William Austin (no relation), "who provided encouragement to be a composer at the point when Reich had to decide between a career in music or going to Harvard graduate school to study philosophy."[44] Given such salient swaps, we seem ready to add biographical details to strips of paper, toss them into a hat, then pull them out one by one to reveal Cavell's biography—or Reich's.

"Against his father's wishes," Reich returned to New York and in 1959 entered Juilliard, where he made analyses of Arnold Schoenberg, among others; he was tuned into contemporary art (crossed paths with Willem de Kooning) and *avant-garde* music ("I was certainly aware of what John Cage was doing [...], and Boulez, Stockhausen, and Berio.")[45] By 1961, Reich set his sights on the Bay Area, almost heading for Berkeley, but instead—for the chance to study with Luciano Berio swerved to Mills College: "Serialism was just then becoming known in this country, and he was a primary member of the team."[46] A final fillip from Reich's uncanny shuffle of Cavellian elements might be resolved into the pieces of music he composed that set Wittgenstein's writing to music, among them *Proverb* (1995) and *You Are (variations)* (2006). Anyone who ponders the vexing folds of accident and intention in one's life course—paths taken, paths forsaken (or unknown)— should be amused by this biographical diversion. Cavell's life, perhaps any of our lives, may feel preordained in retrospect, but the lesson here would seem to confirm that sequences and patterns inform the structure of our personal histories, and that, despite the shocking number of permutations thereof (and whether they are random or fated), we have many ways to get where we're going—however more or less elegantly, nimbly. "The role of temporal intervals, let's say of rhythm," Cavell raises his hand at this point to offer a salutary comment, "in ordering the depth and fragility of human hopes, say, one's conviction in futurity, must be a basis for the profundity of our need for music."[47]

With a formative early life spent in music—training, performing, composing—how could the resonances of such varied work not inform *whatever* path Cavell picked up in its stead? Ministry for Emerson, philology for Nietzsche, engineering for Wittgenstein: early talents and techniques make themselves known in due course, if under the guise of essay writing, or drawing antiquity into the present, or describing how languages structure our "form of life." Though one can look to Cavell's written catalog of essays and books to see the springing up and display of his lifelong commitment to the (continued) study of music, and we might say the philosophical or professional "application" of such lessons (e.g., with a book entitled *A Pitch of Philosophy*), we could also consider, perhaps more gratifying even than scanning his academic library, the way in which *Cavell* tells the story of his own life, albeit through the tantalizing fragments he calls excerpts. In the end, those morsels of memory may be enough to make the point. In *Little Did I Know*, a memoir set out in a complementary dual register of time (present-day experience catching sight of past life events), once the musical motif—counterpoint—is pointed out to readers, the volume's musical affiliations and analogies are undeniable and pervasive—from the first pages and then steadily on through the entire length of the lengthy reminiscence.

Cavell doesn't merely "tell a story" of his life, he creates a musical framework in which to hear his present-day self reflected in relation to the other(s) of his (own) past; something similar is evoked in this book's table of contents in so far as the fractal senses of musical terms—movements, registers, and more—find their sonority as structuring factors (even, after a fashion, Kantian categories) that frame and form the conditions for the compositions to come (as for Cavell, so for we readers and inheritors of his writing). Much as Wittgenstein did in the *Philosophical Investigations* and Cavell varied artfully in his own magnum opus, *The Claim of Reason*, voices are multiplied, placed in conversation with one another. Time is fractured, layered—allowing for moments of harmony as well as dissonance. Yet, *Little Did I Know* innovates such gestures still further—musically, psychoanalytically—by giving many of the instantiations or incarnations of Cavell a voice, a chance to speak. The lesson taken from the composition of Cavell's own reflexive and refracted self-image on this extended occasion, written, little did he know, as he was approaching his final decade of life, shows that, in fact, "excerpts" or extracts from his autobiography will not, at last, serve to fully represent the pervasive extent to which music meant something to him—how it broadly as well as deeply informed his way of inhabiting the world as a teacher of philosophy and as a composer of his work's world-forming lines of prose. Extracts must remain partial, provisional, suggestive—much as a musical phrase. *Little Did I Know* might have been subtitled, if figuratively, "a life in music," or in a veritable Nietzschean variation, "a life in philosophy out of the spirit of music." For if Cavell lived fully with a musician's consciousness of the sounds of the world—in music, in written prose, in the vibrations and reverberations of the human voice—the philosophical and/or autobiographical expression of such deeply felt truths would remain incomplete, still in need of further elucidation.

When Cavell did take up music as a point of (we could add, professional) philosophical interest, as he did with "Music Discomposed" (1967), it was coolly received—equally from traditionalists and from champions of the *avant-garde*. His disappointment in the work's reception was sufficiently pronounced that after replying to (some of) its critics in "A Matter of Meaning It" (also in 1967), he fairly well abandoned writing about music (philosophically or otherwise) for roughly thirty years. In fact, the reception of his work more generally will continue to be a topic of interest to Cavell— and those who read him avidly; what accounts for the ways Cavell's modes of criticism are audible and attractive to some and problematically dissonant to others?[48] In the mid-1960s, though, it would be fair to characterize the kind of writing we find in "Music Discomposed" and "A Matter of Meaning It" as essays with music as their *expressed* topics, but the fact is, in the wake of his disenchantment with their impact, Cavell found other ways of writing about music in disparate medial and textual spaces: when writing on film (where, for example, his remarks on sound garnered attention among cinephiles, critics, and philosophers) and opera (for instance, by linking the artform to its special attributes of vocal recital), and especially when addressing the personal voice as an expression of the autobiographical, the tragic, the skeptical predicament, and the fate of the human condition. Given today's disciplinary categories and professional parlance, the range of Cavell's thoughts on musical or sonic phenomena, broadly construed (by reference to the human voice in ordinary language; the autobiographical and philosophical voice on the page; as featured variously in cinema and opera; and including music as conventionally conceived and customarily treated), should be regarded as contributing broadly and meaningfully to sound studies.[49]

Thinking of inherited disciplines—and the categories and criteria that give shape to them—we could ask how it is one first hears the name "Stanley Cavell." For Stanley Goldstein, the task required a movement from inheritance to invention. Perhaps he heard the rhyme in his adapted and adopted surname—self-consecrated by way of Eastern European origins, suited to his California context—in the pace and thrum of the euphonous *lee / ell / ell.* Though it would take time to recognize it, the composition of Cavell's first philosophical passage—Stan*ley* L. Ca*vell*—was his own new name. Such a moment of recognition (endogenous to the letters and the language of an inventive appellation) seems auspicious and indicative for understanding how his future remarks on music (or sound, more generally) become audible—and remain intelligible—to his readers, his inheritors. If we know how he first heard his name, what of us? —Was it in a philosophy class or one devoted to the criticism of literature and the fine arts? Referenced in league with psychoanalysis or the American transcendentalists? A film seminar devoted to Hollywood's Golden Age? A workshop on Shakespeare? Or in the midst of musical education itself—in some conservatory, in the context of the history of musicology and the performance of music? Most saliently for our line of questioning here, what might it augur about the auspices of such a first hearing—an apt synecdoche for reading—for understanding the way in which Cavell's work works on you?

Cavell's take on, say, Austin or Wittgenstein or Heidegger or Derrida or Emerson, his approach to deconstruction or psychoanalysis or Shakespeare or opera or cinema, could open up something for readers that isn't present in the mainstream trends or curricula of a given field or subfield; in this respect, Cavell's interest in what interests *him* can manifest the particular magic of authorizing *one's own* interest in the material. Thus, one needn't "follow" Cavell, reiterating or defending his points, so much as cite him as an intellectual defender of coming to know, if not also owning, one's own thoughts. Secondly, how one arrives at Cavell can inform what portions of his topics, texts, and methodologies take on a sustained life in one's relationship with his writing. In today's academic argot, this could be spoken of (shifting to an ocular metaphor) as the "lenses" through which we see what Cavell attended to—since terms of musical art, and the abiding tropes they encode, not only shape how we think about Cavell's understanding of music, they also inform his way of thinking about the "sound" of the human "voice" in so far as it is *written.* The cognitive and evaluative energies necessary for the imminent translations involved in *sight-reading* rush to mind. Similarly, the texts and/or the thematics that frame—and filter—one's approach to the page condition one's reception. Coming to Cavell via Shakespeare (or vice versa), for instance, may lead one to see aspects of both bodies of work in terms of incommunicability and tragedy, skepticism and misunderstanding; via Emerson in terms of skepticism and the "steps" we take in the sequentiality, if not the consequentiality, of an everyday life that is lived as if in a dream (sequence) or stupor, not quite spent in wakefulness; via Austin or Wittgenstein in terms of the effectuality (and failures) of speech acts, the deceptions as well as intelligence of ordinary language, and so on. As we would expect from a composer and improvisor, Cavell's literary-philosophical take on a matter is coextensive with the linguistic style—

and sonic sensibility—in which he makes it. Still more, and as a feature of his constitutional proclivities, autobiographical moments continue to inform our impressions and estimations of the distinctive attributes of his intellectual (dis)course.

To wit, there is something telling philosophically about the season when a life in professional music left Cavell, or he left it. "I mean," Cavell tells us in his memoir, "that I found the music I had written to be without consequence. It had its moments, but on the whole I did not love it; it said next to nothing I could, or wished to, believe."[50] What would it mean to write not just music, but anything consequentially? To move, if fitfully, from music composition to "writing words disconsolately in a journal" to composing consecutive philosophical prose endowed with literary finesse, possessed of an unmistakable voice, an inimitable sound? The fact that Cavell could hear the difference in musical performance—hitting the mark or improvising as the case called for—didn't satisfy him, but maybe those talents could be adapted and otherwise marshaled. Or that still further talents—other passionate interests—would announce themselves, as Cavell recalls of his time as an undergraduate writing music for a production of *King Lear* at Berkeley:

I came, not without considerable anxiety, to the first clear inklings, consciously and unforgettably, that I was more interested in the actions and ideas and language of the play, and in learning and understanding what might be said about them and what I felt I had to say about them, than I was in the music in which I expressed what I could of my sense of those actions and ideas and words (though doubtless writing music in response to the play had led me further into its world than, at that stage, I would or could have otherwise found myself).[51]

Observe Cavell's double assessment: that Shakespeare's writing attracted his attention beyond the music, summoning him to a spirit of critical commentary on the "actions and ideas and language of the play," and also that writing music *for* the play "led [him] further" into precisely those actions, ideas, and language than, at the time, he could have otherwise claimed purchase. Cavell studied the shifting calculus of his desire and pleasure at the intersection, at the overlap, of music and philosophy—asking what it would mean to think about the play rather than play its accompaniment. He was slowly, then suddenly, ready to trade his reeds for quills. And yet, despite the realignment, such fortuitous doubling or trebling (the polymath's gift) appears to track Cavell in later stages, since he continues to possess and develop a capacity for a kind of prismatic discernment of layered media and meaning as exhibited by sound, silence, image, text, motion, color, narrative, genre, and so on.

In the precarious and propitious moments of transition from music to philosophy that Cavell recounts, we may also glean a sense of how he comes to terms with his talents—that given talents of a certain sort or selection may not be enough to satisfy (that we may occasionally want to give them up, have given up on them, even if for an alternative to which we have a lesser claim). Cavell's fortune becomes clear in the virtuosity of his movement from music to philosophy, in part, as he has just noted, because training in music bestowed traits beneficial to the study and practice of philosophy (if again, requiring his adroit adaptation in the discipline as he found it). As Kenneth Dauber has written,

> Cavell is somebody who does not want to stop thinking. Rather, he wants to live *in* the thinking about his thinking. He doesn't want a place of rest. Exactly what he wants is to go over and over again the life you are thinking about, the life that you don't have. [...] Cavell wants to *live* in that human condition of a problematical self-consciousness.[52]

For Dauber:

> Cavell's response to [a scene of hearing the differences in a live performance of Bach]—one of the reasons why he decides that he doesn't want to be a musician or have a life in composition—is that he finds he was not interested in the talent that he had, in the fact that he heard it. But he was interested in the conditions which would enable one to hear it or not hear it. One of the things he rejects is his own talent, his own ability, as a resting place. He wants the ability to always be *thinking* about his own talents.[53]

To possess "the ability to always be *thinking* about" the conditions of or for those talents, how they express themselves, why they cause in him a perpetual restlessness about their character. After all, a rest is a musical notation; Cavell opts to indulge his fascination with the tempo of thought—from *accelerando* to *ritardando*—each next word and line inscribed with intention, suspended hopefully, aimed at achieving expressivity and intelligibility, seeking "not the overcoming of our isolation, but the sharing of that isolation—not to save the world out of love, but to save love for the world, until it is responsive again."[54] While he alights from his "laborious path to nowhere," Cavell follows an impulse toward what he will later call Emersonian (moral) perfectionism, a mood or mode of orientation to the world that might be glossed as getting right the pitch of life from moment to moment, as if playing or riffing.[55] The improvisational outlook encodes the sentiment of "nobody's perfect," but enacts such awareness by means of a propulsive interest in forward momentum—coupling rhythm and rhyme, intellectuality and artistry.[56]

* * * *

THE EMINENT INTERNATIONAL LINE-UP of contributors invited to this occasion—all of them seasoned critics of music in some form or fashion (in theory, criticism, performance) and its relationship to philosophy— are *also* all devoted to the ongoing inheritance of Stanley Cavell's legacy. Here they join forces to offer learned and arresting replies to the rhetorical question Wittgenstein posed above. That is, we know that an understanding of music is *essential* to understanding Cavell's work. *Music with Stanley Cavell in Mind* sets out to present a cogent case for why this was so, along the way offering compelling examples of how music found expression in his philosophical achievements, both his written texts and his classroom practice; how music informed his sense of what philosophy was for and how, in turn, we should understand its role in our lives.

As William Day writes in his chapter, italics added: "[i]t is to become even more familiar with the *philosopher* Cavell that our interest in Cavell the *musician* matters." Day continues: "There is a book to be written about Cavell's life with music and its place in his philosophical maturation (even if *Little Did I Know* would seem to satisfy that description)." With a chorus gathered, the present volume may serve as a collective effort toward such an ambition, a supplement of a recognizable sort—or, as a complement to such an as-yet-unwritten work. In our prismatic view of just that life and its maturation, we sustain reflections on why a "musical philosopher," or a philosopher attuned to music, or a philosopher for whom "the sound [of philosophy] makes all the difference," enriches our understanding of his *philosophical writing* and the many realms it touched and expanded. Here, we look to Cavell for lessons in listening, and not just to music, or the philosophical "uses" of music, but also to how sounds inform the nature of human experience and expression. Cavell would have been aware of the ambient presence of Suzanne Langer's work, especially her *Philosophy in a New Key* (1941), and how music is among those "key" meaning-making sign systems that should occupy the attention of philosophers—not merely as an addendum to investigations of art, myth, and ritual, but at the very core of human belief, feeling, and existential commitments. As so often happens, while some philosophers become associated with specific methods or categories—from logic (Kant) to liberalism (Mill), economics (Marx) to psychology (William James)—music, or sound, could be a candidate for being one of the most effective and illuminating ways of thinking about Cavell's diverse projects, across a range of texts, traditions, and media types.

While the proposed, now proffered, book may be belated, its timing is also opportune. Though Cavell first began making the transition (or better translation) from professional musician to professional philosopher in the 1950s, and as it were officially or decisively upon the appearance of "Music Discomposed" (1967, which was later featured in his seminal book, *Must We Mean What We Say?*), a new cache of writing by Cavell on music has been published from the *nachlass* entitled *Here and There: Sites of Philosophy*

(2022). *Hear in the Air*—becomes a lyrical alias and a figure for the happy industry of these pages. Case in point, the title of this editor's introduction is meant to riff on that book's subtitle, hearing in it homophonically also *sights* for which these notes mark off accompanying *sounds*—the audio/ visual as a pairing, assuredly, a marriage Cavell negotiated with unmatched grace. (The dulcet conceptual refrain beneath this book's official title, then, recommends itself in a clandestine variorum: *Hear in the Air: Sounds of Philosophy*.) With ears perked up, *cites* also calls out to the expansive range of Cavell's citations, his diverse thematic, textual, and disciplinary frames of reference—musical, operatic, cinematic, Shakespearean, Emersonian, literary, philosophical, psychoanalytic, Platonic. So abundant and so engrossingly made to speak to one another, at times to sing new songs together, this disparate group can also serve as frames of deference—perhaps especially in so far as such cites spell out Cavell's debts, how he endeavored to repay them with his own consummate contributions. Looking more expansively— to sites, sights, cites, and now also sounds—the present volume, has its own paired objective: to speak in multivocality across the long arc of Cavell's life with music (starting in the 1940s as biography, through the 1960s in a first-phase of foundational criticism that was followed by a series of professional engagements with his varied disciplinary assignments, onward until the 2010s—culminating memorably in his own time with *Little Did I Know*, which, as noted, is saturated with the sensibilities of a musician, and for the 2020s, up to and including the latest revelations of never-before-collected material in the posthumous *Here and There*).

Despite widespread scholarly fascination with the intersection of "Cavell" and "music"—that music is *famously* a core theme for him—no book like ours has yet appeared. Moreover, our efforts here are addressed to serious students (at all levels—from novitiates to seasoned scholars) and general readers alike arriving, as we must, from many precincts of thought and practice—musicology (harnessing, of course, the history of music, musical composition and performance, as well as music theory); cinema, media, improvisation, and sound studies; literary history, theory, and criticism; poetics; linguistics, deconstruction, critical theory; comparative literature; cultural studies; psychology and psychoanalysis; anthropology; and philosophy. The overriding spirit of the volume, as well as the immanent features of how it is written, are pedagogical in nature—aimed at drawing in students and readers (again, at whatever level of interest or expertise, how little or much one knows about Cavell), to provide them with access to conversations already in progress, inviting them to become engaged and excited about the stakes of Cavell's philosophy for our contemporary thinking about music, sound, sonic phenomena, and allied philosophical resonances.

Why Stanley Cavell's philosophical thought matters for the study and performance of music can also be asked in the other direction, as a similarly gratifying prompt: How did Cavell's musical practice and knowledge of music give shape to his most famous philosophical claims about cinema, human speech, opera, psychoanalysis, skepticism, and ordinary language philosophy? *Music with Stanley Cavell in Mind* provides a response with a first-of-its-kind intervention by leading philosophers and scholars of music into an intellectual landscape in need of such charting. As a performer and a devoted student of music, the arc of Cavell's wide-ranging philosophical investigation maps consistently with a proximate concern for the features of human sense that involve music and sound, including the sound of prose, authorial voice (its possession, divestment, and arrogation), the presence/problem/potentiality of silence in communication, and associated features of sonic experience central to life lived at the scale of the everyday.

Thinking of Cavell's writing directly addressed to music puts us in mind of what may be the two founding pieces of his scholarship on the philosophy of music, the aforementioned "Music Discomposed" and "A Matter of Meaning It," which were first published in *Art, Mind, and Religion*, edited by W. H. Capitan and D. D. Merrill (University of Pittsburgh Press, 1967), and later added to Cavell's "book of essays," *Must We Mean What We Say?* (Charles Scribner's Sons, 1969; reissued by Cambridge University Press, 1976).

Sound is a preoccupation early on in *The World Viewed: Reflections on the Ontology of Film* (Harvard University Press, 1971, enlarged edition, 1979) when Cavell considers the medium specificity of cinema—as a marriage of "Sights and Sounds" (chapter 2). And as a coda by way of returning to origins, his concluding chapter declares, "The Acknowledgment of Silence" (chapter 19), thereby drafting a master term from *Must We Mean What We Say?* into the service of thinking about and on film.[57]

As already referred to above, Cavell's *Pursuits of Happiness: The Hollywood Comedy of Remarriage* (Harvard University Press, 1981) achieves a sustained exemplification of the doubleness of musical topic and technique such that music/sound/voice/silence are under discussion throughout its pages even while Cavell's prose demonstrates his virtuosity at the (lettered) keyboard. As one pairing for consideration, first drop into his taxonomical segment devoted to "instances of singing throughout the films of remarriage," a study that culminates with a characteristically Cavellian resolution of antinomies: "film is the mode of modern entertainment in which the distinction between the popular and the learned or the serious breaks down, incorporating both."[58] And then listen to the sound of Cavell's phonemic writing in these lines—in fact, a lone sentence-as-paragraph—concluding his reflections on *Adam's Rib*: "Hatted, as for departure, away from us, they resume their adventure of desire, their pursuit of happiness, sometimes talking, sometimes not, always in conversation."[59] The poetry of the rhyme becomes its own send-off (departure/adventure; they/their/their; sometimes/sometimes not; always), a patterned tune for us to recall for consolation and instruction.

After Cavell presented the Jerusalem-Harvard Lectures, sponsored by the Hebrew University of Jerusalem, in November 1992, his expanded remarks became *A Pitch of Philosophy: Autobiographical Exercises* (Harvard University Press, 1994). In his Acknowledgments, Cavell starts by saying "[e]ach of these chapters represents some degree of departure from anything I have so far published,"—that word, departure (still fresh in mind from his final remarks on *Adam's Rib*), repeating with renewed significance in Part I of *Here and There*, which bears the name as its title (and commemorates his own valedictory moment post mortem). The invocation of *topoi* is felicitous since Cavell traveled upon and traversed so many disparate terrains. We can take care to note that he regarded his work as offering "some degree of departure," not a flight altogether. And so it is, for example, in chapter 3, "Opera and the Lease of Voice," dedicated to Judith Shklar (1928–1992), in which readers can measure the "degree" of distance from—but also proximity to—his earlier thoughts on musical expression and human expressiveness.

Cavell first began speaking publicly about the film *Gaslight* (1944, dir. George Cukor) in 1986, as it happens, also in Jerusalem, with initial reflections refined into "Naughty Orators: Negation of Voice in *Gaslight*," the inaugural chapter of *Contesting Tears: The Hollywood Melodrama of the Unknown Woman* (University of Chicago Press, 1996). "Such work," Cavell tells us, "necessarily contests disciplinary boundaries, sometimes by behaving as if they did not exist, sometimes by asking undivided attention to them. This has, I believe, helped somewhat to stall the hearing I have hoped the work would find."[60] Such a plaintive—sober but also heartfelt—description of circumstances should warm readers to Cavell's ambitions and make more evident the obstacles that were laid in response to them (again, abiding disappointment and consternation about how his work is sometimes uncharitably read). "Contesting disciplinary boundaries" being another theme of Cavell's methodology, not least an instinct he felt and honed when navigating his talents out of music and into philosophy. That is, while away from music per se, but also undeniably born up from it while bearing it, constituted under its aegis.

The gathering of musical affiliations—including performance art and dance—continue in none other than his Presidential Address to the American Philosophical Association, a public hearing (and airing) in Atlanta before a massive audience of professional philosophers just a few miles from where Cavell was born and lived as a child. Like a slow-building dirge, Cavell begins with an excerpt from John Dewey, lines from Nietzsche, acknowledgment of Emerson, Thoreau, film, and ... opera. Shakespeare and Kant follow along with J. L. Austin before the big reveal—what was that "something" you mentioned that was "out of the ordinary," which is to say, in and of it, wrested from the familiar coursings of popular culture and yet also exceptional to the point of exemplarity? Oh yes, Fred Astaire's song, dance, and speaking in Vincente Minnelli's *The Band Wagon* (1953). *S'wonderful, S'marvelous.*

Boundaries would appear to be duly tested, if not traversed and reallocated (earmarked for critical adjustment). When asked publicly "Why?" Cavell was said to have responded: "Because I wanted Fred Astaire to be part of the history of philosophy."[61] Who else would draw together a critique of Willard Van Orman Quine by way of one of Hollywood's premiere song-and-dance men? "Let's begin uncontroversially," Cavell requests, anticipating his possibly puzzled and wary audience.[62] For a later occasion, Cavell defiantly—and delightfully—holds the note a little longer when he turns to the question of "the capacity and right of praise" by returning to Astaire in a partner essay delivered while serving as Visiting Spinoza Professor at the University of Amsterdam (1998) and when speaking before the American Political Science Association (1999).[63] Whether in Atlanta or Amsterdam, Cambridge or Jerusalem, before an agreeable or a circumspect crowd, Cavell's interventions in the history of philosophy make serial contact with the well-springs of his abiding attunement to the philosophical pertinence of music—of melody, lyric, and the affecting potencies of sound.

The third part of *Here and There: Sites of Philosophy* (Harvard University Press, 2022) constitutes an ensemble of previously uncollected pieces on music, including two on opera: "An Understanding with Music" (chapter 21, delivered at the American Musicological Society, October 1998) and "Kivy on *Idomeneo*" (chapter 22, presented at the American Society for Aesthetics, 1999), that is, Peter Kivy (1934–2017) on Mozart's opera; an essay on Arnold Schoenberg (1874–1951) entitled "Philosophy and the Unheard" (chapter 23, 1999) and one on Beethoven, "Impressions of Revolution" (chapter 24, given at the Bard Music Festival, August 2000). The series concludes with "A Scale of Eternity" (chapter 25), also presented at the Bard Music Festival (2002), in which Cavell addresses the work of Gustav Mahler (1860–1911), a composer whom Wittgenstein disliked (even though, or perhaps because, he performed in the Wittgenstein family home[64]), in which Cavell begins by noting Mahler's belatedness—another feature of Cavell's own self-image.

Cavell was a devoted attendee at the Bard Music Festival, beginning in 1990. And by the later part of the decade, he was invited on several occasions—at the festival and elsewhere—to speak at more length and detail about his then-current impressions of music, and not surprisingly, about the role of music in the life of philosophy, if also his own. In 1999, for instance, at a Harvard conference in honor of David Lewin (1933–2003), Cavell returned to the scene of his 1967 essay, "Music Discomposed" with "Philosophy and the Unheard." At this remove, more than three decades later, though, he has the advantage of surveying his various disciplinary border crossings and testings, and how a unity or continuity abides:

[W]hile I have written very little explicitly about music over the ensuing decades, I have known for most of that time that something I have demanded from philosophy was an understanding precisely of what I had sought in music, and in the understanding of music, of what demanded that reclamation of experience, of the capacity for being moved, which called out for, and sustained, an accounting as lucid as the music I loved.[65]

Here, among other places, Cavell and Wittgenstein seem very much of a piece, as when Cavell highlights a line from the *Philosophical Investigations* that may explain why his guide, in fact, didn't pursue a more robust agenda of comments on music (including on its intimate relationship with philosophy—and, by his own account, Wittgenstein's work in particular): "Understanding a sentence is much more akin to understanding a theme in music than one may think" (§527), an echoic line that ramifies throughout Wittgenstein's corpus and *nachlass*, and now Cavell's, as well as in these proceedings. Why is that so? Because music, like the best writing, resists paraphrasing: it demands faithful citation, even if with variations ("interpretations" so-called). If music can serve as an abstraction of human emotion, then writing about music insists on the attempt to articulate with specificity what is at stake. As Cavell said early on, "[c]riticism, as part of the philosophy of art, must aspire to philosophy."[66] It chanced upon Cavell's return to Berkeley—not as a musician but as a Harvard-trained philosopher, and yet to the very place he studied music—that he recognized "music [...] as a figure for the mind in its most perfected relation to itself, or to its wishes for itself"—and not least "contrary to so much in the formation of professional philosophy in those years."[67] Can philosophy become music and still know itself? Cavell's writing career offers a full-throated and mellifluous reply.

As sometimes happens with prophetic writing, the library of subsequent commentary on it can exceed the quantity of source materials. Such may now be the case with remarks on Cavell's writings, including on the twinned topics of "Cavell and music," since the roster addressed to that heading continues to proliferate, for example, and would include—not exhaustively but emblematically—previously published work by contributors to this volume. Beyond that formidable sheaf of dispatches on our appointed pair, doubtless informing the contours of the new research offerings to follow here, we find, again as a measure of representativeness: Stephen W. Melville's *Philosophy Beside Itself: On Deconstruction and Modernism* (1986); Dennis Des Chene's "In Touch with Art: Cavell and His Critics on New Music" (1989); Diana Raffman's *Language, Music, and Mind* (1993, a comparative study of Cavell and Nelson Goodman); Timothy Gould's *Hearing Things: Voice and Method in the Writing of Stanley Cavell* (1998);[68] Roger V. Bell, Jr.'s *Sounding the Abyss: Readings between Cavell and Derrida* (2004); a special issue of the *Journal of Music Theory*, Cavell's "'Music Discomposed' at 40," edited by Brian Kane and Stephen Decatur Smith (2010, vol. 54, no. 1); Arnold I. Davidson's contribution to *The Oxford*

Handbook of Critical Improvisation Studies (vol. 1), "Spiritual Exercises, Improvisation, and Moral Perfectionism: With Special Reference to Sonny Rollins" (2016); Michael Gallope's *Deep Refrains: Music, Philosophy, and the Ineffable* (2017);[69] Lydia Goehr's essay on "What Anyway Is a 'Music Discomposed'?" and the cascade of responses to it collected in *Virtual Works—Actual Things: Essays in Music Ontology*, edited by Paolo de Assis (2019); Adam Gonya's *Stanley Cavell and the Potencies of Voice* (2019); Sandra Laugier's *"The Claim of Reason* as a Study of the Human Voice" (2021); and Vincent Colapietro's "Must We Sing What We Mean?" in *Cavell's Must We Mean What We Say? at 50*, edited by Greg Chase, Juliet Floyd, and Sandra Laugier (2022), where he writes that "Stanley Cavell's voice was one of fluency inflected with hesitancy, of self-affirmation conjoined with self-aversion, one of bold assertion tied to nuanced qualification, and a voice prone to protracted pauses, not all of which were unabashed."[70] Once again, and enduringly, Cavell's self-possession would be tethered to sound, including, as the case may have called for, a taciturn hush.

In such a sketch of the various districts of uptake, we could include especially trenchant appraisals (make those takedowns?), such as the aforementioned George Steiner's *New Yorker* review (1989), and more recently, Joseph Urbas' "How Close a Reader of Emerson is Stanley Cavell?" in the *Journal of Speculative Philosophy* (2017), Marshall Cohen's "Must We Mean What We Say?" in the *Los Angeles Review of Books* (2019), Lola Seaton's "The Sound Makes All the Difference" in *The Point* (2022), and John-Baptiste Oduor's "The Shadows of Stanley Cavell" in *The Nation* (2022), even as we look elsewhere at moments of glancing but productive engagement and willing integration, such as by Richard Taruskin in *Music in the Late Twentieth Century* (2009); Lawrence Kramer in *Expression and Truth: On the Music of Knowledge* (2012); James Buhler and Alex Newton, when they draw Cavell's remarks on sound into their discriminating discussion of the score for the *Bourne* trilogy (2013); or when, in another scene, Kendall Walton conjures a "Cavell-Calvino observation about sounds"—viz., that we treat them as independent entities, whereas we don't accord the same reified status to sights (2015).[71] In *John Cage's Concert for Piano and Orchestra* (2020), Martin Iddon and Philip Thomas, herald Cavell as "the first philosopher to attempt to translate the concerns of the post-war generation of composers, Cage included, into the Anglo-American context."[72]

When Michael S. Roth describes "The Music of the Ordinary" in the *Los Angeles Review of Books* (2022), he tells us there is "nowhere else" to "encounter the sounds one encounters" in Cavell's writing. That elevated election of sonic singularity harkens back to Arthur Danto's sentiments about reading Cavell forty years earlier when he reports to us soon after a deep session of encounter: "This is a voice like no other in philosophy, today or ever," and Danto goes on:

and the only voice it at all resembles is in fiction, indeed, in *Le Neveu de Rameau* [*Rameau's Nephew* by Denis Diderot], the voice of the Musician, seven-eighths moocher and one-eighth genius, who delivers a performance at one point so astounding that Hegel describes it with awe: [...] The style of this speech is the madness of the musician who "piled and mixed up together some thirty airs, Italian, French, comic, tragic, of all sorts and kinds; now with a deep bass, he descended to the depths of hell, then, contracting his throat to a high piping falsetto, he rent the vault of the skies, raving and soothed, haughtily imperious and mockingly jeering by turns."[73]

Danto picks up the point again by saying of *Pursuits of Happiness*, had "Rameau's nephew written an opera, it would be like this book. All the rules of criticism would have to be altered to accommodate it." Thinking back to Robert Warshow's distinctive influence on Cavell, we can add *invented* to altered, since the degree of transformation extends beyond mere adaptation to something like creation. Philosophy had become literature had become music.

The variety of comments on—and criticisms of—Cavell and music, or Cavell and sound, or Cavell on speech and the human voice, provides its own attestation to the viability, versatility, and durability of his writing on these and related subjects. With diverse and dispersed episodes of attention to Cavell and music within close range, the following critical essays complement and capably extend the now multigenerational, that is, ongoing, endeavor to inherit and interpret Cavell, all the while in conversation with his many interlocutors. As we look back—re-view—the scope and spans of Stanley Cavell's work, as we listen anew, it's worth dwelling on how (after Emerson's remark to Fuller at the outset) the Cavellian understanding of "self possession" finds expression in his prose, full of poise, tact, and mindful onwardness. Among other exemplars, we could do worse than manage imitations, but, if we really catch the tune—the fraught power and perspicacity of the instances he provided—we might just be ready for improvisations all our own. Now that would be an enviable legacy.

Notes

1   Stanley Cavell, "Epilogue: Bon Voyage," in *Here and There: Sites of Philosophy*, ed. Nancy Bauer, Alice Crary, and Sandra Laugier (Cambridge, MA: Harvard University Press, 2022), 288.

2   Ralph Waldo Emerson to Margaret Fuller, *The Letters of Ralph Waldo Emerson*, ed. Ralph L. Rusk (New York: Columbia University Press, 1939), May 1, 1839, vol. II, 197.

3   Claude Lévi-Strauss, *The Naked Man*, trans. John Weightman and
    Doreen Weightman (London: Jonathan Cape, 1981), 647 as quoted in
    Michael Poizat's *The Angel's Cry: Beyond the Pleasure Principle in Opera*,
    trans. Arthur Denner (Ithaca: Cornell University Press, 1992; originally
    published as *L'Opéra, ou Le Cri de L'ange: Essai sur la jouissance de
    l'amateur d'opéra* by Éditions A. M. Métailié, 1986). Cited by Cavell in "An
    Understanding with Music," *Here and There*, 251.

4   Cavell, "An Understanding with Music," *Here and There*, 253.

5   For further nuances of this phrasing, see also William Day, "Words Fail Me.
    (Stanley Cavell's Life Out of Music)," in *Inheriting Stanley Cavell: Dreams,
    Memories, Reflections*, ed. David LaRocca (New York: Bloomsbury, 2020),
    187–97. See also, in the same volume, Andreas Tauber, "Cavell's Ear for
    Things," 199–206.

6   For more on Cavell's name change, see "Titles Manifold," in my *Emerson's
    English Traits and the Natural History of Metaphor* (New York: Bloomsbury,
    2013), XVI.12–13, XVI.17; 315–25 and "Autophilosophy," *Inheriting Stanley
    Cavell*, esp., 304–5.

7   Stanley Cavell, *Little Did I Know: Excerpts from Memory* (Stanford: Stanford
    University Press, 2010), 11.

8   Stanley Cavell, "Epilogue: After Half a Century," in Robert Warshow, *The
    Immediate Experience: Movies, Comics, Theatre, and Other Aspects of
    Popular Culture*, Enlarged Edition (Cambridge, MA: Harvard University
    Press, 2001 [1946]), 291.

9   Cavell, "Epilogue," *The Immediate Experience*, 290.

10 Ibid., 291.

11 Ibid., 289.

12 Stanley Cavell, "Freud," in *Cities of Words: Pedagogical Letters on a Register
    of the Moral Life* (Cambridge, MA: The Belknap Press of Harvard University
    Press, 2004), 282.

13 Cavell, "Freud," *Cities of Words*, 292–3.

14 See Cavell, "Introduction: In the Place of the Classroom," *Cities of
    Words*, 1–18.

15 Cavell, "Introduction," *Cities of Words*, 2.

16 Stanley Cavell, "Epilogue," *The Immediate Experience*, 293; italics in original.

17 Stanley Cavell, "Must We Mean What We Say?," in *Must We Mean What We
    Say? A Book of Essays* (New York: Charles Scribner's Sons, 1969; Cambridge:
    Cambridge University Press, 1976; updated ed., 2002; Cambridge Philosophy
    Classics, 2015), ch. 1, 36 n.31; italics in original. Cavell returns to the sound
    of difference between American pragmatism and American transcendentalism
    in "What's the Use of Calling Emerson a Pragmatist?" in Stanley Cavell,
    Emerson's Transcendental Etudes, ed. David Justin Hodge (Stanford: Stanford
    University Press, 2003), 215–23.

18 See my "Autophilosophy," *Inheriting Stanley Cavell*, 275–320.

19 Cavell, *Little Did I Know*, 2.

20   Stanley Cavell, "Performative and Passionate Utterance," in *Philosophy the Day after Tomorrow* (Cambridge, MA: The Belknap Press of Harvard University Press, 2005), 185.

21   Michael Gallope, *Deep Refrains: Music, Philosophy, and the Ineffable* (Chicago: University of Chicago Press, 2017), 164.

22   Cavell, *Little Did I Know*, 200.

23   Cavell, "Philosophy and the Unheard," *Here and There*, 261. Wittgenstein wrote to M. O'C. Drury: "It is impossible to say in my book [*Philosophical Investigations*] one word about all that music has meant in my life. How then can I hope to be understood?" M. O'C. Drury, "Some Notes on Conversations with Wittgenstein," in *The Selected Writings of Maurice O'Connor Drury: On Wittgenstein, Philosophy, Religion, and Psychiatry*, ed. John Hayes (New York: Bloomsbury, 2019 [2017]), 151. See also Béla Szabados, *Wittgenstein as Philosophical Tone-Poet: Philosophy and Music in Dialogue* (Amsterdam: Rodopi, 2014), 20–1.

24   Cavell, "Philosophy and the Unheard," *Here and There*, 261.

25   See again, for example, Szabados, *Wittgenstein as Philosophical Tone-Poet*.

26   William H. Gass, "The Music of Prose," in *Finding a Form: Essays* (New York: Alfred A. Knopf, 1996; first published in *Antaeus*, 1993), 314.

27   See Garrett Stewart on phonemic reading in *Reading Voices: Literature and the Phonotext* (Berkeley: University of California Press, 1990). See also ch. 3, "Literary Graphonics," in *Attention Spans: Garrett Stewart, a Reader*, ed. David LaRocca (New York: Bloomsbury, 2024), 69–76.

28   William H. Gass, "A Memory of a Master," in *Fiction and the Figures of Life* (New York: Alfred A. Knopf, 1970), 247.

29   Gass, "A Memory of a Master," *Fiction and the Figures of Life*, 248.

30   Cavell, "Epilogue," *The Immediate Experience*, 291.

31   Brian Kane, Introduction, *Journal of Music Theory*, Special Issue: Cavell's "'Music Discomposed' at 40," ed. Brian Kane and Stephen Decatur Smith, vol. 54, no. 1 (2010): 2.

32   David Hume, *A Treatise of Human Nature* (1739), II.3.3, 415.

33   Peter Yates, "Two Albums by John Cage—Part I," *Arts & Architecture* (March 1960), 32.

34   Leslie Chamberlain, *Nietzsche in Turin* (New York: Picador, 1999 [1996]), 64.

35   Thirty years later, these two essays—"Thinking of Emerson" and "An Emerson Mood"—will lead the entries in Cavell's book-length study of Emerson, the aforementioned *Emerson's Transcendental Etudes* (2003).

36   Cavell says of *The Senses of Walden*: "This book was written during my tenure as a Fellow of Wesleyan University's Center for the Humanities in 1970–71." (New York: Viking, 1972; Chicago: University of Chicago Press, 1979), ix.

37   Stanley Cavell, *The World Viewed: Reflections on the Ontology of Film*, Enlarged Edition (Cambridge, MA: Harvard University Press, 1979 [1971]), xix.

38 Stanley Cavell, "Knowledge as Transgression: *It Happened One Night*," in *Pursuits of Happiness: The Hollywood Comedy of Remarriage* (Cambridge, MA: Harvard University Press, 1981), 86; italics in original.

39 George Steiner, "Wording Our World," *The New Yorker* (June 19, 1989), 99.

40 Cavell, *Emerson's Transcendental Etudes*, 1.

41 For more on unlived lives, see my review of Andrew H. Miller's *On Not Being Someone Else: Tales of Our Unled Lives*, *Victorian Studies*, vol. 64, no. 3 (Spring 2022): 466–8.

42 Steve Reich, *Writings on Music, 1965-2000*, ed. Paul Hillier (Oxford: Oxford University Press, 2002), 8.

43 Jonathan Cott interview with Steve Reich, New York, 1996, https://stevereich.com/jonathan-cott/.

44 Reich, *Writings on Music*, 8.

45 Ibid., 9.

46 Ibid.

47 Cavell, *Little Did I Know*, 400.

48 For informed replies to such persistent and indispensable questions by dozens of authors, see *Inheriting Stanley Cavell* (2020) and *Acknowledging Stanley Cavell*, ed. David LaRocca, a special commemorative issue of *Conversations: The Journal of Cavellian Studies*, no. 7 (2019): 1–276.

49 See, for example, my "Contemplating the Sounds of Contemplative Cinema: Stanley Cavell and Kelly Reichardt," in *Movies with Stanley Cavell in Mind*, ed. David LaRocca (New York: Bloomsbury, 2021), 274–318; and "From Lectiocentrism to Gramophonology: Listening to Cinema and Writing Sound Criticism," in *The Geschlecht Complex: Addressing Untranslatable Aspects of Gender, Genre, and Ontology*, ed. Oscar Jansson and David LaRocca (New York: Bloomsbury, 2022), 201–67.

50 Cavell, *Little Did I Know*, 223.

51 Ibid., 215.

52 Kenneth Dauber and K. L. Evans, "Revisiting Ordinary Language Criticism," *Inheriting Stanley Cavell*, 149.

53 Ibid.

54 Cavell, "A Matter of Meaning It," *Must We Mean What We Say?*, 229.

55 Cavell, *Little Did I Know*, 225.

56 Those last two words are Cavell's; see *Little Did I Know*, 85.

57 Namely, "Knowing and Acknowledging," which was first presented at a colloquium convened at the University of Rochester in May 1966, offered in reply to a paper by Norman Malcolm. Find it in Cavell, *Must We Mean What We Say?*, ch. IX, 238–66.

58 Cavell, "The Same and Different: *The Awful Truth*," *Pursuits of Happiness*, 248, 251.

59 Cavell, "The Courting of Marriage: *Adam's Rib*," *Pursuits of Happiness*, 228.

60   Stanley Cavell, *Contesting Tears: The Hollywood Melodrama of the Unknown Woman* (Chicago: University of Chicago Press, 1996), xii.

61   The anecdote was relayed to me by John Lachs, though I can't recall if it was he who did the asking.

62   Stanley Cavell, "Something Out of the Ordinary," *Philosophy the Day after Tomorrow*, 22.

63   See Stanley Cavell, "Fred Astaire Asserts the Right to Praise," *Philosophy the Day after Tomorrow*, 61–82.

64   See Ray Monk, *Ludwig Wittgenstein: The Duty of Genius* (New York: Penguin, 1991), 8.

65   Cavell, *Here and There*, 260.

66   Cavell, *The World Viewed*, 202.

67   Cavell, *Here and There*, 260–1.

68   See my review of Timothy Gould's *Hearing Things* in *The Review of Metaphysics*, vol. LIII, no. 4 (June 2000): 931–3.

69   Offering a reply to the question that launches these remarks, if in another context, see Michael Gallope's *The Musician as Philosopher: New York's Vernacular Avant-Garde 1958–1978* (Chicago: University of Chicago Press, 2024).

70   Vincent Colapietro, "Must We Sing What We Mean?" in *Cavell's* Must We Mean What We Say? *at 50*, ed. Greg Chase, Juliet Floyd, and Sandra Laugier (Cambridge: Cambridge University Press, 2022), 148.

71   James Buhler and Alex Newton, "Outside the Law of Action: Music and Sound in the *Bourne* Trilogy," in *The Oxford Handbook of Sound and Image in Digital Media*, ed. Carol Vernallis, Amy Herzog, and John Richardson (Oxford: Oxford University Press, 2013), 325–49. Kendall Walton, *In Other Shoes: Music, Metaphor, Empathy, Existence* (Oxford: Oxford University Press, 2015), 169.

72   Martin Iddon and Philip Thomas, *John Cage's Concert for Piano and Orchestra* (Oxford: Oxford University Press, 2020), 422.

73   Arthur C. Danto, "Philosophy and / as Film and / as If Philosophy," *October*, vol. 23 (Winter 1982): 13–14.

MOVEMENT I

Measures

1

Critical Listening

An Understanding of Cavell's "An Understanding with Music"

JEAN-PHILIPPE ANTOINE

To Lisa, who listens

"Performance is the foundation of Cavell's writing."[1]
—CHARLES BERNSTEIN

I

TO BEGIN WITH I MUST CONFESS my own difficulty in coming to an understanding with Stanley Cavell, partly because of a continuous sense of the intellectual performance at work in his texts, always very upfront, and partly because of the effort required to find my way in the baroque bifurcations of his prose. In the case of his very scarce writings on music, this difficulty is both emphasized and lifted, because of my own strong interest in music and sounds, but mostly because of the very specific and somewhat paradoxical position that music occupies in his world, a position indicated in an exemplary manner by "An Understanding with Music"[2] and its insistence on critical listening.

I would like now to quote two sentences of Wittgenstein that repeatedly anchor Cavell's late reflections on music and philosophy. The first one— in my own understanding the most important—is: "How can anyone understand my thoughts who does not know what music has meant in my life?" And the second one, maybe more of a red herring: "Understanding a sentence is much more akin to understanding a theme in music than one may think."[3] Both sentences appear in quick succession in "An Understanding with Music"[4]; they are repeated, in the same order, in "Philosophy and the Unheard"[5]; the second one makes a third and final appearance, in a new translation, in "A Scale of Eternity."[6]

I will add to these two sentences one of the most famous, and these days most popular statements of Friedrich Nietzsche, a philosopher who, according to Cavell, "[knew] what art is"[7]: "Life without music is a mere error, a calvary, an exile."[8] Both Nietzsche and Cavell started as musicians and apprentice-composers, and their philosophizing arose after the abandonment of their ambitions in composing music. So we may reasonably assume that when Cavell quotes "How can anyone understand my thoughts who does not know what music has meant in my life?," a question that Wittgenstein addressed both to himself and to his readers, Cavell presents a rather poignant plea to his own readers.

To these initial parallels we may yet add another one. The second time Cavell quotes Wittgenstein's question, in "Philosophy and the Unheard," he expresses astonishment at the contrast between significance implied in the question and the very sparse remarks Wittgenstein devoted to music in his writings. This question, once again, could be addressed to Cavell himself: with the notable exceptions of "Music Discomposed," a chapter in *Must We Mean What We Say?* evidently devoted to the posterity of Arnold Schoenberg's atonal music (and just as much to its criticism), and of the third and final lecture published in *A Pitch of Philosophy*, "Opera and the Lease of Voice,"[9] Cavell wrote only the five philosophical essays which conclude *Here and There*.[10]

Of course one may count as another notable exception the smattering of autobiographical fragments concerning Cavell's relationship to music distributed across *Little Did I Know*, his late and moving autobiography, with the provision that these notations of various lengths, kaleidoscopically distributed at aleatory intervals, and, as we shall see soon, mostly concerned with relating facts in a personal life history, do not—and do not pretend to—deliver the same type of critical discourse on music as the essays, as vital as they may be in helping us appreciate how much Cavell's later relationship to music is grounded in an intense experience of mourning.

One may dwell on the fact that the five essays just mentioned are all *responses* to a prompting—an eminently musical situation, not to say a theatrical or operatic situation. But the following pages will concentrate on the term *understanding* that both anchors and haunts the first of these five essays, especially in its multiple relationships to music. All of this inquiry aimed at potentially reaching an understanding with Cavell.

II

Such an inquiry is not an easy task for several related reasons. First, music itself is less present here, in this handful of essays, as an object of study than as a lost object or an expression of loss. To clarify this point it will be useful to go back to the very opening of the third autobiographical exercise included in *A Pitch of Philosophy*, here with my emphasis added:

> When a few years ago I was asked to say how as a philosopher I had become interested in film, I replied by saying, roughly, that *the inflection more pertinent to my experience was how a lost young musician had come to recognize his interests as philosophical*, one whose education (in narrative, in poetry, in song, in dance) had been more formed by going to the movies than by reading books. I might have included listening to the radio along with going to the movies, since, interweaved with many other matters, broadcasts were the primary attestation I had growing up of high culture as a shared world, of ours as a reformable world, not merely endurable. Film was rapturous, as was jazz, but shareable only by marvelous chance; *radio announced itself as originating from some specific elsewhere*.[11]

These remarks tell us two remarkable things. First, Cavell's entry into philosophy was that of a "lost young musician," a youth whose search for a place in the world through music had not succeeded. He was "the only child of a mother who," not content with being a very accomplished pianist and possessing perfect ear, "was next to the oldest of six children, all but one of them musicians, two of them professional,"[12] so the familial and social pressure to become involved in making music must have been very high. Indeed it was enough to bring him to seriously start studying music in view of a professional life as a musician, before he realized that composing music wasn't his calling, and abruptly quit The Juilliard School. At around the same time, improvised music of the highest caliber had also felt out of reach to him, so the pianist, clarinetist, and saxophonist would from then on resort to distinguished amateur practice, mostly playing and improvising from the Great American Songbook on his piano.[13]

A second remarkable point in the opening of "Opera and the Lease of Voice" is the role that Cavell attributes—in his upbringing and especially in his access to what he chooses to call "high culture"—to his listening to the radio, often a communal listening. The importance of radio, with its emphasis on voice—one of the main themes in Cavell's subsequent philosophical reflections—gives us an important clue to the type of relationship with music here at work: not that of a composer or improviser of new music, but rather that of someone foremost interested in listening, and in *critical* listening: an interpreter of an existing text, interpretation being the highest form of critical listening, just as translating may be the highest form of reading. (And it may be germane to these circumstances to recall that Cavell considers philosophy to be "a set of texts" rather than a set of problems). It is quite striking, then, as well as somewhat logical, that Cavell's writing on music issues from the position of listener—a sophisticated, informed listener, but above all an ordinary listener among a community of ordinary listeners, whose commonality is their experience of being affected, and at times deeply affected, by music, often by music embodied in a voice.

At the same time, this emphasis on listening as the core of Cavell's relationship to music doesn't entirely compute: his very few texts on music, written after "Music Discomposed," are all occasional pieces, prompted by invitations and by the reading of recommended books and texts by musicologists or aficionados of opera, as is the case with "An Understanding with Music." All of them deal with "high culture" music, and none with jazz, which comes as a surprise, given the importance of the latter in Cavell's life.

Also, most references to actual pieces of music in the texts from part III of *Here and There*, come up in discussions relating less to the actual shape of the musical discourse than to the moral problems embodied in the characters of this or that opera. Or they arise in abrupt critical judgments and aphorisms, as often as not unsubstantiated by a detailed analysis of the score or of the recording at issue.[14] Music, for Cavell, belongs to the very same territory occupied by film and theater, and it is envisioned in terms that resemble those he used in his texts on, for instance, the comedies of remarriage or *King Lear*. This territory is the territory of culture, whether "high culture," as exemplified in the opening sentences of "Opera and the Lease of Voice," or more popular or experimental cultures such as film and jazz, but always "culture."[15]

Such findings are all the more strange coming from the writer who ends his "Opera and the Lease of Voice" by musing on a quotation from the *The Birth of Tragedy*, where Nietzsche, once again, explicitly separates the scenic apparatus and the text of opera from the sheer emotional power of its music:

I must not appeal to those who use the images of what happens on the stage, the words and emotions of the acting persons, in order to approach with their help the musical feeling; for these people do not speak music as their mother tongue and, in spite of this help, never get beyond the entrance halls of musical perception. [...] *I must appeal only to those who, immediately related to music, have in it, as it were, their motherly womb, and are related to things almost exclusively through unconscious musical relation.*[16]

Cavell asks:

Am I ready to vow, as when Bloch asked us whether we heard through to Bach, *that I have the ear*, that I know my mother's mother tongue of music to be also mine?[17]

The formulation of Cavell's quandary becomes especially significant when one considers his appeal here to two unquestionable figures of authority: Ernest Bloch, the composer and teacher whose "work and presence," which Cavell experienced during his college years at Berkeley, concurs with J. L. Austin's in having profoundly modified his life;[18] and his mother, Fannie Goldstein (née Segal), whose musical gifts and professional practice played a huge role in his early relationship to music. The "mother tongue" of music did indeed come to him through this particular mother's filters and idiosyncrasies, creating an early set of problems and organizing what may be identified as three different moments in Cavell's relationship to music— using the word *moment* here as much in its logical as in its chronological sense.

III

The most archaic of these moments is the early experience of Cavell's "mother's mother tongue of music," remembered as the lost childhood "heaven" of "the Chopin Fourth Ballade and Kreisler encores and the Bach D minor double violin concerto that *my mother and her brothers played when we lived together as a lullaby reward for my going to bed without complaint*,"[19] as well as, later on, regularly and disobediently listening to the Atlanta radio show for whose orchestra his mother played the piano every weeknight.[20] Cavell's early musical culture thus occupies a space delimited on one hand by eighteenth- and nineteenth-century instrumental classical music, from Bach to Brahms through Mozart and Beethoven,[21] *heard at home*, and on the other hand by

a kind of agreeable salon music, most of it drastically familiar, *whose pieces no one would seem to have taken the trouble to compose since they appear to have existed forever*, that formed the basis of the WSB orchestra's repertory. [...] I have an undying intermittent taste, even sometimes a modest craving for this indestructible music, in certain respects an increasing admiration for it.[22]

Although strongly anchored in the classical nineteenth-century canon, this uncomposed salon music, mostly "heard through the radio," points to the more popular culture signaled by its use in twentieth-century cartoons. While pleasant or even at times ecstatic, this early experience of music was no heaven. For Cavell's mother's musical gifts—a perfect ear, playing "like a man,"[23] and an exceptional capacity for sight-reading—as much as they commanded his first accession to music, questioned his relationship to music as a "mother tongue,"[24] thus giving birth to a second moment in an already complex relationship. The second moment develops when the teenage Cavell, until then confined to playing the piano, learns the clarinet, and, soon after, the alto saxophone. This largely self-taught endeavor[25] leads him to perform in various school bands, dance bands, jazz bands, and ultimately musical theater, then to map, with reasonable success, a musical territory of his own, where the names of Benny Goodman (his main inspiration in wanting to learn the clarinet) and Artie Shaw—not to mention Lester Young, Ben Webster, Coleman Hawkins and others—will rival those of Bach, Chopin, Liszt, or Beethoven:

It was clear at once that the clarinet was going to do for me what the piano would, so far as I could see, never do. I would be able to read the single notes of clarinet parts as fluently as my mother could read music at the piano (something I despaired of ever learning to do, something I felt indeed was a mystery that could not be learned), and it would thereby provide companionship.[26]

Cavell's new musical practice of the clarinet, which implied playing together with others for an audience, allowed the young musician to escape both from the domesticity wherein music had previously been contained and from the "high culture" type of music with which its playing was associated. In a more comprehensive way, "the intervention of a new form taken by my musical talent served to rescue me from an intolerable social impasse, a conviction held in place by various sources of confirmation that I belonged in no place that I had so far conceived as some place in which for me to exist."[27] If the new social scene accessed by playing in the various bands, which Cavell was involved with in his late teens and early twenties, helped to eliminate the "intolerable social impasse" that had been, until then, weighing on his existence, it also paradoxically manifested in new ways how for him the practice of music consisted essentially in the interpretation of a written text—a text that must be learned as such, thus explaining the quasi-metaphysical status obtained by the question of sight-reading. Cavell's account of his *apprentissage* here looms especially large:

When I was not practicing the instrument, I was listening obsessively to recordings of the Benny Goodman and the Artie Shaw bands, memorizing and copying down what solos of theirs I felt I could best negotiate, and drawing various configurations of the kind of decorated music stands, with my initials on them indicating the band's leader, used by all the big bands visible in movies of the period, extending to larger and larger imaginary bands on variously deployed platforms.[28]

Exemplary music must be memorized, and in order to be memorized—and later (re)performed—it must be listened to again and again, and its sounds transformed into a written text. The interpretation of a written text, at most tolerating a few augmentations in stride, provided Cavell with a model for the practice of music in which sight-reading more or less occupies the space of improvisation.[29] The continued relevance of music as a written text to be interpreted does explain the transition to the third and in several ways final moment of Cavell's fraught relationship to music: becoming a composer.

Already, while arranging a song for one of the bands he played with, Cavell found himself more interested in the writing of music than in its performance.[30] His preference led to a decision to pursue a bachelor's degree in composition at the University of California, Berkeley—as well as to change his surname before entering college.[31] To the quite systematic "initiation into the theory and composition of music" that ensued in the next three years at Berkeley, including summer classes with Ernest Bloch already mentioned, and a regular activity playing the clarinet in various settings,[32] must be added the unexpected but nonetheless important involvement of the young musician in musical theater.

If Cavell, during his time at Berkeley, never "completed work to be shown to Ernest Bloch and Roger Sessions, the music of both of whom [he] unreservedly believed in, as similar in seriousness as they were distant in procedure and sound from each other,"[33] an initial contribution to the annual Mask and Dagger Revue in 1945 led to two more, and to the regular writing of "incidental music for a number of university productions, roughly one each semester."[34] Cavell's writing of incidental music may in the end have been more important in shaping his future life than the "serious systematic learning" of music composition and the type of music with which it was associated. The "incidental" music was the actual music he wrote and publicly delivered during those years—as opposed to the "serious" music he postponed writing through these assignments. Composing this type of music, through an intense frequentation of theater, brought him to the growing realization that performing (and even writing) music was not, or was no longer, his main interest in life:

Socially the most impressive of these efforts was orchestrating and conducting the music for the Kurt Weill/Moss Hart musical *Lady in the Dark*. [...] Intellectually and artistically, the most lasting of these efforts was writing music for the production of *King Lear* (running, it will emerge, just over four hours, with two intermissions). *It was here, playing music cues at the piano for scene rehearsals, and for run-throughs, and, assembling and rehearsing a small orchestra, conducting dress rehearsals and eight performances, that I came, not without considerable anxiety, to the first clear inklings, consciously and unforgettably, that I was more interested in the actions and ideas and language of the play, and in learning and understanding what might be said about them and what I felt I had to say about them, than I was in the music in which I expressed what I could of my sense of those actions and ideas and words* (though doubtless writing music in response to the play had led me further into its world than, at that stage, I would or could have otherwise found myself).[35]

From this scene of realization and from multiple related experiences, we may date the conscious emergence of the feeling of fraudulence that Cavell finally associated with the writing—and not just the performing—of music. In this sense his subsequent move from California to New York, upon graduation, in order to study composition at Juilliard, more than opening a new chapter in a life in music provides a definitive conclusion to it—an affirmation of an already settled acknowledgment:

My application [to Juilliard] was successful, but I now knew, almost thoroughly, almost face-to-face, almost calmly, that the prospect was irrelevant. I mean that I found the music I had written to be without consequence. It had its moments, but on the whole I did not love it; it said next to nothing I could, or wished to, believe.[36]

It was then a matter of months before Cavell, having started to "play hooky" from his composition classes, decided to quit Juilliard and music altogether:

Music had my whole life been so essentially a part of my days, of what in them I knew was valuable to me, was mine to do, that to forgo it proved to be as mysterious a process of disentanglement as it was to have been awarded it and have nurtured it, eliciting a process of undoing I will come to understand in connection with the work of mourning.[37]

IV

"An Understanding with Music" constitutes yet another mournful attempt—a late one at that—to answer the questions just voiced in Cavell's musical itinerary, or rather to formulate these questions on new terms. The piece supposedly reports to an "outreach panel" of the American Musicological Society on the philosopher's "initial difficulties" in reading two musicological texts dealing with opera. But, as suggested by its title, something other than musicology is at stake here, and this something else takes its time to arrive: the word *understanding* doesn't appear before page three of this seven-and-a-half page essay, in a rather unstable context, mixing problems of Foucauldian historiography, the novelty of the invention of "characters speaking in song," and the question of "the incompleteness of the understanding of another," before coalescing, unsurprisingly under Wittgenstein's patronage, into a by now traditional Cavellian question:

> Now does it make sense in general to frame the question of my knowledge of another soul, as it were the existence of another body possessed of a consciousness like mine, as one in which I *no longer* know or understand an other, can no longer think the thought of an other, as if there had been a *break* between us?

To which a no less Cavellian (and non-Foucauldian) answer is immediately given:

> The break in question may lie in me, without my surmising that my conditions of possibility differ from yours; *our sameness contributes to the anguish.*[38]

The real problems dealt with by the text begin only then, with the introduction of "passionate utterance," Cavell's take on Austin's "perlocutionary force," in which "the interest in language is not primarily in what I do with it as in what I suffer from it." When I perform a perlocutionary act, "the other is, as an effect of my words, wounded, embarrassed, intimidated, fascinated, terrified, horrified, exalted, seduced."[39] In other words the utterance of words by someone produces varied emotions and reactions in another person addressed by that speech. And in Cavell's rendering, we have abruptly switched from the position of uttering (with the illocutionary utterance) to that of listening (with the perlocutionary utterance). The shift involves what Cavell, in the speech where he develops more fully his critique of Austin's use of the perlocutionary, calls "the expressiveness and responsiveness of speech as such."[40]

In "An Understanding with Music," though, speech is being replaced by language, a move explained by the next set of references brought along by Cavell, prompted by his reading of Michel Poizat's *The Angel Cry: Beyond the Pleasure Principle in Opera*, the second of the two texts whose reading he reports on. Cavell singles out from Poizat's book a quotation from Claude Lévi-Strauss' *The Naked Man*:

[T]here would be no music if language had not preceded it and if music did not continue to depend on it, as it were, through a privative connection. Music is language without meaning: this being so, it is understandable that the listener, who is first and foremost a subject with the gift of speech (*un sujet parlant*), should feel himself irresistibly compelled to make up for the absent sense, just as someone who has lost a limb imagines that he still possesses it through the sensations present in the stump.[41]

By accepting the Lévi-Straussian conflation of *speech* with *language*, Cavell immediately destroys the set of Austinian concepts that govern the analysis of perlocutionary force, concepts having to do with speech, with *acts* of language, not with language itself as the object of semiology. At the same time this choice enables Cavell to create a genealogy of music based on its "separating off from language." In music, language survives only in the shape of a ghost: an illusion in terms of knowledge, whose only reality is felt pain.

Cavell's attachment to Lévi-Strauss' formulation of music as "language without meaning," with its substitution of language for speech or discourse, is demonstrated in a further set of remarks:

It is the familiar, almost unnoticeable metaphor of music as a language that perhaps forces the idea of meaning as essential to it. So let's try to capture the insight in Lévi-Strauss's formulation by changing the name "language" to "system of communication." [...] The system of communication called music would be the antithesis of [Wittgenstein's] primitive language [in the second section of *Philosophical Investigations*], music existing in the absolutely sophisticated state in which understanding is endless, in which everything that happens is to be taken as significant, and nothing comes, or need come, as an isolated or incontestable meaning.[42]

Replacing "language" with "system of communication" does extend the domain covered, but it nevertheless remains in the same semiotic territory indicated by the word "language." And of course, the "system of communication" Cavell describes, with its total lack of noise, is just unthinkable ... unless we give it its rightful name: *discourse*. If the adoption of Lévi-Strauss' genealogy of music justifies the status of music as foremost an object of loss and therefore of mourning, it also entails a new emphasis on the semiotic dimension of language to the detriment of the semantic analysis of speech, which would be called for[43]—a move paralleled by the equivalency also posited here between knowledge and understanding.

One cannot but wish that, instead of a book quoting Lévi-Strauss, Cavell had been given, or stumbled upon, a book quoting the French anthropologist's older colleague and mentor, the linguist Émile Benveniste. In his celebrated article on "The semiology of language," a text where the comparison between discourse and music looms very large, Benveniste wrote:

Semiotics designates the mode of signification proper to the linguistic SIGN that establishes it as a unit. We can, for purposes of analyses, consider separately the two surfaces of the sign, but with respect to its signification, it is a unit; it remains a unit. [...] With the semantic, we enter a specific mode of meaning which is generated by DISCOURSE. The problems raised here are a function of language as producer of messages. However, the message is not reduced to a series of separately identifiable units; it is not the sum of many signs that produce meaning; on the contrary it is meaning (*l'intenté*), globally conceived, that is actualized and divided into specific signs, the WORDS. In the second place, semantics takes over all the referents, while semiotics is in principle cut off and independent of all reference. Semantic order becomes identified with the world of enunciation and with the universe of discourse.

That it is a question of two distinct orders of ideas and of two conceptual universes, we can still demonstrate through the difference in criteria of validity required by each. Semiotics (the sign) must be RECOGNIZED; semantics (the discourse) must be UNDERSTOOD. *The difference between recognition and understanding refers to two distinct faculties of the mind: that of discerning the identity between the anterior and the current, and that of discerning, on the other hand, the meaning of a new enunciation.*[44]

Should we accept—quite reasonably—Benveniste's distinction between semiotics and semantics, and therefore between recognition and understanding, we may locate in Lévi-Strauss' thinking, and unfortunately in Cavell's through his quote of Lévi-Strauss, an unacknowledged mixing of semiotics with semantics which ultimately confuses the relationship between meaning and understanding. When Cavell defines music as "language without meaning," we may assume that what he really intends is music as "understanding without recognition," the word *without* bearing no intimation of loss, as implied by another passage from Cavell's text, which states that "music lacks meaning the way the night lacks the sun, it's what music *is*."[45] The sun is as external to the night—defined by the absence of sunlight—as recognition is external to understanding. And meaning here should be identified with recognition, which has little to do with *understanding*, i.e., with "discerning the meaning *of a new enunciation.*"

Interestingly, in "Opera and the Lease of Voice," Cavell had used the much more appropriate expression "understanding without meaning" to define, not exactly what music is, but what music "is supposed to provide." In doing so, Cavell sided this time with Benveniste, who had characterized music as well as the plastic arts as systems of semantics without semiotics.[46] There meaning resides exclusively in enunciation and in its capacity to syntagmatize units, such as sounds or colors, that taken by themselves do not signify anything (as opposed to words, which are immediately signs).[47] The context of Cavell's alternate definition of music is his discussion of Stéphane Mallarmé's description of *Pelléas et Mélisande*, Maurice Maeterlinck's play (not yet set to music by Claude Debussy), as "musical in the real sense":

> Anyone who has heard Mallarmé's description of Maeterlinck's play, in a review written near the time Debussy was deciding to set it, as "musical in the real sense" (as cited in chapter 4 of *Debussy, Pelléas et Mélisande*, ed. Nichols and Smith) is bound to have a guess at what he had in mind. My guess is that he saw in the play its texture of totality yet discreteness of juxtaposition, of irresolution without indecisiveness, very near to and very far from the resonance of our world, always and never over. It is how I see Debussy's perception of the play's possibilities, as providing a human scale for his own intersections of the sensuous and the abstract, the evanescent and the permanent, assertion without the continuities of assertion, significance without consequence, reference without truth, *understanding—as music is supposed to provide understanding—without meaning*, the complete awaiting completion, the before and the after of saying.[48]

These remarks emphasize the ambiguous meaning attached by Cavell to the idea of *understanding* when considered in relationship to music, an ambiguity best summarized in a passage from *Little Did I Know*, where he is once again concerned with his mother's "legendary" or "magic" ability to sight-read:

> My mother's ability to sight-read at the piano was legendary in her musical circles—to me it was for so long purely a display of magic—and a benefit to me of learning to play clarinet and saxophone was, as I had predicted, that the sight-reading of the single lines allotted to these instruments was as immediately available to me as piano music was to my mother. *I was going to say that this made sight-reading as easy for me as reading words. So just this easy was reading piano music for my mother (no doubt within limits I hadn't yet experienced). But if she was reading words then what was I reading? Letters? Or was she reading phrases and sentences?*—as I must have surmised when I turned pages for her, since she always nodded for me to turn well before she had played the last measures on the page.[49]

Cavell's moment of hesitation here, though quickly and rightly resolved (yes, his mother sight-read *sentences*, hence the magic), speaks volumes. Even if his mother indeed read sentences, sentences are made up of words, i.e., signs. Couldn't these signs be or once have been meaningful independently of their present arrangement in this or that particular sentence or set of sentences?

Cavell's memories, as well as his comments concerning Debussy's take on Maeterlinck's play, suggest that the appearance in "An Understanding with Music" of the Lévi-Straussian idea of "music's separating off from language," that is, of "Poizat's use of the idea, or fantasy, of the relation of the present separation of music and language to a preseparative unity," and of "[Gary] Tomlinson's proposal, or reaffirmation, of a state [...] of a musical and linguistic magical harmony prior to one of representative distance,"[50] indeed, has to do with a sense of loss and anguish—and yet a sense of loss not caused by "our sameness." Rather such loss is related to Cavell's personal history, as expressed in the interrogation formerly given voice in "Opera and the Lease of Voice": "Am I ready to vow [...] that I know my mother's mother tongue of music to be also mine?" A question that prompts me to ask what shape this appropriation of the mother's mother tongue of music should ultimately take, when music has taken the mournful shape of the ghost of sight-reading?

V

To answer this last question, my own, it is necessary to switch gears and to privilege the shaping of "An Understanding with Music," rather than its recognizable meaning-as-content, as I have until now. Envisioned as a whole composition, "An Understanding with Music" doesn't begin with the exposition of a theme which is then developed; rather, it builds up by accumulating variegated elements, many of them borrowed from other writers,[51] whose aggregation, in the end—and only in the end—discovers a motif previously repeated in various disguises and never stated in full. For these reasons, I suspect the reference to Wittgenstein's remark, "Understanding a sentence is much more akin to understanding a theme in music than one may think," may be a red herring. Indeed, Cavell's way of composing prose is very much *unlike* the type of mostly classical music here envisioned by Wittgenstein. Cavell's writing has much less to do with presenting a theme and then composing variations of it (and eventually reexpositing the theme enriched by its variations) than with the use of heterogeneous elements that will eventually become a motif recognized *in the end*, and only then, as having been running through the whole piece all the while. This difference may be one of the factors explaining the absence of jazz as a topic in Cavell's writing. The kind of jazz he first practiced and then mostly listened to definitely used themes—"standards"—as springboards for improvisation, or rather ornamentation, a structure closely resembling the approach of "theme + variations," as opposed to the slow building of a motif, which we may for instance find in free jazz.

In "A Scale of Eternity," the last of the five texts on music in *Here and There*, when quoting Wittgenstein's sentence again—here differently translated as "Understanding a sentence lies nearer than one thinks to what is ordinarily called understanding a musical theme"—Cavell suggests we should "take it to mean, whatever else, that understanding a sentence is *hearing the music that shapes its life*"—a much broader concern than the one expressed by Wittgenstein, and one that this time would definitely encompass Cavell's own elaboration of sentences.[52] For Cavell's writing does not start from a problem. It starts from the encounter with a text or, as here, with several texts, assembled and read in order to hopefully arrive at a fully expressed problem. Once it arrives at this point, the text simply stops, tempting one to read it again backwards in order to appreciate how the progressive aggregation of quite heterogeneous elements got us to the final statement, and how these elements, put together in order to resonate with each other, create "an understanding," i.e., the perception of a new enunciation.

In "The World as Things," reflecting on collecting as thinking and musing on a particular episode of Emerson's journals, Cavell wrote: "Everything about Emerson's practice as a writer bespeaks this sense of aggregation and juxtaposition—from his culling from his journals for individual essays, to the sense of his sentences as desiring to stand apart from one another, each saying everything, each starting over."[53] This sentence seems a reasonably good description of Cavell's own way of writing, with the provision that, if his sentences desire to stand apart, "each saying everything, each starting over," they actually do not stand apart, but are, instead, very much a part of a performed flow.

Once again, the understanding here invoked by Cavell doesn't consist in identifying a particular statement; likewise, his conclusions are famously open and will be frustrating to anyone looking for closure.[54] Such understanding concerns, in Benveniste's words, "meaning [*l'intenté*—literally *the intended*] globally conceived," even though in discourse it is "actualized and divided into specific signs." Understanding concerns sentences, the basic units of semantics,[55] but it also looks to phrases, paragraphs, parts, the text shaped as a whole and as a vehicle for "a new enunciation." Understanding is also an understanding *with*, and as such calls for our eventual response.

Cavell's take on understanding introduces us to a lasting paradox in reading Cavell's work and trying to "understand his thoughts," which we well know by now requires "understanding what music meant in [his] life." When we look for what music meant in Cavell's life, we probably shouldn't stop at his writings on music, as interesting and colorful as they may be; nor should we fix ourselves on the "avoidance of music" exhibited by his overall production of written texts. Rather, we should investigate the making of his sentences and paragraphs, their aggregations and bifurcations, blind alleys, the multiple quotes they riff on, the memories they integrate and periodically reshape—and investigate them all for the *understanding without meaning* they are supposed to provide. In these sentences and paragraphs, the activity of critical listening required from musicians and philosophers alike is put to the test, and it is put to the test by the improvisational nature of the writing, the perpetually elusive search for "a new enunciation" over the ruined recognitions of known language.

Beyond coming to understand Cavell's meaning, coming to an understanding *with* Cavell then entails the same capacity for listening deployed in the improvisational character of his writings. Reading him, we are invited, going even beyond sight-reading, to deploy the same type of critical listening his writing attempts to practice, and in turn to make it ours through our own cadences, sentences, and paragraphs. Critical listening invites speech: *our* speech, made up of our own arrangement of sentences. Rather than "participat[e] in the order of law," we are invited, in Cavell's own words, "to improvisation in the disorders of the desire."⁵⁶ And here we enter our understanding with Stanley Cavell.

Notes

1   Charles Bernstein, "Finding Cavell," *ASAP Journal* (July 26, 2018), asapjournal.com/finding-cavell-charles-bernstein/.

2   Stanley Cavell, "An Understanding with Music," in *Here and There: Sites of Philosophy*, ed. Nancy Bauer, Alice Crary, and Sandra Laugier (Cambridge, MA: Harvard University Press, 2022), 247–54.

3   Ludwig Wittgenstein, *Philosophical Investigations*, 3rd ed., trans. G. E. M. Anscombe (New York: Macmillan, 1968 [1953]), §527 (and not §541, as intimated by Cavell).

4   Cavell, "An Understanding with Music," *Here and There*, 253.

5   Ibid., 261.

6   Ibid., 280. See, further down, note 28.

7   Stanley Cavell, "Music Discomposed," in *Must We Mean What We Say?* (Cambridge: Cambridge University Press, 1976), 182.

8   "Das Leben ohne Musik ist einfach ein Irrtum, eine Strapaze, ein Exil." Friedrich Nietzsche, letter to Peter Gast (Heinrich Köselitz), Nice, January 1, 1888.

9   Stanley Cavell, "Opera and the Lease of Voice," in *A Pitch of Philosophy: Autobiographical Exercises* (Cambridge, MA: Harvard University Press, 1994), 129–69.

10 "It was in this same period that I discovered, after some years of resistance to it, the liberation in the teaching of Wittgenstein's later work, centered in the

Philosophical Investigations. I was not exactly surprised to learn eventually of Wittgenstein's remark: 'How can anyone understand my thoughts who does not know what music has meant in my life?' but it makes me wonder the harder why he actually says so little about music." Cavell, "Philosophy and the Unheard," *Here and There,* 261.

11 Cavell, "Opera and the Lease of Voice," *A Pitch of Philosophy,* 131; italics added.

12 Stanley Cavell, *Little Did I Know: Excerpts from Memory* (Stanford: Stanford University Press, 2010), 10.

13 See Charles Bernstein's testimony: "Cavell once told me that once he heard Charlie Parker or Monk, can't recall who, then he knew he could not do that, not as good as them, so had to find another way, via his work as a philosopher (or essayist)." Charles Bernstein, email to the author, June 16, 2022. See Charles Bernstein, "Stanley Cavell on Close Listening," February 2, 2013 (recorded December 10, 2012), *Jacket 2,* jacket2.org/commentary/stanley-cavell-close-listening.

14 An exception in this respect is Cavell's beautiful discussion of Violetta and Germont père's duets in *La Traviata,* which offers a detailed account of the tone modulations and musical progression of the scene in relation to the feelings and social demands expressed by the characters. See "Opera and the Lease of Voice," *A Pitch of Philosophy,* 155. Many small vignettes in *Little Did I Know* further confirm Cavell's proficiency in musical analysis, a proficiency grounded in regular musical practice, whether in jazz and dance bands or, later on, in chamber music and (university) symphony orchestras, as well as in academic classes. See for example Cavell's digression there on "the pain within joy" that characterizes the experience of great music: "I knew that no composer could exhaust this fact of music from the time I realized that even Chopin could not approach by means of a simple diatonic melody (as in the counter-theme of the G major Nocturne, whose excited opening theme is running thirds and sixths) the intensity of expression in, for example, the simplicity of the variation theme in Beethoven's last piano sonata. The limitation of actuality, for example, of sustaining reliable closure with it, seems openly announced in the desperation of the dozens of repetitions hanging on as if for dear life to the concluding C major triad of the Beethoven Fifth." *Little Did I Know,* 165. These scattered notations make all the more remarkable the scarcity of musical analysis in his theoretical writings.

15 See again: "I might have included listening to the radio along with going to the movies, since, interweaved with many other matters, broadcasts were the primary attestation I had growing up of high culture as a shared world, of ours as a reformable world, not merely endurable. Film was rapturous, as was jazz, but shareable only by marvelous chance; *radio announced itself as originating from some specific elsewhere.*" *A Pitch of Philosophy,* 131. Cavell's mention of radio as announcing "itself *as originating from some specific elsewhere*" brings us back, though, to the specific place music may occupy *outside* of this cultural territory.

16   Friedrich Nietzsche, *The Birth of Tragedy and The Case of Wagner*, trans.
      Walter Kaufmann (New York: Vintage Books, 1967), §21; italics added.

17   Cavell, "Opera and the Lease of Voice," *A Pitch of Philosophy*, 169; italics
      added. Nietzsche goes on to ask what could be anachronistically construed
      as a very Cavellian question: "I ask the question of these genuine musicians:
      can they imagine a man capable of hearing the third act of *Tristan und
      Isolde* without any aid of word or scenery, purely as a vast symphonic
      period, without expiring by a spasmodic distention of all the wings of the
      soul?" (translation Dover, 1995, different from the one used by Cavell). The
      dream of a vast period without words permeates "An Understanding with
      Music." Cavell's allusion to Ernest Bloch refers to an earlier passage in *A Pitch
      of Philosophy* (48–50) relating an epiphany of sorts experienced in Bloch's
      classes at Berkeley.

18   Cavell, *Little Did I Know*, 4. See also 85: "Bloch, as much as any teacher I
      have experienced, altered the contour of my life, altered what I was reading,
      how I was reading, what I hoped for from intellectuality as well as from
      artistry."

19   Cavell, *Little Did I Know*, 97; italics added.

20   "It was vaguely supposed that I was to get to bed by 10:00 on school nights,
      but I regularly tuned into the beginning of my mother's program at 10:30 to
      listen to the theme, in which the piano was prominent, and generally to hear
      the orchestra's principal contribution to the show's events." Cavell, *Little Did
      I Know*, 106.

21   Aside from the already mentioned pieces by Chopin, Bach, and Kreisler, *Little
      Did I Know*'s virtual playlist includes Mendelssohn's Rondo Capriccioso;
      Bach's solo violin sonatas; Beethoven's Fifth Symphony, last piano sonatas,
      bagatelles, and Ghost Trio; Mozart's G minor Symphony; Liszt's Sixth
      Hungarian Rhapsody; Brahms' G major Violin Sonata and A major Piano
      Quartet.

22   Cavell, *Little Did I Know*, 113–14; italics added. Among "the most famous"
      and "the best examples of these" pieces, Cavell lists: "Liszt's *Liebestraum*
      (featuring my mother's virtuosity in its two cadenzas), Cécile Chaminade's
      Scarf Dance, the Meditation from *Thais*, Grieg's *Peer Gynt*, sections of
      Tchaikovsky's *Nutcracker Suite*. [...] Certain of their cousins, on the whole
      more ambitious offerings (arias from *Carmen* and from Gounod's *Faust*,
      Chopin's *Funeral March*, parts of Mendelssohn's *Midsummer Night's Dream*)
      were staples of the sound tracks of classical movie cartoons. My children,
      Rachel, Benjamin, and David, without growing up in total immersion in the
      world of classical music, would very early sing along with classical themes
      coming from the FM concert music stations to be found I suppose in any
      university town, that they would not often, if ever, have heard in concert, or
      heard me play, and I had to be told from which cartoon this piece of their
      musical education had been acquired. [...] For years after this enterprise was
      in her past, my mother and I, hearing such a piece over the air, would glance
      at each other and say together, not with unmitigated nor unaffectionate
      condescension, 'WSB.'" Cavell, *Little Did I Know*, 113–14. As we observe

here, the "specific elsewhere" the "radio announced itself as originating from"—see above note 15—also belongs to the mother.

23 "I note that the expression of some particular pleasure in hearing a man's touch at the piano took the form in my mother of her claim, or self-observation, that she played like a man." Cavell, *Little Did I Know*, 210.

24 "Music making, until I began playing in bands, was essentially a separate land from which my mother would intermittently bring back news." Cavell, *Little Did I Know*, 221.

25 "I largely taught myself to play the instrument by working through an illustrated handbook that evidently came with it." Cavell, *Little Did I Know*, 63.

26 Ibid.

27 Ibid., 68.

28 Ibid., 68, italics added. The drawings of the imaginary bandstands bearing Cavell's initials in stylized lettering provide another indication of his personal investment in this new practice.

29 Even his choice of alto saxophone, as opposed to tenor, seems to obey the same logic: "I chose the alto on completely independent grounds—I might say artistic grounds, but they were also in a clear sense deeply prudential. I already knew enough to be fascinated by comparing the undeniable geniuses of tenor saxophone playing of the years around 1940 (Lester Young, Ben Webster, and Coleman Hawkins) and not to be outclassed, even in fantasy, before drawing a serious breath to play, I chose so as to avoid them. (Charlie Parker's alto saxophone was several years in the future.) Moreover, *I had divined that playing lead alto in a swing band, which I had no doubt I would do, required general musicianship more than the ability to improvise, in which I was all but completely untested.*" Cavell, *Little Did I Know*, 70–1; italics added.

30 "The energy I had put into the single arrangement I had written that summer had helped teach me that music now meant to me writing or nothing." Cavell, *Little Did I Know*, 201.

31 For more on Cavell's name change, see David LaRocca, "Titles Manifold," in *Emerson's English Traits and the Natural History of Metaphor* (New York: Bloomsbury, 2013), XVI.12–13, XVI.17; 315–25.

32 "I would spend all night, four or five nights a week, in the music building doing theory assignments for classes, playing one of the several pianos inadequately sound-proofed from one another, listening to the library of recordings, and endlessly writing the beginnings and rebeginnings of compositions or orchestrations. [...] By the fall semester of my first undergraduate year, that is to say, after a spring and a summer semester, I had settled into something that looked more or less like a predictable life of study and performance (performance consisting mostly in playing clarinet in the university symphony, and in various chamber-music recitals—there were plenty of pianists around)." Cavell, *Little Did I Know*, 212–13.

33 Ibid., 223.

34 Ibid., 215.

35 Ibid.; italics added.

36 Ibid.

37 Ibid., 225. This "work of mourning" culminates in what Cavell, very early in his autobiographical endeavor, imagines as "the practice of the renunciation." Reflecting on his renewed interest in the work of fellow philosopher Vladimir Jankelevitch, Cavell comments: "I seem now to glimpse a possible cause of my impulse in invoking so early in the story the work of Jankelevitch. It was not alone because he is one of the rare figures for whom writing about music has been a significant part of a significant philosophical body of work, but because of learning that with the ascendancy of Hitler, Jankelevitch forswore forever reading and mentioning German philosophy and listening to German music. *My recurrent, never really avid, interest in this experiment has been not so much in fathoming its hatred but in trying to imagine the practice of the renunciation.*" Cavell, *Little Did I Know*, 5; italics added.

38 Cavell, "An Understanding with Music," *Here and There*, 249–50; italics added.

39 Cavell, "An Understanding with Music," 250.

40 Stanley Cavell, "Something Out of the Ordinary," in *Proceedings and Addresses of the American Philosophical Association*, Nov. 1997, vol. 71, 23–37, 29; reprinted in *Philosophy the Day after Tomorrow* (Cambridge, MA: Harvard University Press, 2005), 7–27, 17.

41 Michel Poizat, *The Angel's Cry: Beyond the Pleasure Principle in Opera*, trans. Arthur Denner (Ithaca: Cornell University Press, 1992 [1986]), x. See Claude Lévi-Strauss, *The Naked Man*, trans. John Weightman and Doreen Weightman (London: Jonathan Cape, 1981), 647; here is the full quotation in French: "Sans doute la musique parle-t-elle aussi mais ce ne peut être qu'à raison de son rapport négatif à la langue et parce qu'en se séparant d'elle, la musique a conservé l'empreinte en creux de sa structure formelle et de sa fonction sémiotique: il ne saurait y avoir de musique sans langage qui lui préexiste et dont elle continue de dépendre, si l'on peut dire, comme une appartenance privative. La musique, c'est le langage moins le sens; dès lors on comprend que l'auditeur, qui est d'abord un sujet parlant, se sente irrésistiblement poussé à suppléer ce sens absent comme l'amputé attribuant au membre disparu les sensations qu'il éprouve et qui ont leur siège dans le moignon."

42 Cavell, "An Understanding with Music," *Here and There*, 252–53.

43 The notion is quite clearly stated by Lévi-Strauss in the sentences that immediately precede the ones quoted first by Poizat, and then later by Cavell: "In the first place, if music and mythology are each to be defined as language from which something has been subtracted, both will appear as derivative in relation to language. If this supposition is correct, music and mythology become by-products of a structural shift which had language as its starting-point. *Music no doubt also speaks; but this can only be because of its negative*

relationship to language, and because, in separating off from language, music has retained the negative imprint of its formal structure and semiotic function: there would be no music." See Lévi-Strauss, *The Naked Man*, 647; italics added.

44   Émile Benveniste, "The Semiology of Language," *Semiotica*, trans. Genette Ashby and Adelaide Russo (1981), 5–23, 19–20; translation modified, italics added.

45   Cavell, "An Understanding with Music," *Here and There*, 252; italics in original.

46   Benveniste, "The Semiology of Language," *Semiotica*, 20.

47   "Music is made up of sounds which have a musical status when they are designated and classified as notes. There are no other units in music directly comparable to the 'signs' of language. These notes have an organizing framework, the scale, in which they are employed by virtue of being discrete units, discontinuous from one another, of a fixed number, each one characterized by a constant number of vibrations in a given time. [...] There is no limit to the multiplicity of sounds produced simultaneously by a group of instruments, nor to the order, to the frequency, or to the scope of combinations. The composer freely organizes the sounds in a discourse that is never subjected to any 'grammatical' convention, but that obeys its own 'syntax.' [...] We can say, on the whole, if music is considered as a language, it has syntactic features, but not semiotic features." Benveniste, "The Semiology of Language," *Semiotica*, 13–14.

48   Cavell, "Opera and the Lease of Voice," *A Pitch of Philosophy*, 163–4; italics added.

49   Cavell, *Little Did I Know*, 188–9; italics added. The depth of these interrogations is fully revealed in the lines that follow: "That I had decided to understand, nor rather not to understand, sight-reading to constitute a mystery, one revealed to my mother that I was not to attempt to fathom, was not made fully or undeniably conscious to me until some ten years after the sunless late winter afternoon I walked out of my composition lesson at Juilliard six or seven weeks after term began in January 1947, knowing that I would not return." The practice of renunciation takes time—time to mourn.

50   Cavell, "An Understanding with Music," *Here and There*, 251.

51   See Richard Beaudouin, "You're There and You're Not There: Musical Borrowing and Cavell's 'Way,'" in *Journal of Music Theory*, vol. 54, no. 1 (Spring 2010): 91–105. Beaudouin remarks that "Many philosophers and commentators have engaged with *writing about the writings of other writers.* Readers of Cavell know that he can take this practice much further and that his writings often become *writing about another writer's writings about other writers.* This can be enlightening; it can also veer toward mannerism" (94). In his "Reading Cavell Reading Wittgenstein," Charles Bernstein writes perceptively: "While it would be extremely misleading to say that Cavell is creating poetic texts by collage—it would mistake both his genre and his style—it is to the point that his compositional method is one of ordering and arrangement more than exposition, that he is aware that the creation of

the world, as much as writing, is a matter of succession, of conjunction and disjunction, of production, more than approximation and reflection." See *boundary 2*, vol. 9, no. 2, A Supplement on Contemporary Poetry (Winter 1981): 295–306, 296.

52 Cavell, "A Scale of Eternity," *Here and There*, 280; italics added.

53 Cavell, "The World as Things: Collecting Thoughts on Collecting," *Here and There*, 62–3.

54 As noted by Charles Bernstein: "With Cavell, it is just as much a matter of the thinking provoked (or better to say evoked) along the way than any final position that can be summarized." Here again, critical listening is the order of the day. See Charles Bernstein, "Staging Praise / Owning Words," in *Inheriting Stanley Cavell: Memories, Dreams, Reflections*, ed. David LaRocca (New York: Bloomsbury, 2020), 130.

55 "In reality the world of the sign is closed. From the sign to the sentence there is no transition, either by syntagmatization or otherwise. A hiatus separates them." Benveniste, "The Semiology of Language," *Semiotica*, 20.

56 Cavell, "Performative and Passionate Utterance," *Philosophy the Day after Tomorrow*, 185. See also Philip Mills, "Poetic Perlocutions: Poetry after Cavell after Austin," *Philosophical Investigations*, vol. 45, no. 3 (July 2022): 365.

2

Impressions of Meaning in Cavell's Life Out of Music

WILLIAM DAY

STANLEY CAVELL WASN'T THE FIRST TO ARRIVE at philosophy through a life with music.[1] Nor was he the first whose philosophical practice bears the marks of that life. Jean-Jacques Rousseau "testifies to the harmony between his musical work and his philosophy in his *Dialogues*."[2] Friedrich Nietzsche saw himself as "the most musical of all philosophers"—presumably more than even his musico-philosophical mentor, Arthur Schopenhauer— and asserted in all seriousness that "without music, life would be an error."[3] Ludwig Wittgenstein told his friend Maurice Drury, "It is impossible for me to say in my book one word about all that music has meant in my life. How then can I hope to be understood?"[4] (That these are all philosophers Cavell wrote about and cared about shouldn't go unnoticed.) I don't recall when exactly Stanley told me that a highlight of his high school years was playing lead alto sax in an otherwise all-Black jazz band; or when I heard the story of his performing at Berkeley in the premiere of an opera by Roger Sessions during which the English horn player had some mishap and Stanley, seated next to him playing clarinet, transposed and played the English horn solo on the spot; or when he confessed to me late in his teaching career, after the first iteration of his opera course, his nearly unbearable, silent anxiety or fear (somehow traceable to his mother's perfect pitch) that in humming or singing an excerpt from an aria in class he might be reproducing the melody in the wrong key.[5]

Much of Cavell's life with music is confirmed for the world in his philosophical autobiography *Little Did I Know*. The place of that life for Cavell is best captured, to my ear, in the anecdote of what he calls his "impotent gallantry." On leaving a New Year's Eve party in Greenwich Village as 1948 became 1949, he offered to escort a Black singer-friend to her apartment up in Harlem. Recalling her unease and eventual admonishment as they walked together north of 125th Street—"Don't you see that you are in far greater danger here than I am? Please go back."—Cavell writes, in partial echo of Wittgenstein's despairing remark to Drury: "It had evidently never occurred to me that a black person would not know by looking at me what my life with music had been and therewith comprehend that that life of mine exempted me from participation in the tragedy of racial injustice."[6] It's possible to read the autobiographer here as admonishing his younger and naive Juilliard-student self. (The autobiographer calls his book, after all, *Little Did I Know.*) But on what account? Naivete isn't a philosophical error. Self-ignorance, however, is. What strikes the older Stanley in this memory, I think it's clear, is the younger Stanley's youthful failure to recognize that this crucial aspect of his identity doesn't show itself with every step and breath he takes. It is a gentle, convivial admonishment, the kind that a musico-philosophical mentor might give, smilingly, to a student he or she is fond of.

The numerous scattered anecdotes of Cavell's early musical career in *Little Did I Know* are capped off by an entry on April 10, 2004, describing his eventual realization that he was to leave that career behind—for what exactly, he did not yet know. As his description makes clear, it would take the better part of a lifetime for the leaving to arrive at an end:

> Yet this laborious path to nowhere had, I laboriously came to understand, been essential for me. Music had my whole life been so essentially a part of my days, of what in them I knew was valuable to me, was mine to do, that to forgo it proved to be as mysterious a process of disentanglement as it was to have been awarded it and have nurtured it, eliciting a process of undoing I will come to understand in connection with the work of mourning.[7]

Readers of Cavell may well be surprised by the implication that the concept of mourning, a master tone of Cavell's writing from his reading of Thoreau's *Walden* through his essays on Coleridge and Wordsworth and Emerson's "Experience," should have as one of its originary sites the memory-shock of his leaving his musical life behind.[8] There is no mention of mourning, notably, in Cavell's description of his family's move, just before he turned seven, from the south side of Atlanta to its north side—an event often highlighted (including by me) in discussions of *Little Did I Know.*[9] But mourning will become for Cavell an emblem of the perfectionist work of philosophy itself, which "has to do with the perplexed capacity to mourn the passing of the world."[10] If the emblem of that emblem for Cavell is the abandonment or transformation of his life with music for a life of philosophy, a life dedicated to "the repetitive disinvestment of what has passed,"[11] then Cavell's life with music and thoughts about the nature of music ought to be revelatory of Cavell's philosophical life and thoughts.

Is that promising too much? It can seem to overlook the simple, undeniable truth that Cavell's musical performance and improvisational and compositional abilities were after all, pretty completely, when all is said and done, *abandoned*. It is also true that the singular musical experience Cavell writes about most often—his composing, while at Berkeley, the incidental music for a student production of *King Lear*—had its greatest impact on him, as he discovered "not without considerable anxiety,"[12] for the thoughts it engendered about Shakespeare's play rather than for the music it drew out of him. But then unsurprisingly, as Cavell acknowledges, what leads him into *Lear*'s world is exactly his writing and rehearsing and conducting this music "in response to the play." My concern, in any event, isn't to resuscitate Cavell the musician (though some amateur recordings of him at the piano improvising on popular songs near the end of his life are, I found on the distracted occasions of my hearing them, intriguing). It is to become even more familiar with the philosopher Cavell that our interest in Cavell the musician matters.

There is a book to be written about Cavell's life with music and its place in his philosophical maturation (even if *Little Did I Know* would seem to satisfy that description).[13] This essay is not that. It is, instead, an interweaving of remarks and reminiscences of Cavell on music that culminate in a reading of his last published pieces devoted to music, primarily "Impressions of Revolution." The claim I mean to test is that such a life, without variation (if with its own ornamentation), takes on a certain character as it finds a home in philosophy from out of its devotion to music. In Cavell's case, his distinctive orientation in philosophy—call this his lifelong coming to terms with his abandoning a life in music—is guided in part by (1) an interest in those moments in experience where words seem to run out, or veer toward nonsense, leaving in their wake touchstones of ecstasy; and (2) an interest in the education of the senses, without which interest we risk their starvation. While each trait is given some elaboration in each of the two sections that follows, I take them up roughly in order.

Music's Ineffability?

I was introduced to the name "Stanley Cavell" by a musician. John Harbison, the American composer and a longtime friend of Cavell since their meeting at Princeton in 1962, was in the summer of 1981 composer-in-residence at the music festival in Santa Fe, where I was an undergraduate at St. John's College. We met up at one point to talk about music and philosophy (I was making plans, despite or because of St. John's classical curriculum, to write a senior essay on jazz improvisation), and I asked Harbison if he could recommend any contemporary writing on the philosophy of music. That's how I first came to know Cavell's writing voice, a voice I would soon enough learn was indistinguishable from his speaking voice, through the pair of essays Harbison directed me to, "Music Discomposed" and "A Matter of Meaning It."[14]

Seven-and-a-half years later, on leave from my graduate studies at Columbia to spend a year at Harvard,[15] I asked Stanley about musical ineffability. More specifically, I asked whether passages from "Music Discomposed" like the following—passages that picture the scene of exasperation in our trying to explain to someone what we value in some music or other—are depictions of the unsayable:

> [O]ne is anxious to communicate the experience of such objects. [...] I want to tell you something I've seen, or heard, or realized, or come to understand, for the reasons for which *such* things are communicated (because it is news, about a world we share, or could). Only I find that I can't *tell* you; and that makes it all the more urgent to tell you. I want to tell you because the knowledge, unshared, is a burden—not, perhaps, the way having a secret can be a burden, or being misunderstood; a little more like the way, perhaps, not being believed is a burden, or not being trusted. [...] It matters, there is a burden, because unless I can tell what I know, there is a suggestion (and to myself as well) that I do *not* know. But I *do*—what I see [or hear] is *that* (pointing to the object). But for that to communicate, you have to see [or hear] it too.[16]

I remember asking Stanley my question with some urgency, since I had pressed the same question, possibly only days earlier, over lunch with James Conant—Jim was about to make his philosophical reputation disabusing readers of the *Tractatus* who mistakenly find in it a "hidden teaching" that is "inherently inexpressible"—and he had all but persuaded me that the category of the unsayable was a null set.[17]

Stanley was, I'll say, less resolute than Jim in rejecting my suggestion. Still, my reading was off, and in responding to it he offered what I wanted, a rare and detailed gloss on his first essay on music. Stanley's response—I wrote down the gist of it at the time—carried two lines of thought:

1. He said that part of what he was thinking when he wrote that passage was how the imperative "You have to *hear* it" can discount another's claim to have described what is going on in a piece, even if the other person mouths the same words you would use to say what is going on in it. Cavell's recalling this motive turned my focus to the following two excerpts from the same section (IV) of "Music Discomposed":

> What I know, when I've *seen* or *heard* something is, one may wish to say, not a matter of *merely* knowing it. [...] Perhaps "merely knowing"

should be compared with "not really knowing": "You don't really know what it's like to be a Negro"; "You don't really know how your remark made her feel"; "You don't really know what I mean when I say that Schnabel's slow movements give the impression not of slowness but of infinite length." You merely say the words.[18]

The paragraph goes on to discuss what place knowing *has* in these contexts:

The issue in each case is: What would *express* this knowledge? It is not that my knowledge will be real, or more than *mere* knowledge, when I acquire a particular feeling, or come to see something. For the issue can also be said to be: What would express the acquisition of that feeling, or show that you have seen the thing? And the answer might be that I now *know* something I didn't know before.[19]

Knowing in these (moral and aesthetic) contexts doesn't have the shape of a proposition to which is added the appropriate grounding or justifying experience; it has a quite different shape. Knowing here is more like cases of sudden recognition ("I know that face," "I know that move") that can change in a flash every element of one's perception.[20] To express *this* knowledge requires that one *give expression to* those features or that gesture, to that sight or sound. In that light, this section of "Music Discomposed" is not so much about what cannot be said or expressed as about what we mean when we say that we know (or see or hear) a something of this sort. What "Music Discomposed" *does* say about expressing this knowledge is contained in a single sentence: "Describing one's experience of art is itself a form of art; the burden of describing it is like the burden of producing it."[21]

2. Stanley also pointed out, as his teacher J. L. Austin had done, that there is a perfectly trivial sense in which the smell of coffee or the sound of a clarinet,[22] say, can be put into words. (Just like that.)[23]—But those words, of course, standing by themselves, are hardly an expression of knowledge, at least of the kind of knowledge we are tempted to declare beyond words. *Expressing* what we know—or showing it, Tractarian-wise—comes easier in some matters than in others.

* * * *

AND YET: CAVELL RECOUNTS early in *Little Did I Know* a peculiar gesture of his mother's that seems to serve him as a touchstone for what one might well call music's expressible-but-unsayable aspects—"the great secrets," he writes, "I knew I craved to have" and that his musically gifted mother "seemed to divine."[24] The instance he reports occurred at a recital by the great violinist Fritz Kreisler, for which Stanley (aged ten or eleven) traveled with his mother to San Francisco from their home in Sacramento. At various moments during the recital, particularly at the ends of each of

Kreisler's encores, his mother would "suddenly produce (a gesture I knew well and would glory in when directed to something I had done) an all but inaudible high cry and silently snap the fingers of her hand nearer me and thrust it toward her face, which was turned as if to ward off a blow."[25] (Is there an epistemology that gives us a complete account of this species of knowing, a knowing that is neither propositional nor a mere familiarity nor a knowing-how?) If you were to attempt to translate or reduce Stanley's mother's gesture to words—"It is obviously an expression of approval"; "It means, in effect, 'exactly right'"—you would thereby invite the response, "But you have to *hear* it." Part of what that command expresses, we will see, is an awareness that music-making is itself already a kind of saying (for those who have ears to hear). The point is alluded to in Cavell's description of what he took away from Kreisler's playing that day:

> There was a way he stood listening when the piano was playing a solo passage, especially I suppose in a slow movement, his head and body absolutely still, which I retain as an image of total concentration, ending in a single unhurried gesture that brought the violin back beneath the chin and the bow back to the strings at the instant of the violin's next entrance—as if music had been induced to utter itself.[26]

I grant that the "as if" here ("as if music had been induced to utter itself") matters, as the modifier "a kind of" does in my description of music-making as "a kind of saying." But just as the suggestion of a link between music and speech is an ancient and seemingly innocuous one, so is it neither flippant nor mere analogy, not peculiar to Kreisler's somewhat singular and memorable preparation before an entrance. (I clarify or forge the link between music and speech that I associate with Cavell below.)

Words appear to run out at other moments and in other contexts. Twice in *Little Did I Know*, having said all that seems fitting about a particularly striking experience, Cavell is left sensing that not enough has been said to fully convince his reader, and he concludes by simply affirming his conviction, but without any fear that he has thereby undermined it. I am struck by where these moments occur. Taken in tandem, they appear to link the mysteries of sexual awakening and musical ecstasy. The first—in which, admittedly, the moment of wordless knowing is somewhat whimsical— concerns the unspoken connection that the not quite seven-year-old Stanley felt between himself and "a girl of crushing beauty" nearly twice his age who, like him, appeared in a children's talent review in Indian dress, but not before appearing before him backstage undressed:

> I think that is what I saw, although it took some time for me to understand that she had taken off really all of her clothes, upon which recognition I was propelled from the room by an invisible force of nature, something

like a consuming wave of aromatic mist. [...] I tried once or twice during the ensuing week of two shows a day to interest this mythical being in the cosmic fact that we were both Indian royalty, by leaving my costume on and stationing myself by the stairs down to the men's dressing room until she walked off the stage and had a chance to remark the closeness of our connection. Evidently I had failed to place myself in clear enough view for that. But I knew what I knew, and it was satisfactory.[27]

The second occasion concerns the particular, polished, professional sound of the all-Black (except for a guitarist and himself) rehearsal jazz band of the saxophonist–composer Harrel Wiley, in which the fifteen-year-old Stanley played the lead alto saxophone, a band he claims could rival the sound of the best jazz bands of its day:

When he counted off the tempo for a downbeat the ensuing force of sound was so strong that I feared the house could not withstand it, and I was so thrilled by it that I felt I could barely continue playing. [...] Everything we played that morning [...] was an original composition of Wiley's, not simply an arrangement; and the ideas were more advanced than any I had heard outside of the Ellington band. [...] I can readily imagine that someone will think my story remembering our sound in Wiley's arrangements for his black band, as it were invoking comparison with the Basie band of that era, belongs on the side of the delusional. I have to say that on somber reflection I do not really or fully believe that. I place it among those experiences of my life about which I am moved to say: I know what I know.[28]

Finding these passages in a philosophical autobiography called *Little Did I Know*, the reader is all but required to consider how it is that "I know what I know" ("I knew what I knew") says what it does, avoiding triviality.

We can grant that Cavell's story of a secret connection to the Indian princess registers little more than a child's impression, and that the majesty of Wiley's band (absent recorded evidence) is no better than an impression. Given that, the absence of further words, while understandable, can seem protective, even dismissive of doubt, as if the book's title meant, "Little did I know, but I knew *this*." For a different understanding of these invocations of "I know what I know," we should compare them to a remark in Wittgenstein's *Investigations* to which Cavell often turns. In it, Wittgenstein gives voice to that moment in any explanation of my apparent certainties (e.g., in following a rule) when my justifications appear exhausted: "I have reached bedrock, and my spade is turned. Then I am inclined to say: 'This is simply what I do.'"[29] Cavell (reading Wittgenstein) interprets the one so inclined not as dismissing the questioner or voicing despair over the possibility of communication, but as holding that inclination in check, perhaps through an awareness of what our understanding each other, after all, rests on.[30] Taking a cue from Cavell's reading, I want to suggest that "I know what I know" in these passages is not intended by Cavell to silence doubters or to mark where words end, as if out of a false self-certainty or conviction in what he knows. Rather, he employs these words to flag a memory, to draw our attention to it, and to acknowledge where a next question must lead—namely, further down the path of such incandescent experiences. In the wake of these recaptured memories, in other words, words do not come to an end out of necessity, as if in the presence of something ineffable. They simply stop, awaiting the impulse to more speech (whether from himself or, in reading, from his reader). Any continuation calls not for proof but for something like a willing attentiveness. (It may require, for instance, further imagining oneself as an almost seven-year-old boy positioned by the stairs, trying to see thereby the connection between oneself and a mythical being whose aura has the power to command one's thoughts.)

* * * *

WHAT I TAKE TO BE CULMINATING THOUGHTS on the burden borne by words and their failure appear in Cavell's aforementioned late essay on music, "Impressions of Revolution."[31] There the sense of our failure to articulate—or more exactly, to conceptualize—what we hear in music draws inspiration from Walter Benjamin's mid-1920s work *The Origin of German Tragic Drama (Ursprung des deutschen Trauerspiels)*. In this study of German baroque tragedy (*Trauerspiel* literally means "mourning-play"), Benjamin declares at one point that "the spoken word [as opposed to music on the one hand, and written language on the other] is only afflicted by meaning, so to speak, as if by an inescapable disease" so that "meaning is encountered, and will continue to be encountered as the reason for mournfulness," and that "the phonetic tension with speech in the language of the seventeenth century leads directly to music, the opposite of meaning-laden speech."[32] Cavell ties these remarks to his long-posited idea that what is known as philosophical skepticism is fueled by our alternating fear of and wish for inexpressiveness. He then offers this succinct summary of Benjamin's claim and its resonance with his own: "Music allows the achieving of understanding without meaning, that is to say, without the articulation of individual acts of reference on which intelligibility is classically thought to depend."[33] I find in this formulation or epigram a guide for clarifying not only Cavell's thinking about music but the place of musical experience in his thinking about the expressibility of words.

The picture of human understanding ungrounded in individual acts of reference is more than reminiscent of the picture of language that emerges from Wittgenstein's *Investigations*. In that picture, our ability to speak to one another, and to understand one another, does not rest in some fact of language or some fact about a world that our words attach to, as the philosophical tradition to which Wittgenstein is responding argues. Cavell notes elsewhere that the effort to apply the traditional picture to concepts of experience—Wittgenstein "remembers someone striking himself on the breast in the heat of a philosophical discussion, crying out, 'No one else can have THIS pain'"—only appears to make sense if the referring term ("THIS") remains mysteriously unspecified, "an absolute demonstrative absolutely pointing to an absolute object."[34] Absent such absolute connections, understanding happens, and it happens in a world whose actual mystery we overlook. To give the merest indication of Wittgenstein's picture of that mystery: understanding happens through the human ways or forms of life that we inhabit and find ourselves attuned to, and that we also find ourselves desiring (broadly speaking)—ways or forms of life into which we are inaugurated together with language, and that enable language to work on us and to move us (broadly speaking).

But Cavell's epigram is explicitly characterizing music, not language. And it draws its inspiration from Benjamin, who had implied a contrast between music's happier expressivity and that of (spoken) words, which are "afflicted by meaning," "meaning-laden speech" being "the reason for mournfulness." That is, Benjamin's concern is with, not a grief brought on by our words falling short of capturing our experience, but the grief and mourning that follows from speech itself. What we say, we must mean. And yet, what I do with my grief or mourning, my attitude toward words, is not spelled out in this extract from Benjamin's text.

As I read "Impressions of Revolution," we should take "the achieving of understanding without meaning" to be as instructive of the workings of language as it is of music. Cavell is suggesting that we ask: What happens if we let go of the idea that the primary fact of communication is that words carry meanings (fixed by something beyond what we bring to and show in our conversing), or the idea—more to the point—that my understanding you rests on my associating your words with objects in the world, and similar feats of absolute translation? We might, with Cavell, rethink the following analogy, pitched by someone bearing a life with music: "Understanding a sentence is much more like understanding a theme in music than one might believe" (Wittgenstein's words, quoted by Cavell in the penultimate paragraph of "Impressions of Revolution.")[35] Wittgenstein continues: "Why is just *this* the pattern of variation in intensity and tempo [in a musical theme, or in its performance]? One would like to say: 'Because I know what it all means.' But what does it mean? I'd not be able to say."[36] The sense of Wittgenstein's remark, and of Cavell's interest in quoting it (he counts it among the "revolutionary" things Wittgenstein has to say about "the nature of our agreement in speech"),[37] is not to mark where the ineffable or unfathomable enter into our understanding of a musical theme or a sentence. The point is rather to underscore a fact of unending surprise, that "the impress produced in you by things as they pass and abiding in you when they have passed"[38]—that is, your attending, in just these surroundings, with whatever relation you bear to them, and with what has gone before, to just this tone and mood—is the necessary but sufficient condition that structures our understanding (or our failing to understand) one another. As Cavell puts this thought elsewhere:

> The very invocation of the understanding of a musical theme as a guide to philosophical understanding, among the reorientations in this traumatic breakthrough of philosophical imagination, call it the promise of an understanding without meanings, is a utopian glimpse of a new, or undiscovered, relation to language, to its sources in the world, to its means of expression.[39]

Understanding a sentence is hearing the music that shapes its life.[40]

And so similarly, my capacity to mourn the passing of the world (as of time, or a friend and mentor, or the fact of meaning-laden speech itself) does not depend on something fixed in speech or in the world to which I might still return, but is akin to my ability to follow a musical theme without losing the thread.

Animated Hearing

Something that the aforementioned moments of heightened awareness appear to teach the young Stanley as we come to know him in *Little Did I Know*, moments that are mostly occasioned by music (his mother's divining secrets from Fritz Kreisler's playing; the consuming wave of aromatic mist associated with a girl of crushing beauty who, incidentally, would sing "Indian Love Call"; the force of sound of Wiley's band; the "exhilarating enterprise"[41] of composing a musical response to *Lear*), is the recognition that our lives seem to transpire on the brink of ecstasy. Granted, this is not quite a fact, something the recognition of which we can gain by being told. To that extent it is like the recognition of the later Wittgenstein's new method, the understanding of which can't be gained simply by reading Wittgenstein's metaphilosophical remarks, but depends on "the work of changing one's way of looking at things, durch lange Übung [through long practice]."[42] What I am calling Cavell's life "out" of music is the vital source of his understanding of what lies ecstatically next to this life. To understand that a human life contains the possibility of such experiences, and so to try to understand why we might become numb to that possibility, is part of what makes Cavell the philosopher he is. Music is a natural site for this understanding, as one can read in the conclusion to "Impressions of Revolution": "What is at stake here I could perhaps summarize or epitomize this way: The emptiness of the world [...] is to be filled by music, conceived as its willingness to accept assignments of meaning and its power to transcend all its assignments."[43] Here the experience of music as inviting words but transcending all proffered meaning is offered as an experience to be craved, and in the face of which we might exclaim, "Words fail me." (Cavell will come to read the task of the critic to articulate this experience as an instance of a mode of expression he calls "passionate utterance.")[44]

And so several of Cavell's anecdotes about his life with music are to be understood not simply as reports, but as requiring or inviting the reader to share in the (described) experience, as if only in that way can one begin to see the philosophical import of a moment of heightened awareness— begin to see "why philosophy, of a certain ambition, tends perpetually to intersect the autobiographical."[45] These anecdotes are (again) not instances of the inexpressible, but rather locales where an attentive or receptive reader can arrive at the edge of ecstasy with an exercise of imagination. I have in mind such moments in Cavell's text as the following.

* * * *

CAVELL DESCRIBES HOW, when he was about to turn thirteen, he and his mother and two relatives traveled to the 1939 World's Fair in San Francisco. Shortly after they passed through the gates, Stanley heard over the Fair's sound system the Benny Goodman band performing their theme song. In 1939, for a young fan of Benny Goodman, hearing this familiar song broadcast for the Fair visitors would have been both pleasing and unremarkable given the band's popularity. And then, a few minutes further along the entering path, Stanley found himself at the back of a large crowd facing an outdoor bandstand,

> on which the actual Benny Goodman band was playing what we were hearing over the loudspeaker, and as Goodman raised his clarinet for a new entrance, it was not a perfect repetition but a slight variation of something that had become a part of my brain. An ecstasy enclosed me (as if what had only existed for me as sound had of itself materialized on the instant) [...]. I saw a seat open near where we were standing and motioned to my mother that I was staying there. [...] To consider leaving the music of the spheres for a glimpse of earthly innovations seemed unthinkable to me.[46]

Cavell's characterization of this sudden and striking and animating aspect shift ("as if what had only existed for me as sound had of itself materialized on the instant") might best be understood by recalling cinematic efforts at forging similar moments. Think of the palette transformation from sepia to glorious Technicolor at the moment when Dorothy opens the front door to her newly uprooted house in *The Wizard of Oz*, released the same year as Stanley's visit to the World's Fair. A more recent and direct parallel is the Greek chorus of bandsmen in *Woman at War* (2018), whose music we hear at the opening simply as movie soundtrack and then, as the film's heroine runs across the Icelandic highlands and the credits roll, the camera pans not only to follow her but to reveal three musicians and their instruments (harmonium, tuba, drums) out on the highlands in the near distance behind her, creating the soundtrack in real time. Or again, consider the early, farcical moment in *Blazing Saddles* (1974), when the newly appointed Black sheriff is seen riding on horseback across the arid Wild West accompanied, somewhat incongruously, by a famous big band arrangement of "April in Paris." In a moment of cinematic audacity, he rides up to where the entire Count Basie band is seated on a band stage, surrounded by sagebrush and playing the scene's musical background, now gloriously foregrounded.

If I were to further multiply these illustrations of when something familiar or established or recorded comes shockingly to life, it might tempt us to look for a common feature, as if what is being illustrated is a particular technique, a method for making the mundane vivid. But in telling this tale from memory, Cavell is not especially interested in the mere fact of vividness. He wants to convey an *impression*—hoping thereby to conjure some such impression from our own (cinematic or other) experience—so as to make intelligible the (philosophical) insight that followed from it. Here is how he first words that insight:

> To hear the familiar arrangements played live, with inevitable and enlivening alterations in the improvisations, confirmed for me as it were the knowledge of existence, in the form of, or a prophecy of, the reality of happiness. Whatever unanticipated forms the prophecy will recognize, and however many awakenings may be necessary from my coma, I had received proof of a world beyond me.[47]

In this instance, the proto-philosopher's proof of an external world is not effected by a Cartesian medley of the *cogito*, an honest god, and a new method for testing impressions. Rather, it arrives when "something that had become a part of my brain" is revealed to have an unfrozen, ongoing existence ("played *live*, with inevitable and enlivening alterations in the improvisations")—an intriguing template, possibly a definition, of happiness. Let us assume—it seems a safe bet—that this was the young Stanley's first time hearing the Goodman band in person, and take note that he writes, "my fascination with Goodman's playing [...] was the background of my mounting craving to learn the clarinet."[48] If some such consummate experience is what it takes to awaken Cavell or any of us from the cerebral coma of our adolescence, then it is not surprising that we may find ourselves experiencing a related shock of recognition when Cavell the philosopher proposes that the home of skepticism, and the source of the modern wish for stability in our convictions, is our felt disappointment with the world. He speaks of this condition as "the unappeasable human dissatisfaction with each of life's dispensations, the condition I have called 'human restlessness,'" and not surprisingly, he finds this intuition revelatory of some late moments in Mahler.[49]

* * * *

THAT IS NOT THE END OF THE STORY, however, or of the felt aftershock of this particular musical encounter. An intervening memory recorded in the next entry of *Little Did I Know*—drawn from shortly after Stanley turns thirteen and involving, once again, the inadvertent sighting of an older, "extravagantly beautiful," unclothed female—offers Cavell an occasion to note, within the experience of ecstasy, "the pain within joy, not alone the pain of delay, or say, detour, but the pain within the sheer extremity of experience. [...] [It is an experience] of the body's insufficiency to house the materialization of its desire." He then confirms, "This was evident in my response to the Goodman band [...]."[50] Here we have a more developed emblem of the moment when familiar sounds give way to improvisatory variations right before one's ears. The pain within joy comes about not because the body seeks, and fails to find, a way to materialize its desire (the body being insufficient to house it on its own), but because the material representation of its desire (the Goodman band creating the music right there, on stage, "as if what had only existed for me as sound had of itself materialized on the instant") is not the desire itself, and so frustrates even as it exhilarates. The body can't house a *materialization* of its desire; desire alone, inchoate, is the (proper) occupant of its house.

To see uncathected desire as desirable, as not just an element of the human condition to be appeased but as its promise, is one of a handful of differences in outlook between Cavell and Freud.[51] That this experience of uncontained joy is necessarily joined by pain might name the difference in outlook between Cavell's and Kant's views of the sublime. But what deserves underscoring in the continuation of this passage is Cavell's explicit claim that music in its exemplary instances (counting, at least, "great jazz" and "the works, in the other realm of [Western classical] music, that I at the same time loved extravagantly, to the point of pain") is the site where the unappeasable, painful side of ecstatic experience recurs time and again. Cavell offers as illustration of the inexhaustibility of "this fact of music" the secondary theme of the Chopin Nocturne in G major (Op. 37, No. 2), and—exceeding it in expressiveness, as Cavell asserts without argument— the similarly lilting, dotted rhythm, triple time diatonic theme for the set of variations in the second and final movement of Beethoven's final piano sonata (Op. 111). Both are simple melodies, surrounded at first by relatively simple accompaniment. And yet hearing them in their broader surroundings (Chopin's running thirds and sixths of the opening theme; the greater tumult and drama of Opus 111's first movement), the melodies (especially the latter) are, stupefyingly, as weighty and pregnant as certain silences. (Just as with Cavell's readings of individual moments in movies, one needs to go back to a performance, or imagine the sounds here, to hear Cavell's point. Nothing less than that uptake of the sounds can or should count as justification of his claim. Of course, this goes hand in hand with that other fact of music, that any given uptake for any given person may not work, may not instantiate the extremity of experience. Cavell's illustrations are not wholly random, however. Or so I attest.) This entry in *Little Did I Know* closes with a final image of the inexhaustibility of the experience of pain-in-desire. Cavell takes note—as he did a few years earlier in "Impressions of Revolution"[52]— of the incessantly repeated C major triad that concludes Beethoven's Fifth Symphony. He reads the repetitions (covering nearly thirty measures) as signaling not triumph, but Beethoven's uncertainty about endings, his unwillingness to declare the ending as an end, or perhaps his unwillingness to conceive that there should be any experience after this music has ended.

And now consider how such a lesson lends itself to or imparts further lessons of human experience: of the idea that the quest of moral perfectionism, living for one's next self, begins with the painful (or at least, not pleasant) sense of disgust with one's present self, with one's life as it stands. Or that the task of a life is to learn how to mourn each passing, commonplace moment properly. Or that "the human intuition of what Empson calls (and what Adorno calls) 'the insufficiency of existence'" is what the pastoral, whether in poetry or in music, is concerned to ameliorate.[53] It really does not take poetry—though it may take a good live recording—to recognize how the Benny Goodman band's unexpected materialization could guide, as a persistent memory, such lines of thought.

Those lines extend to include the following, written some thirty-eight years after Cavell received at the World's Fair his prophesy of the reality of happiness, but a good ten years before he began to align this vision with the tradition of moral perfectionism:

That to be human is to have, or to risk having, this capacity to wish; that to be human is to wish, and in particular to wish for a completer identity than one has so far attained; and that such a wish may project a complete world *opposed* to the world one so far shares with others: this is a way of taking up the cause of Shakespearean Romance.[54]

A kind of Shakespearean romance is at work in what I count as the most significant feature in Cavell's telling of his "mounting craving to learn the clarinet," a craving he ties explicitly to his desire to overcome his social isolation—his conviction that he "belonged in no place"—and so to his desire for a completer identity than he had so far attained. He mentions the feature twice: he would transcribe (copy down) Goodman's and Artie Shaw's clarinet improvisations from their recordings, a familiar but not universal practice for budding jazz musicians.[55] The time-consuming task of transcribing solos by ear from (at the time) 78 rpm flat disc records, setting the needle down to play short stretches over and over to catch every nuance, "memorizing" and then "imitating" the improvisations, is the wish for, as I might put it, the fullest, exemplary expression of one's understanding of the music one is moved by. The expression reaches its apotheosis not in a description of what one has learned about the solo after the transcribing is done, but in the effort to then play the solo from the *inside*. That is, what the expression of one's understanding demands, as is revealed soon enough to the transcriber–performer and in that sense is internal to the practice, is that one should shift one's efforts from imitation (sounding like) to internalization (sounding out), from what the listener hears to how the performer is thinking, and so to developing one's own vocabulary and voice so as to make the sounds dance.[56] In Cavell's telling, this productive and transformative exercise is joined in his memory with his fanciful drawing of various decorative music stands that would announce to the world the big band he would be leading to musical exceptionality. Cavell sees, in this adolescent fantasy, "I hope with some tenderness, my bursting hopes for wings with which to express myself in the showy form they took of privilege in a perfectly expressive society of artistry."[57] Thus for Cavell, the practice and the fantasy of total expressiveness as a way to combat his awkward isolation in adolescence took form in these preparations for a life of jazz performance.

The other bit of Cavell's ecstasy tinged with pain, both adolescent and performative, in his gradually realized life as the leader of his high school jazz band came about because he and his band (which, unlike Wiley's band, "was not wonderful") were now indispensable to that school's social life, even as he was prohibited, sitting up on the bandstand, from participating in full sociability.[58] Cavell describes the virtues of this circumstance both negatively—as the blessing of averting perplexity and humiliation (he was younger than his classmates, could not yet drive, and was not outgoing, so that attending the dance would have meant his swift defeat)—and positively: "Leading the band annulled this painful dilemma at the first downbeat. I did not attend the dance; I was the dance."[59]

I take it that we are to hear, in Cavell's identifying his performing in the dance with the dance itself, the well-known closing line from Yeats' "Among School Children" that Cavell had dissected years earlier: "How can we know the dancer from the dance?"[60] In his discussion of this line, Cavell (in contrast to Paul de Man in his "Semiology and Rhetoric") proposes that we hear Yeats' question as asking not for a difference (How can we *tell* dancer from dance) but for knowledge, or more exactly, acknowledgment (How can we *know the dancer*, either by means of her dance or apart from her dance). And so in *Little Did I Know*, speaking of the young Stanley performing up there on the stage, Cavell presses the fact of this youngster's unappreciated or unacknowledged expression: Since he was not, could not be, on the dance floor,

> the music was not played for me—except in those instances when, in my disdain, I knew that I was playing better than anyone else present would know, hence in a sense playing for myself, perhaps in a way that made no contribution to the communal effort. What, then, would it be like if the best I could propose came to be recognized as essential to some such effort?[61]

This is the dilemma of musical performance—something requiring extremity in the act but not in its reception—which matches the dilemma of the aficionado, who wants to say what she hears in a performance but faces the threat of not being trusted or believed. The inevitable but still surprising failure of communion, of a shared response, in the presence of the very same stimuli or "facts" about the world, has obvious political importance. (From "The Politics of Interpretation": "Apart from my passion in the dance, my perception is no longer transfigured: Who am I (are we) to take such perception as valid?")[62] That there will be different understandings of the same event, of what counts as the "facts," is of course the lifeblood of moral discourse. (Was it a slap or a slug?) But the *essential* presence of passion in performance, whether in me as audience or in her as performer ("Apart from the other's passion in the dance, the other is no longer transfigured: Is this the one who was there?")[63] is paramount here. If you fail to see it or hear it, that can seem to me as absurd as your failing to notice that the room in which we're conversing has burst into flames.

Here is where skepticism can find a home in a life born out of music, and particularly in the life of a performing musician, even as those on the dance floor greet you as human and navigate their way through doorways and generally, if carelessly or without a care, show themselves accepting of the world and of others in it. That the doubt about our sharing a world should arise so naturally here is no doubt a function of the fact that (to return to Cavell's formula) musical understanding proceeds in the absence of meaning. The blessed truth of music—"the opposite of meaning-laden speech"—is its ontological curse. But then, if musical understanding is rightly taken as the model for sentential understanding, it is unsurprising that we are all cursed, whether we tend to open our mouths to sing or to speak.

* * * *

A FINAL, CRUCIALLY IMPORTANT MEMORY of musical discovery recounted by Cavell in *Little Did I Know*—important for what becomes of the philosopher Stanley Cavell—is tied, surely not accidentally, to his discovery of Freud. As Cavell all but says, it was Freud who filled the void created in his life by his recognition that he was not to be a professional musician. What Freud offered was an answer to the unknown and unacknowledged performer on the bandstand:

> After my consciousness, or I can say the fact, of parting from the imagination of a future for me in the world of music, my reading turned for some time fairly exclusively to reading Freud. [...] I looked forward to each of my sessions of reading Freud's texts as to falling into a kind of trance of absorption and a security of being known, accepted back into the human race.[64]

This memory of welcoming acceptance is then linked to the allure of certain apartment buildings that Stanley would walk past along Central Park West, several exhibiting metal name signs of doctors (or as he imagined, psychoanalysts) offering an emblem of "settled adulthood," of "human beings in command of an orderly existence."[65] It is from the authoritative occupant of one of these "celestial fortresses" that Stanley would take a lesson not only in the blurring of the high and the low (the celestial and the terrestrial) in the arts, but in having his hearing turned around—or as he will say, upside down.

This occupant, who was a relative of an acquaintance of Stanley's, an acquaintance who invited Stanley over to this man's Central Park West residence early in 1949, knew that Stanley was enrolled at Juilliard and subsequently learned of his affection for and experience in swing bands. Thus prompted, the man

> began reminiscing about the time he had invited the Benny Goodman band to be introduced on his radio program. "They turned out to have no opening theme, so I told Benny to make a swing version of *Invitation to the Dance*. [...] He kept it as his opening theme song from then on."[66]

For Stanley, the audacity of this man's assertion was twofold. He was proposing that he was the catalyst for "sounds that had existed from all eternity" (the foxtrot "Let's Dance," Goodman's theme song since the mid-1930s, the song Stanley had heard transfigured when he stumbled across the Goodman band performing it live at the San Francisco World's Fair a decade earlier). And he was claiming that Goodman's piece was a transcription or arrangement of Carl Maria von Weber's *Invitation to the Dance* of 1819, a musical genealogy that made no sense to Stanley—not for implying that

"Let's Dance" was yet another instance of "jazzing the classics" but because the two themes bore no obvious relation to each other.

But then, riding the elevator down from this man's apartment and imagining the Goodman theme's opening bars in his head,

I recognized that I had always heretofore, with evidently willful shallowness, heard the Goodman band's delivery of the tune upside down [...]. When in the past I had found myself syllabifying the Goodman theme, [...] it was uniformly the ornamental, jagged figure for the trumpets I reproduced [...]. But underneath that activity, grounding it, the saxophones, sure enough now in my remembered hearing [...] are playing, as it were calmly, the Weber tune, no longer in three-quarter waltz time, and at about half the velocity of the tempo in which you would expect to hear the tune.[67]

The particular feeling that this discovery produced in Stanley at the time was "chagrin," lessened only by the thought that the connection between the Weber waltz and the Goodman theme song surely went unrecognized by virtually everyone else who bore his classical and swing band devotions.[68] Yet while "the sense of revelation would remain present" even if the Weber–Goodman connection were widely known, the chagrin "in recognizing one's injustices to works, as to persons, that matter to one's life, or cross its paths," would remain. Here again is a memory that joins ecstasy with pain, Proust-like, or like a revelatory insight in psychoanalytic treatment that one may be undergoing. At this moment in *Little Did I Know*, it becomes the exemplar of something Cavell chooses to call "philosophical experience":

The pain so often accompanying an influx of knowledge, exquisitely in the mode of coming to understand what one cannot simply have failed to know is, I suppose, a minor curse upon intellectual vanity [...]. But how could I have known then that this overturning of false assumption by a reversal of listening was a model of philosophical experience? Exactly.[69]

Here ("But how could I have known ... ?") is a better emblem for how to read this memoir's title, *Little Did I Know*. A life, prior to its opening to philosophy, is littered with experiences, ecstatic songs, that in retrospect you may come to recognize as inviting you to cross from the life you were leading to a life whose questions you can find yourself happy to be led by.

But what in this particular experience invites exactly *philosophy*, beyond its exhibiting the Platonic feature of engendering the discovery of one's ignorance?

Begin by considering its musical provenance. Humans aren't typically occupied or preoccupied with ambiguous figures like the duck–rabbit or the Necker cube, yet these figures dominate discussions of aspect–reversals, whether within or outside the context of Wittgenstein's aspect-seeing remarks.[70] On the other hand, many lives are occupied with, even devoted to, music. And a true characterization of musical experience at a certain level of complexity (even at an elementary level) is that our attention is *variously* attracted to features of seemingly equal, or at least arguably equal, interest. To indicate one broad range of examples: the never-ending mystery of contrapuntal music is that we can hear distinguishable and even contrasting lines or voices simultaneously which (unlike the voices of people talking over one another) *make sense* together; and we can attend to one voice, or to the other voice, or to their co-sounding. (This is a distinctive feature of the inexhaustible fascination with different performances of the same musical work, in which, say, one performer brings out a counter-voice that another chooses to underplay.) Music is, in its aspirations, an ambiguous or aspectual construct for the ear's attention. And as with any aspectual phenomenon, one aspect tends to obscure or deafen us to others. But that is an anthropomorphic description. What hides one voice is not the other voice, but my choosing (or my being chosen—the degree of freedom here is obscure) to attend to it, perhaps for a lifetime, or at least whenever I hear it.[71]

Now see this state of affairs in our relation to music as an image of philosophical thinking. What, in Cavell's retelling of his "reversal of listening," brought the reversal about, turning it into "a model of philosophical experience"? A not unimportant feature is that Cavell portrays himself as initially *resistant to believing* that a reversal of listening was possible. This undoubtedly had something to do with his understanding of himself as musically astute, which the preceding pages of his autobiography lay out. (Recall his declaration that "music had my whole life been so essentially a part of my days, of what in them I knew was valuable to me, was mine to do.")[72] His resistance also seems linked to his transparent antipathy to this resident of Central Park West's "rebuking richness," someone whom he describes at the crucial moment simply as "this man," one "no different from the members of my father's generation whom I would have met at the Jewish Progressive Club"; the man's claim "was not a rational proposition."[73] (Then why return to it in thought? What to Stanley does this man represent? His father in a parallel, more luxurious and just universe? The author of *Introductory Lectures on Psychoanalysis?*) The encounter is soon enough followed, however, by a moment of solitude in a descending elevator, a "clear stretch of free time" (*Meditations* I) when, Cavell says, he was "left to my own thoughts."[74] But Stanley's exercise of thought is not spent raising doubts about the man's trustworthiness or constructing a counter-argument to his claim or, for that matter, drawing a lesson about his own fallibility (yet). He uses his solitude as an opportunity to *imagine the sounds* of the Goodman theme song, to

> go over in my head deliberately the then still famous opening bars of the arrangement that Goodman used of his opening theme song, something I

might have done, without deliberation [or prompting], in a certain mood on any number of unremarkable days.[75]

And so it happens that all of a sudden—for this reader of Freud and future reader of Proust, remembering the nature of big band arranging "that I had already surmised" (namely, that the reed instruments take the lead) but in this instance had been "persisting dumbly in turning a deaf ear to"—Stanley hears the melody and the accompaniment of "Let's Dance," the leader and the follower, switch roles in his imagination, and "sure enough now" he hears the Weber waltz in it.[76] Cavell has undergone an auditory aspect shift of some significance, and it proves to be an awakening of philosophy as much as a lesson in listening.

* * * *

IF "LET'S DANCE"—a once wildly popular tune that every American of a certain age and predilection would recognize—could contain an overlooked revelation, a possibility of rehearing that overturned what one took to be the main idea (that is, the theme) and that linked this tune to a different era and a different sensibility, then, really, what is there in experience that one is willing to chance overlooking? What I just mentioned as Stanley's taking the opportunity "to *imagine the sounds*" of the Goodman tune is a version of the critical guidance that Cavell will offer in virtually every one of his readings of works for the theater (including Shakespeare) and of film; it also identifies what is required to employ successfully the procedures of J. L. Austin and of ordinary language philosophy generally.[77] Imagining the sounds is not a poor substitute for *hearing* the sounds; it is, rather, a name for or the activity of a certain kind of reflection, as it were after the fact. If one thinks of the effort to imagine the sounds as an effort that combines the skills of reception and of humility or sympathy, and so skills of criticism and morality, one is soon led to question why we may fail to cultivate these abilities, or choose to withhold them on this or another occasion, or fail to be grateful for them when directed at us; and so one may find oneself drawn, as Cavell is, to questions of skepticism and acknowledgment. (Cavell's discussion of what he calls empathic projection, in relation to skepticism about other minds, leads to the idea that human faces *always* present aspects to be struck by; or better: to the idea that our life with human creatures always invites an animated seeing—and equally to the idea that it invites a refusal of the implications of that seeing.)[78]

And now read "Understanding a sentence is much more like understanding a theme in music than one might believe" in light of this story of a revelation in hearing. Wittgenstein's and Cavell's revelations of language ask that one pay attention to "the voice which says [particular words], and through that to the phenomenology of the straits of mind in which only those words said in that order will suffice," since "in philosophy it is the sound which makes all the difference."[79] We should notice, however, that while the direction to imagine the sounds is key to understanding a sentence, the causal connection between *Invitation to the Dance* and "Let's Dance" is hardly a model for discovering and articulating one's *understanding* of a stretch of music. First, the connection between the two tunes is, as one might say, too literal. The musical connection is rather like Sancho Panza's story about his kinsmen who pronounced on a certain wine that it had a taste of leather and iron, and were then "proven right" when its containing barrel was found to have a leather thong and key at the bottom of it. As Cavell says in countering Hume's reading of this anecdote, the story is no evidence of the kinsmen's critical skills (of either discernment or expression), since a key made of iron is not a *taste* of iron, and the critic's vindication "comes not from his pointing out that it is, or was, in the barrel, but in getting us to taste it there."[80] And second, while discovering the genealogy of "Let's Dance" undoubtedly plays a role in *how* I hear it—not least if I discover it *in* hearing it—you would not want to say, if I merely mention the connection to *Invitation to the Dance*, that I have shown that I *understand* "Let's Dance." (For what if I then go on to tap my foot squarely on the first and third beats of this swing tune as I listen to it? What if I waltz to it?) Showing that one understands a theme in music is much more like doing something (even gesturing with one's words, as the good critic does) than it is like asserting something.

For a better model of musical understanding, we should return, finally, to "Impressions of Revolution." Earlier I highlighted Cavell's formulation that "music allows the achieving of understanding without meaning." But as he goes on to say:

If the idea of "understanding without meaning" is to do real work, then we will have to specify the range of procedures that would *show* understanding [a musical analysis, a narrative, a performance, etc.] [...] and articulate both why we want to, and how it is possible to, relate this apparent motley of procedures to something like addressing meaning, when so obviously whatever meaning they discover is so different from knowing or discovering the meaning of a word or a sentence in speech.[81]

Cavell offers, as examples of how we "*show* understanding" in music, two complementary but contrasting responses to a late stretch in the "Funeral March" of Beethoven's Eroica Symphony. An unnamed panelist at the conference where "Impressions of Revolution" was presented had likened a passage of back-and-forth eighth notes (beginning at mm. 209ff.) to the tick/tock of a clock, "suggesting that time is running, running out." Cavell, hearing the violins here as too low and slow to suggest a clock, offers that it is "closer to rob/rub, more say like a labored heartbeat, suggesting life running out." He concludes that both responses can be taken as exhibiting an understanding of this passage and its role and import at this moment of this impressively long slow movement. But how is that possible, given the evident differences between a mechanism and a human being?

> [T]he fact that both seem to me apt implies that they are to be thought of not as discoveries but as *impressions* and *assignments* of meaning. The philosophical task here then becomes one of showing that this reformulation is not an evasion of the question of meaning in music, but constitutes the beginning of an answer to the question.[82]

What Cavell implies in saying that these expressions of understanding are not "discoveries" about Beethoven's Funeral March is simply that understanding this stretch of music is not a matter of discerning or otherwise learning Beethoven's thinking or feeling, learning what was going on in his head or, as it were, heart as he wrote it. (What other candidate referent could satisfy the fantasy of *discovering* the music's meaning?)[83]

But this beginning of an answer doesn't lead Cavell to the idea that these and other descriptions of music, "*impressions* ... of meaning," are *mere* impressions in a realm of human experience where anything goes. There are two reasons why not. First, when I describe a stretch of music, my description is one not only that I might find apt but that *you* might also; and I care as much that my impression can be shared with you (or with someone) as that I have it. And second, that I *have* this impression (or another more or less articulate, or even possibly inarticulable) is what music that I care about and that occupies my life seems to *require* of me. To listen closely to music and be left with no impression would be a bit like listening to someone speak to you in a language that you don't understand—except that, of course, *that* experience might still leave you with a quite particular impression.[84] Here as elsewhere in his later writings, Cavell is reclaiming with Emerson the concept of "impression" from the Empiricist tradition. Instead of an impression as a more or less mechanical and so determined imprint that sensory objects leave behind in their wake, to speak of "*impressions* ... of meaning" is to recognize my life with things (or here, with music) as reciprocal or conjoined. What impresses its meaning on me is what I *find* impressive or important or to matter to me. To take an interest in these impressions is part—possibly all—of what counts as the education of my senses, "as though without [the arts] we build our knowledge of our place in the world on the basis of sensory deprivation, starving our desires."[85] And my driving interest in wording or otherwise gesturing towards such (possibly ecstatic) experiences is no more and no less mysterious than my driving wish for reciprocal companionship; simply put, wording such experiences is an expression or symptom of that wish. If I see how understanding your sentence (or failing to) is captured by *that* picture, not by one in which

I try to grasp, in or through your words, their overarching or underlying universal meanings, then I may well see why likening linguistic to musical understanding might dawn on someone with a philosophical life out of (or with) music—a Wittgenstein, a Cavell—and why in the end they might find it more fruitful to investigate, not the nature of linguistic meaning or signification, but the nature of human understanding and its vicissitudes.[86]

* * * *

I SHOULD END BY SPEAKING to a conspicuous worry over my claim that Cavell's distinctive orientation in philosophy is guided by his finding philosophy from out of his devotion to music, particularly as that life is revealed in *Little Did I Know*. Have I (has Cavell) demonstrated that some sort of musical life will project itself onto some sort of philosophical life, or have I (has Cavell) projected a philosophical understanding onto scenes from a childhood that happens to have been occupied or preoccupied with music, and then outgrew that occupation along with childhood? To begin, I hope that my use of the word "guided" will help to steer a reading of my claim, so that one might notice, for example, that one can be guided by a star, something distant, dim, and silent (but not for that reason unfit for hitching your wagon to).[87] My claim is also not meant to contravene the truth that many of the five hundred pages of *Little Did I Know* do *not* speak explicitly about music, and yet it is the *whole* of that narrative that is said to tell what "detours on the human path to death" produced the philosophical spirit that is Stanley Cavell.[88] Still, I take encouragement from noting that, in defending his ambition to "test" the idea of entrusting himself "to write, however limitedly, the autobiography of a species; if not of humanity as a whole, then representative of anyone who finds himself or herself in it," Cavell explains that such an idea "is a specific attitude one takes to what happens to the soul, no more pretentious than sitting on a horse, or sitting at the piano, properly."[89] We do not learn in his autobiography what Cavell knows about sitting on a horse properly. But if I were to speak to what Cavell knows about sitting at the piano properly: the attitude that might be mistaken for pretentiousness is the precious moment or two when, sitting in silence, you imagine the sounds you are about to make and then, with the first notes, focus your attention on and become receptive to what each next moment of sound contains, receptive to whatever responsiveness is required of you to invite impressions of meaning. It is an attitude that is a kind of natural primer for the attitude of philosophical or autobiographical reflection. As for the possibility that I (or Cavell) have projected philosophical significance back onto certain musical moments excerpted from memory: that seems as unavoidable, and as necessary to acknowledge, as the very real philosophical significance of those formative, guiding moments themselves.

Notes

1   The present chapter is a substantially expanded version of "Words Fail Me." (Stanley Cavell's Life Out of Music)," that appeared in *Inheriting Stanley Cavell: Memories, Dreams, Reflections*, ed. David LaRocca (New York: Bloomsbury, 2020), 187–97. A draft of this expanded version was presented at the online conference "Stanley Cavell: Constellations of the Ordinary II—International Colloquium," sponsored by Centro de Estudios Filosoficos, Universidad Católica del Perú, Lima, Perú, July 2021. I'm grateful to Victor J. Krebs for organizing the conference, and to conference participants Byron Davies, Nancy Yousef, Paul Standish, Steven Affeldt, and Victor again, for their helpful questions and comments. I especially want to thank Avner Baz for a set of insightful written responses, and Steven again for past and continuing conversations on Cavell's work.

2   John T. Scott, "The Harmony between Rousseau's Musical Theory and His Philosophy," *Journal of the History of Ideas* 59, no. 2 (1998): 287.

3   Georges Liébert, *Nietzsche and Music* (Chicago: University of Chicago Press, 2004).

4   Maurice O'Connor Drury, "Conversations with Wittgenstein," in *Recollections of Wittgenstein*, ed. Rush Rhees (Oxford: Oxford University Press, 1984), 160.

5   Cf. Stanley Cavell, *Little Did I Know: Excerpts from Memory* (Stanford: Stanford University Press, 2010), 73–5, 183; Andrea Olmstead, *Conversations with Roger Sessions* (Boston: Northeastern University Press, 1987), 107–8.

6   Cavell, *Little Did I Know*, 172.

7   Ibid., 225; cf. 209.

8   Cavell doesn't make explicit Thoreau's "morning/mourning" pun in his book on *Walden*—the word "mourning" doesn't appear there—but see Cavell, *The Senses of Walden* (New York: Viking Press, 1972), especially ch. 2, "Sentences," where "morning" is paired with "moulting" (and "metamorphosis" and "leaving"); *In Quest of the Ordinary: Lines of Skepticism and Romanticism* (Chicago: University of Chicago Press, 1988), 44–5, 72–3, 171–2; and *This New Yet Unapproachable America: Lectures after Emerson after Wittgenstein* (Albuquerque: Living Batch Press, 1989), 83–4. See also David LaRocca, "In the Place of Mourning: Questioning the Privations of the Private," *Nineteenth-Century Prose*, vol. 40, no. 2 (2013): 227–42.

9   See my "A Soteriology of Reading: Cavell's Excerpts from Memory," ch. 5 in *Stanley Cavell: Philosophy, Literature and Criticism*, ed. James Loxley and Andrew Taylor (Manchester: Manchester University Press, 2011), 76–91; James Conant, "The Triumph of the Gift Over the Curse in Stanley Cavell's *Little Did I Know*," *MLN*, vol. 126 (2011): 1004–13; Timothy Gould, "Me, Myself and Us: Autobiography and Method in the Writing of Stanley Cavell," *Conversations: The Journal of Cavellian Studies*, vol. 1 (2013): 4–18; and Chiara Alfano, "A Scarred Tympanum," *Conversations*, vol. 1 (2013): 19–38.

10   Cavell, *This New Yet Unapproachable America*, 84.

11   Ibid.

12   Cavell, *Little Did I Know*, 215.

13   Georges Liébert's *Nietzsche and Music* is a model for such a book.

14   Stanley Cavell, "Music Discomposed" and "A Matter of Meaning It," chaps. 7 and 8 in *Must We Mean What We Say?: A Book of Essays* (Cambridge: Cambridge University Press, 1976 [1969]), 180–237.

15   I was by then well on my way to the better part of a lifetime of conversation with Cavell, and also with the remarkable cadre of graduate students studying with him in the mid-to-late 1980s at Harvard, a group he would later describe to me, and then in print, as "permanently inspiring" and "providing a continuity of intellectual purpose unmatched in my decades of teaching" (Cavell, *Little Did I Know*, 476).

16   Cavell, "Music Discomposed," *Must We Mean What We Say?*, 192–3.

17   James Conant, "Throwing Away the Top of the Ladder," *The Yale Review*, vol. 79 (Spring 1990): 328–64, 329; see also "Must We Show What We Cannot Say?," in *The Senses of Stanley Cavell*, ed. Richard Fleming and Michael Payne (Lewisburg: Bucknell University Press, 1989), 242–83. The subtleties of the Diamond/Conant resolute reading may be at right angles to, and so allow for, indeterminate aesthetic experiences that can't be given a name or re-identified, and in that sense are unsayable. Suffice it to say that, at this early stage of our careers, I heard Jim to be making (and he may have meant) a broad denial of a something bearing "ineffable sense."

18   Cavell, "Music Discomposed," *Must We Mean What We Say?*, 192.

19   Ibid.

20   Experiences of sudden (visual or auditory) recognition are the explicit topic of Wittgenstein's late remarks on aspect-seeing, remarks that figure prominently in Part Four of Cavell's *The Claim of Reason* and that he returned to late in his career. See Stanley Cavell, *The Claim of Reason: Wittgenstein, Skepticism, Morality, and Tragedy* (Oxford: Oxford University Press, 1979), 354ff.; and his "The Touch of Words," in *Seeing Wittgenstein Anew*, ed. William Day and Victor J. Krebs (Cambridge: Cambridge University Press, 2010), 81–98.

21   Cavell, "Music Discomposed," *Must We Mean What We Say?*, 193.

22   Cf. Ludwig Wittgenstein, *Philosophical Investigations*, trans. G. E. M. Anscombe, P. M. S. Hacker and Joachim Schulte, rev. 4th ed. (Chichester: Wiley-Blackwell, 2009), §610, §78.

23   "Nearly everybody can recognize a surly look or the smell of tar, but few can describe them non-committally, i.e. otherwise than as 'surly' or 'of tar.'" J. L. Austin, "Other Minds," in *Philosophical Papers*, 3rd ed. (Oxford: Oxford University Press, 1979), 85.

24   Cavell, *Little Did I Know*, 53.

25   Ibid.

26   Ibid.

27   Ibid., 22–3. Stanley's contribution to the review was a piano piece entitled "Indian Drums" which our autobiographer says "I can still play flawlessly on demand," thereby making a rare and explicit gag out of the truth.

28   Ibid., 74, 77.

29   Wittgenstein, *Philosophical Investigations*, §217.

30   Cavell, *Conditions Handsome and Unhandsome: The Constitution of Emersonian Perfectionism* (Chicago: University of Chicago Press, 1990), see p. 70ff.

31   Stanley Cavell, "Impressions of Revolution," ch. 24 in *Here and There: Sites of Philosophy* (Cambridge, MA: Harvard University Press, 2022), 269–78.

32   Walter Benjamin, *The Origin of German Tragic Drama*, trans. John Osborne (London: NLB, 1977), 209, 211; quoted both more and less extensively by Cavell in "Impressions of Revolution," 275. See also Cavell, "Benjamin and Wittgenstein," ch. 7 in *Here and There*, 122–4; "An Understanding with Music," ch. 21 in *Here and There*, 253; "Kivy on *Idomeneo*," ch. 22 in *Here and There*, 258–9.

33   Cavell, "Impressions of Revolution," *Here and There*, 276.

34   Stanley Cavell, "The Wittgensteinian Event," in *Reading Cavell*, ed. Alice Crary and Sanford Shieh (London: Routledge, 2006), 11.

35   Wittgenstein, *Philosophical Investigations*, §527, as quoted by Cavell, "Impressions of Revolution," 278. Cf. Cavell, "An Understanding with Music," 253; "Philosophy and the Unheard," ch. 23 in *Here and There*, 261; and "A Scale of Eternity," ch. 25 in *Here and There*, 280. (The translation in the revised 4th edition of *Investigations* reads: "Understanding a sentence in language is much more akin to understanding a theme in music than one may think.")

36   Wittgenstein, *Philosophical Investigations*, §527. For the later Wittgenstein's conception of language as revealed through the lens of his life with music, see my "The Aesthetic Dimension of Wittgenstein's Later Writings," in *Wittgenstein on Aesthetic Understanding*, ed. Garry L. Hagberg (London: Palgrave Macmillan, 2017), 3–29.

37   Cavell, "Impressions of Revolution," *Here and There*, 277.

38   Augustine, *Confessions*, trans. F. J. Sheed, 2nd ed. (Indianapolis: Hackett, 2006), 253 (XI, xxvii).

39   Cavell, "Philosophy and the Unheard," *Here and There*, 261.

40   Cavell, "A Scale of Eternity," *Here and There*, 280.

41   Cavell, *Little Did I Know*, 216.

42   Letter from Rush Rhees to G. H. von Wright, January 22, 1976; quoted in Christian Erbacher, "Editorial Approaches to Wittgenstein's *Nachlass*: Towards a Historical Appreciation," *Philosophical Investigations*, vol. 38, no. 3 (2015): 184.

43   Cavell, "Impressions of Revolution," *Here and There*, 278.

44   Cavell, "Fred Astaire Asserts the Right to Praise," ch. 3 in *Philosophy the Day after Tomorrow* (Cambridge, MA: Harvard University Press, 2005), 67.

45 Cavell, *Little Did I Know*, 2.

46 Ibid., 163. Cavell may be misremembering the extent to which Goodman's recording of his theme song ("Let's Dance"—see below) "had become a part of [his] brain." While Goodman adopted his theme song in the mid-1930s and it was familiar to radio listeners from his frequent national broadcasts, he didn't make his first and most famous commercial recording of it until October 24, 1939. The Goodman band performed at the San Francisco World's Fair (formally known as the Golden Gate International Exposition) in July of 1939, three months before that recording was made.

47 Ibid., 163–4; cf. endnote 85, below.

48 Ibid., 163.

49 Cavell, "A Scale of Eternity: Gustav Mahler and the Autobiographical," in *Late Thoughts: Reflections on Artists and Composers at Work*, ed. Karen Painter and Thomas Crow (Los Angeles: Getty Research Institute, 2006), 214; cf. *Here and There*, 285.

50 Cavell, *Little Did I Know*, 164–5. Cavell adds parenthetically: "The concept of sublimity was not then in my repertory."

51 In 2013, late in his life and mostly staying at home, Stanley told me not that he was unconnected with the world outside his house but that he was, pleasantly, "uncathected" with it.

52 Cavell, "Impressions of Revolution," *Here and There*, 274.

53 Cavell, "A Scale of Eternity," *Here and There*, 285.

54 Cavell, "What Becomes of Things on Film?," in *Themes Out of School: Effects and Causes* (San Francisco: North Point Press, 1984), 181.

55 Cavell, *Little Did I Know*, 68, 71.

56 For the centrality of transcription to a jazz improviser's self-education, see my "Jazz Improvisation, the Body, and the Ordinary," *Tidskrift för kulturstudier / Journal of Cultural Studies* 5 (2002): 90.

57 Cavell, *Little Did I Know*, 68.

58 Ibid., 73.

59 Ibid., 76.

60 See Cavell, "The Politics of Interpretation (Politics as Opposed to What?)," *Themes Out of School*, 45–8.

61 Cavell, *Little Did I Know*, 76.

62 Cavell, "The Politics of Interpretation," *Themes Out of School*, 46.

63 Ibid.

64 Cavell, *Little Did I Know*, 231, 234.

65 Ibid., 234.

66 Ibid., 235. The man in question, whom Cavell does not identify, was almost certainly Josef Bonime, an Eastern European Jewish émigré (like Cavell's father) and a pianist (like his mother) who made early recordings with famed violinists Mischa Elman and Eugene Ysaye, then went on to work as in-house

composer and conductor for various CBS and NBC radio shows. He put together the "Let's Dance" weekly radio program on which the Goodman band appeared in 1934–5 and is actually credited as co-composer (with Gregory Stone) of Goodman's theme song, "Let's Dance." At the time of his death, Bonime resided at 322 Central Park West (Obituary, *New York Times*, November 10, 1959).

67   Ibid., 235–6.

68   The musical connection between the Goodman theme song and the Weber waltz is in fact, or has since become, somewhat well-known, judging not only from Wikipedia entries and online blog postings but also from the widely distributed if barely watchable 1956 biopic *The Benny Goodman Story*, starring Steve Allen and Donna Reed. (The movie's "Let's Dance" radio show scene depicts the top-of-the-hour transition from the Kel Murray orchestra signing off with a frothy arrangement of *Invitation to the Dance* immediately after which, on a rotating stage, the Benny Goodman band appears performing "Let's Dance.") That said, it is striking that the connection goes unmentioned in perhaps the most authoritative review of the period, Gunther Schuller's *The Swing Era: The Development of Jazz, 1930–1945* (Oxford: Oxford University Press, 1989). When I mentioned the connection to Juilliard faculty member and famed drummer Kenny Washington, known in some quarters as "The Jazz Maniac" for his knowledge of jazz history, he said that he was unaware of it.

69   Cavell, *Little Did I Know*, 236.

70   The *locus classicus* of Wittgenstein's remarks on aspect-seeing is section 11 of Part II (retitled *Philosophy of Psychology—A Fragment*) of *Philosophical Investigations*.

71   Cf. Cavell, *The Claim of Reason*, 369.

72   Cavell, *Little Did I Know*, 225.

73   Ibid., 234–5.

74   Ibid., 235.

75   Ibid.

76   Ibid., 236.

77   On the importance of the demand to "imagine the sounds" in any of Cavell's interpretive efforts, see my "A Soteriology of Reading," *Stanley Cavell: Philosophy, Literature and Criticism*, 79, 82–5.

78   Cavell, *The Claim of Reason*, 421ff. In the abstract that Cavell sent me for his contribution to *Seeing Wittgenstein Anew* ("The Touch of Words"), he wrote the following, related thought: "Experience, as Wittgenstein recounts it in these passages [on aspect-blindness and, relatedly, soul-blindness], is not a peculiar perception of an object but a response to the differences and similarities between objects, even, one could say, to an object's difference from itself, its putting forth, all at once, as it were, a new face (eliciting my response, not awaiting my perception)."

79   Cavell, "The Avoidance of Love: A Reading of *King Lear*," ch. 10 in *Must We Mean What We Say?*, 269; "Must We Mean What We Say?," ch. 1 in *Must We Mean What We Say?*, 36 n.31.

80   Cavell, "Aesthetic Problems of Modern Philosophy," ch. 3 in *Must We Mean What We Say?*, 87.

81   Cavell, "Impressions of Revolution," *Here and There*, 276.

82   Ibid., 276–7.

83   Cavell presents an extensive discussion of where intention (and hence, meaning) in art lies in "A Matter of Meaning It," *Must We Mean What We Say?*, 225–37.

84   Cavell, "Impressions of Revolution," *Here and There*, 277. Cavell's sense of "what we want to explain" in discussing what counts as "understanding music" is echoed in, or echoes, Wittgenstein's remarks on how we convey our experiences of music; see my "The Aesthetic Dimension of Wittgenstein's Later Writings," *Wittgenstein on Aesthetic Understanding*, 13–15.

85   Cavell, "Impressions of Revolution," *Here and There*, 277. The sense of this remark is heightened beyond measure by what Cavell would later write in *Little Did I Know*: "I had characteristically taken it as an unquestionable fact of my life that from the time of that first move [from the south to the north side of Atlanta] until I left Sacramento for Berkeley ten years later I did not draw a happy breath. [...] What is true is that for long periods I spent so much time by myself that a therapist friend of mine will describe something I said alluding to days of that period as expressing a state of sensory deprivation, as if I had been confined in a cave" (54).

86   See, for example, Cavell's condensed appraisal of human understanding and its vicissitudes in his late entry on August 26, 2004 in *Little Did I Know*, 532.

87   Cf. Cavell's late entry on August 27, 2004 in *Little Did I Know*, 533–5.

88   Cavell, *Little Did I Know*, 4.

89   Ibid., 6.

3

Cavell on Music

As Performer, as Writer

JOHN HARBISON

ROSE MARY HARBISON AND I MET STANLEY CAVELL in September 1962, in Princeton, introduced to him in his apartment at the Institute of Advanced Study by Marshall Cohen. We were part of the university's Music Department. I was a graduate student in composition, she was a performer allied with Professor Earl Kim's analysis class. During that fall, Rose Mary's apartment became a meeting place for an intense group of Princeton sojourners: Stanley had formed a bond with a visiting British philosopher, Bernard Williams, and I was spending a lot of time with the composer Peter Maxwell Davies, who was in Princeton studying with Roger Sessions. This Anglo-American group, expanded by other congenial philosophical and musical souls, found much in common. The memory of those evenings is, for me, some sixty years later, still fresh.

Stanley and Rosie soon happened upon a common interest in Brahms. His quarters were without a piano. She had a day job, and offered him a practice space, and soon they were rehearsing the Brahms Violin Sonata in G major. He got back in shape very quickly, they added the Debussy sonata to their repertoire, and soon were playing runouts. Among the first was a house-concert in the country manor of the Duenna of Princeton musical society. While waiting backstage—actually, the kitchen—to go on, Stanley decided to slip out to the living room to grab a snack and coffee, but was quickly arrested by the hostess, who explained that the performers were not to "mingle with the guests" but were confined to the kitchen. Stanley was fond of citing that moment as his true Return to Music.

The next fall, all of us moved to Cambridge, Massachusetts, Stanley to begin his professorship in philosophy at Harvard. His quarters at Adams House soon became a meeting place for many whose thought, work, and sense of adventure still sounds with those long, excited days and evenings.

Early in the spring of 1964 John Mudd, already a veteran of the Civil Rights Movement, was apprised of an initiative to give the faculty of Tougaloo College a summer break. This mainly Black, interracial college near Jackson, Mississippi was directly in the center of the drive for radical change in the south. Rosie and I, together with many of our friends—Tom Gleason, Alan Graubard, Judy Herman, and a very enthusiastic Stanley Cavell—immediately signed on.

The idea was, first, that we would add our presence to a determination for change, but also that we would offer courses in our own disciplines, freeing the Tougaloo faculty for a summer. For Rosie and me, and for my cellist sister Helen, it meant offering concerts of the music we most treasured, and we invited Stanley to join us. He enthusiastically agreed, while also offering his typical course-of-readings seminars.

As one of the anchors for our evening programs at Tougaloo, at Stanley's suggestion, we chose the Brahms A major Piano Quartet. The three of us— Rose Mary Harbison, my sister Helen Abrahamian, and I—had played quite often with each other, but the first rehearsal with Stanley on the Brahms piece was a new experience. He was in prime shape technically, obviously knew how the piece proceeded, but we were most struck by his old-school, deep-in-the-keys sound, and his rich engagement with each change of musical character. To us he sounded like players we had heard on early recordings, un-self-conscious, never decorous, always taking a point of view. He really had no rehearsal mode, he was all in, testing the limits, free and responsive to the moment, highly inflected but clear-minded and intelligible.

When I think back to our journey with the Brahms A major, I remember a passage in the last movement where the viola introduces a vaulting, leaping new tune, immediately after the climactic drive to the end of the first large segment of the piece. I loved reaching that place knowing that Stanley was not going to give me a break, but was committed to the animation of the situation, which had to continue to a breath-stopping general pause. Because he was closer than we were to a grand tradition in this music, we were happy to cede to him important interpretive decisions, feeling that his very detailed rubato and impetuous timing lived closer to the source than we did.

Perhaps of all the members of our summer faculty, Cavell had the clearest sense of why he was at Tougaloo. He was witnessing a test of the resilience of American democracy. Could his South answer this moment? The Atlantan Stanley was our colleague that summer, charged by the heat, the edginess of the situation, the sense that each day it was an important place to be. And with a constant sense of the power of the art and music and literature he loved, he took joy in being at Tougaloo.

It's unfortunate that no recording was made of the performance of the piano quartet. Cavell was close to Brahms—the stoic insistence, the moments of anxious passion, the momentary depressive islands all made sense in his sound. We are fortunate that a rehearsal version of the same composer's G major violin sonata, with Rose Mary Harbison, has surfaced, full of the same mercurial responsiveness to the Brahms' stark shifts of mood and confidence.

There is fortunately another evidence of Cavell as pianist, some of which was wisely included at his memorial events: the player of America Songbook songs, from an improvisational jazz angle.[1] Evening visitors to 27 Monmouth Court, Brookline, might hear such pianistic ruminations as they approached the front door, played with some corrective moments to secure the exact harmony, or doubling back perhaps to confirm the always-remembered words.

This, like most of his piano world, came originally from his admiration of his mother's playing (I heard Fannie Segal, briefly: her pianistic finesse had not been exaggerated). She had honed her craft playing for silent films, improvising according to the plot line, and she moved deftly between all kinds of music, popular and formal. It was from her that Stanley absorbed a certain porousness between levels of culture; there were no hard lines between "high" art and popular. The arrival, toward the end of his life, of the family's fine Atlanta piano, taking up residency in his spartan study, was undoubtedly the inspiration for his renewed enthusiasm in playing. On its lyre were the Chopin preludes he always favored. The standard pop tunes were in his head, and he constantly probed them for their expressive secrets and reviewed them for their exact details.

Sometimes he improvised jazz variations on his favorite tunes.

Maybe it's not too much of a stretch to suggest that his own writing style stretches all the way back to his lead alto days, when jazz etiquette included the option of extending, even exaggerating to make a point, riffing off a thought until it finds (or baffles) more hearers, thinking aloud into new territory, where the drama of expressing an idea can become part of the style, where the shedding of literary convention can mirror the writer's search and even his surprise at discovery.

This is a non-professional philosopher's attempt to describe the exhilaration and occasional despair of this great thinker–writer's bold prose, the place where he never for a moment abandons music.

Cavell on a Life in Music—and Leaving It

"[S]hedding skins of illusion." A "mysterious [...] process of disentanglement." A "work of mourning." These are ways Cavell recalled, in his autobiography, the moment he abandoned hope of a career in music.[2]

So many hours of preparation and study, passionate involvement in every aspect of music, jazz, and classical—performing and composing, listening and absorbing—had brought Cavell to a point he had long defined as a primary goal: enrollment in Composition at The Juilliard School. Music had been his whole life. He was avid in its pursuit, fascinated by its challenges, supported by his distinguished teachers.

But something crucial was missing, something he later summarized in the most unsparing terms, speaking about his own music: "It had its moments, but on the whole I did not love it; it said next to nothing I could, or wished to, believe."[3]

Such a shocking realization left him despairing, unmoored, and initially immobilized. He later remembered the moment, riding in a Manhattan bus, when he knew he was giving up attending those classes at Juilliard. He questioned whether he was going to pieces, which suggested to him that he already had.

For a while he stayed in his room and read, notably Freud, which he perused like a medical textbook. Then, he began to go out, crossing Broadway—going to the shows, clubs, plays, and films.

He also continued to go to opera, orchestra and chamber concerts, and jazz. He continued to stay in good shape as a pianist. We know that he maintained, over many years, a close relationship with the Great American Songbook repertoire (Gershwin, Kern, etc.), constantly bonding him with the keyboard through to his last years.

By the time Rose Mary and I met Stanley, he seemed to have made peace with not pursuing music as a career, instead folding it back near the center of his world, his writing, his teaching, and his private time. He never relinquished the piano keyboard, nor his many connections to music and musicians. Stanley Cavell never truly left music. It may not have been his profession, but it was part of his professional concern. It was a daily part of his inner (and often outer) life, and it remained essential to his writing, thinking, and his friendships.

Composing a Philosophical Criticism of Music

"Music Discomposed" appeared in 1967 and was later included in the collection *Must We Mean What We Say?* (1969).[4] It is still, today, the best known of Cavell's articles on music. I admit staying away from it for decades, because it entered a stream of discourse on music at its low point, when morale and confidence in the new music of the time was in a dangerous state. My fear that Cavell was taking the wrong bait now seems misplaced.

"Music Discomposed" is synchronous with a dark period in the history of concert music composition. Cavell begins with a summary of an article by Ernst Krenek,[5] the Czech composer and music theorist, giving a grim but reasonably accurate picture of a musical community, both audience and professionals, bereft of confidence or even interest in the new, seeking rescue in systematic constructive principles (which generated both interest and faith at the time).

One of these, "total organization"—where all parameters of composition (pitch, rhythm, articulation) are serialized to impose an external control on composition—remains especially emblematic of a spiritual and technical dead end, exemplified by musical and theoretical works by prestigious professionals that stand today as silent witnesses to a creative impasse.

For those of us charged with the teaching of music, that period was dominated by what appeared to be a stylistic imperative, the continuation of a kind of dialectic exploration of the implications of early twentieth-century central European music: a dense, high chromaticism that few performers were able to master technically or imaginatively, and few listeners able to apprehend. Those of us confronting, year after year, groups of student composers alarmingly similar in the language they chose, and equally immobilized by its imperatives, were relieved when Minimalism came along. The resulting pieces, still quite similar to each other, were instead, in their steady pounding rhythms and white-note vocabulary, considerably more pleasant for the listener.

(This change may have been influenced by Pop Art, a cultural moment Cavell seems tempted to address in "A Matter of Meaning It," but stops short.[6] Pop Art appears to have represented the appearance of a salable, critically acceptable semi-art so dubious in its criteria that it helped to bring about a change of atmosphere at the beginning of this century, best described as "All Bets Are Off." Thereafter, composer/new-music gatherings now witnessed young people making concert music with every possible assumption: proto-pop, jazz-fused, Neo-primitive, false or sincere naive, severely plainsong-bare, or anything else that might require fresh premises. With such a hodgepodge of assumptions, genuine and original notions might have a chance to sally forth.)

Cavell doesn't find much interest in Krenek's proposals, or the proposer, and moves instead into his own summary of the state of musical life at the moment of his writing, then veers startlingly to a bold outline of musical aesthetics and, even more surprisingly, offers a kind of composition lesson for those who might look for such guidance.

In re-painting the bleak picture offered by Krenek, Cavell seems to suggest, between the lines, that such conditions may be something of a given in the movement of music's history—composers feeling unheard or misunderstood, audiences pulling away or fleeing, criticism inert or shooting wild, players and composers "fighting for their artistic lives."

Cavell seems to suggest that some or most of that is a natural part of moving forward, finding what is next. In segment VI, which begins "What is composition, what is it to compose?" Cavell moves into a description of the elements that might enable the making of a piece of music—in any time or circumstance. Certain memorable phrases are part of the ensuing paragraphs.

> We follow the progress of a piece the way we follow what someone is saying or doing.
> One makes one's own dangers.
> Every risk must be shown worthwhile.
> You cede the possibilities of excuse, explanation, or justification for your failures, and the cost of failure is not remorse or recompense, but the loss of coherence altogether.
> A continuing improvisation in the face of problems we no longer understand.[7]

In the course of reading this essay, I realize that Cavell is offering something like a guide to composing, expressing his persistent belief that music remains to be written, even under the harsh and demanding terms of the contemporary. He was, throughout his life, always supportive and engaged in the latest musical work—from his devotion to Roger Sessions (enthusiastically playing, listening, and following), through his warm friendship with Seymour Shifrin (whose mercurial, truly unpredictable, oddly phrased music he thoroughly endorsed and supported), to and including younger composers like myself (whose projects he followed closely in progress and in performance). He always believed we were just a few composers away from the start of a new golden age. The main issue was always the lifting of the curtain of conformity.

Cavell's essays on the creation and performance of new music stand among the few serious efforts to define what concert music must confront in order to continue. His writings remain relevant in a field still lacking good criticism, missing the connection between makers and hearers, and experiencing wide disparities of opinion about how to legitimately close these gaps.

Many commentors on "Music Discomposed" focus on Cavell's glancing, somewhat disengaged reference to "fraudulence," which Cavell seems to regard as an age-old anxiety that we must tolerate in order to participate in any phase of the journey. Fraudulence is not really a frequent danger in a field with so few rewards. To willfully and knowingly deceive by causing an inadequate piece to impersonate a good one is not likely, the stakes being so low, the risk so high. Cavell's summary of this topic occasions one of the most essential moments in "Music Discomposed": "the dangers of fraudulence, and of trust, are essential to the experience of art."[8]

With every re-reading, "Music Discomposed" seems like a stealthy, subversive, very philosophic segment of *Must We Mean What We Say?* Of all his remarks on music, this is the closest follow-up to his "departure" from music, a departure which served to clarify music's continuing centrality to his life's work.

The title "Music Discomposed" is important, as always with Cavell essays. He is addressing a discourse within music circles that is in disarray. His stunning assertion about composition, both practical and imaginative, is nothing short of a pronouncement of what music *is*, and what is required to compose it.

Cavell's Late Essays on Music

Here and There: Sites of Philosophy is a volume of Cavell's essays assembled by a team of editors after his death, guided by the author's draft of a possible table of contents. In the preface, Cavell expresses surprise at the appearance of five segments on music, which are placed at the conclusion of the collection. "Music is as old among my cultural practices as reading words or telling time, but except for a pair of forays in my first book, I have until quite recently avoided the issue."[9] ("Recently" in 2001 would include *A Pitch of Philosophy* [1994], in which he deals extensively with opera.)

For the many who knew Stanley Cavell as a musician–philosopher, who kept his musical skills constantly sharp, playing, listening, and discussing music, the appearance of the final chapters of *Here and There* is not a surprise. Those who visited Monmouth Court, in his last years will remember, through the double front doors, the piano sounds of Kern and Gershwin, chord changes improvised and consistently accurate, wafting through.

The concluding essay in *Here and There*, "A Scale of Eternity,"[10] centers on Mahler. Cavell begins by quoting Wittgenstein: "Understanding a sentence lies nearer than one thinks to what is ordinarily called understanding a musical theme."[11] Cavell goes on to consider Wittgenstein and Mahler together in terms of being haunted by doubt, with a shared "fear of inexpressiveness and suffocation."[12] He finds the composer and the philosopher—in spite of their expressed antipathy—to be bravely confronting a common sense of uncertainty, of insufficiency, both eventually finding a way to walk forward (Cavell's frequent evocation of Mahler and walking is a haunting feature of this essay).

Cavell begins "A Scale of Eternity" by noting that Mahler's work was always *late*. There is much to be inferred from this: the admission of banality and repetitiveness; the reluctance to conclude; the expanded, even distorted harmonic and contrapuntal concepts. Above all, we're aware of the imparting of urgent last words, messages close to or perhaps beyond the grave.

Here Cavell the musician–philosopher is at his most eloquent. The "incomplete" conclusions in Mahler have been much discussed, but never with more expressive precision than the sentences offered by Cavell as he describes Mahler "declining to descend to the home degree."[13] At the end of this essay, with a musician's precise technical and affective understanding and a philosopher's gift for analogue and simile, Cavell offers a vivid account of Mahlerian incompleteness, eloquent elisions, extensions, and omissions.

"A Scale of Eternity" is one of the five essays that comprise the concluding section of the posthumous *Here and There*. One thing notable about the entire group is that they never get drawn into a chronicle about the broad sweep of music history. So many commentators about music have spent dutiful pages on Theodor Wiesengrund Adorno, the German philosopher and sociologist active in the first half of the twentieth century, a classically trained pianist sympathetic to the *avant-garde* of his era (serialism at that time), known for his scathing cultural critiques that were particularly derisive of popular music. Adorno's outsized influence meant for a long time that it would not be respectable to say anything about the development of the art without dealing with him.

Cavell wisely does not join in this exercise. Each Cavell reference to Adorno hints that he is not taking the bait, not mistaking colorful polemic for insight, not buying that brand of short-breathed cleverness.

Something Out of the Ordinary: Cavell and Astaire

In December of 1996, Cavell went to Atlanta, to a site only a few blocks from where he had grown up. He was there to deliver, to distinguished peers in his field and in the presence of members of his family, "Something Out of the Ordinary," the Presidential Address to the American Philosophical Association.[14]

And something out of the ordinary is certainly what he offered.

After some (parenthetical) remarks about voice raised to passionate speech in opera, Cavell presented a short bit from one of his favorite films, Vincente Minnelli's *The Band Wagon* (1953), which "readily allows itself to be dismissed as inconsequential; but to my mind that fact precisely fits it to be a memorable enactment of the ordinary as what is missable."[15]

By this point in his career most of his readers were accepting, enthusiastically or reluctantly, Cavell's conviction that the "ordinary," as represented by our country's entertainment culture, especially Broadway and Hollywood dramas and musicals, could be the subject of serious and passionate attention and analysis, in a philosophic context.

It had been long apparent to Stanley that the experience of aesthetic pleasure and assent or, differently described, the enjoyment of something as art, did not have to be the result of the maker's specific intention to Make Art, it could even be the result of a blatantly and joyously commercial enterprise.

This distinction obviously does not need to accompany his essays on *King Lear* and Beckett's *Endgame*. Instead, it suits his frequent address to films and shows, frankly commercial enterprises, or tunes that might be intended to reach the largest swath of listeners. Cavell holds to the premise that "art," especially in American culture, is often achieved, heedlessly, as part of an embrace of an unfiltered audience seldom expected, as in the European operetta tradition, to be culturally literate or aesthetically appreciative.

Cavell encourages himself and his readers to venture, to engage—no matter how appropriate the context. "I keep discovering that I have to go back to collect belongings that others may not have come to care for as I have."[16] This trust and hope in the Ordinary seems very Emersonian.

The talk in Atlanta enfolded a large-screen presentation of the opening scene of *The Band Wagon*, followed by Stanley's rich and detailed account of it. The very personal tone of this speech to his fellow philosophers became clear as he began to narrate the opening sequence, in which we see actor-dancer Fred Astaire arriving in New York to begin work on a new show, but in a defeated, pessimistic, career-in-shambles state. His long traversal down a railroad platform after exiting a train is the essential action of the scene. In it Astaire, with help of the superb song "By Myself" (Arthur Schwartz and Howard Dietz), gradually begins to pull himself out of his depression.

The physical fluency of Astaire is essential here, and Cavell, who always seemed closely identified with Astaire, is able to describe some crucial aspects of the actor's limber, lived-in singing voice and his lightly dance-inflected traversal of the platform.

The song "By Myself"—the very unusual, radically concise song that opens *The Band Wagon*, and thus anchors the beginning of Cavell's address to his philosophical colleagues in Atlanta in 1996—needs a close look. Why this song, why this film, this actor, Astaire, and why this plot line.

The Astaire protagonist is returning to New York to try to re-begin his career. This performance is not high-voltage, instead it glides and suggests and hovers. (For contrast we have the famous performance by Cyd Charisse: brave, combative, triumphant.) Astaire does not insist, he rides the subtle harmonies as an optimistic passenger. The orchestration is lyric, shy, and tuneful. This wistful, conditional tone—encouraging also to the listener (who feels they too might have access to it)—grows naturally with the form of the song.

Cavell rightly describes "By Myself" as exhibiting an "ingeniously modified AABA form."[17] Although it is in four phrases, they are knitted together into a single melody: all of the segments share rhythmic and melodic motives.

The song is presented as it was originally published, that is, with an initial 16-measure A section repeated, the second time with different words. This stretching of the initial segment emphasizes the harmonically most unstable part of the song (the avoidance of its home key). It also prepares for the shorter 8-bar final segments to feel pointed and conclusive, with B reaching the piece's highest note, and A arriving at the lowest, as well as its first full affirmation of the home key. The song is one continuous tune, and the movement from the beginning, through the B section high point to the conclusion is without a seam. The symmetry of the bone structure is hidden by the flow of the melody, and the very unconventional harmonies.

In examining the harmonic structure of "By Myself," Cavell closely considers the unusual opening chord, which hovers at midpoint between D minor and its relative major F. In offering an exact analysis of the sonority—moody and "complicated," momentarily nowhere—he accurately compares it to the famous chord that begins Wagner's *Tristan and Isolde*. Indeed, the harmony, two moves away from a stable tonal location, is pitched only a half-step below the famous string sonority in Wagner's revolutionary second measure. Could the actual context be more different? Hardly, except that the "emotional hovering" emphasized by Cavell's *Band Wagon* discussion is present in both.[18]

"By Myself," at the beginning of *The Band Wagon*, is not conclusive: the achievement is tentative, the protagonist still has to continue to reconstruct. Cavell's engagement with this scene immediately seemed to this listener a talisman of his own early quest to be understood by his peers, for their reading of him to acquire more tolerance for his syntax and his voice. It was, even in his later years, not uncommon for him to return to hover there for a moment.

The Primacy of Voice

An important theme elsewhere in Cavell's writings, appearing in various guises, is the historical "imperative" of opera, its appearance at the end of the great period of English drama, its realization of the need for the release of extreme/sublime emotion as singing, and its various characterizations of the role/plight/transfiguration of women. Cavell notices operatic parallels with the dramaturgy of many of the films he has pondered, and urges certain threads between our perception of an actor on film and an opera singer on a stage.

Since Cavell's philosophy writing is so voice-driven, his growing enthusiasm for opera was no surprise. I'm sure that many others reading him also *hear* him, since he wrote in and for his own speaking voice, since his writing is so personal. Some of the time he seems almost to be writing in the voice of Astaire (with Emerson and Thoreau among his alter egos). My own favorite Cavell moment is in "The Thought of Movies," where Cavell conjures up his adolescent encounter with Astaire in *Top Hat* (1935), singing in his perfect non-singer's voice a song of amazing melodic elegance and formal daring, "Cheek to Cheek." At another place in the essay, Cavell comments on the bold opening word: "Heaven." On this occasion it's the leaping imagination of the first three lines "And the cares that hung around me through the week/seem to vanish like the gambler's lucky streak," about which he says: "a stanza such as this *was* what I thought of as poetry—nothing else will be poetry for me that cannot compete with the experience of concentration and lift in such words."[19]

This is Stanley Cavell, on whom nothing is lost, hearing the music and the poetry in both his ordinary and his shockingly acute way, encouraging his philosophic readers to stay alert.

Notes

1   I'm referring to recordings of Cavell's piano playing that were shared in his honor during a memorial service held at Harvard's Memorial Church, November 2018.

2   Stanley Cavell, *Little Did I Know: Excerpts from Memory* (Stanford: Stanford University Press, 2010), 225.

3   Cavell, *Little Did I Know*, 223.

4   Stanley Cavell, "Music Discomposed," in *Must We Mean What We Say? A Book of Essays* (Cambridge: Cambridge University Press, 1976), 180–212.

5   Ernst Krenek, "Tradition in Perspective," *Perspectives of New Music*, vol. 1, no. 1 (Autumn 1962): 27–38.

6   Cavell, "A Matter of Meaning It," *Must We Mean What We Say?*, 213–37.

7   See section VI, Cavell, "Music Discomposed," *Must We Mean What We Say?*, 197–202.

8   Ibid., 188-89.

9   Stanley Cavell, "Draft Preface to *Here and There*," in *Here and There: Sites of Philosophy*, ed. Alice Crary, Nancy Bauer, and Sandra Laugier (Cambridge, MA: Harvard University Press, 2022), 292.

10 This essay was presented as a talk at the 2002 Bard Music Festival, as part of a panel discussion entitled *Images of Gustav Mahler*. In it, Cavell effects a rapprochement between Wittgenstein and Mahler, a composer whose work Wittgenstein disliked, and who was lauded by Theodor Adorno as the composer of the "breakthrough." See Cavell, "A Scale of Eternity," *Here and There*, 279–86.

11   Ibid., 280.

12   Ibid., 282.

13   Ibid., 285.

14   The address is printed as the first chapter in Stanley Cavell, *Philosophy the Day after Tomorrow* (Cambridge, MA: Harvard University Press, 2005), 7–27.

15   Cavell, "Something Out of the Ordinary," *Philosophy the Day after Tomorrow*, 10–11.

16   Ibid., 7.

17   Ibid., 23.

18   Ibid., 22.

19   Stanley Cavell, "The Thought of Movies," in *Themes Out of School: Effects and Causes* (San Francisco: North Point Press, 1984), 19.

MOVEMENT II

Registers

4

"A Voice Deep Inside"

Cavell, Streisand, and the Reach of Song's Inner Speech

GARRETT STEWART

WHAT FOLLOWS IS AN ATTEMPT AT SYNTHESIS through new evidence: a fusion of Stanley Cavell's writing about female vocal performance with evidence new in particular to Cavell—at least when last we were able to talk, back in 2010. In homage to the titular spirit of this companion volume to David LaRocca's earlier collections—in other words, listening to music in tune with Cavell's trained ear, as before in the project of seeing movies through the philosopher's unique mind's eye[1]—my remarks aim to bring the two attentions together in the more specific consideration of *screen music* and its suggestive philosophic overtones. The approach is further (and more pointedly) Cavellian in taking seriously his emphasis on female "voice" under the sign of both its creative potency and its gender threat. I want therefore to put into dialogue his preoccupation with the operatic vent of passion in female performance—"Opera and the Lease of Voice," that middle noun "lease" indicating not just a voluble release but a short-lived existential license—with musical moments (and their legacy) in the screen rather than the stage genre he so influentially dubbed "remarriage comedy," including his own recurrent stress on the transient song interludes of these films. Pursuing thereby his own interest in vocal performance as it inflects the sexual dynamic of such madcap comedies, I extend consideration into a striking musical-comedy inheritance of the remarriage plot in two touchstone films either anchored by, in one case, or loosely tethered at the end, in the other, to the incandescently expressive vocals of Barbra Streisand.[2]

This path back from operatic tragedy in Cavell's 1994 book, under the punning title *The Pitch of Philosophy*, to the earlier theme of voice in the remarriage films seems glanced at but left hanging at the start of the opera chapter: "When a few years ago I was asked to say how as a philosopher I had become interested in film," he immediately rephrases the question, at a deeper autobiographical level, to suggest that the real question is "how a lost young musician had come to recognize his interests as philosophical."[3] What nothing in the essay actually spells out, however, is how a *philosophical* interest in music leads him later to movies. The case for opera is certainly clear, as I'll summarize it momentarily. But how is an interest in music a redescription of an interest in film? One of the ways Cavell has come closest to answering this question is back in *Pursuits of Happiness*, where he admits that he "sometimes found it useful to think of the nature of film by comparing what camera and projection bring to a script with what music brings to a libretto."[4] So, as it happens, has Barbra Streisand found it useful in turning to the direction of her own voice on screen. In the DVD commentary on *Yentl* she speaks of editing as related to singing, with an alternation between "legato and staccato" registers so palpable in her dexterous camera technique, balancing sinuous dissolves against spatial match cuts. And since the singing is hers in *Yentl*, as well as the writing and directing, such cinematographic rhythm—both in the ligatures of shot transition, and especially in her favored mode of the long take—can seem to figure the found space of and for voice. A space intermittent, hard-won, often cloistered. In the film's break from the mainstream Hollywood staging of musical comedy—as indicated by its subtitle, a "Film with Music"—we might say that bittersweet comedy forces the music inside, socially unwarranted, under repression as withheld song. The details of that process, and the freed-up place of "voice" in it, will, as it were, emerge. And come up for sustained notice in such a way that Cavell's interest in the "photogenetic poetry of film" will be more than ordinarily linked to the auto-genesis of female "creation" in one of his most debated claims about the re-winning of marital rapport.[5]

On just this question, two historical (biographical) checkpoints, first, regarding my "conversation" with Cavell. That is a term I use here in the routine sense, metaphorically and otherwise—as distinct from its elevation by his ordinary language philosophy into a litmus test of marital interchange, with the result that the tireless comic banter of his favored comic scripts, a decade into the medium's technological revolution, work both to epitomize and to thematize the "talking picture." In that special usage of his, "conversation" may seem to operate in unspoken contrast (though with the clear inference of erotic "congress") to the dated legalistic term "criminal conversation" for adultery with another's spouse: the very fear of this (in a flashpoint of the philosopher's career-long interrogation of skepticism) posing one threat to marital stability in these classic screwball films.[6] But that, too, is to come. In the mediated academic "conversation" of scholarly dialogue, which is all I meant above, I was privileged to be a referee reader for Harvard University Press in their eager vetting of Cavell's book on this remarriage genre. My awed and of course laudatory report did, however, take time to worry out loud about a line of thought (somewhat rephrased in clarification, if memory serves, before the book came out) that I suspected would raise issues, indeed hackles, for feminist film scholarship— and, regardless of minor revision, did. The main issue was his crucial sense, quite justified on his own terms, both historical and philosophical, that these films, under marital auspices, involve the "the new creation of a woman."[7] The point wasn't in any way grotesque: that only, for instance, in marriage, and its tested recommitment, does a woman really come to be, nor that without a man she is nothing. Yet his formulation would later, at times, get caricatured as courting that assumption. More generously understood, still the emphasis on female realization under a male aegis, or erotic renovation in the precincts of marital reciprocity, could all too easily be contaminated by the eponymous myth of *Adam's Rib* (1949, dir. George Cukor, among the cinematic test cases in the book), even with pun intended in the Hepburn–Tracy pairing and sparring (the woman as comic foil and goad, ribbing the man's vanity).

Subject versus Object: Toward an "Ordinary Language" Grammar of Remarriage

In this regard, a lynchpin formulation of Cavell's like the following is phrased so as to need almost immediate further comment: "[I]f the creation of the woman is as definitive of the genre as I take it to be, then this phase of the history of cinema is bound up with a phase in the history of the consciousness of women."[8] A gloss comes right on the heels of this assumption: "The formulation 'consciousness of women' is studiously ambiguous," a point he spells out in what a grammarian might trouble to distinguish as the subjective genitive ("women's consciousness" of whatever, including themselves) versus the objective genitive (the "consciousness of women" by whomever, men especially). The fact is that even this acknowledged co-determination in the comedies, and even in a validation of found female "voice," wasn't enough to keep certain 1980s feminists from tuning out—as I well remember, not just from anecdotal evidence in my failures to proselytize this landmark book, but from published complaint. In recurrent celebrations of the "creation of the woman," as perhaps most persuasively in his analysis of feminine disguise-as-revelation in *The Awful*

Truth (1937, dir. Leo McCarey), Cavell might have helped his case by acknowledging that this phrase too, in its grammatical ambiguity, is meant to designate a "creative" recasting of her own persona—in that film's case with a singing and dancing performance of the heroine's earthier and more sexually assertive alter ego—rather than, or at least as much as, the plot's reconstruction of her from a male perspective.

The present chapter may be taken to revisit this contested issue in films of the singing screen star widely hailed in reviews of her triumphant Hollywood debut, *Funny Girl* (1968, dir. William Wyler), less for her vocals, already legendary as a recording artist, than for a voluble comic timing that harked back to the heyday of 1930s comic heroines. Certainly any two-sided center of consciousness in female screen stardom—the woman in view of her own needs under the gaze of male fascination—is a signature effect of Barbara (re-created Barbra) Streisand's suffusedly "self-conscious" comic stardom—as attested to and wrestled with in her own version of the remarriage comedy and its performative discovery of voice, especially when "producing" and directing herself as the fabled "actress-who-sings." And it goes straight to the point of my ventured correlation of Cavell's opera essay, on the one hand, with his searching notice of song numbers in the remarriage comedies, on the other, that the renowned musician Glenn Gould, when adding to his comment that Streisand "is probably the great singing-actress since Maria Callas," wanted the sense that "I hyphenate very carefully."[9] My approach has no interest in arguing that Streisand's feminism had set out to correct some defect in Cavell's prototype comedies, but simply that her inheritance of their energy, including her unmatched vocal enhancement in certain cases, suggests how a rephrased emphasis in Cavell's work—less on "creation of the woman" than on female *self-invention*—might at the time have mitigated a good deal of resistance to his approach.

In any case, as alluded to above, that second conversational moment with Cavell, in live time, led nowhere (at least that I know of)—except to this chapter. It was prompted by sheer curiosity. On the matter of a so-called pursuit of happiness in American marital parable traced out by his 1981 book, a particular kind of happiness already so blocked from possibility in Streisand's man-that-got away films—*Funny Girl* (1968), *On a Clear Day You Can See Forever* (1970, dir. Vincente Minnelli), *The Way We Were* (1973, dir. Sydney Pollack), *Funny Lady* (1975, dir. Herbert Ross), *A Star is Born* (1976, dir. Frank Pierson), later *Yentl* (1983) and *The Prince of Tides* (1991, dir. Barbra Streisand)—I couldn't resist, years later at a conference dinner, asking Stanley what he thought of Streisand's curious mutation of his remarriage paradigm in *Yentl*, and more broadly about her long-anointed role as the true heir of the fast-talking screen heroines of his classic favorites. With passing curiosity he allowed my proposal, though he hadn't himself been paying much attention to the star or her plots. Nor, that is, to her "voice." Hadn't lent a serious ear. So these were two mostly one-sided conversations—once on the page only, then later, in real time, missing the mark; first via anonymous press advice and then in a snatch of friendly but fizzled table talk—whose tacit dialogue this chapter seeks to reboot and prolong. Conversations that might've been.

Since Stanley wasn't, in effect, "conversant" with Streisand's genius, I need to try for myself putting their profoundly shared intuitions about the female voice on screen—and the narrative archetypes that bring it up and out—into fruitful communication after the fact. And to do so first by expanding the spread of common denominators between Cavell's study of marital complications, with their often-claimed Shakespearean ramifications, and Streisand's plotting of their variants, including the reworking of *Twelfth Night* that *Yentl* so subliminally constitutes. This connection happens not by explicit allusion of any sort, but rather through the way Streisand's masterfully crafted film realizes something about the always masked battle of the sexes and the polymorphousness of desire—a desire which, as Shakespeare precedes her in elaborating, a certain tactical disguise can release from straitjacketing: from the costume of custom per se, and in Streisand's case through the bursting-out of song as well. Inevitably, this broadened span of common themes then includes Cavell's interest, contra comedy, in the auditory traumas of female song in the punishing plots of grand opera, dependent on a female abjection that the Streisand voice, as well as persona, and for all the grandeur of her vocals, so utterly rejects. Short of this explicitly musical overlap, a conspicuous number of Cavell's remarriage motifs are there in *Yentl*: maternal absence, paternal impact as a withdrawn magic power (like Prospero's), female desire as self-performance, gender misrecognition and impersonation, erotic blockage in the slump of routine, sexual tension reduced to the symbolism of sibling rivalry, with freedom won at last only when the woman is not given, but claims—that is, creates for herself—a voice in her destiny. Such and more are the convergent paths at issue.

What isn't at stake should be ruled out from the start: namely, incidental (rather than structural) echoes of screwball's word play or certain plot formats—in the broken-marriage archetype—that Streisand's films often share with melodrama. In a deliberate throwback to 1930s screwball, her adamantly madcap character Judy in *What's Up, Doc?* (1972, dir. Peter Bogdanovich)—baffling and infuriating her sudden musicologist heart-throb with her erratic behavior—apologizes that "I know I'm different, but from now on I'll try to be the same." The same as what, he wonders. "As people who aren't different." Such is the trivialized narcissistic introversion of the marital lifeline held out by Lucy (Irene Dunne) at the famous divorce-averting end of *The Awful Truth*, where she offers Jerry (Cary Grant) a chance to deny both his own continued need for erotic roving and his persistent jealousy: "Things are just the same as they always were, only you're just the same, too, so I guess things will never be the same again."

But since Jerry is a man reformed by marital desire itself—his restlessness and skepticism overcome—the marriage can be renewed: "So, as long as I'm different, don't you think things could be the same again?" With the saving extra charge: "Only a little different?" Here is an explicit grammar of remarriage that has, so to say, reconjugated the distinction between gendered subject and object. It is this line (of dialogue and thought) that might have been better borrowed by Streisand the eventual director, not her zany early character Judy, for *The Mirror Has Two Faces* (1996)—and put into the mouth of the returning supplicant would-be husband, Gregory Larkin (Jeff Bridges), precipitating the romantic comedy's musical coda in ways that bear further comparison, so we'll also see, not just with *Yentl* but with erotic "voice" as performed song in *The Awful Truth* itself (including that pair of separate single beds).[10]

Again, though, it's not a matter of allusion at the level of script, or even of plot architecture, that will mainly concern us. Yet in Streisand's catalog, instances do mount up of the remarriage narrative as persistent screen genre. In *On a Clear Day You Can See Forever*, the title song is precipitated at the end from a plot of two dead-ended relationships (Streisand's with her enthralling French psychiatrist and her stodgy fiancé alike), but the marital *reunion* is entirely offstage—as promised by the clairvoyant heroine's hypnotized realization that she and the doctor will be reincarnated as a married couple in the next century. Later comes the sequel to Streisand's debut film, *Funny Girl*, where its subsequent coupling ends up reprising the original film's climactic defeat of marital reengagement in a second divorce plot. Midway in the storyline, the male lead in *Funny Lady*, James Caan as entrepreneur Billy Rose, proposes to Fanny Brice (Streisand) a sequel of their own: that they "get married," long after the actual ceremony. But "we are married," she offhandedly reminds him, only to have him explain: "No, I mean really married"—to each other, that is, not to their once wedded and now separate careers. By the time she agrees, having found that a long-fantasized remarriage with her first husband (Omar Sharif as Nick returning from *Funny Girl*) no longer holds out any thrill for her, it is too late; the current marriage "partner" has gone so far as to actually fall in love with his mistress. Then, too, in another contortion of Cavell's genre format, Streisand as maritally alienated psychiatrist, Susan Lowenstein, in her self-directed *The Prince of Tides* facilitates a remarriage for her lover, not herself, by ironically having helped him (Tom Wingo as played by Nick Nolte) so much in therapy that, despite their passionate and professionally questionable affair, he returns to his estranged wife at the end.

None of these evocations and inversions of the Cavell model, nor Streisand's return to a more canonical variant of it for one of her filmography's rare happy endings in *The Mirror Has Two Faces*, may necessarily be found reaching to the level of "philosophy" in Cavell's genre terms—at least not in any frontal assault, via the ordinary conjugal language of the everyday, on the skeptical bulwarks of sexual anxiety and cultural convention. For this we have *Yentl*, whose heroine's affront to an inveterate mind/body dualism in the skirmish of the sexes is inherent in the voice of female self-disclosure: *Yentl*—with its densely entangled pretzel twist on the remarriage genre—serving in its neo-Shakespearean disguise comedy to double over its subplot of same-sex female desire with an allayed crisis of homosexual panic, thus finally hiving off a displaced if restorative nuptial closure (not the heroine's own) from the unveiled threat of a genuine woman's will. (Don't worry: plot summary coming.) After years of struggle to get her version of the Isaac Bashevis Singer story produced—and cornered by the studio (MGM/UA) when willing to fund it only if it were itself re-created as a musical—the film's appearance soon after *Pursuits of Happiness* hardly means that Streisand had been reading Cavell (nice thought, though), taking cues from the idea of "finding a voice" in the field of amatory desire and intellectual need, working in part from his script regarding the woman's motive to "create herself" anew in the molting of her male disguise. But it does suggest that his work might involve the best reading of hers, and thus that the contours of the film's vocal score, along with the music of its editing, might be best audited not just with Cavell in mind but with his nuanced formulations in earshot.

To appreciate the connection of song, voice, and gender invention that Cavell draws out so impeccably from the marital impasse of *The Awful Truth*, in its subsequent and productive application to the displacement of the remarriage paradigm in Streisand's self-directed plots, one does well to contrast the comedic possibilities of song—as part of a plot's communicative circuit—with its tragic counterpart in so-called high art. This takes us back to "Opera and the Lease of Voice" in registering the main points stressed by Cavell (in close dialogue with the opera theorist Catherine Clément) in respect to the tragic double bind of female song on the operatic stage. They are these—about what the genre's unsparing logic suggests: that the plot-sacrificed female stage persona who dies in or after her break into song doesn't just fail to survive such vented feeling but is, in emotional fact, punished for it; that she dangerously—because threateningly—confirms by vocal extrusion an inner life that gives more proof than culturally tolerable of her autonomy; that this voucher of an Other (female) Mind surfaces from beneath expression from the palpable anatomy of the valorized diva voice itself; and that this voice is isolated as such for the way it cuts across all roles—as being so entirely and specifically *this* particular voice that it becomes, as if by synecdoche on the cusp of paradox, abstractable as the unleashed universal force of any such passional eloquence, such power of speaking out; and that, in such moments of asserted "narcissism" in song, the force of self-thought splits between "ecstasy" and "abandonment" ("beside oneself," according to Cavell's gloss) in the very act of giving voice to (Cavell quoting Nietzsche later under the weight of an extra gendered emphasis) "music as … mother tongue." One might, in sum, have it that every female aria is not just an act, but an allegory, of voice per se. As one always feels with Streisand.

Citing her work in connection with the opera essay, we might think that the best evidence of correlation would be found in her direct refusal, through inversion, of an operatic doom in the non-comic finale of *A Star Is Born*. There, in the unprecedented fixed frame of a seven-minute cathartic lockdown in close-up on the widow's grieving medley ("Watch Closely Now"/"With One More Look at You," her dead husband's signature hit segued into his last and posthumously discovered lyric), we take one more long close look at the surviving star rising phoenix-like from the ferocity of her own pastiched Liebestod. Given the musicology of editing hinted at above by both Cavell and Streisand, here in her driven performance is an unmatched virtuosic "hold" (fermata) of the camera in sync with a fierce resolve—and perseverance. But the rejected abject fatality of that film's closing therapeutic fury is no more a definitive fit with the opera paradigm than is Streisand's vocal deployment in the comic (or semi-comic) instances I'll be considering, where the "lease of voice" answers not just to the rending intensity of ecstasy and abandonment but to the abiding wish, spelled out in *Pursuits of Happiness*, that one might "have a voice in one's own words":[11] some authorizing or signature sound (or sounding) beneath speech, sung or otherwise, in powering the will to self-expression, call it the very *signing* of desire.

Such signature effects are a continuing and self-conscious motif in Streisand's work, hardly just in the eponymous *One Voice* benefit concert (and DVD) two years after *Yentl*, the former "modestly" named for hers as one among a chorus of democratic voices raised in fund-raising support of progressive legislators. This metaphoric sense of voice—as further literalized in song and on this occasion leased out for political purposes—is just as explicit in Streisand's performance logic, and in a more autobiographic frame, long after *Yentl*. And again with a certain Cavellian association. As we've seen in his ruminated link between an early musical interest and his turn to philosophy, Cavell's work is repeatedly alert to moments when autobiography waxes philosophical.[12] Such a moment stands out as well, and on the matter of voice as one of his own main *topoi*, across a dialogue segue in what one might call Streisand's last film(ed) musical, her second live TV concert after decades of stage fright. In that Y2K *Timeless* performance, almost a full quarter century before her own written autobiography, *My Name is Barbra* in 2023, she tracks the arc of her career—in full narrative reminiscence, song by song, from small club dates to big-screen musicals. The two-hour "musical biopic" begins with the metanarrative "Something's Coming" from *West Side Story*, sung in duet with her budding alter ego (played by young teen Lauren Frost). The future-confident verve of the lyric wins approval from the older self and superstar: "Kid, I like what you're saying. Keep listening to that voice": again, song "tamed" metaphorically to unaccompanied inner speech. And before a return to the famous song's lines about the "drumming" of looming possibility, the adult vocalist, looking back on her own performed self-creation, ladders up in dialogue from figurative sonic resonance through embodied urgency to mental conception, self-"knowledge" per se, in the ensuing threefold encouragement for the nurture of that voice: "You'll hear it in your head, feel it in your gut, know it in your heart." Not just a virtual anatomy of motivated voice production in the conceptualized delivery of Streisand's song styling, sketched there as well is a quite Cavellian mind/body resolution: skepticism (in the narrowed version of lurking self-doubt) pictured (sounded) as internally overcome through a career-long thematization of song as expressive gesture. So we turn now, or dial in, to that same "voice deep inside" as it negotiates the technological as well as lyric ingenuity, and stratospheric vocal ambition, of *Yentl*'s psychosexual agenda—and particularly, generatively, to that film's unique wavering frequencies between inner soliloquy and voiced melody.

Female Re-Creation across Gender

In the turning-point song of *Yentl* from which this chapter takes its title— and its context in the plot twists and quasi-operatic recitatives to which I'll be returning—the long-disguised heroine, in gabardine drag so as to study the Talmud in Eastern Europe, circa 1904, is ready to break silence on her gender and her desire. And to do so by metaphorizing, in the process, an inner pressure of voice as other than song: "A voice deep inside" is getting, not "louder," but stronger. And the rhyme pushes it out further—while still holding its volume to a trope—with the admission that "I can't keep it quiet any longer." Voice is strength before music, until finally, in the film's later closure, it reaches out for melodic hearing. At this earlier turning point, however, Yentl can no longer bear, and partly for her bride's sake, that she has married in disguise, without consummation, the one-time fiancée of the fellow male student, and sometime roommate, she is secretly in love with, once his wedding has been forbidden.

It is hard to imagine a plot in which the deliberately "ambiguous" Cavellian phrase "consciousness of women" could be more perplexed and erotically cross-wired. Yentl (played by Streisand) has gone along with the marriage under coercion from Avigdor (Mandy Patinkin). For all the fun she and Hadass (Amy Irving) have together as no-more-than- cohabiting girlfriends, the celibate triangle is bound to come crashing. In terms borrowed from Cavell, only a renewal of the original wedding plans—after a same-sex annulment followed by a proper "remarriage"— can bring enough stability to release Yentl to the "self-creation" of her own

remade womanhood. That at this point the voice of escape is stronger, not
louder—troped as metaphysical not somatic, but in fact bodily manifest
in miked sound—is precisely what brings it into the orbit of Cavell's sense
of voice under skeptical denigration by Derrida and company, for whom
meaning even in language is differential, never plenary and audible. It is
this axiom that, for Cavell, has a way of withdrawing the articulating mind
of the other into a skeptical recess that replays the intractable mind/body
divide of Cartesian metaphysics. This dualism—in the reparative form of its
compelling fusion—is never more tangible than in expressive song, where
the musculature of the body is willfully, rather than unconsciously, mobilized
in the somatic production of intent. This is where the extraordinary
experience of *watching Streisand sing*, as her upper body acts out every
note as well as every line, becomes—the genre of movie musicals aside—a
motion picture of music as meaning. In the only proximate comparison
from the grand annals of post-war American pop performance, music flows
directly through Aretha Franklin's body into song. In Streisand, it passes
through speech via articulation into a different shaping of lyric that retains
its preeminent sense of voice, in a phrasing so vernacular that the blur of
operatic resonance never washes away the ordinary sense of the vocal in the
melody. Retained always is what a Cavellian might hear as the "ordinary
language" of even her bravura turns—thus rendering these vocals as uniquely
ready for metaphoric deployment across a whole spectrum of audiophonic
withdrawals and foregroundings in the musical warp and woof of Yentl's
vocal tapestry. Streisand's is the perfect voice for spanning this gamut, her
lucid enunciation never talky, her big notes never dissolved in sheer music.

Even the most rudimentary plot summary can begin to suggest how songs
become part of a thematic armature in *Yentl* amid the whiplash psychoerotic
transfers of marital irony. And this is of interest for Cavell studies not least
because, beyond the film's unsaid figuration of an America-in-prospect for
the pursuit of gender happiness, or at least authenticity, the knotted storyline
returns to that frequent touchstone of Cavell's in Shakespearean comedy
and romance, in this case *Yentl's* ingenious implosion of the *Twelfth Night*
gender-disguise triangle and its sibling subtexts. It happens as follows. In
this adaptation of the Singer story, Yentl's father Rebbe Mendel (Nehemiah
Persoff) is her only link to the tradition of Talmudic scholarship that has
nurtured her mind, until his death severs this connection. In order to
continue the learning in which he had secretly tutored her, Yentl must go
forth, her long brown hair chopped short, in the disguise of a male student,
eventually taking the name of her dead brother, Anshel. Having met a band
of young scholars on their way to the Yeshiva, and befriending one of them in
particular, Avigdor (Mandy Patinkin), she soon signs on as his study partner
once she is invited to become a Talmud student. She is also subsequently
invited as a frequent dinner guest to the table of Avigdor's extravagantly
pretty fiancée, Hadass (Amy Irving), and her family. It is shortly discovered

by Hadass' parents, however, that Avigdor has made a secret of his brother's suicide, and for this familial stigma of melancholia in the blood he is deemed genetically unsuitable as a marriage partner and potential father of Hadass' child. Devastated, he cajoles Anshel into marrying Hadass instead: a marriage of convenience for his own need, as noted, to keep close (to) his object of desire. To which an agonized Yentl accedes, as mentioned, only to keep *him* near *her*. Alone with the bride on their wedding night, Yentl, still dressed (and still in male garb), convinces Hadass, who is obviously eager to consummate the marriage, that the law prohibits it, given the wife's abiding thoughts for another man. So, pledging Hadass to chastity and patience, Yentl seals the vow of this odd coupling by spilling wine on the sheets to suggest defloration. But when it gradually becomes clear that Hadass no longer pines for Avigdor, but loves her husband, that is, Anshel (Streisand), more after all, Yentl decides to reveal herself to Avigdor at last, hoping they might forge a new life together. But Avigdor is horrified at Yentl's long deception. Even when placated by her confession of love, he rejects out of hand the idea that she should continue her clandestine studies, insisting instead that a woman comes by all the knowledge she needs through sheer biological destiny. The next day the irreconcilable friends part, and months later we see Yentl writing to Avigdor and Hadass, who are now married, wishing them well as she leaves Europe for a new sphere of possibility, by obvious implication America.

Cavell's instinct for finding the archetypal remix (and new matrix) of Shakespearean plots in his remarriage comedies (*A Midsummer Night's Dream* and *The Tempest* figuring notably) could scarcely have been better rewarded than if he had turned later to *Yentl*: especially in regard to his sense of marital lovers grown—in their natural acceptance of the ordinary—too much like siblings under a subsided eroticism that must be rekindled. In contrast, the Shakespearean pall of dead brothers returns in Yentl as the kiss of death for a desire misrecognized as homoerotic—yet also too intense, in its independence, for conventional assimilation. For brotherly absence is precisely what is ironically upended in the percolating eroticism heated up under pressure of normative restraints in this Yeshiva bromance—where Avigdor's affectionate hugging and horseplay is as confusing to him as it is inflaming to Yentl. In the original Singer story, Anshel was the name taken by Yentl in memory of a deceased uncle rather than sibling, so that the whole subtext of the dead brother, with its eventual incestuous and transgender overtones, and its stalling of marital fulfillment, belongs—shadowed by Shakespearean precedent in this motif of the simultaneously mourned and (in a sense) impersonated male counterpart[13]—to the film version alone. In this central strand of Cavell's argument, his sense of sibling deadlock is strikingly intersected three years later, though without mention, by Peter Brooks' psychopoetics of narrative in *Reading for the Plot* (1984) where, exemplified most fully in Brooks' chapter on Faulkner, the cultural transgressions of incest and miscegenation are linked in the grammar of narrative, respectively, with metaphor (too much likeness) and metonymy (too much dispersed association) as enemies of sanctioned narrative advance. It is on this head, in Cavell's figuring the comic dailiness of knowing interchange in marriage, that one better appreciates even the closing wordplay, on his part rather than the script's, of this summary passage about *The Awful Truth*. The structural goal is for the characters to apprehend in their remarital love, to grasp and appreciate, how "what is necessary now is not to estrange ourselves but to recognize, without denying our natural intimacy, that we are also strangers, separate, different"—and thus to overcome skepticism from within—in order to "keep our incestuousness symbolic, tropic, so that it *joins us*, not letting it lapse into literality, which will *enjoin us*."[14] At play between the freedoms of togetherness and the chill of taboo, desire must be re-created, as it were, in each other's eye.

Re-creation: that troubled concept, and all the more in *Yentl* when needing to be extracted from the trappings and trap of masquerade in a world soaked in ancient prejudice. If possible, the overlap of fraternizing and disguise, the travail of exogamous eroticism under wraps, is even more complicated in Streisand's co-authored script than in its Shakespearean prototype. During Avigdor's first meeting with Yentl, it is exactly when he mentions being in mourning for a dead brother that she first conceives the notion of taking her own dead brother's name as a pseudonym. From a zone of unmentioned maternity in the absence of all female modeling (Cavell's sense of family structure in his genre as well), Yentl thus vacates her own place as sister, annihilating her feminine identity, in passing from persona to mask through the border realm of self-effacement. The irony is underlined when, once comparing his own "moodiness" to that of his dead brother, Avigdor is subsequently caught out in his dark family secret about his brother's suicide. By association, we realize that the heroine, née Yentl, reborn Anshel, has also in a figurative sense taken her own gendered life (as a woman) in order to live out her desired independence (because necessary, as a man). She must be reborn, set free again, "re-created" as herself (in Cavell's vocabulary) rather than in the role of her male alter ego—even while the plot's other suspended engagement is reconsecrated in the name of living marital passion rather than some suspected curse of inherited mortal despair.

In a very different version of the plot, Singer's Anshel—in a confession of "his" emotional androgyny, his incapacity for the marriage with Avigdor that might have been—has explained that "I'm neither one nor the other,"[15] a striking anticipation of nonbinary identification, arranging instead for Avigdor's reunion with Hadass. Singer's misfit protagonist, beyond the androgynous *neither/nor* of her spoken disclaimer, is actually more like "mis-assigned" to a girl's body. There is no "consciousness of the woman" (either sense) in Singer's plot. At just this point in the original story, the Yentl/Anshel figure—sexual border case and gobetween—disappears from the plot without further mention, a mere function(ary) of sexual difference and its negotiations: a catalyst evaporated by the chain reaction s/he has set in motion. Her only trace is the namesake son of the new couple, a child who, to the community's general astonishment in the story's last sentence, is named "Anshel." This birth becomes the plot's incarnate principle of a normalized regeneration: a symbolic second start for Yentl as an unequivocal male, a full-fledged inheritor. It is, by contrast, the essence of Streisand's film that the heroic energy should be reborn in the woman herself, that it shouldn't get symbolically redomesticated by patriarchy, but only continue to invoke it in the call for posthumous validation from the missing father that no man has yet to replace. With this re-creation in process, the birth throes of such reinvention are what the innovative sound design of the film has so carefully laid the blueprint for.

Between Monologue and Song: Shaping the Space of Voice

The film opens on the hawking voice of an itinerant bookseller, offering "Picture books for women, religious books for men" as Yentl enters the market square. Alternately, in the original conception for Streisand's comic entrance, testified to amid the DVD's deleted scenes, Yentl's first appearance would have ended in a pratfall from a collapsing woodpile next to the synagogue, where she has climbed to spy yearningly on, and mouth along with, as otherwise forbidden to women, the men's sacred sonorities. This exclusion is seen by the camera through cross barred mullions that partially occlude and subdivide her eager look, as well as through the glass that baffles (in the acoustic sense only) her participation in the solemn vocals, silencing her for us as well as for the men inside. It is one of those engrained "reflexive" moments, so dear to Cavell, and often seen overplayed by his critics, in which cinema instructs us in its own understanding, here technologically as well as thematically. As a prologue to the star's coming vocal arrival onto the musical track, it is as if, in a genre reflex, what we would have been seeing there, in that planned first scene, is the tease of a Streisand song number not yet filled out with its post-sync vocal dub. Long before the "voice deep inside" lyric at the film's turning point, expressive sound is blocked by convention. And is only modestly, gradually, and again reflexively, brought into alignment, into co-presence, with the body that owns and emits it.

In the release print, Yentl's overt exclusion from the sacred song of the learned male is delayed until the end of the first musical number, which, like the one following, begins in address, first to the "Heavenly Father," then, after his death, to "my own Father, who art in Heaven"—respectively, in these paired queries: "Where Is It Written?" and "Papa Can You Hear Me?" Opening its partial release valve for the repressed female voice, the first song is begun in the "stage whisper" motivated by the proximity of her sleeping father. Standing before a candle and a mirror, about to wrap herself in a Tallit—the ceremonial white prayer shawl, striped with black, extended momentarily to its full width—Streisand as Yentl begins to intone the first words of her prayer, call it her recitative: "I'm wrapped in a robe of light." As stressed by this metaphor, the whole *mise-en-scène* now becomes cinematically reflexive in precisely the fabric's slow effacement of the mirror. It is an optical irony of *screening* that is as important in figuring the film's own projective mechanism—a kind of hypnotic industrial light show—as it is in fixing the terms of private devotional craving from this point on in the narrative's musical interlace. The very act of internal framing just before (reversed image-within-image in the mirror's initial field) has markedly situated its star in the symbolic field of self-image. But next, backlit by candlepower, then silhouetted in turn behind a spread "curtain" that, in a slow tracking shot, eventually meets the lateral edges of our own (indeed originally white) plane of perception, the performance of this first song now emerges from an unmistakable screening-within-the-screen. It is an effect that divides the audience from vocal source and, momentarily, from the character's own internally framed image, but that also mediates her privacy, magnifies it in shadow play as occluded visual field. One might speak here, in this glowing scrim, of cinematic reflex supervening upon a private mirror reflection.

Here, then, is the heroine in an iconic parable of her own screen presence. Not only will this scene of mirroring replication (enhanced at the start in secondary shadow duplicate against the prayer shawl) be many times repeated in the film, but the dovetailing of voiced song with interior monologue that ensues sets up exactly those alternating currents of expressive vent that constitute characterization itself in this plot-long performance. Then, too, this variant of the musical comedy norm helps to edit as well as editorialize the narrative, frequently tracking the heroine across space and time. In so doing, these shifts in vocal register offer a mode—and model—of intuitive continuity in its own right, now flashing forward in imagination, now looping back into the present, then again traversing real time to here another room, there a new locale. Voice-over can thus provide a means of passing over, a transition, a momentum—and an unusually clear instance of Cavell's passing transmedial instinct: that cinematography underwrites dialogue like music scores a lyric.

"Where Is It Written?" this first song asks: where is the scripture that forbids Yentl's (female rather than human?) desire for learning? And the question ends up being wrung from her again, without being allowed to ring out, in the song's shift of scene to the upstairs women's gallery at the synagogue. Always this wavering between song in solitude and, by contrast, a subliminal *strain* in company, the agent of longing everywhere on edge because in fact tensely repressed, checked on the very cusp of voice. In neither private nor communal space can "where is it written?" become a viable (voluble) inquiry—in the form of a demand—that the protagonist can aggressively set forth, only a question to sequester. And this first musical scene puts in place the ground plan for recurrent later ramifications of this melodic constraint. Streisand's lips move in articulating the lyric query, and later words to its effect, only when alone, with her mouth instead tightened to the silence of a merely interior if still urgent yearning whenever she moves (in this matrix scene's establishing pattern) into potentially audible range of her sleeping father—or at the song's close, of the women in the temple gallery. The interior wooden framing of the window that would have closed out Yentl's voice in her deleted first scene outside the synagogue does in a sense return here, in the interior gallery shot. This time it serves to bar her quite literally, by a wooden railing, from the space of sacred interchange, behind which her vocals subside against the backdrop of chattering women coming into audition as the musically scored inner voicing fades off into the realist hubbub of drowned-out private sound.

But listen again to that moment in the opening musical number when Yentl's lips must first resist her song, when she first strategically decides to hold her words unshaped, her voice in abeyance. For it sets the template for the way, in Streisand's intricate rethinking of the source story, her Singer gets sung. The first lyrics, in other words, are still framed credibly within the precincts of the narrative space, part of its "ambient" sound—until Yentl's voice can no longer be permitted breathing room within that space, that social diegesis. For the remainder of the song, gone mostly interior, but sometimes given throat, the recording technique switches to a pronounced but subtle reverb, and hence to the precincts of that studio sound of which Streisand is so gifted a manipulator. From here on, whether the sung melodies are dubbed or over-voiced, synchronous or entirely interior and autonomous, they are recorded more or less with this same aural resonance and just slightly artificial reverb. After the first recitative as prayer, what Yentl is therefore felt to utter, even when articulated by her lips as music, are never quite just songs, but rather expressive impulses conveying their own private fiber and vibrancy, motions of the mind with whose pulse we are meant to find ourselves in sympathetic vibration. And not least by analogy with the thrall of the Streisand sound on record. We don't eavesdrop, we are granted access—or better to say we are plugged in.

Technology in *Yentl* thus stands in a multiple and curious relation to psychology. This is because the songs, when voiced rather than just superimposed upon a narrative space by the musical track, still represent only the outer limit of the mere *will* to voice, available to us solely through a privileged vision and audition. Incarnating—in another neo-Cavellian reflexivity—the very paradox of sound on film, in its never more than fictional convergence with the gestural body on screen, Yentl is a character consciously seeking a match between body and voice, striving to motivate the unexpressed exactly through her own physicality. By what convincing logic, though, do we hear her when she is only straining to hear herself? The very raising of that question is the film's deepest ingenuity. The songs, through their subtle reverberation, seem not finally assumed to share the narrative space with her, but rather to open an alternative space. It is our listening, then, that lends the latter its shape and definition, its terrain, and its craving horizons alike.

When the orphaned heroine is encouraged, in the scene following her father's burial, with a matron's bromide that "life" must "go on," the unstated crisis is not a mourning for the father only, but a melancholy incorporation of lost possibility for herself: the life of the mind he embodied and nourished that, for her, cannot go on. When next assured by the neighbor woman promising to house her that she'll be kept so busy she "won't have time to think," the sting of the idiom is registered as a tiny convulsion—Streisand at her most intuitive—on the otherwise blank mask of Yentl's numbed grief. No thinking, no theology, no philosophy, no maintenance of voice in one's daily words. Distilled cause and its precipitated effect: in order precisely "to think," to have contemplative "time" for herself, her image must be remade in the world's eyes. The funeral scene's fade-to-black, followed in dissolve— past a grieving optic drapery—to the liberation of the shrouded mirror, directly prepares us for Yentl's part in a mournful rite of passage in the ensuing scene: the funeral of her father's daughter in rebirth as a male agent. In an adjacent room, she now removes the mourning cloth from her own smaller mirror: this one melodramatically cracked on the diagonal. Yentl's having a piece of her lapel ceremonially ripped at the gravesite, just before, can thus appear in its own right "mirrored" in what happens next within the frame of this fractured looking-glass. For in front of this second and baldly symbolic mirror, wielding an oversized pair of female sewing scissors, Yentl slices through her luxuriant tawny locks, dividing herself from herself across the split of that same fissured plane.

We now follow the ghost of Yentl in the "figure" of Anshel, the dead brother and double, to her first night alone on the road, a disguised female picaro seeking shelter in the forest. Here the second song ("Papa Can You Hear Me?") begins again in a prayer that is voiced but invisibly received. And that reverses direction in the lines of sight: "I see a million eyes," Yentl sings, asking "Which ones are yours?" The song is sung out loud, but half to herself, half to an unseen spiritual auditor. Translated from its theological status as prayer to the dead, this is the secular nature of musical expression in the film: a melodic, pre-conversational monologue that must ordinarily suppress its intent and intensity behind closed lips. Only when alone, as in this second number, can Yentl discharge her energy without fear of detection and reprisal. Yet played by Streisand, it is the figure's exact situation before the rapt gaze of the camera, as well as the italicizing of the *mise-en-scène* by the lyrics about "stars" and "illumination," that turns this second song setting into another parable of the cinema: of its rectangular robe of light, its specular basis, the special aura of its star performances. The supplicant is overheard in song (and ultimately from overhead) at the center of an omniscient 360 degree shot. As a single wind-fluttered candle casts light on her from a makeshift tree-stump altar, this musical setting comes once more into manifest alignment with the cinematic projection that materializes it. The scene even closes with an overt effect of cinematographic processing: a dissolving close-up of Streisand superimposed over a withdrawing reverse-zoom that dims and distances a second image of her to no more than a single glimmering dot, a point of light indistinguishable from the candlepower that discloses her in the first place. The optic parable is hard to miss. An expressive presence alone in the dark, illuminated by a single flickering source of light, stared upon by a "million eyes" out of the impalpable blackness past the zone of the image: this is the cinema staging its own conditions as unrestrained star vehicle, even as its heroine remains a self still held in reserve by the narrative.

Fast forward through the charming comedy of her meeting up (cute) with a cartload of Yeshiva boys and testing her masqueraded way into Yeshiva matriculation, we come to the first rousing, rather than plangent number in the film, once it is clear that Avigdor has developed an unusual attachment to his charming young study buddy. In the build-up to this moment, where Anshel has sheepishly corrected one of Avigdor's own Talmudic answers, an over-voiced "Yentl within" sings out (while still holding in) her joy at being at last able to "listen to the lesson of the leaves"—with its acoustically suited slant rhyme (*lissn* against *lessn*), as well as its pun on her beloved bookish page "leaves." As celebrated in the spirited "This Is One of Those Moments" number, she has indeed come to inhabit, in serial montage, exactly "one of those moments" she's dreamed of, with "certain things" achieved that "no man can take away." But even that momentary feminist confidence sweeps forward into a fuller litany of possibilities rounded out by the ringing ten-second last syllable of those ineffable things "about to be"—at last and after all—"miiiiiiiiine." The "I" hiding there in a rising lustrous enunciation like this will return magnified—or further dialed up—in the phonic lift of the film's last vocal note.

But this midpoint elation doesn't last. For it is here that the convoluted marriage plot kicks in, plummeting Yentl from this prospect of realization to a network of desperate erotic deception. Should we wish to claim such a thread, it is certainly a richer allusion to the same-but-different trope in *The Awful Truth* than anything *What's Up, Doc?* had glibly in mind that brackets the lyric trajectory of unchecked "voice" in that pivotal "No

Matter What Happens (It Won't Be the Same Anymore)." Too true, that break from sameness: dashing her hopes rather than rewarding her courage. For when Yentl, weary of deceptions, gives voice to, and delivers physical evidence of, her female body, Avigdor recoils in complex horror, traumatized by what he sees. In the sponsoring song's refusal of further self-suppression, Yentl's own motive is precisely "to see myself" and so "to free myself" and thus, bloomingly, to "beeeee myself at laaaast." Leading up to this ladder-rungued "see, free, be" crescendo—in the convergent vectors of recognition and release—is one of the best of the many crisp lyrics in this Alan and Marilyn Bergman ballad. Yentl's avoidance of a "sunlight" that would reveal too much has been put into cross-word rhyme with the moon as the "one light" that "I walked in," a fact we see presently—if now transitionally, vanishingly—enacted in the final striding performance of the song. Where in fact "be myself" can be heard gleaming (in reflected moonlight and vocal projection alike) with "beam myself": on Cavell's cinematography-as-music model, the hint of a melodic "hold" superimposed on the lyric in the build-up to a long "legato" tracking shot. But here grammatical rhyme takes over from sound rhyme, so that this moonlight is also both what "I bathed in" and what, we next assume, "I held in"—until that sense of internalization is immediately switched instead by syntactic swivel, a kind of internal poetic volta, to the new grammar: "held in ... my feelings." This is just the repression refused for the future, as the swelling lyric now moves to prove.

Dys/Closure and the Marriage Plot

Yentl is ready at last to render her relation with Avigdor, in the words of the precipitating ballad, not "the same anymore"—in fact to explode the ruse of sameness by opening both her heart and her shirt (or should we say blouse?) to him in the confession of her long subterfuge. As if to stress her supposed beardless youth in the original Singer story, Avigdor's "eyes widened" when she vows to "get undressed" so as to prove her point. Boyhood on the line, it "occurred to him that Anshel might want to practice pederasty."[16] Panicked and enraged at first in the film (whatever his wide-eyed reaction might have implied in the story), he can warm to the idea of desiring her only once he cools off regarding the previous deception, about which his outrage is in itself a revelation. In Yentl's attempted "normalizing" of relations, the film thus enters upon its genuinely queerest nest of inference. Once his fury has subsided, relief is at one with new desire. At first one might say the skepticism of the other has gone into panicked overdrive, so that the unknowable secret of her body has rendered her less than human in her deception, a "demon," as he screams. Yet relief comes quickly as well. At least he wasn't smitten all along with a real boy! So long confounded and deferred in the warring factions of Avigdor's mind, but now divided further by ethnic and cultural as well as gender entrenchments, the hetero/ normative regime struggles to assert itself. Predictably enough, his desire for a woman so much like a beloved pal is bested by his expectations for a culturally valorized femininity. Hadass is bound to resurface again, a check on untoward desire: the renewed and normative fallback option. Yentl is willing to run away with him—but not from her dream of institutional learning. This he refuses, and so she refuses him.

The very possibility of sex is over before it has been allowed to surface fully. With a last chaste embrace the next morning, this detachment from Avigdor in the name of Yentl's own self-determination is now soliloquized, and in deliberate reversal of her congratulatory hug from him back at the Yeshiva, by the leading refrain from that "One of those Moments" anthem. What she'll "remember" all her "life" is the parting of their ways and lives. This emphasis on affect already memorialized, just by saying (or singing) so, thrusts all romantic feeling into the bracketed, the always unactionable, past: a node of closure in going forward. Life must still be lived—must be made, if possible, further memorable. And the next reprise of the film's first lyric, asking as it did where the limit on desire is "written," is at once folded into the film's multi-staged climactic aria. This is a song of local severance and forward-looking self-asseveration that begins, in a detached voice-over, as if further back than we've ever been privy to. "It all began," we hear at the start of "A Piece of Sky"—initiating a kind of retrospective loop, catching up the psychogenesis of her disruptive desire even before we encountered her obstreperous energy in the early mirror scenes. It all began, that is, when she noticed that her domestic horizons were limited by the vantage of a lone "window" on only one slice or sector of the outer world, a mere "piece of sky." Just before this retrospective lyric—inaugurating Yentl's exuberant shipboard departure—the now aptly re-bonded, contentedly married couple, Avigdor and Hadass, remade (thanks to Yentl) for each other, read a letter superimposed over Yentl's writing of it, just her hands in frame moving across the reframed paper rectangle, taking charge of the script (she is writing twice over, as character and visible screen-writer), wishing the new couple well and hoping that Hadass will continue with her study. This image begins to fade forward over Yentl's closing of that well-wishing goodbye letter with a modest mention of herself: "As for me, I'm going to a new place, where I hear things are different. Anyway, we'll see." Certainly not "the same anymore"—with the onward force of such implied *hearsay* idiomatically split down the middle into "hear" and its potential "see": two key terms lyrically redeployed, as well as cinematically realized, in the spectacular audiovisual euphoria of the film's last song.

On a wintry day under leaden skies, the camera seeks out, from behind, a single windswept figure. She is wrapped tight still, but now in female coat, cap, and muffler. She stands alone on the stern cargo deck of the freighter, taking her bearings by looking back, then steadying herself at one point on an auxiliary steering wheel—as if to suggest that she is now warily charting her own course. After reviewing her life ("It all began") in synchronized lyrics, open-mouthed, fully voiced but still uttered in solitude, Yentl soon moves to the crowded upper deck for the second phase of the finale. What follows is of course deliberately reminiscent of the tugboat staging for the Broadway showpiece "Don't Rain on My Parade" that closed the first half her debut film. Surely this harking back to probably the most famous musical number in Streisand's career is a deliberate and considered self-aware attempt at what might be called corrective allusion. In *Funny Girl*, Fanny Brice leaves her stage career in dry-dock to chug after her man, trying to intercept him on an ocean liner bound for Europe. In passing the Statue of Liberty in New York harbor, as everyone remembers, she mimes it with a torch of wilted roses, comic emblem of her supposed liberation. In *Yentl*, Streisand reverses the pattern. Reconsidered, an emotional turning point has become closure, satisfying in its very attitude of latency. This time out, Streisand as Yentl—leaving Europe behind, as well as the man to whom she could not capitulate—moves toward a mythic New World alone, a self in waiting but no longer in hiding. The other corrective allusion might well refer the film back to the tragic close of Greta Garbo's famous "trouser role" in *Queen Christina* (1933, dir. Rouben Mamoulian), a movie that also brings the transvestite heroine and the hero together for the first time in a country inn, and that ends with the indelible fixed close-up of Garbo at the prow of a ship, her lover dead astern, her face blankly turned from him, looking forward but mostly away.

But no intertexts can erode the force of Streisand's finale. Nor the way it invites us, in the Cavellian spirit, to let the film's own technical provisions instruct us, "reflexively," in its own optic—and ultimately ocular—impact. From her initial isolation on a lower deck, Yentl now maneuvers her way through the cargo hold onto the upper passenger deck, traversing the latter in public singing for the first time in the narrative. She is openly moving her lips as she moves among the huddled transients, at home on the ship's quasi-performative "boards"—marking another "stage" in her pilgrim's progress. Other passengers seem to notice this animated figure—as if talking to herself—at just about the point in the song where she exclaims, "Papa I've a voice now!" And just that sung power is heard resonant there in the lyric voicing itself: its confidence powered, in such a typifying Streisand nuance, by the contraction from "Papa I" to the enunciative flutter of "'ve a voice now." In her visible march forward, putting the stride of assertion back in an always mellifluous stridency of desire, the heroine is redoubling the ship's momentum with her own: her mission manifest in vocal emission. It is tempting here to recall Cavell's reference, in his opera chapter, to Emerson's sense that one can never see the "breath" of one's own "extension" into speech.[17] Not as such, perhaps—but in *Yentl*, as figure, that extension, that final reach, is made manifest, at least to us if not the heroine. For when she announces that she has found "voice," for the first and last time in Streisand's film career, quintessentially, we can literally *see that voice*, that expressed breath, in the Atlantic chill: an aerated will to song in, so to say, double condensation. Passing through the cold sea air, breathing it in, and in her freedom giving it back warmed as melody, Yentl, no longer suppressing a swallowed desire, permits her voice to be made visible at last as a hovering, vaporous presence on the screen. Exhalation as exaltation. Yet the musical action of this number, it must be remembered, is not an act, a singing performance inside the drama: the film has not taken a generic turn into a standard musical finale. Threading her way through the crowd to keep up with the camera, Yentl is still only singing as she might be talking or humming to herself, full of her own thoughts, incautious as never before, as she could never before afford to be, about their incidental overflow. *Yentl* the film has hereby opened itself to a social space without becoming diegetic spectacle, song transformed within the narrative to an expressive gesture of personality without becoming shipboard show. Part of a communal exodus to a new land, nevertheless the heroine does not provide through song the stabilizing social focus on which generic musicals tend to close. In genre terms, the communal space at the center of which such a ritual moment would be possible has not yet been achieved in Yentl's search for a new home. Filial structure, or rather a single paternal bond, is still the largest social unit consolidated by her lyrics. In a second and last call to her father only, the heroine asks no one else's attention—but is not afraid of it either.

Paternity in Absentia

To the full force of this last number in its closing cadences we will return, via the shared theme (so much in the Cavellian spirit) of the paradoxically absent fatherly presence. But one best comes round to this after considering Streisand's later and last self-directed film, *The Mirror Has Two Faces*—and its own rehearsal of a career-long personal mythology (the fatherless aspiring daughter struggling to make her own way) more important for the star (more autobiographical, hence ultimately more philosophical?) than the motif of incestuous closeness in sibling familiarity. What remains so Cavellian here in what we might call the "post-marriage" phase of the plot, despite the presence of the (bad) mother and the absence of the modeling father, is that, as all the more so in *Yentl*, there is no one waiting, in any remarriage turn, to "give the bride away"—only the chance of her being turned over, and back, to her own female sufficiency.

In *The Mirror*, Rose Morgan, played by Streisand, is the down-to-earth and supposedly frumpy English professor at Columbia University (why wear make-up, she wonders, since she'd only "look like myself, but in color") whose hunk mathematician husband Gregory (Jeff Bridges) has married her only because, amid the good fun they have together, and the ongoing professional conversation, she doesn't excite and distract him sexually, or so he at first assumes—having been so often smitten, burned, and dumped in his affairs with students. Reversing the dimming of conjugal passion in the screwball plots, here, when the hero is aroused, he works hard to repress it. This is as far-fetched as the heroine's response falls short of funny. There is none of the delightful symmetry Cavell captures so well from *The Awful Truth*, where the "creation of a woman"—in and by herself, concocting an alternate version of her feminine sexuality—is made unmistakable. After Lucy Warriner (Irene Dunne) performs beautifully an art-song recital— which her jealous husband Jerry (Cary Grant) bursts in upon thinking it is a private tryst in the teacher's apartment, embarrassing himself in a wrestle with collapsing furniture—she brings the melodics of laughter up into her last notes of the love song (an effect familiar from the giddy denouement of many Streisand numbers). There is room for both, lyrics and laughter, in such a musical/comedy interlude. And the phrasings of desire are more openly erotic in the comic performance of the later answering scene. When divorce is under way and a new, highly publicized flirtation is begun on the husband's part, Lucy stages a counter-performance by vamping it up as his pretend sister, not only (as Cavell reads it) to horrify his apparent new intended and her stuffy society family, but also to win him back by showing her openly erotic side, however vulgar, in a second and this time tawdry vocal performance ("My Love is Gone With the Wind"). Such is the remade "sister act" she had, in Cavell's terms, lapsed into as a too-familiar spouse. "Her solution is to create her identity so that the very thing that repels the proper Vances is what attracts Jerry, that he has a hidden, improper sister."[18] Wonderfully: "Her incorporation of familiarity and eroticism redeems both."[19] Indeed, this "new creation of herself" models the "same but different" of the dizzy closing dialogue.

When Rose in *The Mirror*—and too much in the mirror only, at that— "creates herself" after her husband's misconstrued connubial repulse (read: defensiveness), it is only a conventional "make-over" that we watch—in an exercise regimen and cosmetology montage. This is a too self-centered reinvention, far riskier than the comic vamp act in *The Awful Truth*: answering as it does to the playbook of Streisand's detractors when she squelches the self-mocking "funny girl" side of herself to release, and without obvious irony as yet, the glamorous fashion-plate diva—a re-creation in the debased form of a body-sculpting vanity agenda straight out of a spa brochure and couture magazine supplement. Yet even here the Cavellian paradigm is buried deep, as we'll see, in the absent father motif. It is just this psychological lacuna—exacerbated by the present but affectively disengaged mother played by Lauren Bacall, caught up in her own vanity (the mother figure so structurally excluded from female reinvention in the 1930s comedies)—that is meant to humanize this plot and that, in our return to it, will help inflect the revisionary patriarchal allusions at the climax of *Yentl*'s. And even on its own terms, the later film's dialogue is at least as directly plugged into screwball reversals as was "the same as those who aren't different" in *What's Up Doc?* When the former boyfriend and now ex-husband (Pierce Brosnan) of her glamorous sister tries coming on to the "new Rose," realizing out loud that he "must've loved her" all along, she corners him into saying that he loved her, without really wanting her, for "being who she was." Her sarcastic comeback, in mock confusion, is immediate—and familiar to students of the genre's logic-chopping subtexts: "So now you want who I am because I'm not who I was anymore?"

By an irony that can't quite redeem the blatancy of Rose's routine cosmetic transformation, the result of this casual-rags-to-black-sheath trajectory backfires within the plot by intimidating the self-distancing husband, who now, back from a long European lecture trip, misses his no-nonsense academic bride. In order to achieve closure as a remarriage comedy, the now toned, blonde, and chicly coiffed Rose needs to be humbled a notch in the mystique of her new dieted and polished look. This happens when, in the closing scene, she is interrupted in her sleep, disheveled as she races to the street to stop Gregory's braying for her, promising on the spot an inevitable reversion ("aging here" by the second, she insists, as he fumbles for words, things "falling" as we speak). But, in the spirit of Cavell's paradigm, the reversion is not just to sag and flab, but to the sibling-like fun they used to have, ignited this time by sex but without the confusions of glamor. Here the second-honeymoon effect will involve the deferred consummation of the original marriage. The corrective plot closely resembles Cavell's model, where the return to passion is triggered by the disruptive enlivening of a friendly marital routine that had grown too much like sheer familial comfort—or even sibling rivalry. As usual, though, marital recovery takes its own plot-long good time.

Well along in the relationship, and long after their unconsummated honeymoon, finally claiming her marital due in a way that Hadass never openly did in *Yentl*, Rose is miserably rebuffed when Gregory curtails his own obvious desire for her. Understandably enough, she immediately mistakes his vocalized restraint as indifference: "I don't want to do this, Rose." He doesn't want to spoil the camaraderie with erotic complications. In tears, she retreats to the bathroom, throwing a towel over her tearful face in the mirror: reversing the mourning shroud lifted from the bedroom mirror in *Yentl* before which, shears in hand, she begins her empowering male disguise (defeminizing herself, as the Streisand character does before a mirror not long after in *Nuts* [1987, dir. Martin Ritt]). And again here in *The Mirror*, the dead father—in another Cavellian version of the Shakespearean patriarchal image—reaching out, in this case, as in *Yentl*, with a kind of supportive sorcery from beyond the grave. Far more explicit than the mirror's metafilmic intertext in *Yentl*—the star here framed in self-scrutiny on the verge of transformation—there's a further autobiographical nod at this point in the later film. On exit from her sexual humiliation in the apartment she can no long share with Gregory, Rose has retrieved a photo of her father and mother from the short-lived marital bookshelf. It is a black-and-white studio portrait in which Mr. Morgan, with his pencil thin moustache, looks strikingly like Streisand's own father—as often seen in biopic segments over the years, even concert montage. This is the father who (the screen father, that is) is later learned, the mother admits, to have doted on Rose as the favorite child, rather than the nominally prettier sister. And if beautiful in his eyes, she can become beautiful in her own. But instead of the proto-feminist defiance of cultural norms in Yentl's self-refashioning as a male in search of a learned life, in *The Mirror Has Two Faces*, the Ivy League professor, fully credentialed, has launched a militant campaign of glamorous self-enhancement in order to embody the modern-day version of comparable female stereotypes.

This can't in itself be allowed to succeed, to win the man back. The trim chic of the make-over must be humbled by self-deprecation, in a quintessential Streisand double play. But only after the man's having heard from the meddling mother-in-law that his wife is seeing someone else, inducing the familiar Cavellian doubt at the heart of the remarriage test. In the last scene, wrapping her bathrobe around her on the deserted, pre-dawn street, make-up off for the night, hair mussed, Rose jokes her husband free from the panic of undue allure, rather than, like Lucy in *The Awful Truth*, comically exaggerating a raw eroticism staged to win him back. Gregory finds it "comforting" that all the body-toning will wither away into droop. But the double bind of this rom-com plot needs one more move of celebratory rescue from the corner into which it would otherwise have painted its heroine, eyeliner and all. What follows is every bit as unrealistic as its one-sided celibate build-up. But when riding in on Streisand's usual uncanny gamut of expressions, from impatience to sudden joy, it is nonetheless a contagious pleasure to watch. And a prolonged one. Its distended playful bliss (and deferred private climax) continues behind the credits—with a sudden freeform editing, by dolly and crane, capturing the reunited couple quite literally dancing in the street, in the twirls and dips of a new relaxed pleasure in each other.

In a *Criterion* interview, Streisand explains that she wanted to make at least one movie where she gets, rather than must give up, her man. As if evoking as well the song-and-dance duet that no musical comedy actually made space for in her overmasting solo career, this impromptu pop ballet may be narratively unearned, but there was a deliberate down payment early in the script. In a moment of professorial comic relief in what we hear of Rose's sappy and implausible Columbia lecture on romance literature, our

Professor Morgan, when Gregory is first spying on her from the auditorium balcony, has suggested that the clichés about romance, or call it the music of love, are so powerful that if we don't hear the New York Philharmonic in our head on a first kiss, we "dump the guy." Gregory leaves after hearing this heartening cynicism about romanticized sex and its Hollywood illusions, missing out on the ludicrous student ovation she shortly receives for her corrective rhapsodic peroration (and latent tautology) on how "fucking great" love does in fact feel when it strikes. We are expected to remember the previous jokey turn of the lecture at the end when, with the couple embracing on the street in their new sexual rapport, they are stunned in mid-kiss by Pavarotti's "Nessun Dorma" filling the cavern of the avenue from (we see in cutaway to an upper window) a lone sleepless guy's combination of amorous approval and karaoke indulgence.

But opera isn't going to stand as primary musical touchstone in a Streisand film. Her own music will soon take over. It is telling here that in Cavell's chapter on opera he returns to screwball Hollywood farce and its own interpolation of the "higher" art for an extensive digression on the place of *Il Trovatore* in the Marx Brothers' *Night at the Opera*, including the operatic plot's reliance on a surplus of brothers.[20] The punctilious phrasing of his question about what "the incorporation of just this work" in the work of "just this" comedy comes back to mind. It could well arise in regard to "Nessun Dorma" breaking the pre-dawn air in *The Mirror Has Two Faces*, if with no other answer than the titular "none shall sleep" stripped of its tragic overtones in Puccini. None are to sleep in this moment of coupling either, reawakened instead to a desire conversant with unguarded fun—and accompanied by the pop soundtrack of Cavell's valorized "everyday" in a top-ten register. To secure a second chance with the guy for once, Streisand's recruiting of the remarriage plot can seem to put her entire film career into rehearsal for it—screen autobiography as philosophy, Cavell might say—including even, as plausible intertext, the early raptures of Glenn Gould about her interpretive genius as a vocal artist, singling out her finessing of the high C in the "Puccini-like" concluding splendor of "He Touched Me" from her second album.[21] After the diegetic interpolation of actual Puccini, and rising now behind the end titles, is the winning percussive beat of "I Finally Found Someone," Streisand's co-written duet with Bryan Adams. The remarriage comedy takes on that form of diurnal "festival" (Cavell's term) most fully identified in genre terms not just with the "musical accompaniment" constituted by film editing (as Cavell has put it) but with song itself.[22] Here the contemporary couple, suddenly caught up in a "musical" of their own making, needs to bond over a Streisand song—indeed a song and dance. So the two of them whirl away across the still mostly deserted street, with traffic coming slowly to life, yet the couple still uncurbed in their fun, all to the accompaniment now of Barbra and Bryan in audible overlap with the hugs and dips of Rose and Gregory. Some deep instinct must have suggested to Streisand that the anomalous and more formulaic happy ending she had for once in mind could best be achieved by some measure of return to the genre that screen history's commercial determinations had forced her to leave behind. So in getting her man she also gets to sing with one, if not the same one she's dancing with.

The number recurs directly to the kind of festive conversation that animated their first dates (reflexively rerun as a script turn itself: "My favorite line: Can I call you sometime?"). Now the erotic charge of those moments can be accepted—without debilitating skepticism (his fear of female motive and its rejections, let alone jealousy) or self-doubt (her insecurity about inducing desire). "Did I keep you waiting?" is one of Adams' lines in the bridge patter of the song's recurrent dialogue format, answered soon by his partner's swelling vocal revision in very sense of the verb: "I can't *wait*," now that love has struck, "for the rest of my li-i-IFE"—an eagerness emblemized in her voice's own exponential lift-off. A similar melodic boost, along with the everyday ("ordinary language") sense of compatible intercourse, inflects the shared Cavellian lines, sung at first in unison, about it being "better than it's ever been" because "we can talk it throuuuugh"—where Streisand's sound eventually breaks through from talk to song's high note, with its extra little fillip of "oohooh." In this endpiece as a whole, script has pushed past dialogue into the melody of conversation, including its own explicit version of diurnal routine in finding "someone to be with every night." When unfreezing the closed-down story line (a stop-frame image on their last embrace behind "A Film by Barbra Streisand"), the quick-cut to the ensuing musical coda offers up an exit scene whose narrative motivation may well seem flimsy, including all these giddy improvised spins in the street, but, with the poetic license of a momentarily recovered genre, it's close to irresistible. Pitted against Puccini booming from that upper window, this is the boon of everyday song and its "lease of voice." Rose's Papa should only see—and hear—her now.

So back to *Yentl* via the more indirect motif of a deserting (rather than just missing or dead) father and the invalidation threatened by such absence in Streisand's debut musical, *Funny Girl*. In perhaps the most famous opening line in post-war American cinema, Streisand as Fanny Brice—awaiting the return from prison of the husband with whom a desired "remarriage," she too well knows, is unlikely—addresses herself, a tear glinting visibly in one eye, with "Hello, gorgeous." This is spoken in a frame narrative, after which only a two-hour flashback can explain to us, in context, how she might in fact be addressing the handsome husband as such in a gloomy rehearsal of the pending backstage reunion—and destined split. The evidence to this (chronological) end is easy to overlook in passing, masked always across the unfolding flashback in broad comedy or light banter. When she first meets heart-throb Nick Arnstein (Omar Sharif), her spontaneous outburst "gorgeous" is quickly redirected to his ruffled dress shirt. Soon the dashing

Nick catches the eye even of Fanny's mother in just those terms: the third repetition of "gorgeous." And more, too, as we may now remember from this passing ethnic schtick. For Mrs. Brice (Kay Medford) admits to the awed Mrs. Strakosh (Mae Questal), a lower East Side neighbor, after the latter's "Frankly, that's a good-looking man," that she's putting it mildly. The mother's gloss on the praise is as immediate as it is dubious: "Gorgeous—reminds me of Fanny's papa, my ex—also gorgeous!" A point hardly mitigated by the inverted Jewish lilt of good riddance: "wherever he is, he should only stay there." And then there's Fanny's later line to Nick himself, as father, about the daughter he hasn't stopped to see when he's released from prison in his final scene with Fanny: "She's gorgeous—getting to look just like you." We've only seen her doted upon in the cradle, and, with no clear timeline in this part of the film, she may well be not much older than Streisand herself was when, as only a toddler, she was emotionally orphaned by her father's early death. What *Funny Girl* stages, in short, is a second-generation feminine presence gradually embodying—as if in the course of maturation itself—the special beauty, the enduring lure, of paternal magnetism. If this is still no more than one wrinkle of an intermittent dialogue motif in the first of Streisand's films, it will of course have become the dominant strain of her self-scripted *Yentl*. Operating in *Funny Girl* more starkly, Fanny's pending divorce anticipates her having only a Cavellian "created" self left to embody the gorgeous. Such is her otherwise bereft incorporation of sexual disparity: a male loss colonized in despair as self-image in the mirror of imposed deficit. The mirror has had two faces from the start of Streisand's career, negotiated potently by the songs that fill out its frame.

While only a latent ironic subtext in *Funny Girl*, this tacit thematic has become openly validated and inescapable in *Yentl*—from the Talmudic teacher–patriarch's death forward. Deserted again by a man at the end— by a transitional and slightly older mentor figure in the person of Avigdor (after his having passed through the inverted looking-glass of repressed gay desire)—the heroine will need to go it alone. Or almost. Not, it is true, without some measure of fantasized audiovisual reciprocation from the still-licensing realm of paternal absence. It is a point commentary need not belabor in the way the star herself has done in personal reminiscence. But if those first spoken words from *Funny Girl* operate as a distilled gender matrix whose inferences about the lost father are only unfolded in flashback, they certainly have their own patrimony going forward. Granting that the handsome absent father and the handsome absconding husband of that first film intersect upon the site of the heroine's incorporated loss, we find this logic strenuously fleshed out not only in *Yentl* but then again in *The Mirror Has Two Faces*. The fact that Streisand's own father (dead before she really knew him) has in effect always been absent for her—not long-adored and then torn away by death, but only a missing and idealized validation from the start—is what can most forcefully authorize Streisand's own ongoing appeal to an unseen audience as a disembodied abstraction (From "Watch Me Now" in the finale of *A Star Is Born* to "Watch me fly!" at the end of *Yentl*).

Long before defying Hollywood norms and asserting her right to the megaphone (see *The Way We Were*) as well as the microphone, Streisand first went before the Hollywood camera in a way we can now more fully apprehend. For in the light of hindsight, within *Funny Girl*'s flashback dialogue and within Streisand's career at large, tears are welling up in these first-seen eyes not just because of the impending marital separation—and the "hello"-again and final goodbye to male glamor it will involve. Those eyes can seem to be responding to the wry formulation itself of "Hello, gorgeous" in its impinging gender irony: Fanny being, by erotic default, the only one left to bear that epithet—if she can bear up under it. As punctuated by that scene's mirror reflection, then, and in the form of voice before flashback song, are not just the star's first screen words but their epithet's compressed and double-edged summary of the whole narrative melodrama—including the absconded father figure. And of the career to which this debut musical was such a meteoric boost. As an autobiographical storyline Streisand has repeated to herself over the years, the void of paternity can only be called monumentally empowering. The surprise, in a rescreening of *Funny Girl*, is that its scaffold was all there in her first film—though trussed with irony at every turn. As initially played out in the form of desertion and cross-gender internalization for her character, rather than sheer rebound, Streisand's own continuing force of artistic will is a drive that has, for decades, shaped ambition into a recuperative mission, a force compensatory as well as lucrative, re-routing familial trauma into vocal and theatrical drama, redeeming narcissism as catharsis.

It is in this way, when Streisand's debut vocative is taken as a rehearsed goodbye to a derivative patriarchal beauty and support (the divorcing husband as surrogate for "her father, also gorgeous")—while also offering a self-welcome to the recuperative energy of its survived loss—that model of address helps us to understand a pivotal rephrasing in the most salient lyric refrain of *Yentl*. And to find consolidated there certain patterns familiar from Cavell's remarriage comedies as well as the operatic "lease of voice" in diva performance. This refrain involves a shift, easy to miss from within the overriding sense of iteration, from a prayer-like appeal to the absent father's hearing, after his death, absent but still superintending, to Yentl's final sense of channeling his voiced pride in her own gendered release. "Papa, can you hear me?" is the interrogative title line of the earlier ballad, its metafilmic treatment in the second musical number framing the lone daughter as the specular object of what one might call an acousmatic gaze. But by the end, she needn't ask: she knows there's something decisive to hear. "Papa, I've a voice now." And so we return to the film's last shot, and operatically scaled high note, for its transmutation of the missing father into sheer figure.

Vocal Flight

What's easy to miss in this climactic moment, given the camera's final riveted fixation (its own hold and release) on the closing phrase of this star aria, is that the question of "hearing" and "seeing" has been reversed—and we might well say philosophically reoriented, turned from skepticism concerning the spiritualized male other to a confidence in the "created woman" and her integrated self-sufficiency. So now the "voice deep inside" takes to the air this way, floating up from "Papa I can hear you" through "Papa I can see you" to the assonant third term of self-asserted internalization: "Papa I can feel you." With the supervening ear and eye of loving validation having been embodied and rechanneled on the inside of voice, the final appeal to a ratifying and approving gaze ("Papa, watch me FLY!") may be heard to embed protectively—in its high "flight" to places unknown but unfeared—the doomed subject of "I want" in the outcrop of opera's threatening female "autonomy" according to Cavell. But the force of vocalized will is lightened here within the vocal levitation of Streisand's immaculate vernacular delivery—in its preternatural transfiguration of everyday speech. With gender simulation no longer needed, in this flight there is no longer fleeing, only a freeing new direction. Restored to outward (outed) feminine identity, with another couple's "remarriage" behind here, Yentl has in effect, in a variant of Cavell's Hollywood paradigm, become her own father substitute. And in the lyrically figured verticality of this ascent from deprivation, echoing Cavell's lines about Irene Dunne's Lucy when donning a particular female disguise rather than, like Yentl, shedding its opposite: "So she gives rise to herself, recreates herself"—but not this time in "his image," not in any man's guise, since in Yentl the marital prompt has been forgone. Beyond sexual difference as well as its opposite in "the same [anymore]," she just seeks out "difference" itself (as rumors have it about America): change in the form of a further becoming.

Here, in Streisand's longest-held screen sound, that dissevered assertion of the "I"—when loosed from within the twenty-second last syllabic updraft of the vocally polyvalent "Papa, watch me flyyyHIYIGH"—can be taken to encapsulate, with the synesthetic fusion of sight and sound in its punning "high" note, something very much like opera's "narcissistic" cynosure of solicited attention. Solicited and returned, in a piercing instance of Cavell's reflexive "acknowledgment," technical as well as affective. Unlike Garbo's slightly averted gaze as the private vessel to her own elsewhere at the end of Queen Christina, Streisand looks almost straight into the eyes of the film audience at the start of this last note of appeal. Her giddy, ecstatic stare seems narrowing in medium close-up toward some metanarrative vanishing point—until that far-away look in her eyes, vision of a "new creation" elsewhere, is answered, or more like troped, by a reverse helicopter zoom. Aesthetic distance is sweepingly put between star and camera as if to make space for the radiant volume of her sound. The film's teleology of sung monologues is complete in this unequivocal convergence of the heroine's impetuosity with the star's pyrotechnics, sealed with a knowing glance of tacit cinematic recognition. Yentl's virtually meeting the gaze of Streisand's audience is not a flaw, a crack, in the fiction, through which credibility is inadvertently bled away. Rather, it is an admission, even from within the labor of "re-creation," that performance is its own mode of agency, inward and outward at once, inbred—thus self-same—in its very liberation. And the music of cinematography (Cavell again) underscores the lyric straight through to its final sonic rather than optic fade. As the freighter steams off into the distance, the last prolonged vowel of "fly" might well be a ligature to some whole new predication ("I ... ") about what the re-created first-person subject of the woman has in store.

For all her talent, despite and because of its outsize proportions, Streisand has never managed to find a comfortable niche in a movie genre ordinarily centered upon the communal and the socially harmonized, has never claimed easily the generic legacy to which her talents as a singing comedienne were natively suited. The lack even of duets in her musicals is a recurrent symptom of this—achieving some fleeting compensation at last in the remarital coda of *The Mirror Has Two Faces*. Earlier, the structure of *Yentl* has found one incomparable way around the impasse, not just by its seamless quilting together of song and interior monologue, but by backdating the crisis to a point of historical precondition, indirectly alluding to that Jewish immigration at the turn of the century that helped shape the musical comedy tradition on the American stage and thereafter the founding of Hollywood by Jewish émigrés. The film would thus be historically situated to precede—and thematically anticipate—even the Hollywood genre of which its particular narrative is a provisional rethinking. In these terms Streisand's masterwork can be thought to close by opening up(on) its own formal lineage. We do not have to imagine Yentl on her way to New York in 1904 to become a vaudevillian and eventual Ziegfeld star—and age handsomely into a supporting role among screwball talkies of the 1930s (of which her role in *What's Up, Doc?* is a studied throwback)—to feel the film driving toward, while stopping short of, a generic vision of integrated singing on screen. This holding back, it should now be clear, is required even at the last by the film's whole logic. The force of this solitary drive leaves the film (behind), in Cavell's terms, hovering in the telos of the heroine's own uniquely American "pursuit of happiness," claimed as an inalienable right in her declaration of (her sung declamation of) independence.

The pervasive motif of "a voice deep inside," and its finding of some hospitable social space, has sustained a sense of private expressiveness for which the complexities of the soundtrack have provided metaphor as much as transmission. Such a voice can preserve its figurative integrity through to the end only by anticipating, not yet accomplishing, its own literalization in and as straightforward "song," its registers still oscillating in shipboard passage between public and private release. Not in operatic tragedy but in a closer approach than before to musical comedy in *Yentl*, we are still struck, with Cavell again, by the divide within "narcissism" between "ecstasy" (self-displacement) and "abandonment" (not just of self, here, but of its gendered constraints). In similarly etymological as well as autobiographical, and thus ultimately philosophical, terms (Emerson: all language begins in figure, in metaphor), the very measure of voice as avowal, in *Yentl*'s re-creation myth, is validated not by a lost father figure but by the *figuration* of an internalized strength of origin, its stamp of authority implicit in the urge to self-determination. Call it, let Cavell insist after all, the creation of a woman. The "introjection" of the Other, the internalization of the father, has gone beyond mourning and melancholy alike—into redoubled purpose. In Yentl's epochal feminist transit to intellectual and gender freedom—dredging the depths of Streisand's talent in catapulting it to new heights in this last unmoored heave of sound—one hears figured in the all-out ecstatic ring of her shipboard vocal delivery, not just a *transport*, but a *deliverance*. "Nothing's impossible," as the film's tagline has it. In this case, certainly, hearing is believing.

Notes

1   See *Movies with Stanley Cavell in Mind*, ed. David LaRocca (New York: Bloomsbury, 2021); and *The Thought of Stanley Cavell and Cinema: Turning Anew to the Ontology of Film a Half-Century after* The World Viewed, ed. David LaRocca (New York: Bloomsbury, 2020).

2   See my *Streisand: The Mirror of Difference* (Detroit: Wayne State University Press, 2023) and "The Legible Voice," ch. 20 in *Attention Spans: Garrett Stewart, a Reader*, ed. David LaRocca (New York: Bloomsbury, 2024), 261–70.

3   Stanley Cavell, *A Pitch of Philosophy: Autobiographical Exercises* (Cambridge, MA: Harvard University Press, 1994), 151.

4   Stanley Cavell, *Pursuits of Happiness: The Hollywood Comedy of Remarriage* (Cambridge, MA: Harvard University Press, 1981), 52. It is the suggested utility of this "thought," tucked away in his opening chapter on *The Lady Eve* (1941, dir. Preston Sturges), that may shed light back on Cavell's sense in the Introduction that his "reading" of a given film produces not a secondary commentary on a primary text so much as a "tertiary text" (37) in itself, what he calls a "performance" (37) of the film as if it were a score to be "interpreted" in the very process of execution, both play or of course replay.

5   Cavell, *Pursuits of Happiness*, 52.

6   Cavell alludes to this legalistic term in *Pursuits*, in connection with Milton on divorce (87), in part to suggest the implication of "intercourse" even in his

own sense of the quotidian dimension of spousal "conversation"—rather than stressing the concept's actual narrative links to the place of feared adultery as a crisis of skepticism in his chosen genre. Idiom and dramatic turn are, of course, reversible pictures of each other.

7 Cavell, *Pursuits of Happiness*, 2.

8 Cavell, *Pursuits of Happiness*, 16.

9 Jonathan Cott, *Conversations with Glenn Gould* (New York: Little, Brown, 1984), 113.

10 Two decades before this mad-capping exchange in *The Awful Truth*, there is a more explicitly gendered model for the kind of constraint Judy's line has a way of merely travestying in Streisand's deviant stardom, rather than fully acknowledging or probing—and that is its bleak rather than comic variant in the social norming of earlier American mores, captured here in Edith Wharton's 1920 *The Age of Innocence*. Insists the repatriated Countess Olenska, in dialogue with the enamored Newland Archer:

"I want to cast off all my old life, to become just like everybody else here."

Archer reddened. "You'll never be like everybody else," he said.

She raised her straight eyebrows a little. "Ah, don't say that. If you knew how I hate to be different!"

11 Cavell, *Pursuits of Happiness*, 162.

12 For more on this connection see, for example, David LaRocca, "Autophilosophy," in *Inheriting Stanley Cavell: Memories, Dreams, Reflections*, ed. David LaRocca (New York: Bloomsbury, 2020), 275–320.

13 In *Twelfth Night*, Shakespeare's plot has a man (the Duke Orsino) commissioning a woman who loves him in secret while dressed as a man to woo a woman in celibate mourning for a dead brother as well as father (Olivia, the latter, as the near anagram of the disguised Viola)—against whose passion for her cross-dressed self Viola must remain on the defensive. She also is in mourning for a dead brother (a twin supposedly lost in the shipwreck she survived), so that the play's blocked courtship possibilities—a kind of problematized *pre*-marital comedy—seem indirectly to make Cavell's point, twice over, about the risked cross-purposes of the companionable and the amatory, the filial and the connubial. All this menless grieving for dead brothers and fathers (replayed symbolically in *Yentl*) marks a loss to be in one way or another overcome, in Shakespeare, through a matured marital pairing. More specifically rooted, for the later trials of marriage, in familial crossed wires and closed circuits, Cavell's comedies—and *The Mirror Has Two Faces* as their late-century inheritor—work out how the downside of spousal brotherliness must be enlivened by the woman's "created" sexuality as narrative agency (a newly inflected "sister act") in the drive toward re-marital closure. It is only then that the everyday might become again a prolonged if intermittent holiday.

14 Cavell, *Pursuits of Happiness*, 260; italics added.

15 Isaac Bashevis Singer, "Yentl the Yeshiva Boy," in *Collected Stories: "Gimpel the Fool" to "The Letter Writer,"* ed. Ilan Stavans (New York: Library of

America, 2004), 457, though in the story Yentl's misfit status is closer to gender dysphoria, registered by her secretly dressing up in her father's clothes long before his death (439)—and by her being recognized by him otherwise as having "the soul of a man" (439). When asked by Yentl how that could happen: "Even Heaven makes mistakes."

16 Singer, "Yentl the Yeshiva Boy," *Collected Stories*, 456.

17 Cavell, *Pursuits of Happiness*, 150.

18 Ibid., 251.

19 Ibid., 252.

20 Ibid., 159–60.

21 See "Nice to Meet You Glenn!" at glenngould.tv (May 6, 2020); https://tinyurl.com/37usefuu.

22 Cavell, *Pursuits of Happiness*, 262.

5

Cavell as Halted Traveler

The Experience of Music

RICHARD ELDRIDGE

EARLY ON IN *HERE AND THERE*, in the Prologue entitled "A Site for Philosophy" and originally delivered as an address on "the place of visual art" at Harvard and, more broadly, in the university in general, Cavell observes that, as he sees things, "there is an internal relation between philosophy and sites or spaces that is mostly unthematized in philosophy."[1] This lack of attention to specific sites (and experiences in relation to them) that Cavell notes is at least close to non-accidental in relation to more or less typical conceptions of philosophy. All but constitutively, philosophy seeks timeless answers to timeless questions: what are knowledge and justification?; what is the fundamental nature of reality?; what is justice?; what is virtue? These are typically taken to be questions that might be raised by anyone at any time, and satisfactory answers must take the form of necessary truths, invariable across all contingencies of time, place, culture, or history. In challenging this typical conception of philosophy, then, Cavell has evidently set himself a monumental task of calling philosophy back to its true nature as a kind of open-ended, specifically situated criticism of important commitments that have somehow fallen into question for someone in a particular time and place. His effort must be to awaken philosophy and philosophers, or anyone who might seek justification for a fundamental commitment, from an enchanting dream or nightmare (or both) of absolute authority, freed of anything personal, local, or contingent.

If the relation between philosophy and occasioning sites that Cavell proposes is generally unthematized in philosophy, however, it is far from

unthematized elsewhere. As Geoffrey Hartman has shown at length, the
topos of the halted traveler—arrested in a specific spot of time and place
and thereby given over to thought—is central to Wordsworth's poetry.[2]
As Hartman puts it, Wordsworth's poetry is typically precipitated (though
not yet completed, since completion requires "emotion recollected in
tranquility"[3]) when "what others might have passed by produces a strong
emotional response in him."[4] The strong responses in question are not
simply materially caused by the scene of experience, but instead are the joint
product of the scene and the poet's attentive mind, "which actively desires
the inauguration of a totally new epoch"[5] or new joint habits of thought,
feeling, and activity wherein things will at last make sense and significant
reconciliation with others and with oneself is possible. These responses
typically alternate between wild hope in a prospective, transfigurative
apocalypse, promised by a sublime, fearful moment of experience, but
haunted, too, by a sense of its unshareability, hence a sense also of its risk of
madness, and calm rebinding to the earth and to what is common, or what
Hartman calls *akedah*: "a soul," as Hartman puts it, "has to renaturalize
itself"[6] in order to lead a life on earth with others in time, as opposed to
escaping into empyrean but potentially empty liberation.[7] The body of
Wordsworth's poetry as a whole and in particular *The Prelude* presents "no
argument [for a settled conclusion] but a vacillation between doubt and
faith."[8] In seeking justified reconciliation with and within a radically new
form of earthly life, Wordsworth "carried the Puritan quest for evidences of
election into the most ordinary emotional contexts"[9] and gave expression to
the experience of that quest as unconcluded rather than resolving it under
any settled doctrine.

Cavell gives frequent expression to a similar desire or ambition for
radical transfiguration, both individual and cultural, alternating with a
competing desire for settlement with and within the common. The genius
of Austin's practice of ordinary language philosophy, as Cavell saw it,
was to answer to both desires, as one could speak (and hear) freely and
intelligibly, in redemptive escape from conceptual confusion, while also
remaining within the sways of the common. The limitation of that practice
was its ultimate failure to move beyond particular ranges and construals
of examples (mistakes vs. accidents; succumbing to temptation vs. losing
control of oneself) in a way that quieted the desire for systematic theory. The
great discovery of *The Claim of Reason* is that rehearsing criteria of identity
does not settle questions of existence, so that *if* questions of existence (of
the world, of the minds of others) have to be raised (from within a prior
experience of alienation), *then* they cannot be settled by the procedures of
ordinary language philosophy: the skeptic is equally a master of ordinary
language, and *if you have to ask* whether the occluded side of an object is
really, absolutely there beyond all possible doubt, then the honest answer
is that you don't know, not absolutely. "The human creature's basis in the

world as a whole, its relation to the world, is not that of knowing, anyway not what we think of as knowing,"[10] and if trust in the world and in others in it is lost (perhaps partly through one's own misbegotten but natural and motivated directions of desire, ambition, and effort), then it is by no means clear how it can be recovered. The force of appeals to the ordinary is inadequate to undo fundamental distortions of ambition and desire.

In *Here and There*, Cavell expresses a joint sense of a continuing desire for philosophy—that is, for its putative achievement of timeless and impersonal authority—and of the impossibility of satisfying this desire, insofar as one remains always belated and self-opaque in coming to one's words, which are in shifting circulation within the common. "The arrogance of philosophy is to show that I can speak universally, for everyone. The confidence of psychoanalysis is to show that I do not so much as speak for myself."[11] Here Cavell finds himself, and (many or most modern) human subjects as such, fated to live between and with both this arrogance (in undertaking to speak for everyone) and this confidence (in psychoanalytic doubt).

How, then, might this fate be lived with aptly? In a central leitmotif that runs throughout both *Here and There* and his work as a whole, Cavell finds some materials for an answer in the experience of music, which offers something like the satisfaction of the ambition of philosophy for full, grounded, confidence and cathexis to activities under commitments, coupled with a registration of finitude and incompleteness. As Cavell remarks in a crucial passage about the course of his life with philosophy:

> While I have written very little explicitly about music over the ensuing decades [since ...] I graduated with a major in music from the University of California at Berkeley [in 1946, ...] I have known for most of that time that something I have demanded from philosophy was an understanding precisely of what I had sought in music, and in the understanding of music, of what demanded that reclamation of experience, of the capacity for being moved, which called out for, and sustained, an accounting as lucid as the music I loved.

This crucial passage is difficult both conceptually and grammatically, and it is worth some extended paraphrase. Cavell had sought something in music. Evidently enough, he had frequently enough found it, had found his experience in general reclaimed (from dullness, lack of meaningful presence) by the experience and understanding of music as a temporally unfolding order that moved him and that engaged both his intellect and his ear (and his body) in what he was doing (playing or listening). Initially, at least, this experience, while entrancing, was also obscure—as though Cavell himself were a Wordsworthian halted traveler, stopped in his otherwise wandering through life by an overwhelming experience of unfolding sound that in its suddenness and force demanded that it be reflected on, tested, and worked through. "What," Cavell must have asked himself, "has just happened to me? What does it mean? Is it trustworthy? Is it repeatable and shareable? Or am I mad or otherwise the victim of an unintelligible fit of transport?"[12] He turned to philosophy in hopes of carrying out this working-through and of finding a language for this experience and assessing its value. In seeking that understanding of music, he hoped further to understand what in life otherwise—a matter of idleness, drift, and lack of orientation (such as he may have experienced in breaking off from the formal study of music at Juilliard in New York in 1947)—demanded the compensations and redemptions that musical experience afforded. "What is (my) life, such that it needs music in order for me to bear it?" And the account of this would, itself, have to be as lucid—that is, as convincing, continuously absorbing, and moving—as the experience of music itself. Hence the philosophical account of music would have to have something like distinctively musical structure. To sum up schematically:

1. Cavell sought and found in music (both playing it and understanding it) an overwhelming but obscure and fearful experience of transfigurative, engaged, absorption and meaningfulness.

2. He turned to philosophy in order to work through, understand, and assess this experience.

3. In doing so, he remained in the grip of the thought that the account he sought must be as entrancing and nonartificial—as lucid—as the experience of music itself, must, in effect, itself be musical.[13]

In short, Cavell takes music to provide "a figure of the mind in its most perfected relation to itself, or to its wishes for itself,"[14] and philosophy is to parse that figure conceptually, but without dominating it, that is, while itself repeating, echoing, or participating in that figure.

An obvious question to ask is *how* music works as a figure of the mind in its most perfected relation to itself. (Answering this will require the philosophico-musical parsing of that figure.) In the essay "An Understanding with Music," the title of which implies all of understanding music (what it is, how it works, why we have it), coming to terms with one's experience of it (how it affects one, working through that arresting experience), and doing all this in a musical way, Cavell comments on a passage from Lévi-Strauss' *Introduction to a Science of Mythology*, volume 4, as cited by the French music theorist Michel Poizat in his book *The Angel's Cry*. Here is the passage from Lévi-Strauss:

There would be no music if language had not preceded it and if music did not continue to depend on it, as it were, through a privative connection. Music is language without meaning: this being so, it is understandable that the listener, who is first and foremost a subject with the gift of speech, should feel himself irresistibly compelled to make up for the absent sense, just as someone who has lost a limb imagines that he still possesses it through the sensations present in the stump.[15]

Cavell then further cites Poizat's own comment on this passage: "Is it perhaps this primordial act of separation that opera speaks of, letting us know that it is paid for with suffering? And is it perhaps in the nostalgia for a paradisiacal unity of preseparation that the opera lover's ecstasy resides?"[16]

What guides Cavell's attention here, I conjecture, is the more or less psychoanalytic idea that the experience of music provides the individuated subject (the subject with the gift of speech) with a kind of reminder of or reconnection to a lost unity, insofar as the listening or playing subject is caught up in and cathected to the musical development, together with the critical sense (registered in the development's drive toward its final cadence, where it will break off) that one remains nonetheless a finite, individuated subject. Cavell remarks in particular that:

Poizat's hypothesis of a primordial connection relies elsewhere than evidence [from human prehistory] for its conviction, presumably upon a more or less unspoken theory of the psychic development of singing as stretching between speech and the cry, under the demand for pleasure and for an enjoyment beyond pleasure, linked with the identification of this beyond in moments across the history of opera.[17]

This suggests that singing, or the hearing of singing in certain high moments in opera, both responds to and satisfies that demand for an enjoyment beyond pleasure in a specifically bounded way. In doing so, it makes available to the singer or hearer a partially reparative all but reconnection to what Julia Kristeva has identified as the semiotic: the register of experience that is prior to ego individuation and that is marked by bodily–emotional involvement and responsiveness to a maternal (not quite) other, where discursive structure is absent and where rhythm and melodic contour predominate and support diffuse *jouissance*, as opposed to the pleasurable satisfaction of a discretely articulated desire.[18] This register of experience is prior to the symbolic, understood as the register of experience of the now individuated, discursively structured ego, with its now distinct plans, goals, and specified pleasures. That something like this partially reparative experience is what Cavell has in mind as afforded by music is evident in his going on to observe that Poizat's account of "the cry as the epitome of opera's expressiveness, the final anguish that transcends both language and music to reach an expression of pure voice," recalls Nietzsche's account in *The Birth of Tragedy* of "the cry as the suffering of individuation, that is of finite existence, of which music allows the expression, as if we should, without such expression, suffocate from our words, buried alive."[19] Here the thought is that without the cry that expresses the suffering of individuation—the cry that resummons pre-individuative libidinal energies and investments that are cathected to rhythm and melody—our words threaten to become not ours, less than fully felt and meant, or things that suffocate us under the demands of conformity.[20] In moving into song, with words, but remaining shaped as a melodic contour of passion, an operatic aria simultaneously recovers and liberates original libidinal energies and registers of experience, while also reenacting and compensating for their loss via conventionalization and submission to language and authority. In this way, it functions as a vehicle for becoming more present as a distinctive individual both to oneself and to others in one's words and life. It brings remnants of originary libidinal pre-ego identity into the ambit of conventionalized expression. This is the source of its redemptive power. And the same thing is true of purely instrumental melodic and harmonic development. Or, as Cavell puts it, "one might see the possibility of understanding without [compositional, linguistic] meaning," in cathexis to a melodic contour of passion or to other forms of musical development that gesture toward but exceed linguistic meaning—Lévi-Strauss' "privative connection"—"as redemptive, like losing one's chains,"[21] in an experience of what one might call meaning for the subject beyond (linguistic) meaning. "We could say that the instance of music defeats the idea of a certain *theory* of meaning, the one Wittgenstein seeks to defeat as expressed in the opening paragraph of *Philosophical Investigations*, according to which every word has a meaning which is the object it refers to."[22] Wittgenstein himself once remarked "[i]t is impossible for me to say in my book one word about all that music has meant to me in my life. How then can I hope to be understood?"[23]

Notably, however, cathexis to musical development—feeling one's powers of thought and feeling wedded to the course and cadencing of the music—provides no possibility of full, enduring escape from self-doubt and the feelings of being hostage to conventions and sealed within one's privacy. Any piece of music with hearable development[24] comes to an end, its final cadence achieved. After that, the rest is silence, at least until a new piece occupies one's attentions. In the intervals that constitute the bulk of anyone's life, one will again be within the orbits of language and discursively structured experience and activity, and one will again face whatever problems of distance and difference from others and of personally felt inexpressiveness and isolation that made the experience of music so absorbing and redemptive. Can that experience, in its particular guided raptures, be trusted? Which, if any, others share it? What significance, if any, does it have for the rest of life, apart from being a bounded compensation?

Nor is this kind of cathexis to development that affords a distinct, intense mode of experience limited to music. Cavell wonders how it is that the arts in general "show, or remind us, or expand our horizons, so that we see, or remember, or learn what truly matters to us?—as though without them we build our knowledge of our place in the world on the basis of sensory deprivation, starving our desires."[25] There is sometimes, as in lyric poetry, or in richly attentive conversation, or in following the development of a movie, what Cavell calls "the music of [...] the dense contexts in which speech makes its specific sense."[26] Theoretically minded, arts-and-music-scanting philosophers in pursuit of a guiding *doxa* arrived at and sustained on the basis of deductive argument, are, Cavell claims, characteristically deaf to and unable to enter into this kind of music of and in speech. Or as Cavell puts the thought that he finds in Wittgenstein: "Wittgenstein takes philosophers, succumbing to the temptation to metaphysics or false transcendence or skepticism, to torture human speech, to madden human encounter, unable or unwilling to imagine, to participate in" that kind of musical speech and mutual sense-making.[27] One way out of this self-torture is then specifically to trust works of music and art along with intimate conversational life and experiences of them—to open oneself to their development, rather than standing on formulas that restrict significance to literalness—however one might manage that trust and however much these works and experiences remain bounded and their affordances remain less than fully sustainable.

Yet here too, trust proves less than perfectly sustainable, and when uncritical it verges on idolatry, which will not do as a mode of meaningful, individual life with others. One must also think and feel for oneself, actively engaging with what one encounters. As Cavell comments on Allan Bloom's dogmatic defense of the authority of classical texts:

[T]he *distrust* of reading—[that is, of the authority of "mere letters," in comparison with the serious work of science and of "analyzing and solving problems"]—is half of the philosophical spirit. A devotion to thinking by reading—however great the books in question—will not count, in my corner of things, as a philosophical devotion, unless it knows at each moment how to distrust reading.[28]

It is ongoing interaction with others and with works of the various arts, involving both joint sense-making and critical engagement, both similarity and difference, both community and isolation, that is the genuine vehicle of fuller, more active life for a human subject.[29]

Achieving this fuller life is more a matter of imagination and investment as open-ended skills whose fit exercises blend responsiveness (taking seriously the commitments and feelings of others) and originality (having the courage of one's own affections and aversions) than it is of living according to formula or rule. For Cavell, at least, there remains, always, "the unappeasable human dissatisfaction with each of its dispensations, the condition I called human restlessness,"[30] as we find ourselves always moving into new regions of doubt and experience and self-assertion, whatever temporary absorptions we have achieved. Hence our lives remain marked by both "the torment in human restlessness [...] and [...] the dream of peace," as we remain in the grip "of an urge to misunderstand" (and to mark out one's own way, leaving the work of music, or the work of art, the metaphor or the other behind, going one's own way) and also of the possibility "of understanding as knowing how to go on" (with them).[31]

In Book II of *The Prelude*, Wordsworth comes to articulate his sense that with the death of his mother just before his eighth birthday "The props of my affections were removed/[...] I was left alone/Seeking the visible world nor knowing why"[32] in continuing experiences of an ongoing lack of direction and investment in meaningful activity that might enable him to sustain a sense of the worth of his own life in a world with others. This sense of a lack of direction or orientation sharpened in him as a young adult into the sense that he might be "Unprofitably travelling toward the grave, / Like a false steward who hath much received /And renders nothing back,"[33] with his human powers of meaning-making and significant action blocked or stultified. Thus are we all, sooner or later, betimes cast into the world.

Yet Wordsworth retained a sense of the possibility of, and sometimes took himself to have achieved, "that peace /which passeth understanding," involving "the consciousness/Of [who one] is, habitually infused /Through every image and through every thought [...]: /Hence endless occupation for the Soul, /Discursive or intuitive /Hence cheerfulness for acts of daily life / Emotions which best foresight need not fear /Most worthy then of trust when most intense,"[34] as he found himself as a halted traveler first undergoing alternating moments of intense, calming absorption (*akedah*, the beautiful) and intense, unsettling disturbance (*apocalypse*, the sublime, the fearful) and then later working them through, articulating them—locating and assessing their places in his life—in reflection. As I have elsewhere put it, "[o]ur humanity, Wordsworth's example suggests, is lived out within [and amidst] these [experiences and] articulations, between the sublimities of partial transcendence into individual vision and the beauties of partial community in shared valuations and engagements."[35] Cavell's life and writing—his ongoing experiences of being stopped in various ways by works of music and art (and by others)—and his ongoing reflections on them confirm this suggestion. There are, always, occasioning circumstances for renewed reflection, "events of a life that turn its dedication toward philosophy"[36] *as* reflective criticism that courts transcendence and yet always founders—none of them more powerful for Cavell than the experience of music.

Notes

1   Stanley Cavell, *Here and There: Sites of Philosophy*, ed. Nancy Bauer, Alice Crary, and Sandra Laugier (Cambridge, MA: Harvard University Press, 2022), 14, 16.

2   "The Halted Traveler" is the title of Part I: Thesis, of Geoffrey Hartman's
     epochal *Wordsworth's Poetry 1787–1814* (New Haven: Yale University
     Press, 1971 [1964]). Cavell and Hartman both participated in a ten-month
     symposium in Jerusalem on the play of negativity in literature and literary
     theory that culminated in a conference in June 1986. That conference in
     turn yielded the volume *Languages of the Unsayable: The Play of Negativity
     in Literature and Literary Theory*, eds. Sanford Budick and Wolfgang Iser
     (New York: Columbia University Press, 1987). The symposium participants
     included, in addition to Cavell, Hartman, and the editors, Jacques Derrida,
     Frank Kermode, Gerald Bruns, Jonathan Culler, Shira Wolosky, and Neil
     Hertz, among others. Hearsay as it reaches me has it that Cavell was the
     central figure to whom others deferred.

3   William Wordsworth, "Preface to *Lyrical Ballads*," in Wordsworth,
     Selected Poems and Prefaces, ed. Jack Stillinger (Boston: Houghton Mifflin,
     1965), 460.

4   Hartman, *Wordsworth's Poetry 1787–1814*, 3.

5   Ibid., xxii.

6   Ibid., xvi.

7   *Apocalypse* and *akedah* are Hartman's two master terms for describing
     Wordsworth's primary, competing registers of precipitated but active response
     (*Wordsworth's Poetry 1787–1814*, 225–33). *Apocalypse* names the unleashing
     of potentially world-transfiguring imaginative energies; *akedah* names the
     rebinding of agency to the earth and communal life.

8   Hartman, *Wordsworth's Poetry 1787–1814*, 218.

9   Ibid., 5.

10   Stanley Cavell, *The Claim of Reason: Wittgenstein, Skepticism, Morality, and
     Tragedy* (New York: Oxford University Press, 1979), 241.

11   Cavell, "Finding Words," *Here and There*, 145.

12   Cavell writes in "Philosophy and the Unheard," an entry in *Here
     and There*, of his "vision of the human as caught between a sense of
     inexpressiveness suggesting suffocation and a sense of uncontrollable
     expressiveness threatening exposure" (262) and of "the modern ego
     entangled in its expressions of desire" (267). Evidently, actively maintained,
     continuously meaningful, and emotionally apt human life is more or less
     continuously absent or under threat for Cavell.

13   In their Introduction to *Here and Now*, the editors Nancy Bauer, Alice Crary,
     and Sandra Laugier, commenting on the crucial passage, nicely observe that,
     for Cavell, "it makes sense to hold that philosophy, and more exactly ordinary
     language philosophy, can be asked to supply the kind of reclamation of, or
     reconciliation with, sensibility that we may also seek in music," 11.

14   Cavell, "Philosophy and the Unheard," *Here and There*, 260–1.

15   Cavell, "An Understanding with Music," *Here and There*, 251.

16   Ibid.

17   Ibid.

18 See Kristeva, *Desire in Language: A Semiotic Approach to Literature and Art*, ed. Leon S. Roudiez, trans. Thomas Gora, Alice Jardine, and Leon S. Roudiez (New York: Columbia University Press, 1980).

19 Cavell, "An Understanding with Music," *Here and There*, 252.

20 Ibid., 253. Compare Wordsworth's paradoxical attempts to reconnect his now individuated sense of self to an originary, libidinally suffused naturalness, projected onto Dorothy and onto numinous nature more generally, while yet retaining a mature identity. For an account of this, see my *Literature, Life, and Modernity* (New York: Columbia University Press, 2008), 95–7, drawing on and revising the work of John Barrell, *Poetry, Language, and Politics* (Manchester: Manchester University Press, 1988).

21 There is an echo here of Wittgenstein's phrase "das erlösende Wort [the redemptive or liberating word]" in the *Big Typescript*: "The philosopher strives to find the liberating [*erlösende*] word, that is, the word that finally permits us to grasp what until now has intangibly weighed down our consciousness" (Wittgenstein, "Philosophy: Sections 86–93 of the so-called *Big Typescript*," in Wittgenstein, *Philosophical Occasions, 1912–1951*, ed. James Klagge and Alfred Nordmann [Indianapolis: Hackett Publishing Company, 1993, 165, 164]). Martin Luther uses "Erlöser" for what the King James Bible renders as "redeemer," as in Job's "I know that my redeemer liveth" (Job 19:25, KJV). See James C. Klagge, *Wittgenstein in Exile* (Cambridge, MA: MIT Press, 2014), 125–6.

22 Cavell, "An Understanding with Music," *Here and There*, 253.

23 Wittgenstein to Maurice Drury, as reported in M. O'C. Drury, "Conversations with Wittgenstein," in *Recollections of Wittgenstein*, ed. Rush Rhees (Oxford: Oxford University Press, 1984), 160.

24 John Cage's "Organ2/ASLSP (As Slow as Possible)," in "performance" (mechanical sound generation with rare human interventions) in Halberstadt, Germany, since 2001 and scheduled to conclude in 2640, interestingly lacks hearable development.

25 Cavell, "Impressions of Revolution," *Here and There*, 277.

26 Cavell, "A Scale of Eternity," *Here and There*, 280.

27 Ibid.

28 Cavell, "Who Disappoints Whom? Allan Bloom at Harvard," *Here and There*, 212.

29 Ted Cohen nicely captures this point in writing that "being human requires knowing what it is to be human, and that requires the intimate recognition of other human beings" in both their shifting likenesses to and differences from oneself over time. This requires "investing your self" imaginatively and emotionally in what is going on with them, a kind of investment that is also required by metaphors and works of art. "The metaphors, the art, the people would all be dispensable if their measure could be taken by a formula. There are no formulas for this, thank God." Ted Cohen, *Thinking of Others: On the Talent for Metaphor* (Princeton: Princeton University Press, 2008), 85–6.

30 Cavell, "A Scale of Eternity," *Here and There*, 285.

31 Ibid., 282.

32 William Wordsworth, *The Prelude Or, Growth of a Poet's Mind*, in *Selected Poems and Prefaces*, Book II, lines 279, 277–8; page 213.

33 Ibid., Book I, lines 267–9; page 199.

34 Ibid., Book XIV, lines 126–7, 114–16, 119–23; page 359.

35 See my "Internal Transcendentalism: Wordsworth and 'A New Condition of Philosophy,'" in Richard Eldridge, *The Persistence of Romanticism* (Cambridge: Cambridge University Press, 2001), 123.

36 Stanley Cavell, *A Pitch of Philosophy: Autobiographical Exercises* (Cambridge, MA: Harvard University Press, 1994), vii.

6

The Sound of Reality

Jocelyn Benoist

IN "SILENCES NOISES VOICES," Stanley Cavell describes philosophy as the journey from one silence to another: a silence out of which philosophy arises and one in which philosophy finds its achievement. "The silence in which philosophy begins," he says, "is the recognition of my lostness to myself [.... T]he silence in which philosophy ends is the acceptance of the human life of words."[1] The first silence is somehow *below* the voice: I experience something that is not really a voice, or, if things like voices are to be found there, it is impossible for me to appropriate them. The second silence sanctifies a recovered voice: the utterance of the one who recognizes himself or herself in his or her own words. *Prima facie*, this characterization of philosophy as leading us from one silence to another seems paradoxical.

In the first place, one could be tempted to say that at the beginning, certainly, there is no silence. For a philosopher starting from a critical dialogue with the philosophy of ordinary language like Cavell, it is quite clear that *it speaks before philosophy*, and even that it speaks *essentially* before philosophy: there is no philosophy except in relation to this basic fact of speech. For philosophy to *start* from a silence, it is therefore required that, in some way, this silence be made. Very particular conditions are probably required to this effect, which does not mean that these conditions are no part of the very nature of our existence. Secondly, one could say that what one reaches at the end of philosophical therapy, if it succeeds, is not silence, but speech: speech that one makes one's own and that is freed from the impediment that may have hindered it. If philosophy ever leads to silence, it is at most, if it is ever possible (which is not clear), to *the silence of philosophy*.

In fact, such a diagnosis is quite consistent with the background over against which Cavell advances this motto: indeed, in this text, when mention is made of a "beyond of the voices," which would be the true meaning of this silence, it is about the two conflicting voices that Cavell hears disputing throughout Wittgenstein's *Philosophical Investigations*.[2] Silence, on the one side and on the other, would then be nothing else than the silence of philosophy, in senses that are certainly different in one case and in the other. In fact, much, as far as the reading of *Philosophical Investigations* but also the self-understanding of philosophy itself is concerned, would depend on our capacity to correctly assess how one silence is not the same as the other. I think, however, that, in order to make such a distinction, we can and must go further, and reflect on how, on both sides, it is *really* about a silence: that is to say, a silence in the ordinary sense of the term, or at least in dimensions of what is ordinarily called "silence," and not only "the silence of philosophy," as far as, precisely, one aspect of Cavell's view is, both against traditional philosophy as well as the philosophy of ordinary language, that it essentially blurs the division between what is philosophical and what is ordinary.[3] If there is philosophical silence, in the sense of one or more silences that play a role in philosophy, this one or these ones should also be ordinary silence(s), and vice versa.

In the first place, what is this silence out of which philosophy arises and that, if we accept the kind of teleology that Cavell seems to suggest, philosophy seems to have the vocation to overcome, or to help us overcome? It is essential to note the constitutive ambiguity of this silence presented as that of the origin. On the one hand, this silence is the one of philosophy itself, in the sense of the one philosophy maintains ("it maintains silence") first of all.[4] There is silence only insofar as philosophy keeps its silence. On the other hand, however, by keeping its silence, philosophy makes audible a certain silence, which without that, perhaps, would have passed unnoticed, or at least would have remained non-thematic. Very strikingly, Cavell describes philosophy as an exercise of *wakefulness*. It remains "awake, after all the others have fallen asleep," and thus have fallen silent. Its original silence is, thus, not only its own, but the one of other discourses, and in a certain sense the one of speech in general.[5] The picture according to which there is philosophy only where *it speaks/they speak* before philosophy should thus be completed in this way: on the other hand, philosophy starts where *it does not speak/they do not speak* anymore. The question is then to know what there is to hear in this silence, as *the silence of speech*. What else than the non-propositional murmur of the title of this essay, without syntax and without commas: "silences noises voices"?

Voices are there, to be sure. However, their apposition to the "noises" establishes a continuity and an encroachment of the ones to the others. We are in the gray zone of the listening where it is difficult to distinguish sounds and voices: where, in fact, voices themselves echo as sounds, and where the sounds, potentially, are always suspected to be voices. Indistinction between what is voice and what is not voice is systematically related by Cavell to another indistinction: that between the proper voice and some "other voice" (that is not my own). Who speaks? One does not know well anymore. So much so that one does not really know any more if one speaks or not.

Philosophically, this anxiety responds to the fear of a certain kind of alienation of the language, where I do not find myself anymore, where it is impossible for me to recognize *my voice*, and which by this very fact loses its meaning as language for me. However, it is significant that this anxiety takes the shape of a certain experience of *noise*. Indeed, beyond the voice, what else but noise? It is noteworthy, in this respect, that Cavell, in this brief presentation on the French translation of *The Claim of Reason*, which he chooses to entitle "Silences Noises Voices," selects in his book, in which, contrary to what he now suggests, noise is not very present, a quotation of a quite strategic passage from Wittgenstein's *Philosophical Investigations* (§261), where noise plays a pivotal role in the reinvestment of ordinary language by an irreducibly metaphysical problem. In fact, it is not the only example given in this portion of *The Claim of Reason*, but to be sure this mention of noise is anything but insignificant. A certain experience of noise, indeed, surfaces then as something that calls *reality* into question. It is about the "humming in the air" or a "noise at midnight in the basement" summoned against the Austinian securing of experience, whose invocation of ordinary ways of speaking perhaps plays the role of a placebo rather than a real remedy: "I was also recalling specific occurrences of noises in my book [in fact, there are not so many ...], as when it justifies the traditional epistemologist's fastidiousness (however much it seeks to avoid the animus of skepticism) by remarking, 'There are not *just* noises in the air.'"[6] Let us return to *The Claim of Reason*:

> There is this humming in the air; or a noise at midnight in the basement—there it is again. Shall I say: "I don't by any means *always* know ...", and let it go at that? But there aren't *just* hummings in the air; it is *imperative* that I find out whether there happens to be one in the air now or whether it is only in my ears. Certainly I may not be able to learn the answer in this case, to convince myself one way or the other. But it won't help my condition to say that sometimes I *just* don't know. I am left with the question; it stays in me, until it decays in my memory or I overlay it, perhaps symbolize it, with something else. It is imperative that our experience of the world *make sense*, that loose threads get taken up by some explanation or other.[7]

In a famous passage of "Other Minds," J. L. Austin advocates a deflationary treatment of the dramaturgy of human finitude that permeates modern philosophy. He argues against the idea that the fact that it is always possible that circumstances are exceptional and that, despite all the legitimate reasons I may have for thinking something, this thing is false or rather inadequate, should render void any claim to knowledge:

> "When you know you can't be wrong" is perfectly good sense. You are prohibited from saying "I know it is so, but I may be wrong," just as you are prohibited from saying "I promise I will, but I may fail." If you are aware you may be mistaken, you ought not to say you know, just as, if you are aware you may break your word, you have no business to promise. But of course, being aware that you may be mistaken doesn't mean merely being aware that you are a fallible human being: it means that you have some concrete reason to suppose that you may be mistaken in this case. Just as "but I may fail" does not mean merely "but I am a weak human being" (in which case it would be no more exciting than adding "D.V." [*Deo Volente*]).[8]

Cavell's point is that sometimes a lot may be put in this *Deo Volente* and excitement may be in order: the tragic excitement of life. Now, in some way, this may be the same with the uncertainties of epistemology. Perhaps, there is something equivocal in Cavell's vindication of what he calls "traditional epistemology," since he restores it not as far as epistemology but as far as he reinterprets it as imbued with the feeling of *the limitation of epistemology.* In fact, the idea that our knowledge of this or that is always limited has something to do with the fact that knowledge as such is limited as far as it puts us in relation with *something that is never only an object of knowledge,* and that the very possibility of knowledge requires that certain conditions are met for knowledge to make sense.

In this regard, Cavell makes a point of distinguishing between *identity* and *reality.* Austin, in his famous discussion of "if you like, the Nature of Reality" in the seventh chapter of *Sense and Sensibilia,* insists that "real" is a "substantive-hungry" word that always applies to something definite and is defined by some standard for this thing.[9] Then, it seems that the question of reality is a mere matter of identity. Something is said not to be real as far as it is not *a real something of some sort,* and as far as it might be *mistaken for* that kind of thing. Cavell is not satisfied with this manifestly deflationary reduction of the question of reality to a mere question of identity and Cavell's dissatisfaction forms the basis of his vindication of metaphysics as a part of the ordinary itself. To be true, reality is a metaphysical concept, but, still, we cannot expurgate our existence from such worries about reality. In this sense, metaphysics is part of our life, of the so-called "ordinary," and the invocation *of* the ordinary is no defense against it.

In fact, it is important that Cavell's demonstration shows how the question of identity might prove to be trickier than it seems—to such an extent that the problem is no longer to know whether the thing in question is a false or a real x, but whether it is *real* at all. We cannot jettison the absolute use of the word "real"—and, in some cases, the question whether it is "real" or not lies at the end of the question of identity, because far from knowing by which standard the thing must be measured and assessed as a real something or not, we really do not know anymore which standard to rely on. In such cases, we are doomed to wonder whether "is it real or not?" There are no criteria to deal with that kind of situation: for, to enforce criteria would mean to have a standard already in view.

The strength of Cavell's demonstration rests on his use of Austin's own examples in order to destabilize the epistemic comfort claimed by the British philosopher. In fact, what would we say if the goldfinch we see starts quoting Virginia Woolf?[10] Probably not only—and not necessarily either—that it is "not a real goldfinch." As Austin notes: we just *don't know what to say*. In fact, Austin's works are full of this kind of nonsense, most often imbued with some kind of British humor. The philosopher of ordinary language considers a lot of situations that are *not ordinary at all*. Of course, the point is to build, so to speak, a view from outside regarding the limits of ordinary uses. However, could the extraordinary be systematically taken so lightly, with such Oxonian armchair humor, and neutralized as such? Are we satisfied to say that "we don't know"? And is nothing more involved by the fact that we are at a loss for words?

The gist of Cavell's argument is that such situations, such examples— which he calls "surreal"—are in fact much less exceptional than the British philosopher wants to suggest they are, and have certainly not the artificiality of a mere philosopher's game.[11] In some way, this strangeness is anchored in the interstices of the ordinary itself; it is essential even that the ordinary might face such concerns. Thus, the extraordinary, in the sense of what makes us break out of the usual routines and hesitate as to which standard is relevant and even as to whether any standard is really relevant, is essentially *part* of the ordinary. It surfaces, one might say, at the edge of the ordinary and is so to speak its "other side." It is a theme, no doubt borrowed from psychoanalysis, which constitutes, so to speak, *the other voice* of Cavellian thought—as is still to be seen in the final part of "Silences Noises Voices"— that is, of *the uncanniness of the ordinary*.

Thus, noises enter the scene. The first figure of this familiar strangeness is indeed the noise in the basement. A very common experience, but one that nonetheless opens up another dimension in our relationship to things. Indeed, in such conditions, the first question "What is it?" transforms quickly into "Is it real?" To use big words—and Cavell does not always shy away from them—we pass quite naturally, silently even, from ontology to metaphysics.

Wittgenstein says we can ask ourselves: "was it a thunderclap or a gunshot?" but not "was it a noise (*Lärm*)"?[12] And of course, we should qualify this assertion: after all, we can invent scenarios—exactly what

Cavell would call "surrealistic scenarios"—in which it would not always be clear whether we are dealing with a noise or not. Let's imagine that the noise only comes to us under the guise of vibrations. Is this not exactly what we wonder about when we have the suspicion that maybe we are experiencing tinnitus: was that a noise or not? It is, however, true that usually we would rather ask whether *we really heard something or not*. Interestingly, it is precisely by its poverty—of not giving a *thing* or at least not immediately a thing—that the sense of hearing can in a way become a sense of reality, that is to say the sense through which reality as such is at stake: the sense with regard to which the right question is to know if it is real or not. A question which sounds a bit like "Is it safe?" in *Marathon Man*. Because, in the first place, we do not know what *it* is. Such scenarios have something to do with what we might call the purely *symptomatic* character of sound experience as a detached experience broadly speaking, reduced to the one category of a *noise*. In another passage, Wittgenstein remarks:

> I hear noises in the next room and say there is probably someone therein. I infer it from those signs (*Anzeichen*). Now somebody could ask me: and what is that, what you infer, how is that, if a person is really in this room? As an answer one could show a man in that room. This would be the answer to the question: "under what circumstances do you say that a human being is in the room?" And these circumstances could also be called the *criteria*. This in contrast to a *symptom* like the sound (*Geräusch*) I had heard from the next room.[13]

Turn out, this is exactly Cavell's point. *There are no criteria about noises,* at least as long as they are received as those orphan sounds of which it is not immediately obvious *of what* they are noises: as *symptoms*. At the same time, when there is no more obvious criterion to apply, in some sense, reality itself is at stake. The question becomes: *is it real?* Have I *really* heard anything?

Now, a striking aspect of the matter, according to Cavell, is that, when it is impossible for me to make sense of the existence of something, I may always be tempted to think that it depends on me: that this noise is a mere internal noise. That is the constitutive ambiguity of noise. Because, at the same time, noise is essentially aggressive: it is some kind of break-in of exteriority, and still, when it is not known to be the effect of any material thing, the sound itself always raises the suspicion that it may be something merely internal.

In fact, this is precisely the way in which Cavell rewrites Thoreau's story about the cock crow in the wonderful chapter on sounds in *Walden*. The case is even more striking, because, strangely enough—or maybe significantly enough—Cavell doesn't pay much attention to this pivotal chapter in his beautiful commentary on the book in *The Senses of Walden*. In fact, Cavell wants to retain only the disappearance of "domestic sounds" in Thoreau's surroundings, which he sees as a symptom of Thoreau's turning his back on the register of writing a "novel." Cavell interprets Thoreau's point about cock-crowing precisely along these lines, but in order to do so, he twists it in some way. In Thoreau's description, the point is about the absence of cock-crowing at Walden Pond, and about the fact that, finally, he is not missing the dear presence of that sound, although it is of high value to him. The most striking and paradoxical aspect of the passage in *Walden* is Thoreau's fantasy of releasing a cock into the wild—in which case it may turn out to be the singing prince of the forest, that is, if it could itself become "natural": if such cocks "could be naturalized without being domesticated."[14] And yet nothing like that is needed. Thoreau is perfectly content with the natural sounds he is already surrounded by. He does not miss "the singing of the kettle" or "the sound of the cock-crowing." When, at the beginning of the paragraph, he writes: "I am not sure that I ever heard the sound of cock-crowing from my clearing," the meaning of the observation is unequivocal: as his clearing is far enough from villages and other human habitations, he is *not sure*—not sure—to have ever heard such sounds there.[15] As finally he appreciates this fact—this *absence* of a certain kind of sound—he decides he doesn't need to add it back. In fact, in this context, he does not need this sound anymore.

In *The Senses of Walden*, Cavell suspects in Thoreau an uncertainty about what he hears. The hermit *is not anymore sure* whether he hears a cock crowing—or not. "How can this observer and experimenter and accounter," Cavell asks,

> be unsure whether he ever heard the sound of a rooster from his clearing? Perhaps because the sound is so familiar and frequent to his ear, and at once so faint and so unmistakable, that he is not sure it is a sound heard, i.e., that it comes from outside. But then you may find yourself conjecturing whether one is quite sure one hears, or knows, the sound of one's own voice.[16]

Cavell elaborates Thoreau's text in the very same terms as he does the unfamiliarity of the noises (one thinks one hears) coming from a basement, which—in this picture of skepticism—might always turn out to arise out of the basement of consciousness.

One may experience a noise one does not manage to identify immediately, or a noise such that it does not make even sense to identify it—because it is a mere noise, product of a darkness that steals us *things*. One may as well hear the crowing of a cock that is not there, or that *there is not*. Cavell treats all those experiences in the same way and sees in them as many proofs of an uncertainty about one's voice. Is there really any external sound or is it not rather *my* voice that I hear? Or rather, precisely, my voice in so far as it is not a voice—that it does not manage to be one or is always also something else, someone else's? The noise that we cannot identify as the noise *of anything*, is bound to be confused with this haunting of a voice that does not manage to accept itself *as* a voice, or as one's own. This going beyond the subjective and the objective to which the experience of the mere, or orphan noise confronts us, is, according to Cavell, essentially connected to a crisis of subjectivity, a crisis which is the very condition of subjectivity itself. One must know how to lose oneself in order to find oneself, and the test of such losses and discoveries can always turn out to be an ordeal constitutive of the subject. Interestingly, this test takes on the shape of experiencing noise.

Indeed, how to describe Cavell's philosophy as a whole if not as a constant search to know *how to cope with noise?* What could be more normal for a musician indeed, as music can be described in a certain sense as *a way to control noise*: to restore a voice where there is none by accepting one way to play or another.[17] In a sense, Cavell's issue with modernism in music has to do with the presence—or eruption—of noise into it. From late Beethoven onwards there is noise in music, i.e.: what is not immediately recognized as music, because it is no longer defined by being based on a shared, pre-existing standard of listening, but is supposed to establish a new one.[18] The result is the impression of an estrangement of music, with which Cavell constantly struggles in his reflections on what he calls "music discomposed." Such music can no longer pass for an improvisation or in other words, be received as the mere expression of what is already recognized as a voice—a way to speak, musically. The listener has to find a way to recognize a voice in it, and it can in no way be taken for granted. It is working or not. In other words, music speaks or not. This seems to depend essentially on our willingness to let it speak. Cavell understands the problem of modernism in music in these terms.

The general problem of Cavell's philosophy—to pass from one silence to another—can thus be rewritten in the terms of a dialectic of voice and noise. At the beginning there are voices, the voices of others in relation to which the silence of philosophy indicates a kind of stalling, like an inability to recognize oneself in them. "Every word they say chagrins us," as Emerson says, a remark to which Cavell refers one more time when delivering a first kind of experience of "noise" at the beginning of "Silences Noises Voices."[19] When these voices are suspended, noise is heard, at which point, I can never completely exclude the possibility that I am just hearing my own voice— not as a voice, however, as it is mere noise. The problem is to regain the conditions of an *enunciation then*: to come to terms with the fact that by using words that, by definition, are taken from others, I can speak for myself. To "find one's voice," as they say. Finally, when I have taken responsibility, that is, accepted my capacity to use language as a *common* language and to express myself in it, we find silence in the sense that what is uttered is no longer mere "noise" but meaningful utterance, and this in such a way that the noise it makes is not anymore to be heard *as* noise. The noises in the basement of consciousness were just the other side of inexpressiveness.

When inexpressiveness is overcome, there is no longer noise, but *a speaking voice* that is capable of entering into an interlocutory relation.

Now, the question that should be asked is whether this philosophy, which is essentially *a philosophy of expression*, governed by the dramaturgy of expressivity versus inexpressiveness, has not bracketed out too fast one dimension of our "experience"—and in fact, of being. Cavell reminds us in a very Kantian way how the metaphysical need and requirement is irremissible: "It is *imperative* that our experience of the world *make sense*, that loose threads get taken up by some explanation or other."[20] Thus, "there aren't *just* hummings in the air; it is *imperative* that I find out whether there happens to be one in the air now or whether it is only in my ears."[21] And yet, *why should we make sense of everything?* Why should living be a business, to paraphrase the words of a famous Italian writer (*Il mestiere di vivere*)? Isn't there a relaxation in existence—the other side of tragedy—where it is appropriate to *let it ring*? The question, of course, involves one of the *limits* of responsibility. Why is Cavell obsessed with voices? Because *we are*—and it is a part of what our existence is about. However, it is just a *part* of what our existence is about. And, anyway, why should our existence on the whole be about anything? I mean: nothing like aboutness can be found in other very important parts of our existence—and also as something that we should want to miss. Such a situation is just *what we have to live with*. In this sense, we should ask: why doesn't Cavell want Thoreau to be happy with his *nondomestic* sounds? Why should he invent a dramaturgy of a hallucinated cock-crowing into a story of quietness—a story about the fact that finally Thoreau *does not miss* the cock-crowing that he loves so much and just *does not care* anymore about it in this context? In fact, the author of *Walden* does not care because he has *other* sounds to listen to.

Sounds are not noises because we do not mind them. However, they are not necessarily different in nature. The point is just to learn to live with them—things that, at last, have very little to do with language. Between my own silence—as my incapacity and/or unwillingness to make common words mine and the silence of speech in which no inarticulate noise is left over—if anything like that even exists—there is not only the unbearable inexpressiveness of those *noises* that echo in our desperate need for expressivity, but there is also the mere enjoyment of what is *not* expression: the *sounds of silence* as such.[22] To the silence of *expression*—as that which is no longer noise, and has so to speak, reduced the noise in itself—we may contrast that other kind of silence regained by *silencing* expression as such, taking a break from it. In this wordless silence, noises may be heard but they are to be heard as sounds. Some sounds may even themselves be the essential condition for opening up that dimension of experience. In an interview with Tony Schwartz, Paul Simon tells us how he wrote "The Sound of Silence": "I used to go off in the bathroom, because the bathroom had tiles, so it was a slight echo chamber. I'd turn on the faucet so that water would run (I like that sound, it's very soothing to me) and I'd play."[23]

Notes

1   Stanley Cavell, "Silences Noises Voices," in *Here and There: Sites of Philosophy*, ed. Nancy Bauer, Alice Crary, and Sandra Laugier (Cambridge, MA: Harvard University Press, 2022), 114.

2   Ibid., 113.

3   See what Cavell calls "traditional epistemology" in *The Claim of Reason*, in particular ch. vi. Stanley Cavell, *The Claim of Reason: Wittgenstein, Skepticism, Morality, and Tragedy* (Oxford: Oxford University Press, 1979).

4   Cavell, "Silences Noises Voices," 113.

5   Ibid.

6   Ibid., 112.

7   Cavell, *The Claim of Reason*, 60; italics in original.

8   J. L. Austin, *Philosophical Papers*, ed. J. O. Urmson and G. J. Warnock (Oxford: Oxford University Press, 1961), 98.

9   J. L. Austin, *Sense and Sensibilia*, reconstructed from the manuscript notes by G. J. Warnock (Oxford: Oxford University Press, 1962), 68.

10 Austin, *Philosophical Papers*, 88.

11 Cavell, *The Claim of Reason*, 61.

12 Ludwig Wittgenstein, *Nachlaß*, The Bergen Electronic Edition (Charlottesville: InteLex Corporation, 2003), MS 214 b 10.

13 Wittgenstein, *Nachlaß*, MS 178 b 8.

14 Henry David Thoreau, *Walden, or Life in the Woods* (New York: Library of America, 1991), 103.

15 Ibid.

16 Stanley Cavell, *The Senses of Walden* (Chicago: University of Chicago Press, 1992), 38.

17 This is in fact at the same time a very classical take on what music is; in this sense, according to Cavell, jazz is "classical"—and a very *particular* take. And yet, why should music be or have a *voice*—or anything *like* a voice? Some music certainly has a voice—for instance, the part of Beethoven that Cavell likes, which contrasts to the part from which he recoils, or at least to which he has trouble adjusting. To be sure, music can be many things, and depending on how it is made, heard, and listened to, *sound* as such matters in it more or less. In this Cavellian context, Giacinto Scelsi's tenet that "music is made out of sounds" is anything but obvious. At least, Scelsi's view sets the standard for a specific musical poetics that Cavell's anthropocentric view cannot countenance. On this alternative poetics, see ch. IX of my *L'Adresse du réel* (Paris: Vrin, 2017), "La nature poétique du sensible."

18 See late Beethoven as a turning point in "Music Discomposed," in *Must We Mean What We Say?: A Book of Essays*, updated ed. (Cambridge: Cambridge University Press, 2002), 186.

19 Ralph Waldo Emerson, *Essays and Lectures* (New York: Literary Classics of the United States, 1983), 264; Cavell, "Silences Noises Voices," *Here and There*, 112.

20 Cavell, *The Claim of Reason*; first italics added; second italics in original.

21 Ibid., 60; italics in original.

22 The *unartikulierter Laut* in Wittgenstein's *Philosophical Investigations* (§261).

23 Paul Simon, "Love, Hate, and Art Garfunkel," *Playboy*, February 1984.

MOVEMENT III

Recitatives

7

Something Called Perfect Pitch

Cavell and the Calling of
Ordinary Language to Mind

PAUL STANDISH

HOW DOES ORDINARY LANGUAGE PHILOSOPHY relate to perfect pitch? This is a question that arises, in fleeting but telling ways, in Stanley Cavell's extended reflections on what constitutes the ability to follow and produce Austinian examples of ordinary language. In turn, it raises still further questions that are themselves of no little significance regarding moral (or Emersonian) perfectionism, which occupies such a prominent position in Cavell's later work.

In the wake of *The Claim of Reason* (1979), the theme of moral perfectionism becomes more fully articulated. Cavell's return to Emerson is a revisiting of texts first encountered in high school and of ideas elaborated in the summer of 1971, when Cavell wrote his "little book" on Thoreau, *The Senses of Walden* (1972).[1] The consigning of the works of those authors to a strictly *literary* heritage was, as Cavell has been at pains to show, a characteristic form of America's repression of its own best cultural—in this case, *philosophical*—achievements.[2] With the publication of *A Pitch of Philosophy* (1994), perfectionism becomes linked expressly with the theme of autobiography, a literary form upon which repression inevitably encroaches. In that book, Cavell makes the connection to his mother's giftedness as a musician and to her perfect pitch. From here there unfold, naturally enough, further connections with the significance of the ear, in music and in ordinary language philosophy.

Perfectionism is not perfectibility.[3] Perfectibility, specified by some abstract ideal and dependent on a substantive conception of human nature, would be the notion that with appropriate social engineering perfection can be realized by humans, here on earth, in the span of a given life. The burden of *perfectionism*, by contrast, is precisely the imperfect nature of forms of human settlement, which brings with it the realization that America, for instance, has not yet been discovered and (true) democracy is still to come. Unlike conceptions of ethics that compartmentalize human experience, perfectionism takes the human condition to be forever open to criticism and, thence, to possibilities of betterment. Not to see this fundamental attribute of perfectionism would be tantamount to hubris and complacency. Cavell's coining of the phrase "Emersonian moral perfectionism" brings together several strands of an outlook he finds in Emerson; in Cavell's understanding, its instances span great literature and perennial philosophy as well those Hollywood "talkies" of the 1930s and 1940s in which the possibilities of conversation are characteristically pushed to the fore. Emerson's perfectionism exemplifies, then, the criticism of democracy from within. *Conditions Handsome and Unhandsome* provides a gloss on what Cavell has in mind:

[A]n outlook or dimension of thought embodied and developed in a set of texts spanning the range of Western culture, a conception that is odd in linking texts that may otherwise not be thought of together and open in two directions: as to whether a text belongs to the set and what feature or features in the text constitute its belonging.[4]

The list of "candidate features" that then follow are indicative and open-ended, not definitive. Morality is not the subject of a separate philosophical field of study, set apart from the imagination of the good city, for to conceive it thus would be to acquiesce to a kind of moralism. It is of the utmost significance also that such perfection is held to exist in an intimate relation with writing, specifically with a conception of writing committed to:

[T]he achieving of an expression public enough to show its disdain for, its refusal to participate fully in, the shameful state of current society, or rather to participate by showing society its shame, and at the same time the achieving of a promise of expression that can attract the good stranger to enter the precincts of its city of words.[5]

The writing of philosophical prose then comes into competition with poetry such that it claims for itself "the privilege of the work poetry does in making things happen to the soul."[6]

These are powerful thoughts. My particular issue is with how they connect with music and especially with the faculty of perfect pitch.[7] Good fortune has it that Martin Gustafsson's thoughtful discussion in "Perfect Pitch and Austinian Examples: Cavell, McDowell, Wittgenstein, and the Philosophical Significance of Ordinary Language"[8] provides an appropriate staging-post for thoughts I want to pursue further. Gustafsson's paper begins in resplendent fashion with a substantial quote from *A Pitch for Philosophy*, the first part of which runs:

> It was familiarly said that the point of Austin's stories, those examples apart from which ordinary language philosophy has no method, required what you might call "ear" to comprehend (as in, more or less at random, setting out the difference between doing something by mistake or by accident, or between doing something willingly or voluntarily, carelessly or heedlessly, or between doing something in saying something or by saying something, or between telling a bird by its call or from its call).[9]

The tentativeness of Cavell's "what you might call 'ear'" points to the difficulty of specifying whatever it is that grounds ordinary language philosophy, and it is towards this important matter that Gustafsson's discussion gravitates.[10] The paper progresses with some assurance to the Wittgensteinian insight, shared by Cavell and John McDowell, into that very human desire for "a kind of practice where justification comes to an end, not just at a different place, but, as it were, at an absolutely stable place. But now, it is becoming increasingly clear that the idea of such an 'absolutely stable' foundation is an illusion."[11] It does this via a thought experiment, the prompt for which can be found in "Philosophy and the Arrogation of Voice":

> My mother had something called perfect pitch, as did one of her brothers. That I did not was a source of anguished perplexity to me, one of the reasons I would eventually give myself for withdrawing from music, particularly after I found that the only role I conceived for myself in music was as a composer. Yet I felt there must be something I was meant to do that required an equivalent of the enigmatic faculty of perfect pitch. Being good at following and producing Austinian examples will strike me as some attestation of this prophecy.[12]

Gustafsson recalls his own experience when, at the age of fourteen and attending a music theory class, the idea of perfect pitch came home to him, leaving him bewildered. The thought experiment envisions a world in which everyone has perfect pitch (and subsequently one in which no one does), and he ponders the significance of these inverted options for thinking about the kind of evidence and experience upon which ordinary language philosophy relies. His discussion is intriguing and thought provoking, but the eloquent elaboration of what it is to "have an ear" in ordinary language philosophy ends up occluding the early focus on perfect pitch, the subject of which is pivotal for my own discussion here.

Identifying Perfect Pitch, Naming Notes

"Perfect pitch," or "absolute pitch," typically refers to a person's ability to identify any musical note by name after hearing it, or to sing a given note when it is named, without reference to other notes. The faculty is quite rare, being found in about one in ten thousand of the population, and with an occurrence of 4 percent in music students. Though there is reason to think that it can be acquired, especially in early childhood, it is generally regarded as innate. Given the extraordinary quality of memory it seems to involve, it is not surprising that there is some correlation with autism; the trait appears to be something more specific and other than having (merely) a good ear for music, the robust sense of relative pitch that enables someone to sing perfectly in tune with others, to sing F# to a given C, and so on.

Musical ability in Western music depends upon having an appropriate sense of the relationship between pitches and, from there, what constitutes harmony. To say "sense" here implies the hearing of the relationship as concordant, discordant, as colored in a major or a minor key, and the like; this capacity to differentiate does not require that the instruments be correctly adjusted to standards of absolute pitch. Two further factors warrant consideration. First, a piece may be played in "the wrong key," yet one in which those relationships still persist. An accomplished musician may well notice this difference, most probably through familiarity with the characteristics of, say, G major and C major—at minimum, recognizing that the tune is likely to come in at a much higher pitch in the former than in the latter case? Perfect pitch is not needed for this "coloring" of the different key signatures to be recognized. Second, atmospheric conditions may affect the pitch at which instruments play, a fact to which those without perfect pitch easily adjust; moreover, it is a common practice for a soloist, in a violin concerto, for example, to play fractionally "bright" in order to stand out from the orchestra. These factors show that having perfect pitch is not an unequivocal advantage for a musician and that it may even prove to be a problem.

That perfect pitch is typically identified in relation to the ability to *name* a particular note certainly warrants attention. Such a trait is especially apparent when someone can immediately recognize the key of a given piece of music or can sing a B$^\flat$ on demand. The nature of this ability— extraordinary to those who do not have it, not to those who do—can seem like an attunement to the fundamental physics of the world, to the Music of the Spheres. But naming depends upon there being sound frequencies that have been nominated within a regular system. Developments in technology have made it possible to reproduce those sounds reliably with, for example, tuning-forks. Along similar lines, innovations in musical instrument-making have made it possible to create instruments with pitch that cannot be readily altered. Unlike a guitar or a trumpet, a piano or a pipe organ needs expert technical tuning, and this is not of a kind that can be carried out during a performance. In musical traditions that rely on instruments, including the human voice, where variations in pitch can be tolerated easily, there need be no precise consistency in the pitch at which, on different occasions, a piece is played. In the large symphony orchestra that developed in the nineteenth century, by contrast, there is an imperative to adhere to standard pitch (where the A above Middle C is 440 Hz). It is to this frequency that the piano in the orchestra will have been tuned ahead of a given performance.

Let us imagine a performance of Franz Schubert's Trout Quintet (*Forellenquintett*, A major, D. 667). As it turns out, the piano has not been correctly tuned and is, in fact, playing nearly a quarter tone lower than it should. It is quite possible that the players of the stringed instruments (violin, viola, cello, double-bass), all of whom have very good relative pitch but not perfect pitch, will adjust painlessly to the pitch set by the piano, perhaps not even realizing that the piano is playing flat. To anyone who happens to have perfect pitch, however, the music will sound all wrong.

Many musical traditions have not depended on this standard regulation of pitch, and there has been no expectation that the repetition of a piece should be at exactly the same pitch as when first created or first performed. So what would be the position of a person with perfect pitch native to a society of that kind? Presumably she would have quite different expectations for the expressions of sound. When she became familiar with a folk song, she would realize that it sounded different with each iteration; to some extent this would just be an extension of the variation in performance of all music, except perhaps the most highly scripted (say, computer-generated music, where the very idea of performance is put into question). Provided there was consistency in the piece (in the tonal relationships in melody and harmony), she would still think of it as the same piece and not have reason to object to this variation; she would perhaps be at a loss as to why others did not notice this difference. If a musically educated outsider with perfect pitch from a society where standard pitch was the norm came onto this scene and heard these same iterations of the song, she would have a similar awareness of the variations in pitch from performance to performance but notice that while one performance was clearly in D major, another was in B♭ major, and another—probably to her discomfort—somewhere between E♭ and E major. In fact most performances would probably not settle into the familiar key signatures. As far as the locals were concerned, the relative attunement of the voices would be all that mattered. To the extent that this is a correct portrayal of such matters, it starts to seem that the musically educated person with perfect pitch from the society where standard pitch is dominant (viz., in which A is 440 Hz) has been disciplined by an authority that is culturally specific and in some degree arbitrary.[13]

Relatedly, it is worth noting that children who are musically educated from an early age in cultures with tonal languages are more likely to have, or to develop the faculty of, perfect pitch than those speaking non-tonal languages. In some respects the deep connections between music and education that such considerations imply is not surprising. In Plato's *Republic*, that children become familiar with music is considered an important part of the education of their character: "[R]hythm and harmony permeate the inner part of the soul more than anything else, affecting it most strongly and bringing it grace, so that if someone is properly educated in music and poetry, it makes him graceful, but if not, then the opposite."[14] The learner will "receive them into his soul, and, being nurtured by them, become fine and good." Of course, no reference is made here to perfect pitch, but Plato's account resonates with what will become later responses to the phenomenon.

When thinking of Plato's concern with the formation of character, consider F. R. Leavis' description of an incident when Wittgenstein called unexpectedly at his house in Cambridge. Wittgenstein had apparently been looking for someone else. Not having had success locating the person he sought, but finding himself in front of the Leavis' house, he decided to knock on their door, to bide his time there before looking again. Upon entering the house, he immediately peered out through the window, onto the street. Yet after a moment, he turned and said abruptly: "You've got a gramophone, I see—I don't suppose you've anything worth playing." And "then," so Leavis continues the description:

with a marked change of tone, he exclaimed "Ah": from the repository just at hand he pulled out the album of Schubert's Great C Major Symphony and put the first record on the machine. A moment after the music began to sound he lifted the tone-arm, altered the speed, and lowered the needle on to the record again. He did this several times until he was satisfied.

What was characteristic about the performance (Wittgenstein's) was not merely the aplomb with which he ignored our—my wife's and my— apprehensive presence, but the delicate precision with which he performed the manoeuvre. He was, in fact, truly and finely cultivated, and, as part of his obvious cultivation, very musical, and, having absolute pitch, had judged and acted instantaneously on hearing the opening bars.[15]

Leavis' careful, rather beautiful description of what Wittgenstein did, and his seeing in this behavior a reflection of the qualities of someone truly and finely cultivated, are linked with a kind of admiration for Wittgenstein's having judged and acted instantaneously. In the "single-minded coolness" of "I don't suppose you've anything worth playing," Leavis found a "disinterested regardlessness" and an "innocent egotism."[16] In such a moment, while looking back at the lines in Plato's discourse, we are meant to judge something significant about Wittgenstein's education and, by extension, his character.

The Leavis passage is worth reading also alongside Cavell's elaboration of his comment on his mother's perfect pitch in his broader celebration of what he saw as her natural talent. "In my rapidly increasing sophistication," he writes:

what genuinely surprised me was to realize, acquiring means to measure it, how extraordinary a musician my mother was. My new acquaintances were educated [...]; but none could reach past what I still think of as my mother's natural talent [...], a talent gaudily attested in the assured fire with which she played.[17]

Cavell's parenthetical comments, which I have omitted, attest to both the range of her repertoire and her taste. The elaboration goes further, however, when Cavell recalls her "legendary" and "uncanny" ability to sight-read. "I am talking," he writes:

about my image of this [sight] reading, my interpretation of this woman's ability to bring to life whatever notes were put before her. It was precisely not to my mind a knack of interpretation, but something like the contrary, a capacity to put aside any interference, as of her own will, and to let the body be moved, unmechanically, by the mind of those racing notes. The lapse of distance—say that she was the music then and there; there was nothing beyond her to read into—is captured in my mind by an image of a certain mood that caused her to play the piano for herself.[18]

There is surely some resonance between the qualities Cavell highlights here, the attunement of character to the music, and those observed by Leavis in Wittgenstein—the fine cultivation, the lack of any gap between judgment and action, the unmechanical, unmediated response to the music itself. Again, Plato's ancient model appears to receive illustrations from these more contemporary scenes of music playing, and the qualities of the people doing the playing (in the case of Fannie Segal, Cavell's mother), or listening (in Wittgenstein's scene at the Leavis').

The almost explicit implication, by Leavis and Cavell, of a connection between perfect pitch and these qualities of character is compelling, and yet it is difficult to fathom. The former is subject to precise measurement, the latter is not. So is there not a sense here of the willful projection of the phrase—defiantly pitching it, as it were, into further contexts of use, and in the process implying that perfect pitch in the conventional sense would be of less interest if it did not connect with musical practices that, by their very nature, extend aesthetically beyond anything that could be simply measured? Cavell's reference to his mother as having "something called" perfect pitch suggests a degree of caution around the term, but it can also create a kind of aura around the idea, as of something one seeks that is difficult to understand. (Recall the title of Cavell's essay "Something Out of the Ordinary," which registers the subdued power in one Fred Astaire's dance sequences in *The Band Wagon*.[19]) But this specification still scarcely lays the way for the elaboration that ensues, since it is not obvious that the faculty of perfect pitch has *any relation* to the capacity to sight-read. And it is surely ironic that the instrument his mother played, the piano, is one for which the pitch of the notes *cannot* be altered by the player.

Then there are Cavell's recollections of moments of perfection, or what he calls "an equivalent of perfect pitch,"[20] in the teaching of Ernest Bloch:

[H]e would cover both long walls of staved-lined blackboards with different dispositions of a C-major triad to warn against believing in simple or academic definitions of harmonic correctness [...] or he would interrupt himself to read an excerpt from Plato, or from Confucius.

He would play [...] a Bach four-part chorale, with one note altered by a half step from Bach's rendering; then he would play the Bach unaltered. Perhaps he would turn to us, fix us with a stare, then turn back to the piano and repeat, as if for himself, the two versions. [...] "You hear that? You hear the difference?" [...] "My version is perfectly correct; but the Bach, the Bach is perfect; late sunlight burning the edges of a cloud. Of course I do not say you must hear this. Not at all. No. But."[21]

After the classes, Cavell would walk alone in the hills for an hour, finding almost that he could not breathe.

The remarkable nature of perfect pitch is typically seen against the kind of background I have sketched above: an exceptional psychological phenomenon, on a par with other manifestations of autism, becomes aligned with a remarkable list of musical talents—Beethoven, Pierre Boulez, Bing Crosby, Ella Fitzgerald, Glenn Gould, Fannie Segal, and in a sense Wittgenstein. But bringing together the psychological phenomenon with these examples of musical excellence seems to threaten the distinction between perfectibility and perfectionism. It should also occasion puzzlement about the aligning of the idea of perfect pitch with having an ear for the kinds of examples that Austin addresses—that is, with the very basis of ordinary language philosophy. This is my principal concern.

Having said something about "something," however, and about what and how it is "called," I want to pause, for the space of a paragraph, in order to lay the way for pursuing further this principal concern. Let me unpack the burden of the phrasing in my subtitle—"the calling of ordinary language to mind." Something that came to my mind, as I was reflecting on these matters, was the title of Emmanuel Levinas' *De Dieu Qui Vient à l'Idée* in its inspired translation by Bettina Bergo: *Of God Who Comes to Mind.*[22] Equivocating between "to mind" as noun-phrase and as verb reveals at once the way the thought of God crosses my mind, and the fact that God thereby comes into my mind, which in turn suggests that God becomes part of or a quality of (my) mind, and further, attending now to the verb, the way he comes with the purpose of minding or looking after me, and minding what I do! My appropriation replaces "God" with the "calling of ordinary language," retaining a trace of the idea of a religious calling but supplying a double-genitive form that again multiplies the implications. We call upon ordinary language (as grammatical object), as we search for and produce Austinian examples. Ordinary language (as grammatical subject) calls to us when we are persuaded, as by Wittgenstein, to turn away from the *philosopher's* language: we are released from bewitchment, clouds of metaphysics condensing in drops of grammar;[23] and a new realism, middle-voiced, comes into the mind, ordinary language re-minding us. As if this were not already enough, a proper recollection of the ordinary calls us to mind about things, to care about them. The ordinary is a matter of what matters, of the ethical as going all the way down. Such a point is surely recessive in Austin; it was a certain tone-deafness that enabled Oxford philosophers to think he was talking exclusively about the logic of ordinary language and not about human life as a whole—a far grander project than Austin wanted to declare. But implications of such kinds become more explicit in Cavell and, for example, in Sandra Laugier's ambitions for a care ethics that would "re-center moral philosophy on ordinary language and expressiveness."[24] In my view, such a grammatical investigation needs to be seen, in a fashion not far removed from Levinas, as descriptive of the very structuring of human relationships and of the phenomenology of the world. Thus, the grammar of "the calling of ordinary language to mind" illustrates the intimacy of the concepts of the human and the ordinary as Cavell understands them.

Cavell's Ear

At the age of six, Cavell was hit by a car, and as a result he suffered damage to his left ear. At the age of about sixteen, he lied about his age in order to enlist in the navy. Even so, he was turned down on medical grounds related to the damage to his ear. Some time in his sixties, as he was closing *A Pitch of Philosophy*, he asked himself:

Am I ready to vow, as when Bloch asked us whether we heard through to Bach, that I have the ear, that I know my mother's mother tongue of music to be also mine! The hills are different ones now, but the world is, I'm glad to say, the same when I have to catch my breath at such promises. Are they mine? Have I, throughout these pages, been asking anything else?[25]

Cavell has aligned his mother with perfect pitch. But while music may be *her* mother tongue, Cavell's father "had no natural language left." He did, however, have an unusual ability to tell stories and a capacity for conversation.[26] Cavell sees his own fascination with Austin as drawing, in some respects, with comparisons and contrasts, on each of his parents' separate but distinctive talents.

At one level this conjunction of influences seems plausible enough, and Cavell's autobiographical variations on the theme of perfect pitch are enthralling. But what is happening when the fundamental problem I have identified—the unyielding nature of perfect pitch—is forgotten or occluded? In language—at least in ordinary language philosophy—there is no space for such rigidity. Having an ear depends upon attunement to the conversation of others, not in the manner of a study in linguistics, of course, but on the strength of a continual attentiveness to what we do with words; and here, contra Plato, there is no equivalent of perfect pitch, no equivalent of "A is 440 Hz." Cavell surely wants to acknowledge that there are moments of perfection, moments in conversation where one finds a phrase that is apt, a chord progression that could not be surpassed, the realization of a promise in the city of words. But this is a different order of perfection. His investment in the idea of ordinary language philosophy is an affirmation of democracy, and here the point is amplified: political attunement will depend upon something *beyond* the natural. Thoreau's naming of "the father tongue" comes into the picture of what this might comprise, and suggests writing when one is out of breath. I am not suggesting that Cavell's father provided the father tongue to answer to this need: it is difficult to imagine that he would have had the ear to follow and produce Austinian examples. To the extent that Cavell gained his ear from his mother, it was implausible that it was from her having perfect pitch.

So is this a blind spot in Cavell? One he simply has not noticed? Something running too deep in the family drama to be articulated? Perhaps such features cannot be confronted head on, cannot be said but must be shown. As far as I can see, Cavell's excellent commentators and critics have not made anything of the matter that I am struggling with. Is Cavell's text reenacting the "despair of harmony"[27] he observes between his mother and his father? A pragmatist might recognize the problem and move on, with due consideration for those involved. For Cavell, more psychoanalytically invested, it will be necessary to preserve the tension. If this approach is right, such tension cannot simply be spelled out—not, that is, without a kind of repression. His ordinary language philosophy, born of "anguished bewilderment," existentially if not religiously inflected, is an "attestation" to the "prophecy" that there would be something "equivalent to the enigmatic of perfect pitch" that he was "meant to do."[28]

In an interview with Giovanna Borradori, published in 1994, the same year as *A Pitch of Philosophy*, Cavell remarks how "[s]kepticism as a search for the inhuman is a search for a means of the perfection of the ear, to the extent that the ear is no longer required to listen. It is the denial of having to hear."[29] Remarkable and rare though perfect pitch is, does it signify a faculty where justification comes to an end—an absolutely stable place? Remembering the attraction and the illusion of such a fixed point of orientation, remembering the philosophical seductiveness of (the Platonic or Socratic recollection of) true forms, remembering the all-too-human compulsions of perfectibility will be dimensions of recognition of the truth in skepticism. This, in the way I am pitching it, is what the pragmatist cannot, or will not, do.[30]

Notes

1 Stanley Cavell, *The Senses of Walden, an Expanded Edition* (Chicago: University of Chicago Press, 1981).

2 For a unified approach to Cavell's recovery of Emerson and his sense of Emerson and Thoreau's philosophical achievements, see his *Emerson's Transcendental Etudes*, ed. David Justin Hodge (Stanford: Stanford University Press, 2003).

3 For further discussion of perfectionism and perfectibility, see Paul Standish, "'Language must be raked': Experience, race, and the pressure of air," *Educational Philosophy and Theory*, vol. 50, no. 4 (2017): 428–40.

4 Stanley Cavell, *Conditions Handsome and Unhandsome: The Constitution of American Perfectionism* (Chicago: University of Chicago Press, 1990), 4.

5 Cavell, *Conditions Handsome and Unhandsome*, 7.

6 Ibid.

7 I made an earlier brief attempt to address these matters in Paul Standish, "A Pitch of Education. A response to Naoko Saito, 'Finding Perfect Pitch: Reading Perfectionist Narrative with Stanley Cavell,'" *Philosophy of Education 2009* (Urbana: Philosophy of Education Society, 2010).

8 Martin Gustafsson, "Perfect Pitch and Austinian Examples: Cavell, McDowell, Wittgenstein, and the Philosophical Significance of Ordinary Language," *Inquiry: An Interdisciplinary Journal of Philosophy*, vol. 48. no. 4 (2005): 356–89, https://doi.org/10.1080/00201750510022853.

9   Stanley Cavell, *A Pitch of Philosophy: Autobiographical Exercises* (Cambridge, MA: Harvard University Press, 1994), 21.

10   For more on Cavell's notion of "what you might call 'ear,'" see Andreas Teuber, "Cavell's Ear for Things," in *Inheriting Stanley Cavell: Memories, Dreams, Reflections*, ed. David LaRocca (New York: Bloomsbury, 2020), 199–206.

11   Gustafsson, "Perfect Pitch and Austinian Examples," 360.

12   Cavell, *A Pitch of Philosophy*, 21.

13   The notion of perfect pitch as it is commonly understood plays havoc with the idea of following a rule. Sometimes analogies are drawn with the perception of color, but their value lies primarily in showing how different these faculties are.

14   Plato, *The Republic*, in *Complete Works*, ed. John Cooper (Indianapolis: Hackett, 1967), 401d–402a.

15   F. R. Leavis, "Memories of Wittgenstein," in *Recollections of Wittgenstein*, ed. Rush Rhees (Oxford: Oxford University Press, 1973), 50–67; 58. For further discussion of this episode in relation to perfect pitch, see Paul Standish, "Absolute Pitch and Exquisite Rightness of Tone," *Philosophy and Literature*, vol. 40, no. 1 (2016): 226–39.

16   Leavis, "Memories of Wittgenstein," *Recollections of Wittgenstein*, 58–9.

17   Cavell, *A Pitch of Philosophy*, 17–18.

18   Ibid., 18.

19   Stanley Cavell, "Something Out of the Ordinary," in *Philosophy the Day after Tomorrow* (Cambridge, MA: Harvard University Press, 2005), 7–27.

20   Cavell, *A Pitch of Philosophy*, 48.

21   Ibid., 48–50.

22   Emmanuel Levinas, *De Dieu Qui Vient a l'Idée* (Paris: Vrin, 1986); *Of God Who Comes to Mind*, trans. Bettina Bergo (Stanford: Stanford University Press, 1998).

23   Cf. "(A whole cloud of philosophy condenses into a drop of grammar.)" Ludwig Wittgenstein, "Philosophy of Psychology—A Fragment," §315, in *Philosophical Investigations*, trans. G. E. M. Anscombe, P. M. S. Hacker, and Joachim Schulte; revised 4th ed. by P. M. S. Hacker and Joachim Schulte (Oxford: Wiley-Blackwell, 2009).

24   Sandra Laugier, "The Ethics of Care as a Politics of the Ordinary," *New Literary History*, vol. 46, no. 2 (Spring 2015): 217–40, 218.

25   Ibid., 169.

26   For a related discussion, see Paul Standish, "The Philosophy of Pawnbroking," in *Stanley Cavell and Philosophy as Translation: The Truth is Translated*, ed. Paul Standish and Naoko Saito (London: Rowman & Littlefield, 2017), 171–82.

27   Cavell, *A Pitch of Philosophy*, 21.

28   Ibid.

29   "Apology for Skepticism," an interview with Giovanna Borradori, in *The American Philosopher*, trans. Rosanna Crocitto (Chicago: University of Chicago Press, 1994), 133–4.

30   I would like to thank Gordon Bearn for helpful comments in an early discussion on this topic and both Suzy Harris and David LaRocca for helpful comments on drafts of this chapter.

8

Understanding Music, Understanding Persons

Cavell and the Necessity of Intentional Content

GARRY L. HAGBERG

THE AESTHETIC DOCTRINE, THE CRITICAL APPROACH, of New Criticism was in full swing when Stanley Cavell first presented his now-classic paper "Music Discomposed"[1] in 1965, first published it in 1967, and then included it in his collection *Must We Mean What We Say?* in 1969. New Criticism was greeted, especially by the literary community but also throughout the humanities and the arts, as an interpretive credo offering (1) a new and sharper focus in aesthetic perception, (2) an intellectually hygienic methodology, (3) a criterion for determining what is, and what is not, interpretively relevant, and more generally as a result of these three, (4) a prescriptive procedure for rightly engaging with a work of art.

Regarding the idea of a new and sharper focus: this was intrinsically attractive because it introduced an ocular metaphor that at once promises a clearer vision (or in the case of non-visual art such as literature and music, "vision") of any aesthetic object. And it can suggest an increase in magnification—indeed like a higher power-setting on a microscope—that would allow the perception of subtle features not previously discernible. Regarding the idea of a hygienic methodology, New Criticism promised to separate the "noise" from the "signal," removing the veils of cognitive content—biographical, artist-circumstantial, social-contextual, and so forth—that would intrude on the mind of the perceiver. And so, regarding the idea of determining, *in advance,* what is and is not relevant to the appreciation and understanding of a work of literature or art, New Criticism was reductive by means of exclusion: what was left after such exclusions was then identified in a new phrase: the work itself. The promise (if, as we shall shortly see, a false promise in Cavell's view) was of purification; in this sense, each work contains its own essence, to be revealed through a process of cognitive-perceptual veil-removal. With those thoughts in place, New Criticism then reduced, or at least encapsulated, its own position to its essence in a prescriptive slogan: artistic intention is irrelevant (where that intentional content can include biographical and circumstantial, and broad cultural content as the mind of the artist incorporates them.)

Cavell wrote: "I cannot accept such a resolution, for three main sorts of reasons."[2] His first reason is the initially counterintuitive but actually clarifying point that a focus on formal properties does not in and of itself imply the exclusion of intentional content, his example being Kant's formal approach that still includes intentional content (or purposiveness, as Kant calls it). What Cavell sees here, I take it, is that formal properties, and here more importantly relational properties internal to the work, may emerge only when we recognize that those relations were intended to be perceived a certain way. I would offer here the example of Mozart's *Six Quartets Dedicated to Haydn,* where we only hear the structural content of those works by simultaneously imaginatively "hearing" within them the Haydnesque character of both the melodies and the harmonizations. Then beyond that, when we hear Mozart developing (harmonically and rhythmically) the pieces here beyond what Haydn did or could have done, we hear how the formal interrelations of the parts use Haydn as in this sense a launching pad.

Consider then Cavell's second reason (which warrants quoting at length because it captures so well what is fundamental to what I will discuss below):

The denial of the relevance of the artist's intention is likely not to record the simple, fundamental fact that what an artist meant cannot alter what he has or has not accomplished, but to imply a philosophical *theory* according to which the artist's intention is something in his mind while the work of art is something out of his mind, and so the closest connection there could be between them is one of causation, about which, to be sure, only a psychologist or biographer could care. But I am far less sure that any such philosophical theory is correct than I am that when I experience a work of art I feel that I am *meant* to notice one thing and not another, that the placement of a note or rhyme or line has a *purpose.*[3]

Here I would offer the example of Béla Bartók's (1881–1945) phenomenally intelligent integration of folk themes. Because those themes, as they lived and circulated in cultural practices both outside Bartók's composition and outside his classical compositional world, were external to the work itself (as we shall see below, whatever that is), their origin would be excluded from the hygienic formal New Critical mind. But those melodies, with those origins, can only be understood, only heard for what they are within Bartók's works, as transfigurations of musical content. The fact that we are intended, we are *meant*, to hear that transfigurative inclusion is, as Cavell is suggesting, something we are surer of than we are of any theory designed to purify, to reduce to essence. It would be as if we claimed that the knowledge of what a butterfly is can be whole and complete without any knowledge of the caterpillar and the cocoon. Part of our perception of the great beauty of the butterfly includes imaginatively present knowledge of where it came from (in a way visually or perceptually external to what we are presently perceiving). And then, as Cavell is also suggesting, we know in many works that we are meant to perceive relations between parts, relations that are constitutive of the meaning of the piece. Strong examples are plentiful, but particularly striking ones present themselves within the late quartets of Beethoven. The quartets, initially often derided as senseless cacophony, revealed their profound sense in exact correspondence with the gradually increasing perception of the contrapuntal structural–formal relations between melodic phrases. One, indeed, *makes sense* of those great works of art as one recognizes those internal relations and thus comes to hear those interweaving lines as they were intended to be heard, intended to be understood. One does not, and in these cases, cannot hear strictly one thing at once and still discern the sense within the work. Again, as Cavell is directing us to consider, one is much surer of this fact than of any theory designed to purify the perception of a musical work. And of course: following out what Beethoven intended here yields genuine (if initially demanding) musical experience and deep musical understanding; following out the desiderata of a theory, in this case of intentional exclusion, yields perceptual impoverishment. But another message from Cavell emerges here as his third reason:

"Why does Beethoven put a bar of rest in the last line of the fourth Bagatelle (Op. 126)?" The best critic is the one who knows best where to ask this question, and how to get an answer; but surely he doesn't feel it necessary, or desirable even were it possible, to get in touch with the artist to find out the answer.[4]

This connects directly to what I meant just above by the activity, the active work, of making sense of musical works. Now, we might need to ask John Cage what he meant by *4:33*; because of the extremely minimal content of such works, we may feel a need to consult the mind of the artist to discover meaning. But many, most, almost all works of music are not anything like that (and it is, I believe, because of this special need that such works are often held in aesthetic suspicion—they are not created in such a way that they speak for themselves). Rather, with Cavell implicitly refining the model of what artistic intention is and how artistic intention is conveyed, we consult not intentional content within the mind of the composer, but intentional content as discernible within the work—where the phrase "the work" does not mean the reduced work of hardline formalism. The best critic, he is claiming, is the one who simultaneously knows where precisely to place the question and how and where to look into the work to answer it. It proved too easy for the New Critics to reduce the concept of intention itself—reducing it to a mental object in the mind of the artist that prefigured what we will then see as that mental object's material manifestation in text, image, or sound. With this simplified dualistic schema in place separating mind from matter, drawn in accordance with the classical metaphysical distinction, it was then for them a conceptually straightforward matter to construct a theory based on the exclusion of the former with what they then thought was a clarifying focus on the latter. Cavell was among the first to see the drastic oversimplification of the concept of intention that was involved in this methodological initiative, and, having read Wittgenstein's remarks on intention, Cavell understood that intention is not ontologically the kind of thing that acknowledges and behaves in strict accordance with the classical dualistic template. Intention, as he is saying here, can be discerned in the work, very often without which we cannot answer good and well-placed critical and interpretive questions—or indeed, without which we cannot make sense of, cannot understand, the musical work. And although Cavell does not say this here, it is important to see that there is usually no single way to express, to bring out, that intentional content in one singly correct way; one cellist might emphasize one particular set of relations between contrapuntal lines in Bach's cello suites, while another cellist brings out others. The same is of course true of conductors; we are interested in differing and contrasting performers and performances for precisely this reason. This is parallel to differing ways of articulating the implied content of an utterance or literary passage; different interpretations will bring out and display relations within the work in ways distinctive to that reader, critic, or performer. And we understand that it is the performer's intention to do so and thus understand that performer's distinctive contribution to the performance history, to the ongoing elucidation of the ways of assembling and presenting the intentional content, of that work.

Cavell also sees how a new style can transform the way we see, or what we see in, the earlier style preceding it. This is a change that invites two streams of descriptions. Again Cavell:

And a new style not merely replaces an older one, it may change the significance of any earlier style; I do not think this is merely a matter of changing taste but a matter also of changing the *look*, as it were, of past art, changing the ways it can be described, outmoding some, bringing some to new light—one may even want to say, it can change what the past *is*, however against the grain that sounds. A generation or so ago, "Debussy" referred to music of a certain ethereal mood, satisfying a taste for refined sweetness or poignance; today it refers to solutions for avoiding tonality: I find I waver between thinking of that as a word altering its meaning and thinking of it as referring to an altered object.[5]

It was Arnold Schoenberg (1874–1951), who in one sense discovered, in another sense created, and in a synthesized sense evolved, a novel system of musical pitch-organization that was not internally determined by the rules of classical harmony, by the overtone series, by the fundamental stacking of thirds in the generation of diatonic chordal interrelations. And post-war serialism, after Alban Berg (1885–1935) and Anton Webern (1883–1945), developed that musical language intensively. That development, as Cavell is insisting, did change our conception of what Debussy did, much in the same way that Picasso changed the way we see Cézanne—as opening a door to cubism by representing features in the landscape and the built environment as geometrical volumetric masses. The way that the new style can cast the preceding in a new light can be like the verbal phenomenon of a speaker endorsing a paraphrase of what she or he said as a further elucidation or articulation of what was intended. But it can also be like this: the speaker's language carries implications that the speaker, at the time of speaking, did not explicitly realize, but later recognizes as a furtherance of significance that is now endorsed but that was not at the time of speaking foreseen. This complicates the picture of intention: it allows phrases such as "Yes, that development is consistent with what I intended, and it does capture one aspect, one line of significance that was indeed contained within my work, but I did not fully realize that at the time." Had Debussy lived into the age of post-war serialism, it would have been possible for him to have said such a thing. Or he might have said that, had he been presented with this line of significance stemming from his work, he would have strongly endorsed it (not as what he with full cognizance meant at the time, but as what his *work* meant—or (after Cavell on Debussy) could *now* mean given that the circumstances *around* his work had changed). So, what is later endorsed as intentional content need not have been cognized at the time of the original utterance, on the linguistic side, or at the time of the original composition, on the musical side. And of course, refusals of endorsement can function in the same way, expressed in sentences such as, "No, that is not at all what I meant." Here we begin to see the connections between understanding a person and understanding a work of music.

The two streams of description I mentioned just above are: (1) the name "Debussy" has had its meaning altered, and (2) the work of Debussy has been altered. Cavell wavers—but I would say for an interesting and instructive reason. One kind of philosophical sensibility will demand that we decide: it must at bottom be one or the other. Another kind of sensibility, perhaps aware of Wittgenstein's remarks in section xi of Part II of his *Philosophical Investigations*, might see this as a complex and irreducible phenomenon exhibiting two central aspects. The connotations and associations that are awakened by so much as hearing the name "Debussy" have altered; those connotations can now include elements including "one who initially pointed the way toward a breakthrough musical structure that was not dependent for its coherence on triadic harmony." But the power of this description—Cavell does not quite say this, but almost does—reaches into the work being heard: we now hear differently because we say differently. It is in this sense that Cavell spoke of an idea that goes against the grain: what he could have said is that it is of course impossible to change the past—but it is not impossible to change how we see, how we hear, how we understand, how we articulate the past (in the present). Those features of experience are not separate: a change in understanding possesses the power to change seeing or hearing; a change in description possesses the power to change understanding; and so forth. The New Critic's idea of "the work itself" becomes ever more opaque the more one tries to define it, since the work is, itself, evolving as our understanding of what it "is" evolves.

And so, what is within the thematic logic of the ideas assembled so far—what is contained within their range of implication? As Cavell put it:

I am in effect claiming that the answer to the question "What is art?" will in part be an answer which explains why it is we treat certain objects, or how we *can* treat certain objects, in ways normally reserved for treating persons.[6]

This idea opens two avenues. Obviously, it is an invitation to think our way into the parallels between the modes of perception—perhaps more accurately the modes of engagement—that we bring to persons and to works of art. But less obviously, it's a comparison that implicitly argues against the conception of the work of art that is at the core of the New Critical view— the conception of "the work itself." Under the influence of that theory, we may convince ourselves that the hygienic reduction is a clarifying step forward. But with the comparison in mind, where similarities between our parallel modes of engagement are surfacing, we can ask the question, What is "the person itself?" That is a disorienting question, because we know without argument that to strip away all of the knowledge of a person's personal history, the person's experiential background relevant to the present consideration at hand, the mode of speaking, of self-presentation, of interacting, of patterns of thoughtfulness, of kindness, of generosity, of aspirations, of desires—to lose all this (and of course much more) is to lose the conditions and the content of our knowledge of, our understanding of, that person. What could "the person itself" so much as mean? Our sense here is either that this phrase is incoherent word-salad nonsense, or that it names a stick figure, a robot, an entity so far reduced that we no longer can or would use the word "person," so that the conjunction of "itself" and "person" is a kind of oxymoron. And so traveling back across the parallel from persons to music, one feels the greater force of the question: what do we actually mean, what can we mean, by "the work itself"?

Cavell presents this thought, this question, in the context of discussing the possibility, the threat, of fraudulent art and music (with, again, his focus being on post-war, post-Webern serialism). Although Cavell does not discuss this matter in this way, the parallel between how we treat artworks and persons deepens in an interesting way here. Fraudulence in art and music, he observes, is not detectable in the way we detect forgeries or counterfeit money—that is, by comparing the forgery with the genuine article. The sense of fraudulence he is exploring has no genuine article, has no original as the standard of comparison. So he wrote, "The emphasis is not on copying a *particular* object, as in forgery and counterfeit, but on producing *the effect* of the genuine, or having some of its properties."[7] The fraudulent person is not a mime, not a stand-in, not a body double, not an exact twin posing. The fraudulent person desires to achieve an effect, to create a convincing impression of sincerity, of genuineness. We do not in such cases compare the fraudulent person against a genuine article. A misplaced phrase, a fleeting but odd facial expression, an unexplained avoidance, an over-eagerness to rephrase something said that might cause doubt, and countless other things in the interactions of human life that awaken suspicion are how we start a process of reconsideration. If, at the end of such a process, we learn that we have been used as a pawn in that person's game while living under that person's description of helpfulness and kindness, we know that a fraud stands before us, and that the intentional content is very different from what we trustingly took it to be. What we do not do is quickly apply a general criterion, a general litmus test, to such cases. And this is due to a simple fact: there is no such single criterion. Interweaving strands of our experience form a fabric within a particular circumstance or setting, a fabric in which we can see the genuine intentional content emerging from behind the veil. With the parallel between artworks and persons in mind, we can begin to see that there is no reason to expect the musical case to be any less complex. Stripped of everything in the musical case that stands parallel to the person case, how could we ever proceed in a parallel process of reconsideration? Listening reductively to—what is a musical work itself?—the sensory sonic experience, the sound alone, shorn of a surrounding world of cognitive and cultural content, would and could show us nothing, reveal nothing, about the sincerity or genuineness of the work. It would be as bereft an exercise as having a total stranger presented to us and, without a word, trying to assess the sincerity, the genuineness, the character, of the person. Cavell does not discuss these parts of the parallel, but I believe they are implicit within his work in this essay and bringing these considerations out helps to uncover why he regarded the promise of New Criticism as a false promise, and a promise that may initially sound good but that, given the deepening connection between the special way we treat persons and the special way we treat works of art, cannot be fulfilled. Cavell mentions the example of the sentence, "You don't really know what I mean when I say that [Artur] Schnabel's slow movements give the impression not of slowness but of infinite length."[8] That is the kind of perception that runs far beyond anything an exclusionary focus on "the music alone" (again as just sensory sonic experience) could capture, and it runs far beyond the anemic descriptions we could offer from that point of view (or a phrase we don't use, but should: point of listening.) Of course, the description of music is itself an expansive, intricate, analytically demanding, culturally enmeshed enterprise; it too resists reduction. Cavell thus wrote, "Describing one's experience of art is itself a form of art; the burden of describing it is like the burden of producing it."[9]

But there remains another, and perhaps still more informative observation about the nature, the character, of music and art that is implicit within this essay. Cavell asks, "Could someone be interested and become absorbed in a pin, or a crumpled handkerchief?"[10] Were such a situation to occur, Cavell observes that it would require or call for explanation in a way that, say, seeing someone listening in a deeply absorbed way to Mozart would not. The underlying point here is not traditionalist—it is not that new objects of aesthetic attention should be held in automatic suspicion. Rather, it is that we come, with our aesthetic attention, with a set of often unspoken but experientially embedded expectations concerning the kind of thing, the kind of object, we have before us. They must have, in the sense of intentional content discernible within the work as discussed above, the kind of content that we recognize as, through the parallel, human and of humanity. A pin, without a separate and superadded theory designed to add to the object something that it does not internally possess, will not have that. To suggest, in theory, that anything can be art, is I believe for Cavell (again, in his implicit message here) to conflate the artistic or musical parallel to saying that robots can be every bit as interesting as persons. And so here again, the parallel is instructive; it brings to the surface the necessity of intentional content. And not only that, since, as Cavell noted:

> But objects of art not merely interest and absorb, they move us; we are not merely involved with them, but concerned with them, and care about them; we treat them in special ways, invest them with a value which

normal people otherwise reserve only for other people—*and* with the same kind of scorn and outrage. They *mean* something to us, not just the way statements do, but the way people do.[11]

It is a challenge to speak of meaning without either explicitly speaking of or implicitly relying on the concept of intention (where, again, the answer to why Beethoven has a bar of rest at just this point in the music is found in the musical work itself, not in Beethoven's mind). It would be bizarre, actually beyond our comprehension, to imagine a person with a life devoted to pins (but not to the monetary profit derived from owning a manufacturing plant for pins, which is an entirely separate matter). However, "People devote their lives, sometimes sacrifice them, to producing such objects just in order that they will have such consequences; and we do not think they are mad for doing so."[12] The nature of the engagement is distinctive, and it connects to what Wittgenstein discussed as "an attitude towards a soul."[13] As if reflecting on the aesthetic significance of Wittgenstein's phrase, Cavell wrote:

We approach such objects not merely because they are interesting in themselves, but because they are felt as made by someone—and so we use such categories as intention, personal style, feeling, dishonesty, authority, inventiveness, profundity, meretriciousness, etc., in speaking of them.[14]

The work of music has to have what the robot does not: we can imagine a robot being programmed to reply to instructions with phrases such as "Am getting it now," "Coffee coming." "Will sweep floor now," and so forth. But never will we say to each other, "Is the robot alright? Did you hear how it said 'Am getting it now'? It seemed somehow crestfallen, somehow quietly saddened by something unnamed."—Why not? Because the preconditions for that mode of attention, of responsiveness, of caring, of sympathy, of understanding, are wholly missing. Our understanding of persons is based upon, built upon, everything humane that the robot lacks. Works of music need something very similar.

Notes

1 Stanley Cavell, "Music Discomposed," in *Must We Mean What We Say? A Book of Essays* (Cambridge: Cambridge University Press, 1976; originally published by Charles Scribner's Sons, 1969), 180–212.

2 Cavell, "Music Discomposed," *Must We Mean What We Say?*, 181.

3 Ibid., 182; italics in original.

4 Ibid.

5 Ibid., 184; italics in original.

6   Ibid., 189.

7   Ibid., 189–90.

8   Ibid., 192.

9   Ibid., 193.

10   Ibid., 197.

11   Ibid., 197–8; italics in original.

12   Ibid., 198.

13   Ludwig Wittgenstein, *Philosophical Investigations*, ed. G. E. M. Anscombe (New York: The Macmillan Company, 1953), Part II: iv, 178.

14   Cavell, "Music Discomposed," *Must We Mean What We Say?*, 198.

9

Punk Discomposed

Staging Sincerity and Fraudulence

DAVID LAROCCA

MUSICIANS ENCOUNTER A RANGE OF CIRCUMSTANCES in which improvisation is necessary, in which deviation from a plan becomes part of artistry itself. An opera soprano finds that by chance one evening she'll be singing with not one substitute tenor, but two (this happened to Renata Scotto, who performed with three Rodolphos during a Met production of *La Bohème* in 1977—a production that served as the Met's first live television broadcast[1]); a sextet with a prominent trumpet part suddenly becomes a quintet when its trumpetist gets sick (this happened when Johnny Cole collapsed leaving Charles Mingus & co. to scramble on April 19, 1964, a set that went on to be deemed *The Great Concert of Charles Mingus*[2]); an orchestra member leans over to whisper that his instrument, an English horn, has malfunctioned, to which the nearby performer—a clarinetist—responds by "asking him to turn his music stand so that I could read his part," whereupon, as Stanley Cavell relates the story of the opening night of Roger Sessions' first opera, *The Trial of Lucullus*, in 1947, "I produced his ensuing solo on the clarinet, which contained an essential cue for the singers on the stage."[3] Cavell speaks of a "perception of an anxious strangeness" that arose in response to a task that "one would be unlikely ever to have had occasion to calculate, let alone execute, all magnified by the difficulty of Sessions' music." These emergencies calling for on-the-spot, in-the-moment responses are examples of what Lydia Goehr defines as instances of improvisation *impromptu* (in contradistinction to improvisation *extempore*).[4] Such acts exemplify, as she puts it: "wit and fit, of doing exactly the right thing or wrong thing *in the moment*" and "how we live our lives precariously and contingently—on the edge."[5] Whether a person shows "a cool head and competent musicianship," as Cavell describes it, is a pressing matter that, effectively, never dissipates (e.g., thinking again of Goehr's theorizing, a string may always break).[6]

All of the above case studies could be listed under the ledger of accident (e.g., last-minute substitutes, performer illness, instrument malfunction, etc.), and the itemization can get very long, very fast. But there is another phenomenon to consider—changing one's mind—and how it should be classified. Can a *thought* be an accident, as when an invasive idea arrests or contests performance? Changing one's mind could at times present an obstacle (to whatever has been rehearsed) and also an opportunity for moving beyond the scope of the familiar, the repeated. In the case of changing one's mind, then, accident and intention blur. A thought is not authored so much as appears in consciousness—the question, then, is how to respond to it, how to play in the light of it. Accident, in this sense, needn't be in the moment, like a broken string, but a condition that shapes experience. *When* the thought to change occurs makes a substantive difference: before the gig begins or while one is on stage singing the tune, the band in full swing? The timing of such thoughts—and the actions they inspire—alters the very qualities of improvisation in question, yielding a still further range of queries about the form of a live event itself; the nature of upsetting a pre-established agenda; the risks and virtues of spontaneity in performance; whether an interruption is sincere or a bit of invented stagecraft aimed at heightening crisis and thus drama—perhaps creating in onlookers (onlisteners?) a sense of their own "anxious strangeness." Though a performer can *plan* on improvising (e.g., decide in advance that a change of course is in order), no one can plan how the improvisation will go, still less how it will be received—so even the premeditated deviation would appear to place the artist (and audience alike) in a precarious position, once again and always, living on the edge.

* * * *

ON DECEMBER 17, 1977, ELVIS COSTELLO performed live on television with his band, the Attractions—including musicians Steve Nieve (keyboards), Bruce Thomas (bass guitar), and Pete Thomas (drums)—on *Saturday Night Live*, only three years into the sketch-comedy show's ongoing, by now nearly half-century operation (and for a further sense of temporal continuity, featuring a host, Miskel Spillman, who was born in the nineteenth century).[7] Within a few bars of starting to play the band's debut single, "Less Than Zero," Costello suddenly ceases to sing, and tells his band "Stop! Stop!," then turns back to the live audience (in the studio before him and watching and listening elsewhere) and declares: "I'm sorry, ladies and gentlemen, there's no reason to do this song here."[8] Then he turns again to address the band anew, audibly whispering "Radio, Radio," and with that prompt, the Attractions launch into a spirited rendition of the band leader's alternate song selection. Because extemporizing is often simply defined as improvising, consider afresh Goehr's nuancing of her distinction: "improvisation *extempore* asks us to attend to what is achieved in the performance as a whole, improvisation *impromptu* picks out the inspired or exemplary *turn* in a performance when, on the spot, one does (at best) the right or winning thing."[9] The fact that Costello keeps (literally) turning— playing for his audience, then addressing his band, then, after another pivot, returning to the audience—only rounds out the trope (which itself, etymologically, is defined by this very same action). Our investigation follows after the nature and effects of Costello's turn (by way of Castiglione's moment of *sprezzatura*: a "particular nonchalance and wit [...] that makes it seem as though all he does—with perfect fit—he does effortlessly").[10] Costello's "turn" distills something particularly punk: a gesture of confident—if bold, also oddly polite—address against the standing order of things.

For decades, Costello's scene on the *SNL* stage—amounting to only a dozen or so seconds of air time—has proved a scandal, one on par, perhaps, with Sinéad O'Connor's daring act of ripping to pieces her mother's photograph of Pope John Paul II on the same stage in Studio 8H after singing *acapella* Bob Marley's "War."[11] Assessing the professional fallout of such acts is a separate project—but in brief, we can see that Costello was invited back to perform at the *SNL* 25th anniversary, while O'Connor appears to have been more aggressively punished for her defiance (with her vehement protest of the Catholic Church's scandal of sexual abuse only recently being vindicated). Rather, on the present occasion, it's worth considering how Costello, who in 1977 was not a punk rocker himself, but a New Wave innovator in the presence of punk, a musician who, on *SNL*, made a particularly punk act in his self-appointed role as a proxy for bona fide punk, living adjacent to and claiming for himself its energy and ethos. In those few seconds of shifting course, changing his mind, going off script, Costello borrowed a punk move and made it his own. For us, the drama encodes philosophical lessons about improvisation and invention, freedom and conformism, authority and creativity, constraint and authorship, sincerity and fraudulence.

What does it mean to deviate from pre-planned television programming? Given the strictures of the Federal Communications Commission (FCC), we are familiar with the "bleep" that sonically covers over profanity, but what about stopping a line of thought altogether—and starting a different one? Should such actions, when taken on live television, also be censored? While considering the (apparent) freedom of such an act, what if the deviation was, in fact, planned? Does premeditation change the meaning of the detour— make it less, or differently, problematic? With such questions, we are launched in a philosophical study of de-programming and reprogramming on live television—and how such a moment may become emblematic (an icon for an age or a movement, or at the very least, in today's parlance, a meme that captures a quintessential temperament). In those few seconds, Elvis Costello and his band provide a clinic on the aesthetics and ontology of punk defiance and creativity, one whose philosophical significance still radiates through our musical and wider popular culture.

Making It New, Again

From our vantage, how do we know the act on live TV in 1977 sustains cultural significance, even if we are not yet sure what that significance might amount to? Consider that the iconicity of Costello's move was reinforced in a metareferential moment during SNL's 25th-anniversary show in 1999, in which Costello burst in on the Beastie Boys during their live performance of "Sabotage" and, after reprising his famous introduction of the song from the original performance, played, you guessed it, "Radio, Radio" with the obliging Beastie Boys as his back-up band.[12] This recital of interior homage—where a show decides to celebrate itself, even its most controversial moments—and playful "sabotage" is coupled with outside applications too, such as when fans and imitators make it their own: from a "Weird Al" Yankovic parody to the way indie rock musician, St. Vincent started a version of her song "Cheerleader" on Conan, again on live television, but interrupted herself to say, as you will by now expect, "I'm sorry ladies and gentlemen, there's no reason to play that song"—and thereupon plays not an alternate selection from her own oeuvre, but in knowing reference/deference, Costello's "Radio, Radio." During an opening monologue while hosting SNL, Jason Sudeikis stirred awe at the prodigious talent that has graced the SNL stage, pointing to the place "where all the music happened" and offering a short list of exemplars: "Elvis Costello, Kanye, Nirvana, The Rolling Stones."[13] Not to be missed in the shuffle: two weeks after her SNL appearance, Sinéad O'Connor was on stage again, this time for a 30th-anniversary tribute concert for Bob Dylan, where she was slated to sing his "I Believe in You." Instead, in a variation of Costello's SNL exploit, O'Connor ignored the band, which had started to play, and sang acapella, once again, Marley's "War."

At each moment of iteration and invocation, we may pause to wonder if the repetition or re-application of the act defangs it—in Costello's loaded lyric "anesthetizes" it—creating a gimmick, where once it was a potent marker of defiance. Indeed, reflecting on the incident many years later, Costello himself deflated the transgressiveness of the stunt when he said "It felt good, but it was hardly a revolutionary act."[14] No doubt, we are left to parse what a "revolutionary act" is—what we mean by the phrase, or why we should care about creating one—when thinking of Costello's *SNL* hijinks. In short, we could say that the interruption-and-reprogramming's status as a punk act may have nothing at all to do with its revolutionary quality. Indeed, the trope of the "revolutionary"—as Hannah Arendt wrote about the decade before the *SNL* broadcast—means, simply, ending up where you began (since revolving brings one full circle, if perhaps changed for the trip). Better, perhaps to speak to punk's capacity to agitate. And in 1977 punk music did agitate; Costello's defiant leap from his predetermined assignment made many unnerved. Perhaps by now—approaching a half-century later—even Costello himself has lost touch with the energy of the song-as-protest and the counter-programming as a punk act of consequence.

Rather than the "revolutionary," a more fitting punk mentality may come from a different metaphor—unsettling. As Ralph Waldo Emerson, a punk transcendentalist wrote: "I unsettle all things. [...] People wish to be settled; only as far as they are unsettled is there any hope for them."[15] Bravery amounts to being sanguine about living in a condition of perpetual change, and in those endless "moments of transition" finding our orientation to taking "next steps." Still, we must be on guard, as Emerson also counsels, whether an act, say, of (apparent) norm-challenging risks yet another "foolish consistency"—this time of anti-social behavior, or the expression of a prevailing spirit of the *agon* (the contest, contesting, the contested) merely for the reaction one gets from others—stirring trouble as a *modus operandi*. Costello's apology and, indeed, his formality ("I'm sorry, ladies and gentlemen, there's no reason to do this song here.")[16] may hardly seem like a moment of punk rudeness, but then there is often something paradoxically *polite* about punk actions—like a friend who calls you on your stupidity, or a teacher or spouse who interrupts your speech to save you from what troubling thing you are about to say. And if in addition to seeming polite, the interruption is planned or staged, that's fine too! Such performativity—such meta-ness—adds yet more layers to the probity of the punk gesture and its kind of care: yes, we can be *thoughtful* about such transgressions.

Some viewers have suggested that Bruce Thomas lets the "secret" out by halting too quickly, almost as if on cue (and to a lesser extent, so does Steve Nieve). Indeed, the band doesn't seem *that* surprised by their band leader's boldness. Others have intimated that it was Costello's own manager who recommended the stunt as a way for the British band to get the attention of an American audience. Yet, as we have seen elsewhere, even if it's fraud, it's still instructive. Consider Casey Affleck's heavily rehearsed provocation, *I'm Still Here* (2013)—a species of what I have called hoax *vérité*, and different from the fabrications found in Orson Welles' *F for Fake* (1973) and Sarah Polley's *Stories We Tell* (2012).[17] In Affleck's conspiratorial effort at performance art, the running time of the film doesn't resolve the status of the film *as* fake. Likewise with Costello's radical interruption of his own work, all these decades on, we remain unsure how to understand the scene.

And in that state of indeterminacy—admittedly, we remain unsettled—we are granted much latitude to explore the power of punk behavior and its effects on the making and reception of art.

Inherited Order and Imposed Improvisation

As it happened, a genuine punk band—the Sex Pistols—was scheduled to perform on *Saturday Night Live* that evening in 1977 for the show's Christmas special. However, drug convictions led to Visa problems that prevented the band from traveling to the United States from their home in Britain. (Take note how Attractions' drummer, Pete Thomas' T-shirt reads "THANKS MALC"—a gesture of gratitude to the manager of the Sex Pistols, Malcolm McLaren, who failed to get his band to the gig.) Elvis Costello and the Attractions became a last-minute replacement, which in itself lends interest to the sense of Costello and his band as punk, or better, as a suitable replacement for an emphatically, emblematically punk band such as the Sex Pistols. Maybe Costello felt emboldened by the trade—and with it, anointed by a kind of peer-esteem baptism that filled him and his band with intentions and methods to unsettle the establishment. Consider that when Costello switched songs, the almost-always cool-headed producer of the show, Lorne Michaels, was so incensed that he rushed to the side of the main camera filming the band and gave Costello the middle finger throughout the performance of the song—a strikingly punk gesture on Michaels' part! History revealed that Michaels didn't mind "Radio, Radio" being played (the record company wanted Costello to do another song, though), but it was longer than the time slot and so threw off the show's tight schedule; like a good arts manager, he was upset by threats to planning, not from content.

    The enemy of planning, then, appears to be spontaneity, so what we have in this case is a question about inherited order and imposed improvisation: something that was and remains at the core of live performance, perhaps especially live television, which is constrained by time, number of songs allowed (in this venue, two), by marketing interests (such as commercials), and by the nature of rehearsal. *SNL* is an institutional exemplar of all of the above: the crew rehearses all week; sponsors are lined up and their advertisements are set in place; and yet in the open spaces of live presentation, there is room for improvisation. Of course, there are moments when actors "break" (e.g., usually laugh, but smiling can be enough to show a seam) or drop a violating-and-bleep-commanding f-bomb. Yet, as the charge of the live broadcast also affords, there is space and time for the achievement of comedy of an order altogether different from the pre-recorded.

    As we think about Costello and the Attractions performing "in the place of punk"—that is, as proxies (for the Sex Pistols) and perhaps as self-appointed emissaries from another genre—let's look to Stanley Cavell's still-generative reading of modernist music in a moment of modernist philosophy, his "Music Discomposed," which first appeared in 1967 (and was added to *Must We Mean What We Say?* two years later). Indeed, Cavell's own punk moves in this essay transform the familiar senses of "improvisation" such that we find ourselves thinking of Bach and Beethoven as *improvisers*, e.g., "[an] ethnomusicologist will have recourse to the concept [of improvisation] as a way of accounting for the creation-cum-performance of the music of cultures, or classes, which have no functionaries we would think of as composers, and no objects we would think of as embodying the intention to art."[18] We may find an analogue in the figure of music itself—that is, as a set of notes set on staves, written on sheets—such that we recognize it *as* music even if we are not ever sure how such music will sound given different artists, instruments, venues, and other contingencies. Thus, Cavell speaks of "improvisation" in the work of music (e.g., the manner of its performance on a given occasion); and also on film (e.g., the way actors behave, showing, in fact, "a natural dominance of improvisation over prediction"[19]); as well as on television (e.g., where the "amount of talk" involved seems to demand a persistent improvisation of content).[20] So, as Cavell has us consider "what is composition, what is it to compose," or for us to treat "compositions as objects *composed*,"we are wondering about those moments—such as the live performance of music on live television—when improvisation intercedes on planning, rehearsal, and the assignments of the composition.[21] Cavell insists that intention is present in the whole range of music-making, including traditional music, even when improvised, as opposed to what occurs in pieces defined by "chance" procedures (in this latter sense, a work is not "composed" at all).[22] As Cavell puts it, it may seem paradoxical that "[r]eliance on formula should allow the fullest release of spontaneity," but "[t]he context in which we can hear music as improvisatory is one in which the language it employs, its conventions, are familiar or obvious enough. [... A] mistake is clearly recognizable as such, and may even present a chance to be seized."[23] Costello's self-interruption could be treated as a variety of mistake, an intriguing one, as when a speaker says a word, then stops herself cold—"I don't mean that; that's the wrong word. I mean this word instead." Mistake as clarification, but crucially in this moment of live performance on TV—"a chance to be seized," one a seasoned musician is poised to exploit.

As Rosalind Krauss tells us, other compositional options on offer include "absolute mechanization of chance" (John Cage) or "utter submission to total organization" (Ernst Krenek's, Pierre Boulez's, and others' methods).[24] With Cavell, then, and in our scene with Costello, we have this productive coupling of being entirely sure of the context of the performance and yet also utterly unsure how the artist's interruption in that space—his improvisation—will turn out. Will the band falter or disobey? Will the audience revolt? Will a manager enter the stage and silence the band? Will the broadcast cut the feed? —Or will, as actually happened, we in the audience (in the studio and at home) be given a chance to hear what's on Costello's mind? We thus recognize the form, yet, for the way the content is treated (e.g., inserted, replaced, etc.), both realms are transformed: the venue is suddenly a space for countermanding the "programmed" (e.g., the fated set-list) and an occasion in which the well-known song is given a radiant new valence of signification (e.g., what does this song mean now, played in this way, selected to displace a previous choice, etc.?). We are *suddenly in danger*, and that is precisely what Cavell recognizes in the performance of art: "Within the world of art one makes one's own dangers, takes one's own chances—and one speaks of its objects at such moments in terms of tension, problem, imbalance, necessity, shock, surprise."[25] It shouldn't be lost on us that being "in danger" when there is no genuine danger (say, to life and limb) is precisely how Kant understands the experience of the sublime. The aesthetic potential for improvisation, therefore, is as enormous as it is unpredictable.

In this arrangement, we have Costello and his band, the songs, the show *SNL*, and also the audience (again, in studio and at home). Something crucial is happening *in relation to* those who would "receive" the act as one meriting comment, one somehow suffused with the capacity for impact—in a word, the power to unsettle. As Cavell puts it:

> [...] in art, the chances you take are your own. But of course you are inviting others to take them with you. [... A]nd your invitation incurs the most exacting of obligations: that *every* risk must be shown worthwhile, and every infliction of tension lead to a resolution, and every demand on attention and passion be satisfied—that risks those who trust you can't have known they would take, will be found to yield value they can't have known existed.[26]

There are risks taken in improvisation and in music generally; yet, there is also—from the moment of the act onward—a process of *reception* of those risks, a cultural history of their significance. At the time, of course, Costello himself couldn't know how the legacy of his act would cash out—what it meant in the moment or what it would still mean decades later, but then artists are rarely the best critics of their work, perhaps especially if the art in question is improvised, since they too are experiencing it for the first time, just like us.

We, the audience, we the inheritors of this act, are in the position—have the time—to reflect on whether the incident was and remains "worthwhile." Perhaps most crucially for our purposes here is the sense that the risks Costello took (as an artist) were taken by someone we trusted, perhaps still trust, risks we "can't have known [he] would take," nor—even now in the third decade of the twenty-first century—"will be found to yield value [he and we] can't have known existed." As each successive generation sees Costello and the Attractions on the *SNL* stage, each also has to come to terms with what the act—including that trust—amounts to. We have seen that the Beastie Boys and Lorne Michaels as well as Weird Al and St. Vincent, and Costello too, have all placed themselves in relation to the act, that is, as settling on its once and ongoing significance. And yet, they are all artists, so the question of how such a punk act "discomposes" is the work of the critic, of the reader (as TV watcher, as music fan) who comes to these moments in musical history in a spirit of inquiry.

Still, for Cavell, the meaning of the artistic act and the reflections a critic offers on those acts (her assessments, her judgments, etc.) are nevertheless productively and necessarily entwined, since "the modernist situation forces an awareness of the *difficulty* in avoiding prescription, and indeed of the ways in which criticism, and art itself, are ineluctably prescriptive—art, because its successes garner imitations [...]; criticism [...] because the terms in which [the critic] defines his response themselves define which objects are and which are not relevant to his response."[27] In turn, our criticism is creative too—its compositions generate the conditions in which art—even transgressive, or perhaps especially transgressive art—finds intelligibility for audiences, that is, as individuals coming to new work, groups seeking to find emblematic instances, or cultures gathering exemplars for future reference, repetition, reconceptualization, including for canonization.

TV Made the Radio Star

Think of the scene of Costello's interruption as also illuminating something distinctive about the medium of television, here in the light of Cavell's observation that each television format—such as the serial/program we have since October 1975 called *Saturday Night Live*—offers "the establishing of a stable condition punctuated by repeated crises or events that are not developments of the situation requiring a single resolution, but intrusions or emergencies [...] each of which runs a natural course and thereupon rejoins the realm of the uneventful."[28] Costello's prank is just such an intrusion or emergency in the life of the live show. Even though we have always watched the show live—even if "behind" the protection of an FCC-imposed delay (that monitors for prohibited language, wardrobe malfunctions, etc.)—we watch, in part, because of the particular charge all of this improvisation (however scripted and rehearsed it may be) reveals to us in novel moments, such as when, as noted, a comedian or guest "breaks," or a musical guest suddenly replaces a stage for repetition with a stage for innovation. Given our attunement to sonic phenomena, recall that television as a live medium owes the evolution of its programming to live radio. As TV becomes increasingly scripted and pre-recorded, therefore, *SNL* is at once a throwback to the radio era and an outlier among its current on-air rivals.

Indeed, according to Cavell's logic, when the show functions without "errors" it is, alas, "uneventful," much as a newscast that adduces things that have happened, one thing after another—leaving us with the paradoxical sense that the news is not, in a word, newsworthy. In our case, with this TV show, with this moment in its history, the notoriety of punk actions—call them anarchist, anti-authoritarian, etc.—are beautifully and fittingly glossed by the Cavellian tandem "intrusion and emergency" in which we are faced with what amounts to news, to the new, to the shocking and thus eventful.

Costello said later that the inspiration for the last-minute song change did not originate with him, but came instead from a moment he saw on BBC's *The Lulu Show* in 1969 when Jimi Hendrix concluded his performance of "Hey Joe" by announcing on air, "We're going to stop playing this rubbish."[29] Unlike Costello, who played another of *his own* songs, Hendrix played Cream's "Sunshine of Your Love"—a band that had recently broken up—until his air was cut. Costello recalled, "It was like watching your television go out of control."[30] And so, nested in what appeared to be Costello's seminal scene of television defiance is this autobiographical reflection that finds an even earlier instantiation. Though Hendrix's and Costello's are not identical acts, we are, with Costello, closer to the space of homage and imitation, the planned and predetermined and not the nominally improvisatory. And yet, Costello's very premeditation—with a heavy dose of punk-inspired appropriation—is generative, since, as Cavell notes about music generally, "[r]eliance on formula seems to allow the fullest release of spontaneity." Consequently, constraint itself can provide an artist pathways to creativity—including to provocation, and, indeed, to pedagogy in new forms and modes.[31] Costello had set about applying or repurposing Hendrix's act as a "formula" of a sort—call it an inspiration—in order to manufacture an "intrusion and emergency." Costello himself was obviously and strikingly impacted by Hendrix's interruption (Was Hendrix's halt-and-swap planned too? Did he also have an antecedent in mind?), and so, in his own moment on a live TV stage, he sustained the disruptive energy in the guise of an imported punk statement for American audiences. In time, inspiration and intrusion become culturally solidified as innovation—a new benchmark that lays the ground for future imitation.

When Costello forces his own show to "go out of control" in 1977, he doesn't denigrate his song like a self-effacing and self-knowing Hendrix ("We're going to stop playing this rubbish"), but instead suggests the pre-planned "Less Than Zero" is inappropriate, out of place, even a scandal: "there's no reason to do this song here." So we are invited to presume that there *is* a reason for him to sing "Radio, Radio" on live television, on *SNL*, and at that location in the history of music and of technology. The band

The Buggles formed in that same year, and the following year, wrote "Video Killed the Radio Star,"—as legend has it, in an hour. The song, released in 1979 describes the events of the title, which happened "[i]n my mind and in my car" (a combination of changes to one's mental soundtrack and those happening to broadcast radio as found in one's dashboard). And there's no turning back, since "we've gone too far." Alas, "Pictures came and broke your heart / Put the blame on VCR." The acronym—VCR—holding and hiding twin phenomena (video and recording) that vaunted and vaulted the visuals to the fore.

Meanwhile, back in 1977, "Radio, Radio"—with its own duplication and repetition firmly in place—admonishes its listeners even as, in a moment of metamusic, Costello sings of listening to the radio himself ("With every one of those late night stations / Playing songs bringing tears to my eyes"). And yet, those are *not* tears of longing or joy (from listening to his favorites) but tears of frustration (from listening to the kinds of songs that get played by bottom-line driven station owners and programmers): "And the radio is in the hands of such a lot of fools / Tryin' to anesthetize the way that you feel." Costello counter-programs the cultural moment by insisting that "[r]adio is a sound salvation," yet slumps at the fact that song selection is out of our hands (since "they don't give you any choice 'cause they think that it's treason"). When Costello takes the stage, then, he stages a comeback for all the radio enthusiasts out there in the form of jockeying the songs—shaking up the playlist to suit his tastes and the delivery of his message. Treason is his reason. The few seconds of Costello's shuffle appear from our vantage as an embodiment of the two songs just invoked: when the video star sang his heart out for the radio star but found himself for decades thereafter the subject of a video clip—played and replayed for its brash act to preserve a dying aspect of culture.

"Radio, Radio" and "Video Killed the Radio Star" share sensibilities as late 1970s meditations on the emergence of new media—and on their contestation by New Wave performer–critics. MTV broadcast for the first time in 1981. Radio—the dominant live medium of the prior century—and especially the popular music of the post-Second World War era, would be suddenly challenged for dominance, influence, and relevance. Soon enough, in the 1980s, a song often *needed a video* in order to be launched into wide circulation and rotation on the radio. The radio star, then, became the video star; the video star absorbed the radio star.

Given all the punk and New Wave credentials of the song "Radio, Radio," and Hendrix's influence on the *SNL* act, it's surprising to learn that the song began in 1974 as "Radio Soul," a piece Costello described as Bruce Springsteen-inspired—especially by songs on *The Wild, the Innocent & the E Street Shuffle* (1973).[32] Lyrically, this early version was, according to Costello, about "the idea that the radio broadcasting from within you was ultimately of more value than the radio in the dashboard or the wireless on the shelf."[33] An eerie premonition of the spiritual elements of the Walkman and iPod to come—the way we create soundtracks for our own lives, become our own "radio programmers." In 1977, however, Costello revised the song to make it more aggressive and a more pointed critique of British radio, especially in the wake of the BBC's attempt to censor the Sex Pistols' song "God Save the Queen." (And so we come full circle to the band that was originally set to appear on *SNL*, and does appear on the cover of the volume *Punk Rock and Philosophy*.[34])

With the context of the song's compositional development, and the history of its release in mind, "Radio, Radio" presents as a pre-Clash "public service announcement" *and* as an homage to the Sex Pistols.[35] Not surprisingly, it also functioned as an affront to Costello's own record label, Columbia: they insisted he play "Less than Zero" on *SNL*, but Costello wanted to assert more control over what he sang, and he believed "Radio, Radio" was a better fit for the occasion; not only was he writing his own songs, he was programming them too (another bid for becoming one's own radio station, internal or otherwise). Perhaps, not surprisingly, the fate of "Radio, Radio" *on the radio* was dire: once the advertisers realized the song was *anti*-radio (that is, the problem with radio as status quo rather than radio as *avant-garde*), stations stopped playing it. "I want to bite the hand that feeds me. I want to bite that hand so badly," sings Costello. Ryan Prado declared "Radio, Radio" to be "Costello's punk-as-fuck dissertation on corporate radio," one that "still seethes as red-faced to this day."[36]

Our lives are heavily repetitious, as Kierkegaard memorably reminded us, and people—especially those in positions of authority: parents, schools, governments, and perhaps most of all, corporate entities—tell us what to do (and increasingly so these days via social media and other forms of digital surveillance, including algorithmically informed directives, enticements, and monitoring). All the more reason to continue thinking about Costello's "punk-as-fuck" move to cancel a song, pick another, and play it loud, fast, and with conviction. Here we have a worthy aid to reflection in our own times: though our days are full of the same tasks, thoughts, and patterns, they can be interrupted, new things picked up, a new course chosen. And this unsettling can be occasioned even if the move is itself rehearsed or faked. The act of improvisation within constraints remains one of the central functions of art, whether as artist or critic, performer or audience. We are all positioned to draw lessons from biting the hand that feeds us.

Doing Art

We may think there is a question about the matter of the song—Costello's choice to sing this song and not another. When he abruptly stops a song-in-progress, comments on its inappropriateness ("there's no reason to do this song here"), offers no explanation for his decision, and then cues his bandmates to begin another song, thereby making the choice of *that* song also an issue—the choice may be about the artistry of the separable acts we can discern in this string of performative moments. In short, the starting, stopping, re-starting amounts to a kind of art event (what may travel under the name "object of art" insofar as we are able to discern it as a continuous phenomenon). "The question, therefore, if it is art, must be," Cavell begins: "How is this to be seen? What is the [artist or performer] doing?"

The problem, one could say, is not one of escaping inspiration, but of determining how a man could be inspired to do *this*, why he feels *this* necessary or satisfactory, how he can mean *this*. Suppose you conclude that he cannot. Then that will mean, I am suggesting, that you conclude this is not art, and this man is not an artist; that in failing to mean what he's done, he is fraudulent. But how do you know?[37]

There's some intriguing conceptual or linguistic slippage here, which may be a distraction, or may turn us to the heart of the matter. Notice Cavell's conclusion that "this is not art, and this man is not an artist," followed by "*he* is fraudulent" [italics added]. What of the art ("object of art")? Is it *also* fraudulent? And if fraudulent, does a recursive logic hold that it is, in fact, *not art*? Let those questions hang for a moment while we note that the problem of the modern in the tradition of Western-composed music is a preoccupation in "Music Discomposed." Yet, the "modern" is not identical to the problem of whether a particular *moment* in a performance is pre-planned or spontaneous, since Cavell claims that both (traditionally) composed music and music improvised from within a tradition, such as jazz, provide ways "to act coherently and successfully" in creating music that delivers the satisfactions associated with art.[38]

In Cavell's serial reflections on Krenek's "total organization" procedures, or for that matter, Cage's "chance" procedures, he doesn't conclude that such music is worthless, or that these procedures aren't themselves understandable responses to the problem of the modern that composers marshaled in the mid-twentieth century (and still confront, if not always knowingly or explicitly). Cavell's point is that the pseudo-scientific or pseudo-philosophical writings *about* these procedures do nothing to justify them as solutions to the problem of the modern—and that the *only* justification that such procedures can gain—as thinking about them may allow us to discover, as it did for Cavell—is through an experience of listening that we can recognize as associated with the pleasures we take in art.[39] With Cavell's "contempt [...] for Krenek's pseudo-technical writing" in mind, Richard Taruskin claims that Krenek's total serialism admits a "nihilistic defeatism" and a mood of "existential despair."[40] —Now back from the brink to the question of fraudulence, Cavell contextualizes the term this way (with respect to the modern) when he takes up some of his critics in "A Matter of Meaning It":

> [In "Music Discomposed,"] I was not directly concerned to condemn any given work as fraudulent, but to call attention to (what I took to be) the obvious but unappreciated *fact* that the experience of the modern is one which itself raises the question of fraudulence and genuineness.[41]

That is, the modern has given us a preoccupation with the *object* of art, or better, the *status* of the art object, in terms variously, on the one hand, of its sincerity and authenticity and on the other hand, of its artifice and duplicity. For Cavell, as Eric Drott has written, "the uncertainty regarding both the status and the sincerity of contemporary art gave the lie to the formalism that dominated midcentury Anglo-American aesthetics."[42] Consequently, "Cavell has argued at length," notes Stephen W. Melville, "that this risk of or openness to fraudulence is more crucially defining of the modern than the apparent positive terms of sincerity or authenticity or demystifying truth telling insofar as it is the omnipresent possibility of fraudulence that determines our countervailing valorization of authenticity."[43] A large measure of that "length," it's fair to say, almost too obvious to notice, is how the notion of sincerity (and its opposite, insincerity) are what's being asked after in the ordinary language prompt-question of the book's title—in which the motive to sincerity may be mobilized as a duty or (moral) obligation to mean what we say. To be sincere—and not, as modernity might have us model: cynical, ironic, self-deluded, or "fraudulent."

Part of the force propelling modernism (and the instincts of its would-be practitioners), one that appears to gather intensity over time, is the drive to tease authenticity with the threat of artifice.[44] I often keep in mind that Cavell published "Music Discomposed" and "A Matter of Meaning It" in 1967, at the dawn of our contemporary sense of the meta—with art's persistent deployment of reference and reflexivity.[45] And now, in the 2020s, entering an asymptotic rise, an ascent into the hyper-meta—a period that may be defined by taking reference and reflexivity for granted as an essential, required part of what art (in our day) is and does. When we look at the period between 1967 and the present, we see performances and art and performance art that appear to *build in* fabrication and fraudulence; actor/performer doubleness (or blurring or erasure of that demarcation); narratives *en abîme*; mimesis of existing intellectual property or characteristics (such as found in satire, impersonation, evocation); and the troubling of (inherited or presumed) boundaries between art and history, fiction and nonfiction. From Andy Kaufman to Charlie Kaufman, Woody Allen to Andy Warhol to Sacha Baron Cohen, mockumentary to metacinema, a dominant strain of art making—from museums to movie theaters, on stages and on screen—has taken up fraudulence ("faking it") as a mode of art and art making. Elvis Costello's stunt then appears on this continuum as a bit of stagecraft vying for its own kind of claim to a work of art. The *music* being played—stopped or started—is on a secondary level, while, in this live, televised moment, the art at issue is the *presentation* of the music itself. The dramaturgy interrupts the music, introducing a *Verfremdungseffekt*, in effect, breaking our concentration on the songs and shifting it to the drama of the space between them—the very nature of the interruption, arguably our new object of art. The "presentation," of course, turns us to some of Cavell's principal nomenclature in "Music Discomposed," namely: composition, improvisation, and chance.[46]

Art, Audience, Tradition

What Costello does in the space between "Less than Zero" and "Radio, Radio" is not music, and we should add along Cavellian lines, not part of the performance of music. If it is performative—in an embodied sense, which it is—then we can think of it in terms of *an event that conditions the reception of the music* (in this case, two different songs, one "authorized" by the show's programming, the record label, the artist, and so on; and one "unauthorized"). The interruption can be usefully treated as a kind of paratext; and if identifiable in this way, then on my reading or reception, it appears to function as a work of art, however brief, slight, and transient. By framing the scene this way, we are encouraged to look as much at Costello's act (on stage) as we are to recognize ourselves as one among several *audiences* for the music he plays with his band (along with the moment when he stops playing and calls our attention to the music stopped and re-started). We are told that Lorne Michaels, *SNL*'s showrunner, was livid—that he was furious at Costello's break from agreed-upon terms. But what of the audience in attendance in Studio 8H or at home—of course, both part of *a live audience* (one "on TV," the other watching the TV set)? What were they thinking? And how might thoughts on their reception enrich the significance of the paratext thus called to our attention?

Cavell marks out a distinction between two types of audiences: "The philistine audience cannot afford to admit the new; the *avant-garde* audience cannot afford not to."[47] Cavell is troubled by the state of affairs in which these are the options: "This bankruptcy means that both are at the mercy of their tastes, or fears, and that no artist can test his work either by their rejection or by their experience." In short, there is *no shared standard of judgment* that rests beyond these two audiences. Cavell admits of his own dyad: "[t]hese may or may not exhaust all the audiences there are," so let's conjecture at least one other dominant category of audience, something along the lines of a conservative audience (a class that would include experts, trained professionals, keepers of tradition, and so on). Such a group or class would be at the mercy of its tastes, perhaps its fears too (e.g., the fear of change, deviation, innovation, etc.), but imagine that it is precisely its prior experience (of music) and its development of a standard of judgment that would place it in a position to test the proffered work (and as a result to accept or reject it). Thus, "[t]he philistine audience cannot afford to admit the new" because it doesn't know better (or have a standard of judgment upon which to consider admissions), whereas the conservative audience possesses a wealth of experience that makes its judgments informed. Even so, both types of audience may reject the new as a matter of habit—the former from ignorance, the latter from a kind of intelligence.

"Punk" wasn't a category of musical experience for Cavell in 1967, so let's place its dominant sensibilities within the realm of the *avant-garde*—befitting the punk even in an etymological sense, as the leading edge of a disposition or movement. Quick takes made in the moment—live on TV and in the studio in 1977—could range from a certain thrill in Costello's intervention/interruption of his own singing, of his band's much sought-after slot on the show, to some version of the philistine and conservative reactions to the events of that Saturday night. In the context of network TV circa 1977, simply featuring Elvis Costello and the Attractions on TV was *enough* of an *avant-garde* act for Lorne Michaels or the National Broadcasting Company (NBC) to take (as was their invitation to the Sex Pistols); having Costello shift abruptly to an unauthorized song went too far. Whether Michaels and NBC and the FCC are philistine or conservative is secondary; they are, like content moderators on today's social media platforms, simply trying to abide by established (and ever-evolving or contested) social and moral guidelines for programming and broadcast. Whether those guidelines make sense—are fair, are designed by informed taste-makers or reactionaries, and so on—is again, beyond the scope of concern for the context of live music broadcast on live television.

Modern/modernist/modernism form a trinity that pervades the discussions throughout *Must We Mean What We Say?* (first published in 1969 with a subtitle that begins "modern philosophical essays ... "), and they remain words or terms with currency in our time, in the 2020s. Our point of focus—a few seconds-or-so on *SNL*—takes us back about forty-seven years, and so the nexus of modern/modernist/modernism may be taken up as a *lingua franca*. When Cavell writes here about "modern artists," then, I think we can class Elvis Costello in that group, and extend the discussion by asking whether his music—or at least this staged act on *SNL*—places him in the company of the modernist, or of modernism:

What modern artists realize [...] is that taste must be *defeated*, and indeed that this can be accomplished by nothing less powerful than art itself.

One may see in this the essential moral motive of modern art. Or put it this way: What looks like "breaking with tradition" in the successions of art is not really that; or is that only after the fact, looking historically or critically; or is that only as a result not as a motive: the unheard of appearance of the modern in art is an effort not to break, but to keep faith with tradition.[48]

We've already introduced the question of Costello's *sincerity* (i.e., whether he means what he says in saying to stop the music; whether the act was fraudulent, a put-on), and we could add how we (may) remain skeptical about who knew what when (e.g., if Lorne Michaels was truly in the dark, did other people know what Costello would do—his bandmates? people other than his bandmates?). To work within Cavell's framework as we think about Costello on *SNL*, we could draw from concepts that are proximate, such as seriousness and intention.[49] Even in an untutored way, invoking their demotic senses, we can profitably ask: was Costello serious about his action (in stopping the song)? Does his intensity convey a bid for the seriousness of his decision to do so? When considering the nature or prehistory of such a "decision"—Costello's "reason" for the substitution, including his own post-facto recollections of the matter—he did appear to *intend* something significant by the act (e.g., "Columbia [Records] insisted that the second song should be 'Less Than Zero.' The song had already proven to be obscure to many American ears, and if this was supposed to be our 'I Want to Hold Your Hand' moment, I thought the song was too low-key."[50]) It seems worth noting that Costello's way of taking the moment seriously, or taking his art seriously, entailed interrupting the plan, especially if he had visions of a (still-unrealized) Costello-mania on his mind. Instead of "the show must go on," he defiantly offers: "the show must *stop* … in order to go on."

Naming himself after that "other Elvis," we shouldn't be too shocked to imagine that the re-anointed Declan Patrick MacManus would be attracted to mixing his music with aggrandizing showmanship and a Beatles-like fan base to match. While the "other half" of his name, Costello, derives from his father's stage name, Day Costello, it also whispers a lineage to Abbott's Lou—and thus a propensity for tricksterism and the comedic familiar to the younger MacManus' lyrics, aggressive genre-blending, and far-ranging musical curiosity. Here Elvis Costello was, on December 17, 1977, just a few months after Elvis Presley's death on August 16, 1977, taking on— without any introduction by Ed Sullivan—the mantle of troubadour and troublemaker. And though Costello was at the time, and has since been, associated with the New Wave—and not punk—it's not hard to see elements of crossover between the two trends, or genres, in his work. Such "crossover" music may be celebrated for its achievement of satisfying amalgams, or it may scandalize for its transgressiveness, or both. David Bowie, Lou Reed, Frank Zappa, and others concomitantly ingest and transform myriad other genres, each making, in turn, their own iconic dominions. Though none, given available alternatives, would likely be taken as exemplars of punk or New Wave per se, they could be invoked to illuminate and complicate the rendering of genre assignments, including the sincerity with which they inhabit them; moreover, moments of gender fluidity further inform the variability of genre definition.[51] Abruptly inserting Barbra Streisand on this point (no doubt a bit of irreverence in line with our topic) so we don't lose track of the role androgyneity plays in her work—on stage, on screen, and in song.[52] Though Bowie, Reed, and Zappa (even when, say, Zappa satirizes punk and New Wave[53]) would never be mistaken for Iggy Pop, they still operate on a register of musical experimentation and unfettered invention that nevertheless accords with an underlying punk outlook. David Byrne and Talking Heads could prove an intriguing additional test case—depending on *when* you listen—perhaps offering an amalgamation amounting to a *tertium quid* or a designation of *sui generis*. Picking up with Cavell, we recall him saying how "I was claiming that in modernist art the issue of the artist's intention, his seriousness and his sincerity, has taken on a more naked role in our acceptance of his works than in earlier periods."[54] All of the above artists and musicians might be profitably interrogated for the extent to which seriousness and sincerity interact with name changing, gender-inflected make-up and costuming, dramatic staging, musically informed genre-mashing, and more.

Given Cavell's formulation or phrasing above, we can propose asking whether Costello's act is part of a "moral motive of modern art" in which "taste must be *defeated*"—in which Costello is schooling us from the stage—or whether his lesson(s) appear(s) "only as a result not as a motive." Either way, though, it seems plausible, given what Cavell says, that whether from motive or result, such interventions/interruptions, such "breaks" in the prevailing order of things—in art, in music, on television—count as instances of illumination by which we can better see and hear and appreciate tradition. These "breaks" are Brechtian moments in which the plied fabric of experience—whether in our living rooms or on the television screen— is given a stitch, or in digital terms, a glitch. When the screen is perfectly painted with pixels, the illusion is complete, but a single dead pixel will nag at the eye like a splinter—breaking the spell. In related fashion, Costello's brief but bold, abrupt but lasting, "defeat of taste" reminds us that taste remains an open issue for us (regardless of audience type), that tradition is there to be drawn from *and* antagonized.

Criticism For/Against Art—and of Itself

Cavell recognized how modern art was becoming increasingly meta art— that the work of art as object, as process, would circulate back upon itself, ouroboros-style. As he said in 1967, "maybe it just is a fact about modern art that coming to care about it demands coming to care about the problems in producing it."[55]

Whatever music can do, modern music is concerned with the making of music, with what is required to gain the movement and the stability on which its power depends. The problems of composition are no longer irrelevant to the audience of art when the solution to a compositional problem has become identical with the aesthetic result itself.[56]

Already an innovation beyond historical trends, the "modernist situation" evolves still more, adds a further fillip, in so far as it includes the criticism written about the art—where criticism constitutes what it is we think of as the art, the art object, and the various achievements and disappointments that flow or follow thereafter.[57] Criticism, as Cavell casts it at this point in the history of art, is "internal [...] to the experience of art."[58] Even if none of the examples I've offered here—Elvis Costello, *SNL*, live music, live television, live music on television, etc.—casts any sway with contemporary readers, our *responses* may end up being what interests us most. Namely, that the "art" or the "object of art" is not nearly as fascinating as what it occasions in us as critics, as audience(s) for the event or performance. The parsing of these few seconds of television from the late 1970s is potent, even if—and perhaps because it—has pushed criticism back upon its heels, destabilizing what it is we are said to assess when we "write about music." And so the matter of writing criticism is a particularly modernist preoccupation. In a word, criticism for modernists is not just "about art" but about *itself*. The reflexivity here appears to be a veritable definition of the situation—the predicament—the modernist finds herself within. As Cavell observes: "a central importance of criticism has become to protect its art against criticism"[59]—pausing with pleasure over the doubleness of "its art": meaning at once *the art of criticism* and *the criticism of art.*

In our televised test case, as noted, we may be most interested in what happens *between* the music, between the songs, in the interval when Costello is not singing at all, but speaking to the audience. Holding in mind for the moment whether Costello is making a moral or evaluative statement, let's simply note the Cavellian yield on the notion that his time on stage is turning the sheer performance of music—or its stoppage—into a question for music (as above: "Whatever music can do, modern music is concerned with the making of music"). A salient way of noticing what Costello occasions arises when asking what it is we think he is "composing"—or *dis*composing, or perhaps un- or re-composing—in the moment when he stops singing and starts speaking. The interruption—and the commentary between songs—is not an act of composing music in any way we would recognize it. Hence the *avant-garde* moment, call it the punk de/dis-composition of the authority of tradition; Costello undoes, then re-does. The terms, or better, terrain of "composition" have evidently changed in this modern(ist) scene: the audience of art is suddenly, radically implicated in adjudicating what to do, say, think—how to react, how to value/evaluate, to offer a *criticism* of the art (what art?). We are told that Lorne Michaels' response to the act was anger and frustration, but what did we (the audience) think then, what do we (the critics) think now? The fact that we can ask such questions— formulating them as questions for or proximate to music—means that, as Cavell has said above, "the solution to a compositional problem has become identical with the aesthetic result itself." We are *in* the music, implicated in its making. On this account, the audience/critic is *witness to* as much as *creator of* outcomes—reading as much as read by the texts at hand, on stage, on screen. Costello is, of course, the composer of the music, creator of the event in which the music starts and stops and starts again, and yet, in our modernist predicament, we listeners/viewers are also constituting— *composing*—the meaning of the moment in our response to it, including in these belated pages.

Cavell is preoccupied throughout "Music Discomposed" with the state of musical composition and the composition of criticism (about art, including music). "This is particularly urgent," Cavell cautions, "or perhaps particularly clear, in the case of music, because, as suggested, the absence of a strong tradition of criticism leaves this art especially vulnerable to whatever criticism becomes established, and because the recent establishment of criticism is peculiarly invulnerable to control (because of its technicalities, its scientific chic …)."[60] We have on the one hand the prospects for new musical expression and on the other hand (or in parallel) the creation of new modes of criticism. Do they advance in sequence or in tandem? And what do they do for one another? Cavell, for his part, believes philosophy ought to be a helpmeet to the truths music may contain.[61] Meanwhile, the figure of the composer weighs on him as he considers "[t]hat a few composers might, because of this distraction and discouragement, cease trying to write, is doubtless to be expected in a difficult period. But it is not unthinkable that next time all on whom the art relies will succumb to that distraction and discouragement."[62] Throughout "Music Discomposed" Cavell is preoccupied with the thinking and writing composer, that is, with the composer who writes music (of course) and who *also* (more remarkably, more problematically) writes criticism. "The particular phenomenon I wanted to make surprising," he says retrospectively in "A Matter of Meaning It," reveals that "composers have come to feel compelled to defend their work in theoretical papers, a phenomenon I take, in turn, to be characteristic of the kind of work they are compelled to produce."[63] At the same time, Cavell, with a bit of knowing humor in place, must find himself burdened with such a role as well, on some variation of the theme—for he too is a composer-turned-critic. And yet, in his onward position as a philosopher, he does not write, or no longer writes, music, but instead criticism about music, contributing to a philosophy of music, to aesthetics, a general theory of value, and so on. (As he says in "A Matter of Meaning It" about his ambitions for "Music Discomposed": "the oblique and shifting relations between an art, and its criticism, and philosophy, is a major theme of the entire paper."[64])

As television—and its heirs on streaming platforms and apps, such as TikTok—has taken on an increasingly prominent role in contemporary life, we are aware of how the language of TV producers has entered the fray of everyday speech.[65] As Megan Garber writes, "People who are deluded, we say, have 'lost the plot'; people who have become pariahs have been 'canceled.' In earlier ages, people attributed their circumstances to the will of gods and the whims of fate; we attribute ours to the artistic choices of 'the writers' and lament that we may be living through America's final season."[66] Looking back to *SNL* in 1977, we'd be right to say that Elvis Costello got "canceled"—as Ralph Waldo Emerson was by Harvard after declaiming the "Divinity School Address." Neither Costello nor Emerson were "invited back" to those respective institutions for a long time (nearly three decades in Emerson's case; twelve years in Costello's). Though we often wonder about the fate of the canceled in the present day, when we look back we can appreciate how such diversions (or punishments, as the case may be) shape the course of a life, embolden subsequent work, or hasten the end of a career. Emerson kept writing and speaking publicly—likely addressing and reaching a more widespread audience than if he remained a pastor devoted to the proximate needs of his Boston congregation. Elvis Costello, for his part, has since his first *SNL* appearance, released more than thirty studio albums (plus another half-dozen live albums, a half-dozen tribute albums, and sixteen compilation albums). So Costello did not "succumb to [...] distraction and discouragement," though he was denied for a time a platform suited to his gifts. His memorably staged interruption—and its aftermath—became a cautionary tale for the television age and, in our own so-called social media age, a meme.

Meme-ification itself illustrates a tendency (however much it has antecedents in other technologies and techniques) to draw a lesson from, or impose a lesson on, a *fragment* of art. Thus the proliferation of phrases and sentences drawn from books written fancifully upon coffee mugs, tote bags, and posters: the reduction of literature and philosophy to "sayings" (and the pronounced malapropism: "Nietzsche has a quote about how, 'without music, life would be a mistake.'"). "We know," writes Cavell, "that criticism ought to come only after the fact of art, but we cannot *insure* that it will come only after the fact. What is to be hoped for is that criticism learns to criticize itself, as art does, distrusting its own success."[67] While Costello's *SNL* stunt has entered the meme bloodstream, becoming its own cultural signifier (and thus shorthand), "Music Discomposed" unsettles our habits of reception, helps us see the event anew—perhaps in the context of multiple musical traditions, not least the confluences of New Wave, punk, rock 'n' roll, pop music, and their coexistence at the dawn of MTV. In this case, criticism didn't come after the fact of art but was *internal to the object of art itself.*

Art and Its Aftermath: Meaning (It) in the Moment (and Afterwards)

Watching Costello's interlude, we may wonder about the *tone* of his intervention. He doesn't smile. He doesn't seem like he's having fun. The cessation of playing music appears—in the company of his narration ("there's no reason to do this song here")—to be on the order of a moral imperative or an even political declaration. Had the Sex Pistols instead made the flight and performed as scheduled, and also been moved to make such a live, unscripted change in the set-list, one can imagine the act would have been done with a snarl and wink—and been played for its jesting best. This counterfactual seems to better capture the Cavellian hope for criticism capable of criticizing itself, "distrusting its own success." Meanwhile, Costello's actual act can come off as righteous, doubling down on the exhilaration of making a power move in the midst of a live broadcast.

Cavell may give us a propitious clue to our deliberation in so far as we could take the interval between Costello singing "Less than Zero" and "Radio, Radio" to be a bit of modern theater. "A writer like Samuel Beckett," writes Cavell, "does *not* want what is communicated easily to be what he communicates—it is not what he means."[68] Calls this Beckett's brand of esotericism.

> So his effort is not to find belief from his audience, but to defeat it, so that his meaning *has* to be searched for. Similarly, modern dramatists do not *rely* on their audiences, but *deny* them. Suppose an audience is thought of as "those present whom the actors ignore." Then to stop ignoring them, to recognize them explicitly, speak *to* them, insist on the fact *that* this is acting and this is a theater, functions to remove the status of *audience* from "those out there who were ignored."[69]

As earlier "taste must be *defeated*," so now the *audience* must be defeated also. But defeated in a modern way, which is, I suppose, an ironic way: the language is unstable here, of course, since to *deny* the audience the artist/ playwright must *address* the audience, acknowledge it, "break" the so-called fourth wall (a hallmark of the meta and the *mise-en-abîme* that so often travels with it). Recall how polite, how sincere, how stern Costello presents himself in the moments between two raucous songs: "I'm sorry, ladies and gentlemen, there's no reason to do this song here." He's calling out how

"Less than Zero," with its modulated reggae rhythm namechecks a person few Americans had heard of, the unrepentant fascist Oswald Mosley (1896–1930); meanwhile, "Radio, Radio" is a protest song with a prospective rather than a retrospective momentum; a song about the radio as we know it (and were losing it; not yet knowing how forcefully MTV would dominate the coming decade—as noted, an era officially and ironically inaugurated by The Buggles' "Video Killed the Radio Star" in August 1981).

There's a long tradition of hucksters and fakers—from those featured in Melville's *The Confidence-Man: His Masquerade* (1857) to Casey Affleck's *I'm Still Here* (2013)—so we've been warned, even if we haven't taken notice or cared much to protect ourselves in the face of new instances. In the penultimate paragraph of "Music Discomposed," Cavell writes:

> I've been insisting that we can no longer be sure that any artist is sincere— we haven't convention or technique or appeal to go on any longer: *anyone* could fake it. And this means that modern art, if and where it exists, *forces* the issue of sincerity, depriving the artist and his audience of every measure except absolute attention to one's experience and absolute honesty in expressing it. This is what I meant in saying that [modern art] lays bare the condition of art altogether. And of course it runs its own risks of failure, as art within established traditions does.[70]

Cavell replied to his critics, Monroe Beardsley and Joseph Margolis, by glossing the notion of "modernism laying bare its art" (in "A Matter of Meaning It") by saying it "is meant not as an interpretation of history (the history of an art), but as a description of the latest period of a history, a period in which each of the arts seems to be, even forced to be, drawing itself to its limits, purging itself of elements which can be foregone and which therefore seem arbitrary or extraneous."[71] And if I may gloss the gloss, this picture of heading for "limits," or evacuating "elements," aligns with my sense of this "latest period of a history," now more-than-half-a-century-on, in which the sheer or mere status of a work of art is enough to summon a question about its presence *and pretense*—to notice it *as* art, to take stock of its status as that sort of thing, and so on. I don't wish to overstate the extent to which the meta qualities of art (as object, as medium/media, as category, as practice, as process of inheritance, as part of/apart from an authorizing institution, etc.) are present, but the *trend* appears doubtless: irony and self-referentiality, repetition, recycling, and recursion have increased as functions of art perhaps, especially in response to the collapse of tradition, institutional authority, and de facto guardians of taste and value. The dawn of generative artificial intelligence appears to complete this ascendant phase with its aggressive plagiarism and free-wheeling reconstitutions of intellectual property; copyright has been replaced by the algorithmic right to copy (without negative recourse or consequence)—perhaps delivering, at last, the apotheosis of a punk dismissal of authority. Fraudulence may be a sign of protection, a way to undermine threats upon sincerity; it may be an admission that decadence befalls cultural life—and as suits ironic overload, becomes its signature. Even so, if we notice trends, we can also slow down sufficiently to study individual cases, as we have done here.

The meta moment—asked as if in reply to the (playful) question "What's the meta here?"—reminds us of the quarrel between the New Critics and Cavell (especially as he dramatized it in "A Matter of Meaning It"), in short, coming to terms with the former's focus on the art object itself (say, a poem) apart from authorial intention, historical context, and the like, and the latter's modernist twist: showing us how "the issues of intention and seriousness and sincerity are forced upon the reader by the poem itself."[72] In other words, the reflexivity and referentiality of the modernist poem reconceives of its status as a work of art; it cannot be siloed, made an island of meaning unto itself; instead, its meta-ness *demands* a connection to the world beyond it, the world it inhabits and from which it has necessarily emerged. Cavell presents these effects as "religious" in nature and as calling us to a "more personal" response to the art we encounter and interpret.[73] A New Critical reading of Costello's interruption would be peculiar and impoverished compared with the varied levels of meaning available to critics open to context, among other facts and notions discussed above: Costello's proxy status for the punk band the Sex Pistols; his sense of occasion (not just as *his* British landing in America, but also his admiration for a bit of mischief caused by Jimi Hendrix); his evolving status in the climate of late-1970s music (as punk-adjacent, or post-punk, or proxy-punk, etc.); his dedication to commenting on media while using it (e.g., singing about the radio on TV); his showmanship (as another Elvis, arriving just months after the original Elvis' demise); and so on. "[T]he issues of intention and seriousness and sincerity are forced upon" the viewer by Costello's performance itself. The crux of the moment's meaning lies in the overlapping nature of these three mental dispositions. When Costello stops the music, does he mean what he says?

All along, that is, from the late evening of December 17, 1977 to the present hour, we've been wondering about what Cavell calls "further relevances" of a given act or work of art (since, as Cavell says, "works of art are intentional objects.")[74] Costello may have an idea of what he wanted to do, wanted to achieve, but the act is bigger than his intentions (though it includes them). Rather, "when further relevances of what you are doing, or have done, are pointed out, then you cannot disclaim them by saying that it is not your intention to do those things but only the thing you're concentrating on."[75] Costello's intentions for the evening broadcast are seductive if enigmatic—worth exploring as aspects of history—and with such investigations, we'll have to assess, if not summarily conclude upon, a sense of his seriousness and sincerity. Of course, part of the stunt—the playfulness and anti-authority charge of punk—is about "taking the piss" on the matter of seriousness, such as FCC rules and record label dictates, manners that govern how bands perform on stage, who's in charge, what gets played, etc. What remains fascinating, endlessly rewarding about Costello's *SNL* appearance resolves itself in our relation to what Cavell calls "the shift of events"—how there were things that were *done, meant*. And as time—decades, in fact—went on, other events (including further thoughts on the matter, referential improvisations, for example) reveal themselves. "In art," writes Cavell,

> our interest in intention, given the fact that we are confronted by someone's work, is to locate ourselves in its shift of events. In all cases, the need is for coming to terms, for taking up the import of a human gesture. In all, I may use terms to describe what someone has done which he himself would not use, or may not know.[76]

Like Cavell's hypothetical reading of Federico Fellini's *La Strada* (viz., as "a version of the story of Philomel"), we are drawn at once to the immediate conditions (and terms) of that late night in December 1977, and in *returning* to the scene all these years later, we come equipped with strange and welcome abundances (among them Costello's prodigious decade-spanning career; *SNL*'s continuous run ever since; uptakes and meta-references to the evening made by others).

To be sure, Cavell's famous last words (in "Music Discomposed") are: "Of course, I may be taken in." We linger to appreciate the double sense in play here: to be tricked, sure, and also to be absorbed—a fitting pair of sensibilities for our encounter with Costello, since it is a riveting, multiform moment even as it may be a manufactured one. So, what do we *do* about it—a word that has proximate resonance with the diction of Costello's own mercurial declaration, my emphasis added: "There's no reason to *do* this song here." Does "doing" a song mean the same thing as "playing" it? In the "grammar" of his art (and vernacular speech), *yes* in so far as Costello is stopping and withholding the song—and then starting another, *doing it*. But we were talking mainly about an artist's sincerity and by association, or by way of Cavell's admonition and admission, our degrees of gullibility.

Costello's sincerity in the interstitial moment—this breach, this Brechtian break—is, it seems, after watching it for more than forty years, not something we can settle once and for all. Indeed, that this perpetually unsettled state, which Emerson praised as the only one in which there is any hope for us, is the very condition of modern art—how we know, at least, that it *is* modern art.[77] When Cavell shares with us his "perception of an anxious strangeness," he brings the predicament of the modern artist into proximity with the fate of modern art, including what may be, at this late stage, a ratification of those instances Goehr deems improvisation *impromptu*.[78] We have left total serialism as well as any resolute New Criticism to make a fuller encounter with existence as we find it, "how we live our lives precariously and contingently—on the edge."[79] Hence the aesthetic and ethical urgency of achieving "wit and fit,"—"of doing exactly the right thing or wrong thing *in the moment*."[80] Making that call—whether it means "there's no reason to do this song here," or some other act of judgment, including missing the moment—remains, or has become, the purview of the (modern) artist.

Though Cavell concludes, in the final lines of "Music Discomposed," that "[t]he task of the modern artist, as of the modern man, is to find something he can be sincere and serious in; something he can mean," Cavell also introduces uncertainty, a degree of deferred resolution, since "he may not at all" find it.[81] The modern artist/the modern human may come up short—or discover the thing she "did" is neither sincere nor serious, not something she can mean after all. In the end, which is to say at the end of Cavell's "Music Discomposed," we are encouraged to study any given work of art not (only) for its bespoke traits and characteristics but also for "how such works are made and the reasons for which they are made"—all the while remembering that "some are sincere and some counterfeit."[82] We cannot be sure if Elvis Costello's stagecraft imbued with *sprezzatura* eschews affectation for a few seconds of genuine frisson. But he has stirred and unsettled us enough that we are compelled to give an account of those fraught moments. Such a kinetic scene—with its iconic lessons in rehearsed spontaneity, studied nonchalance, and artful artlessness—may yet leave us ambivalent about pursuing the etiology of origins and intentions. Distracted *and* entranced by wit and fit, we readily submit to the supervening truths of fiction, to the realities inherent in the fabrications of art—phenomena worth taking seriously, worthy of addled attention spans.

Notes

1　https://tinyurl.com/33bxxaea.

2　https://tinyurl.com/38mcycke. I am grateful to William Day for sharing these two apt examples (viz., Scotto and Mingus).

3　Stanley Cavell, *Little Did I Know: Excerpts from Memory* (Stanford: Stanford University Press, 2010), 183.

4　Lydia Goehr, "Improvising *Impromptu*, Or, What to Do with a Broken String," in *The Oxford Handbook of Critical Improvisation Studies*, vol. 1, ed. George E. Lewis and Benjamin Piekut (New York: Oxford University Press, 2016), 459. See also Lydia Goehr, "What Anyway Is a 'Music Discomposed'?" and responses to Goehr collected in *Virtual Works—Actual*

Things: Essays in Music Ontology, edited by Paolo de Assis (Leuven: Leuven University Press, 2019).

5   Goehr, "Improvising *Impromptu*," *Critical Improvisation Studies*, 459, 462; italics in original.

6   Cavell, *Little Did I Know*, 183.

7   Elvis Costello and the Attractions appeared on *Saturday Night Live* with host Miskel Spillman (1897–1992), s3:e8. Spillman won the "Anyone Can Host" contest. The risk and rawness of inviting a person who may still be the show's only non-celebrity to host would appear to ratify this episode's even wider experimental and improvisatory attributes.

8   See https://youtu.be/eD_24nDzkeo.

9   Goehr, "Improvising *Impromptu*," *Critical Improvisation Studies*, 464; italics in original.

10   Ibid.

11   Sinéad O'Connor (1996-2023) performed on *Saturday Night Live* October 3, 1992; s18:e2.

12   See https://youtu.be/22wwbTQYKxc.

13   Jason Sudeikis hosted *Saturday Night Live* October 22, 2022; s47:e4.

14   Elvis Costello, *Unfaithful Music & Disappearing Ink* (New York: Blue Rider Press, 2016), 308.

15   Ralph Waldo Emerson, "Circles," *Essays: Second Series*, vol. 2 of *The Complete Works of Ralph Waldo Emerson* (Boston: Houghton Mifflin & Co., 1904), 318, 320.

16   For more on *agon* and generational contest, see my "We Were Educated for This?" in *Girls and Philosophy*, ed. Richard Greene and Rachel Robison-Greene (Chicago: Open Court, 2015), 199–218.

17   See my "A Reality Rescinded: The Transformative Effects of Fraud in *I'm Still Here*," in *The Philosophy of Documentary Film: Image, Sound, Fiction, Truth*, ed. David LaRocca (Lanham: Lexington Books of Roman & Littlefield, 2017), 537–76 and "The False Pretender: Deleuze, Sherman, and the Status of Simulacra," *The Journal of Aesthetics and Art Criticism*, vol. 69, no. 3 (Summer 2011): 321–9.

18   Stanley Cavell, "Music Discomposed," in *Must We Mean What We Say? A Book of Essays* (New York: Charles Scribner's Sons, 1969; Cambridge: Cambridge University Press, 1976; updated ed., 2002; Cambridge Philosophy Classics, 2015), 200.

19   Stanley Cavell, "Cons and Pros: *The Lady Eve*," in *Pursuits of Happiness: The Hollywood Comedy of Remarriage* (Cambridge, MA: Harvard University Press, 1981), 53.

20   Stanley Cavell, "The Fact of Television," in *Themes Out of School: Effects and Causes* (San Francisco: North Point Press, 1984), 253. See also *Television with Stanley Cavell in Mind*, ed. David LaRocca and Sandra Laugier (Exeter: University of Exeter Press, 2023).

21 Cavell, "Music Discomposed," *Must We Mean What We Say?*, 197–8; italics in original.

22 Ibid., 202.

23 Ibid., 201.

24 See Rosalind Krauss, "'The Rock': William Kentridge's Drawings for Projection," in *The Sharpest Point: Animation at the End of Cinema*, ed. Chris Gehman and Steve Reinke (Toronto: YYZ Books, 2005), 103.

25 Cavell, "Music Discomposed," *Must We Mean What We Say?*, 199.

26 Ibid.; italics in original.

27 Ibid., 208; italics in original.

28 Cavell, "The Fact of Television," *Themes Out of School*, 253.

29 Costello, *Unfaithful Music & Disappearing Ink*, 307–8.

30 Ibid., 308.

31 For notes on the creative use of constraints, see my "The Limits of Instruction," *Film and Philosophy*, vol. 13 (2009): 35–50 and "Teaching without Explication: Pedagogical Lessons from Rancière's *The Ignorant Schoolmaster* in *The Grand Budapest Hotel* and *The Emperor's Club*," *Journalism, Media and Cultural Studies*, vol. 10 (2016): 10–28.

32 See my "Suicide Machines: Bruce Springsteen, Ballard, and Broken Heroes on a Last Chance Power Drive," in *Transportation and the Culture of Climate Change: Accelerating Ride to Global Crisis*, ed. Tatiana Prorokova-Konrad (Morgantown: West Virginia University Press, 2020), 123–50.

33 Costello, *Unfaithful Music & Disappearing Ink*, 306.

34 See *Punk Rock and Philosophy*, ed. Joshua Heter and Richard Greene (Chicago: Carus Books, 2022).

35 See The Clash, "Know Your Rights" (1982), which begins: "this is a public service announcement … with guitar."

36 Ryan J. Prado, "The 20 Best Songs by Elvis Costello," *Paste*, May 24, 2014, https://tinyurl.com/ypbfvfpz.

37 Cavell, "Music Discomposed," *Must We Mean What We Say?*, 203.

38 Ibid., 198.

39 With thanks to William Day for helping me articulate these claims.

40 Richard Taruskin, *The Oxford History of Western Music: Music in the Late Twentieth Century*, vol. 5 (Oxford: Oxford University Press, 2009), 43.

41 Cavell, "A Matter of Meaning It," *Must We Mean What We Say?*, 214.

42 Eric Drott, "Fraudulence and the Gift Economy of Music," *Journal of Music Theory*, vol. 54, no. 1 (Spring 2010): 61.

43 Stephen W. Melville, *Philosophy Beside Itself: On Deconstruction and Modernism* (Minneapolis: University of Minnesota Press, 1986), 29.

44 See my "From Authenticity to Authentication: Cinaesthetics and Auteurship in the Age of AI," in *Aesthetic Authenticity in Cinema*, ed. Filipe Martins (Porto: Faculdade de Letras da Universidade do Porto [FLUP], 2023), 33–58.

45 See, for example, *Metacinema: The Form and Content of Filmic Reference and Reflexivity*, ed. David LaRocca (Oxford: Oxford University Press, 2021).

46 Cavell, "Music Discomposed," *Must We Mean What We Say?*, 193.

47 Ibid., 206.

48 Ibid.; italics in original.

49 See, for example, ibid., 225.

50 Costello, *Unfaithful Music & Disappearing Ink*, 307–8.

51 For more on gender and genre, see *The Geschlecht Complex: Addressing Untranslatable Aspects of Gender, Genre, and Ontology*, ed. Oscar Jansson and David LaRocca (New York: Bloomsbury, 2022).

52 On this score, see especially Garrett Stewart, *Barbra Streisand: The Mirror of Difference* (Detroit: Wayne State University Press, 2023) and in this volume, Chapter 4. See also ch. 20, "The Legible Voice," in *Attention Spans: Garrett Stewart, a Reader*, ed. David LaRocca (New York: Bloomsbury, 2024), 261–70.

53 See Frank Zappa, "Tinsel Town Rebellion," *Tinsel Town Rebellion* (1981).

54 Cavell, "A Matter of Meaning It," *Must We Mean What We Say?*, 228.

55 Cavell, "Music Discomposed," *Must We Mean What We Say?*, 207.

56 Ibid.

57 Ibid.

58 Ibid.

59 Ibid., 208.

60 Ibid., 209.

61 Ibid., 209–10.

62 Ibid., 209.

63 Cavell, "A Matter of Meaning It," *Must We Mean What We Say?*, 223.

64 Ibid.

65 Caroline Mimbs Nyce says "the app is basically just broadcast TV now," in "You're Looking at TikTok All Wrong," *The Atlantic*, March 1, 2024, theatlantic.com.

66 Megan Garber, "We've Lost the Plot," *The Atlantic*, January 30, 2023, theatlantic.com.

67 Cavell, "Music Discomposed," *Must We Mean What We Say?*, 209; italics in original.

68 Ibid., 210.

69 Ibid.

70 Ibid., 211.

71 Cavell, "A Matter of Meaning It," *Must We Mean What We Say?*, 220.

72 Ibid., 229.

73 Ibid.

74   Ibid., 236.

75   Ibid., 231.

76   Ibid., 236.

77   Emerson, "Circles," *The Complete Works*, 320.

78   Goehr, "Improvising *Impromptu*," *Critical Improvisation Studies*, 459. See also n.4.

79   Ibid., 462.

80   Ibid., 459; italics in original.

81   Cavell, "Music Discomposed," *Must We Mean What We Say?*, 212.

82   Ibid.

MOVEMENT IV

Intervals

10

Listening In

Cavell, Krenek, Cage, and Reich
at the Limits of Musical Meaning

KEVIN C. KARNES AND JOHN T. LYSAKER

STANLEY CAVELL'S "MUSIC DISCOMPOSED" was initially presented at the sixth annual Oberlin Colloquium, hosted by the Oberlin College Department of Philosophy on April 16–18, 1965. It was one of several symposia concerned with matters derided by positivist trends in Anglo-American philosophy such as mystical experience, Anselm's ontological argument, and, in Cavell's case, a "number of large questions about art and philosophy and the ways they bear on one another."[1] While Cavell's presentation concerned art in a general sense, his focus was modernism, and music at that, and then, specifically, the "*avant garde* composers who regard themselves as the natural successors of the work of Schoenberg's greatest pupil, Anton Webern."[2] Cavell's paper received responses from two leading aestheticians, Joseph Margolis and Monroe Beardsley, to which Cavell responded with what became "A Matter of Meaning It." The Colloquium was later edited by W. H. Capitan and D. D. Merrill and published in 1967 under the title *Art, Mind, and Religion*. Cavell then reprinted both of his contributions in *Must We Mean What We Say?*, first published by Charles Scribner's Sons in 1969.

A colloquium convening three leading aestheticians is an event unto itself. Cavell's papers have gone on to a more lasting impact, however, and not just in the field of philosophy. The *Journal of Music Theory* celebrated the essay's forty-fifth anniversary with a special issue in 2010.[3] We also wish to return to it and reflect on some of its chief motifs, which remain generative. One is methodological. Cavell proposes that art requires engagements that weave together (or move between) theory (or philosophy) and criticism: "an aesthetician incapable of producing criticism is simply incapable of recognizing and relevantly describing the objects of his discourse."[4] Aesthetics, like all fields of philosophy, proceeds by way of examples. If we do not know whether the object being considered is an example of music or painting or how it exemplifies those classes of things, we cannot proceed.

We share this commitment. Aestheticians (or philosophers of art) should have a concrete feel for how art works work. A poetics without some feel for prosody, for example, isn't really a poetics but a procedure that leaves a good deal of the patient on the table. But we also wish to thicken this commitment, albeit in a manner friendly to Cavell's essay. Competent critics are historically informed. They know, for example, what comes with presenting a work as a successor to Webern's inheritance of Schoenberg. We might debate what contexts are germane to this series of acts, but some context that links them must be in play. Otherwise, we proceed like botanists unaware of ecosystems.

What follows is a dialogue between a historian–critic, Kevin Karnes, and a philosopher–critic, John Lysaker, about Cavell's seminal essay. We proceed in this way because we feel it exemplifies the kind of scholarly bearing that art requires. Karnes is a musicologist who studies various musics of the twentieth and twenty-first centuries as sounding expressions of identity, difference, and belonging. His work spans archival research, oral history, and ethnography, engaging such adjacent fields as anthropology, ethnomusicology, and sound studies. He has published on subjects ranging from Arnold Schoenberg and post-war Jewish émigré culture to Arvo Pärt and Soviet disco. His newest work focuses on musically inspired exchange across the post-war East/West European divide, highlighting DJ culture, electronic music, and other manifestations of vernacular *avant-gardes*. Lysaker is a philosopher working in the philosophy of art and other areas, including ethics and philosophical psychology, often in an Emersonian manner. In art, his interests include philosophy's relation to poetry, ambient and minimalist musical works, and a broad range of twentieth-century aesthetics and art practices.

I. The Post-war Environment

JOHN T. LYSAKER: The essay is bold. Cavell the critic is frustrated by a series of works presented as genuine successors of Schoenberg's so-called serial compositions. He can't find any way to listen to them, anything to listen for, and the writings surrounding these works, some by the composers themselves, leave him even more disoriented. "One comes to realize," he says, "that these professionals themselves do not quite know who is and who is not rightly included among their peers, whose work counts and whose do not. No wonder then, that we outsiders do not know. And one result clearly communicated by these periodicals is that there is no obvious way to find out."[5] Cavell the philosopher then charges "fraudulence" and accuses the composers, particularly Ernst Krenek and Karlheinz Stockhausen, of "nihilism." I hope we can test these claims.

KEVIN C. KARNES: Already in Cavell's line about "*avant garde* composers who regard themselves as the natural successors of the work of Schoenberg's greatest pupil, Anton Webern," referenced in our opening words above, there is a lot of history to unpack. While origin stories are always more complicated than their common telling, Schoenberg's name is widely associated with two signal moves in twentieth-century composition. First, there was his self-conscious break from what is often called common-practice tonality, a way of organizing notes and harmonies hierarchically around a single, referential key, which had governed the composition of Western classical music since the sixteenth century or so. Around 1910, he started experimenting with ways of writing music such that neither successions of notes nor their simultaneous sounding made sense within this tonal framework. He thus began composing what we call *atonal* music. (Compare, for instance, his *Verklärte Nacht*, a tonal piece from 1899, with his atonal *Sechs kleine Klavierstücke*, op. 19, from 1911, both widely available online.)

His second big move came in the early 1920s, when he sought to systematize a method for composing atonal music, which he had previously been writing in an intuitive manner. What he hit upon, he called "twelve-tone composition." He wrote about it in 1923 and demonstrated it in his *Suite for Piano*, op. 25, that year.[6] With the twelve-tone method, he tried to capture, in an atonal context, something akin to the unifying effect of the referential key that tonality had provided. In lieu of choosing a central key, the twelve-tone method required the composer to begin their work by creating a series of twelve distinct chromatic pitches, and then to derive all further pitch relations in the piece from that series, via such manipulations as playing the series forward, backwards, and upside down, and by superimposing different transpositions of the series on top of one another. This manner of composition is widely called *serial*, in reference to the pitch series that defines it. Some, however, have always felt that Schoenberg's adherence to the serial method lacked rigor, owing to his inability to surrender fully to the system. Theodor Adorno charged him "assault[ing]" his own twelve-tone rows, reigning "sovereignly over them" as he created.[7] In contrast, Schoenberg's pupil, Anton Webern, was a purist when it came to serial composition. Those who followed *his* path were Cavell's concern.

Before elaborating further on the musical issues Cavell confronted in "Music Discomposed," I should say that I'm struck by what I read as his lack of curiosity about the critical environment he was entering. Take his principal source, the journal *Perspectives of New Music*, founded three years before the Oberlin Colloquium. He writes of the "rancors and rites in [its] pages" and a "sense of conflict [that] is unmistakable." "The air," he observes, "is of men fighting for their artistic lives."[8] Well, yes, and for good reason. Its founding vision was largely laid by figures whose creative lives were literally saved by fleeing wartime Europe for America: Bolshevik Russia in the case of Igor Stravinsky, Nazi Germany in the case of Ernst Krenek, occupied France in the case of Darius Milhaud. The journal's principal patron, the philanthropist Paul Fromm, was a German Jew whose family fled the Nazis in 1938. Over half of its editorial board was Jewish, and all of them looked to Schoenberg as a spiritual father—a figure who, as an Austrian Jew himself, escaped to the States in 1935. For many of these composers, the fight Cavell references was real, and it was recent.

Cavell's main target was a case in point. Born in Vienna in 1900, Krenek found early fame in interwar Germany with his opera *Jonny spielt auf* (1926), the success of which was massive. It drew official ire almost immediately upon Hitler's rise to power in 1933, owing to both the opera's jazz-like idiom and its Black protagonist. Bureaucratic hounding, public protests, and the canceling of professional opportunities came to a head in 1937–38 with the Nazi campaign against "degenerate" art and music, a famous poster for which featured a racist caricature of the saxophone-playing Jonny wearing a Star of David on his lapel. That year, Krenek emigrated to America and took up a post at Vassar College, having already traded his jazz-inspired musical language for post-Schoenbergian serialism.

Landing at Vassar, Krenek took part in a fundamental transformation in music faculties and curricula then under way at some of America's leading colleges and universities, which welcomed a tide of European émigrés and refugees, many of whom studied, practiced, and taught serial composition—and not just serialism as Schoenberg understood it, but so-called integral or total serialism, which I'll explain below. This distinctive variety of post-war serialism also took root in post-war Western Europe, where the Darmstadt Summer Courses and the journal *Die Reihe*, which Cavell also references (its title was German for "the row"—i.e., the twelve-tone-row), celebrated integral serialism as an ostensibly rational, even scientific way around the romantic subjectivity then widely deemed to have enabled if not led to the advent of Nazi ideology in music, among other fields.

Whereas Schoenberg's serialism consisted of deriving a work's pitch material from a germinal twelve-tone row, leading figures at Darmstadt—Pierre Boulez, prominently—extended that principle across multiple parameters of musical structure simultaneously. They accomplished this by assigning each pitch of the twelve-tone row a unique integer, thus converting the pitch series into an integer series, and then assigning each integer in the series to one of any number of other musical parameters: note durations, timbres, dynamics, and so on. This gave rise to the phenomenon of *integral* or *total serialism*, which not only differed from its precursors by degree but entailed, in fact, a compositional process fundamentally unlike any that had been imagined before. Schoenberg's method had left everything but the moment-to-moment selection of pitches up to the artist; while the row and its manipulations determined which pitch should come next in a work, the composer retained their customary right to select at will among forms, phrase lengths, dynamic gestures, orchestration, and everything else. Boulez's integral serialism, in contrast, required the composer to surrender *all* those choices to the dictates of the integer series and its systematic manipulations. In effect, the system generated a work *algorithmically*; the composer designed the integer series and selected initial inputs into the system (the starting pitch, dynamic marking, and so forth), and then they watched, as it were, as every sounding element of the work was generated by the system itself. Boulez's *Structures* for two pianos (1952–61) is often regarded as an exemplary model of the style, though the advent of electronic sound synthesis was already making even more musical parameters available for serial treatment, as in Krenek's *Spiritus intelligentiae, sanctus (Pfingstoratorium)*, op. 152 (1955–56), which Cavell encountered in the composer's essay he cites at length. This was the approach to composition to which *Perspectives of New Music* was dedicated, and to which Krenek himself was devoted in the 1950s and 1960s. It was this mode of composition that inspired Cavell to write "Music Discomposed."

LYSAKER: This is a rich context, and it shows that the struggle and rancor are not merely formal but tied, at least in the minds and hearts of the participants, to historical, even existential circumstances. In one of the Krenek passages you found, he says: "Actually the composer has come to distrust his inspiration because it is not really as innocent as it was supposed to be, but rather conditioned by a tremendous body of recollection, tradition, training, and experience."[9] The protagonists are emigrating from more than homelands, therefore. They are fleeing a culture in ruins, one whose artistic currents they find tainted if not bankrupt.

KARNES: This really can't be overstated. This was literally post-war music.

LYSAKER: Cavell's overall disorientation was far from unique to him, however, and listeners were not only perplexed by serial compositions. In May of 1958, John Cage's work received a twenty-five-year retrospective concert at Town Hall in New York, and at certain points the crowd was effusive in its disapproval. At its conclusion, his *Williams Mix* for eight tracks of ¼" magnetic tape (1952) met with a reciprocal volley of applause and boos, each contingent trying to outdo the other.[10] The work splices together six groups of sounds, such as city, country, and electronic according to patterns determined by *I Ching* chance operations. To the ear, it sounds like a jumble of sounds without any discernable structure—although, as in a serial work, a rigid structure is in fact present, with Cage notating pitch, loudness, and timbre according to a rhythmic structure, admittedly an elusive one, with successive phrase lengths of 12, 16, 28, 26, and 18 beats.

KARNES: Both the distinction and the intersection you point to are important. Cage's method of composing by chance operations was also a kind of algorithmically determined process, but it was emphatically not a serial process. In Boulez's serialism, every detail is determined according to rational, quasi-mathematical manipulations of initial inputs. In Cage's chance music, every detail is left to the casting of dice, as it were. In both cases, the composer cedes control of the generation of their scores to a system. And in both, the logic and structure of what's produced is often deemed inscrutable.

LYSAKER: Then in 1964, Arthur Danto published "The Artworld," now one of the most celebrated essays in philosophical aesthetics. As he sees it, a revolution in art requires a revolution in theory that renders the new intelligible. This happened with the advent of impressionism and post-impressionism, he thinks. People learned to stop looking for imitation and to regard painting as a "freshly opened area between real objects and real facsimiles of real objects," in which one might explore color, basic shapes, the multifaceted nature of human perception, even the unconscious.[11] But, and here Danto's concerns dovetail with Cavell's, how does one approach an art object that is materially identical to a non-art object? What distinguishes the art version from the non-art version? Warhol's *Brillo Boxes* also appeared in 1964, which in part provoked Danto's reflections. "Where is the art in that?," one could, probably should ask. And not simply to police galleries. Rather, one is asking: to what should I direct my attention? I thus feel the pull of Cavell's disorientation and admire him for working through it. And I am struck that whereas Danto aspired to make room for what he was witnessing, Cavell felt compelled to draw a line in the sand.

II. How Music Moves Us

LYSAKER: Before we address the charges of fraudulence and nihilism, I'd like to consider a different, more general claim about why art matters, although it will help us understand Cavell's accusations. "But objects of art do not merely interest and absorb," Cavell writes, "they move us; we are not involved with them, but concerned with them, and care about them; we treat them in special ways, invest them with a value which normal people otherwise only reserve for other people—*and* with the same scorn and outrage."[12] I wish he had said a bit more about how they move us or move him or made more of the analogy he draws with investing value in other people. But he does enough to assemble a general picture. I don't think he means that we think that artworks and people have the same, let alone equal, value. Rather, it's as if we can be encouraged or let down by artworks in a manner akin to being encouraged or let down by people. But what are artworks up to such that we puzzle over them and find them good company or bad?

Cavell distinguishes artworks from typical statements and the intentions they might express as with: "I love the color blue." His claim, therefore, is that artworks are not simply conveying facts about the maker, as if Beethoven wrote his Seventh Symphony to convey his love for A major. Cavell also distinguishes how artworks move us from how technological skill or moral action moves us. While I hesitate to class both sets in the same category (*praxis* isn't *technē*), Cavell's concern is nevertheless clear: some actions achieve goals, and we praise them for achieving them effectively. But art, Cavell insists, doesn't move us through its effectiveness. A composition may hush a room but those listening intently are not seeking, with admiration, its room-hushing powers.

But what then focuses our attention and moves us to cheer or decry an artwork? Cavell suggests that art "celebrates the fact that men can intend their lives at all (if you like, that they are free to choose)."[13] Such a remark only seems possible after the onset of modernity. Established traditions of conduct are no longer sacrosanct. In fact, they have become suspicious. People now must find their own way, hence novels, according to Lukács, which depict individuals finding their way through the collapse of divinely sanctioned social orders and vocations, which underwrote epics. Modern artworks are thus like characters in a novel. They exemplify the effort to make their own way in a world of "indifferent nature and determined society," to return to Cavell. Such works thus move us with how they find their way, and through how their way resonates or fails to resonate with our own. But what matters is that they have a way that we can track and assess and so share in. What do you make of this?

KARNES: Attempts to discern the composer's intention have been so roundly pilloried in musicology for so long that we've all mostly just stopped talking about intention at all. Part of the problem derives from what's often described as the non-representational nature of much (some would say all) music. Musical notes and their conglomerations simply do not—cannot—convey ideas with anything approaching the concreteness of words. This has led some, starting in the nineteenth century, to describe music as an "absolute" kind of art, with the score inscribing nothing more or less than arrays of notes, and with its realization in performance consisting simply of *tönend bewegte Formen*—"forms moved in sounding," as Eduard Hanslick wrote in 1854. Mark Evan Bonds' book on absolute music is a great source for this history.[14]

But it's important to realize that however unknowable a composer's intentions may be, and however limiting or not those intentions may be to our own experience of their work, listeners have for two centuries been listening in ways a lot like what you describe above, especially with respect to a work's perceived resonance with their—or our—own experience. In 1810, E. T. A. Hoffmann heard in Beethoven's Fifth Symphony an "infinite yearning" that was, for him, the essence of a peculiar form of "romanticism" he described—which, importantly, happened to have impelled his own life as author and composer.[15] A little later, Adolf Bernhard Marx described what he heard as the narrative unfolding of Beethoven's *Eroica*, complete with the dramatic interaction ("battle") of contrasting themes ("armies"), as a heroic confrontation with the unknown and hostile forces lurking within.[16] Still today, as Tia DeNora and a generation of ethnomusicologists and sociologists of music have shown, we often identify with music that seems to us to echo or resonate with aspects of our own lived experience, with our present sensibilities, our memories and nostalgia, our imagined futures.[17] We describe what we hear in terms of "surprises" and "interruptions," "introductions" and "recollections," "expectation" and "closure."

When Cavell writes of our concern for artworks being akin to our concern for people, I think he's revealing his attachment to this kind of listening, a deeply human kind of listening. He *expects* that whatever music he listens to will be amenable to hearing in these ways: it will accommodate narrative description in relation to some kind of imaginable, inhabitable journey, or at least it will be describable in terms of some sort of relatable experience. It's only fair that Cavell would approach the challenge of listening in this way. After all, prior to the 1950s, just about every work of Western classical music accommodated listening along these lines. And although he never tells us exactly what he was listening to when he wrote "Music Discomposed," total serialism, to which he responds, absolutely refuses such accommodation. If you haven't done so yet, you should listen now to Boulez's *Structures*, or to Krenek's *Spiritus Intelligentiae Sanctus*. As Boulez's title suggests, the music is more architectural than processual: athematic, without repeating elements, denying the listener even a sense of beginning, middle, and ending. Cage's music also refuses to accommodate this kind of listening. For Cavell, this refusal of accommodation is a problem.

LYSAKER: A poetic analogue, namely voice, might also apply. Cavell expects, I think, that someone has *their* way of generating art and that their way is an essential part of what is on offer. I like this up to a point and have tried to capture some of it by claiming that artworks have a bearing that one can track, say Anselm Kiefer's way of inhabiting the history of German culture, including but not limited to painting, or the clear pleasure Wallace Stevens takes in the iambic patter of English. But Cavell has something more ambitious in mind. According to Cavell, every word counts in an Emerson essay. It's as if Emerson is there in every word, assuming responsibility for every word, answerable for every word. And that provides something of a measure for authorship, one already operating in "Music Discomposed" when Cavell writes that "art plays with one of man's fates, the fate of being accountable for everything you do and are, intended or not."[18] Boulez's *Structures* as well as Cage's *Williams Mix* are the antithesis of this. Let me talk about Cage's piece, which I know better. His use of the *I Ching* to determine when and where tape is cut and spliced effaces "Cage" just where we might expect to find the composer's signature, as it were. And for Cavell, that prompts a justifiable disappointment.

KARNES: I agree with you about Cavell and Cage, with the philosopher's judgment extending to Krenek and presumably others as well. But to extend your reading of Kiefer's work as suggesting a way of inhabiting the history of German culture, I think the widespread post-war turn to integral serialism was also precisely that, as I'll elaborate below, however differently its artistic products were widely deemed to meet those listening or observing. Kiefer's work is devastating. Krenek's is incomprehensible.

III. Fraudulence and Surprise

LYSAKER: We've worked our way into the issue of fraudulence, which is central to "Music Discomposed." Cavell says that the "dangers of fraudulence and trust, are essential to the experience of art. If anything in this paper should count as a thesis, that is my thesis."[19] The issue isn't forgery, as if someone might present a work as Krenek's or Cage's when it isn't. In fact, that might be impossible in some sense. Regardless, the issue is closer to counterfeit—someone is trying to pass something off as bona fide when it isn't. Although even that isn't quite right, given that Cavell claims that the line distinguishing the genuine from the counterfeit is beginning to fade, which is why he wished to redraw it.

Cavell is "insisting that we can no longer be sure that any artist is sincere— we haven't convention or technique or appeal to go on any longer: *anyone could fake it.*"[20] This reminds me of various remarks gathered for a box set of Ornette Coleman's albums for Atlantic, *Beauty is a Rare Thing* (1993). Several accuse Coleman of fraudulence. Consider this from trumpeter Roy Eldridge (1911–89), who was speaking to *Esquire* in 1961: "I listened to him all kind of ways. I listened to him high. I listened to him sober. I even played with him. I think he's jiving baby."[21] What does that mean? There might be no reason why a given note is played when and how it is played. And if you listen as if there were, you've been had. And interestingly, Coleman himself testifies to the issue. Speaking in 1963 with Martin Williams from *Jazz*, he declares: "It was when I realized that I could make mistakes that I decided I was really on to something."[22] If anything can go anywhere, if nothing is a mistake, nothing like a work or even a phrase is on offer. But Coleman is insistent that something is on offer, which leads me to wonder what kind of mistake one might make in total serialism. You could break a general rule in setting up initial conditions for your system, but could one really make a mistake within the work? The work seems to have disappeared under the dictates of general rules.

KARNES: For me, as a listener in 2023, fraudulence is not a major concern. Or even an issue. If a work proves uncompelling or impenetrable, I simply turn away, and listen to another. I do not assume the kind of compact with the composer that would lead me to register my disappointment or indifference as having been defrauded. But I think it's important to reflect here on the radically different worlds in which I and Cavell are listening, and the substantially different investments that listening to music requires of us in turn. First, when he wrote in the 1960s, the music he confronted was radically different from anything that had come before—and, importantly, both its sounding idiom and its manner of creation were very, very new. Krenek himself acknowledged it as such. Writing of serialism in the very essay of 1960 that so stoked Cavell's ire, he admitted, "we have to face the fact that under the influence of the constructive rigor that was the very consequence of Expressionistic roaming[,] serial music has turned away from its rhetorical past."[23] Nothing, in short, had prepared Cavell—or the broader world—for music like that which Krenek or Boulez composed. And many listeners shared Cavell's frustration.

But there is also a second factor at play here, namely the sheer amount of labor that acquiring and learning to understand music required in Cavell's day, as opposed to ours. I noted above that recordings of Boulez's *Structures* are widely available online, and anyone with borrowing privileges at a library can freely read *Perspectives of New Music* on their home computer. Cavell, in contrast, had to seek these things out: purchasing concert tickets, ordering records, visiting the listening collection in a library, browsing physical copies of journals whose collective contents were, if you were lucky, cataloged in a card file at your local branch. And then there is the problem of *Perspectives* itself. On the first page of the essay that opens the very first volume of the journal, we read that it was established as an "expression of our interest in opening avenues of communication between composers and interested performers and listeners."[24] I can just imagine Cavell, feeling adrift as a listener, reading these lines and thinking, "Well, this is for me!," only to move beyond its opening lines to discover little other than esoteric and sometimes pompous prose by serialist composers only writing for each other. And then Krenek's statements, which we'll address below, basically acknowledge that engaging listeners was not, in fact, those composers' project at all. The journal could not have seemed anything but a classic bait-and-switch. The whole experience would reasonably leave anyone who'd undertaken Cavell's quest for understanding feeling duped.

LYSAKER: I too pause when Cavell invokes "fraudulence." In part, I rarely wonder about it (in general or when confronted by particular works). And that makes me wonder: why is this a focal concern in 1964? I very much appreciate your contextualization, therefore. And keeping to the thought that questions have histories too and limiting myself to Cage and those composing in his wake, I think we have grown used to listening for and to the activity of sounds, that is, to sounds relating to one another outside traditional or even settled musical structures. More particularly, I think many now find more to hear in the attack and decay of sounds, in their textures and resonances or timbre. When I think about what I like in Brian Eno's ambient works, that's it, more or less: sounds coming and going arrhythmically, resonating in a particular space.[25] By treating them in various ways (say by playing a tape at half-speed, thereby lowering pitch), the simple becomes complex. But there is no score behind those albums. No pre-existing work is being performed let alone recorded. Could Eno be joking? No doubt. But I trust my ear, as it were, and I will let my recounting vindicate what I find unfolding. Not that it means what I say it means. But if I can work into something and articulate why it thrills, I'm good.

But a deeper concern is probably circulating. If one takes artworks to celebrate the "fact that men can intend their lives at all," then all is lost when the intention is either to defraud or disappears in a swirl of effects that never were, maybe never could be intended. While I appreciate approaching art with this in mind, namely, an image of the very effort to intend, my own feel for works attends to how they conspire with their fatedness, as it were (say the acoustic facts of a room or the size of a gallery or the history of the genre—or with a diverse set of receptive capacities, including my own) and with what results. Not that I consider intention irrelevant. For me, an artwork needs to be intended as "art" to be a work of art. Wind in dry grass is not a "Field Symphony," although subjecting it to a kind of sonic organization might be, say by recording those sounds (which inevitably arranges them) and presenting them through some form of playback (which marks a second arrangement). That said, there remains, always, a gap between the realized work and what the creator imagined it would be, even upon finishing it. And that gap impacts how I take it up. It's as if, with unsettled syntax and semantics, I've been invited to consider something gathered in the work, initiated by the work, say, the activity of sounds. More specifically, I've been encouraged to root around in whatever the work generates through the interactions of its elements, and to report on what I find, some of which, no doubt, was not intended but nevertheless can be credibly found in the work as it interacts with and refracts its history and environment.

Looking at criticism from this theoretical angle, one that takes each work as a kind of experiment in search of a collaborator, I'm less worried about fraudulence as a general threat. But experiments can fail, and so, if the metaphor holds, there will be times when I'm disappointed or let down, and can articulate why and how. I thus want to affirm Cavell's larger claim that artworks matter in ways that allow us to be grateful or disappointed for the work and what it enables in and for us. Is this true for you, and if so, what are some of the ways in which musical works disappoint you, and do those ways indicate some generalizable ways in which artworks matter?

KARNES: I'd much rather talk about what I'm grateful for! I'm grateful for works that surprise me, or that challenge me in ways I can't easily respond to, that I keep returning to in my mind when I'm not listening, and that draw me back to listen again. I'm grateful for works that challenge me to listen to *other* works in new ways, or even to think of myself *as a listener* in ways I didn't before, or maybe don't even want to. I'll give some examples.

Schoenberg's *Sechs kleine Klavierstücke*, which I mentioned above: fleeting, freely atonal, not yet serial. How can I hear these works as statements that resonate with my own wayfinding as a listener and a person? Is there a narrative unfolding of events and ideas, however obscured on the first (or hundredth) hearing? In the second of the six works in the collection, for sure, and also in the sixth, a funereal tribute to Gustav Mahler. And I think I've found something to hold onto in all the others in the set but the first. But the *first*: it eludes me. Yet my experience with the others convinces me that *something must be there*. So, I keep listening, searching.

Sometimes the challenge is simpler: "Mumbly" from Richard D. James' (aka Aphex Twin's) *Caustic Window* LP from 1994. What kind of modulation is it that makes the principal line sound so fuzzy, so urgently unfocused, like a grainy, partly faded photograph somehow translated into sound? I'm just now getting into analogue synths, and it's a challenge—a technical challenge—that's had me stumped for months.

Sometimes the challenge is deeper, prompting me to question my own sense of myself as a listener. Like in the final number from Philip Glass' *Einstein on the Beach* (1975), the second half, "We have need of a soothing story to banish the disturbing thoughts of the day." The music here, coming after everything we've heard thus far, is to me just so hauntingly, devastatingly beautiful. But the words are so cheesy that I feel embarrassed to be listening to it even by myself. ("How much do I love you? Count the stars in the sky ....") And yet I do listen, again and again, drawn back as much (I imagine) by the sheer beauty of the musical lines and texture as by the spectacle of myself, present before myself, listening to such undisguised schlock. Am I really the kind of listener who listens to such stuff? Obviously, I am. (I guess?) Or wait, maybe I'm missing something here, selling myself or the music short. I'd better listen again.

I'd say that what disappoints me as a listener is *not* being challenged by what I'm listening to. But I'm not sure how generalizable this is. I'm mindful of the fact that I'm just one person, listening in relation to my own present concerns and questions, my own past, my own life. (Not everyone is just now getting into analogue synthesizers.) And I feel certain that what doesn't challenge me must surely challenge someone, somewhere, in relation to their own experience. Also, there is a difference between being challenged and being cast out into the open ocean, with no ties to anything we might claim as our own, with no horizon line in sight. I think that's where Cavell found himself, reading Krenek and maybe listening to him as well. What about you? How do you chart a course between gratitude and disappointment as a listener, and how might that course condition how we respond to Cavell in the present?

LYSAKER: "I read for the lusters," Emerson says; and so, should we listen.[26] I thus love your emphasis on gratitude. I too like to be taken somewhere, which is how I hear surprise within something like a hearable arc of development or interplay. And I doubly love how what grabs you puts you into question—who am I to be moved by this?, with equal emphasis on the "I" and the "this." That openness requires a kind of vulnerability, which is something I hear in Cavell's essay, in his concern over being taken for a ride that doesn't go anywhere. This is partly why his essay still moves me.

What moves us or fails to move us is often tricky to articulate, however, and even trickier to offer as persuasive in some generalizable manner, although assuming the task of a critic requires one to do so. As with philosophy, mood matters. Sometimes certain works are not available to me because I am not available to them. And as with love, there is something accidental in the attraction, something one should never insist on universalizing, despite Kant's insistence in the *Critique of Judgment* that judgments of beauty, while subjective in origin, seek, even expect universal acknowledgment. But there is still something there to indicate and share, as you do with the closing bits of *Einstein on the Beach*, even if that leads to a discussion of whether the lines, textures, and rhythms outstrip the lyrical cheese. (I don't remember my relation to this work. I too will have to return and listen again.)

Regardless, in being moved I want to be able to recount what the fuss is all about, and that is part of being moved for me. I'm compelled to testify, to register and track the movement, chase it. That's a way of being in it, intimately, of respecting it. And if I can't, no gratitude. I might even feel irritation. Clichéd writing or playing also disappoints, particularly when a composer seems to have a "style" that almost overwhelms whatever they do.

I really struggle with Philip Glass' symphonies, for example, even though I thrill to some of his piano works, say "Mad Rush" (1989), and still find myself drawn into a tone poem, "The Light" (1987). The difference is a kind of singularity to those works. Being in them is not like being anywhere else, even though each is instantly recognizable as his work at a harmonic and rhythmic level. I do not want to fetishize novelty, therefore. The issue concerns what happens when you give yourself over to the work, attentively. "The Light" seems to absorb many elements from the *Koyaanisquatsi* soundtrack (1982) but nevertheless stands on its own. It is rhythmically gripping and intriguing in its syncopations, rich in coloration, and immanently dynamic— the brass wells up from within as if something is breaking through and around you.

That said, I share Cavell's impatience with what he calls "the constant search for effects."[27] After being introduced to the Big Ears Festival in Knoxville, Tennessee, I've been listening to a lot of free jazz over the last few years, including works and performances by some amazing contemporaries such as Mary Halvorson, Jason Moran, and Tyshawn Sorey. It's a fantastic time for jazz, less a renaissance than a period of growth, with artists taking risks, say by composing in a manner that maybe begins in a so-called classical idiom but invites and leads to improvisation, which John Zorn has been doing for some time as well. But when there are genuine risks there will be "mistakes," to recall Coleman. In live improvisation, this often entails efforts to sound *free*, but which seem little more than flights from dead-ends or laziness or an inability to get-with the other players. Squawk, squawk, squawk, mash, mash, mash, louder ever louder, and the audience roars. That's not "free" to me. When it erupts discreetly out of what had come before and leads nowhere, it's flight. Freedom is a capacity to be with the instrument, a history of composition/performance, and other players in a living, generative manner that can carry—possibly transport—an attentive, open audience. And those capacities, discoveries, and resulting creations bring joy and prompt gratitude.

IV. Nihilism

LYSAKER: Our emphasis on challenge and surprise, particularly in discernable contexts of change and transition, drops us right into the question of nihilism. Let me quote Cavell's concern at length, in part because I could imagine someone saying something very similar today.

> Nothing we now have to say, no *personal* utterance, has its meaning conveyed in the conventions and formulas we now share. In a time of slogans, sponsored messages, ideologies, psychological warfare, mass projects, where words have lost touch with their sources or objects, and

in a phonographic culture where music is for dreaming, or for kissing, or for taking a shower, or having your teeth drilled, our choices seem to be those of silence, or nihilism (the denial of shared meaning altogether), or statements so personal as to form the possibility of communication without the support of convention. And then, of course, they are most likely to even seem to communicate. Such, at any rate, are the choices which the modern works of art I know seem to me to have made. I should say that the attempt to re-invent convention is the alternative I take Schoenberg and Stravinsky and Bartók to have taken; whereas in their total organization, Krenek and Stockhausen have chosen nihilism.[28]

I appreciate that Cavell locates an aesthetic concern within a more general one: we lack shared conventions against which something personal might appear. Ideologies in the sense used here efface the personal at a thematic level. Sameness allows for participation rather than sharing, which moves among differences. Slogans and the like, at a performative level, undermine communication from the inside. Many do not mean what they say, and not just because they favor irony. Some talk in code, others lie, and still others seem to have abandoned communication altogether in favor of manipulation. In this context, it seems valiant to intend anything, let alone something that can challenge addressees rather than manipulate them. Moreover, here the aesthetic floats like a life-preserver in a sea of noise. Not that art will provide generalizable meanings in the manner of a new mythos. But it might exemplify a process of generating shared but novel meaning and so stand, almost allegorically, for the effort to find one's way by conversing with one's past and with one's contemporaries. The rhetoric of nihilism thus concerns more than artworks that turn their back on the audience or slide into counterfeit. To Cavell, Krenek and company seem to abandon precisely what they hoped to rescue from the ruins of European totalitarianism—something still recognizably human.

KARNES: I think you're pointing to something important when you speak of a work as an aid to finding one's way by conversing with one's past. I pointed to something along those lines with reference to ideas of narrative listening, above. But listening for habitable traces of a past that is shared with others is also crucially important. And it's with respect to that, I think, where Cavell makes a point that is absolutely relevant to our listening today. Krenek is key to his argument, so I'll answer your long quotation from Cavell with a similarly lengthy statement by the composer, from an essay he published in the very first issue of *Perspectives of New Music* in 1962.

As soon as everything from pitch succession to density to dynamics to time values is regulated by serial statements derived from one single archetype [...] so that literally everything is intricately and inextricably related to everything else, these relationships are no longer conducive to establishing individually profiled thematic shapes susceptible of "progressive variation," because predetermination has already covered all details of the musical process in a manner that precludes further "inspirational" elaboration. The panthematic concept carried through to the extreme leads to athematic, nondevelopmental, subjectless music, wherein a parallel to nonrepresentational painting may be seen. This evolution indeed does away with most of the fundamental concepts that had traditionally dominated the creation and perception of music since its rise in Western civilization. [...] The result of such far-reaching predetermination by serial statements is a condition of imperceptibly manipulated chaos, where attention is drawn not to the dramatized destinies of personalized themes taken through easily discernible peripeties, but to the infinite fluctuations and subtle mutations in the numerous aspects of the sounding matter.[29]

In this passage, Krenek describes a listener's encounter (his own encounter?) with the very kind of music he was then writing, and he lays his cards out on the table. To compose by means of the algorithmic systems essential to total serialism, which derive every sounding element of a work from the ordering of a generative series of pitches, is to confine the composer's work to the so-called pre-compositional labor of designing the algorithm and determining its initial input (i.e., the series of pitches itself). To work in this way is thus to deny the composer any possibility of shaping the work as it takes form in time; its form, down to its most subtle details, is determined by the algorithm itself. This manner of composing, this way of a creative subject relating to the object produced through their labor, was wholly new in Western music. And the sounding forms it gave rise to, as noted above with respect to Boulez's *Structures* and Krenek's *Spiritus Intelligentiae Sanctus*, were so absolutely novel as to seem to stand, as Krenek himself suggests, outside that tradition itself. No amount of listening to Western classical music composed beyond this particular niche of post-war Euro-American culture will prepare a listener to grasp the relation of the part to the whole in such compositions, or to hear the unfolding of the work in narrative terms, as nearly the entirety of the tradition had invited them to do.

But it's important to note that Krenek did not regard this move as abdicating his responsibility to respond to Europe's twentieth-century catastrophes. Quite the opposite. Only, the terms of his response were different from those Cavell may have imagined. While some might well regard the artist as charged with somehow trying to salvage something human from amidst the wreckage, Krenek—and here I'm leaning partly on Richard Taruskin's own response to Cavell—saw the human foremost as the origin and cause of the catastrophes themselves.[30] It was human reason, history, prejudice, custom, and self-regard—above all, collective self-regard—that brought us

Hiroshima, Auschwitz, Holodomor, and countless other horrors. It was *that* humanity, in this view, that one must work to transcend. Krenek comes close to conceding this openly in a passage Cavell quotes as evidence of his nihilism. "The composer has come to distrust his inspiration because it is not really as innocent as it was supposed to be," Krenek writes, "but rather [it is] conditioned by a tremendous body of recollection, tradition, training, and experience. To avoid the dictations of such ghosts, he prefers to set up an impersonal mechanism which will furnish, according to premeditated patterns, unpredictable situations."[31] For Cavell, this elevation of the "impersonal" might well have been proof enough of Krenek's nihilism.

But to give Krenek what I think he's due, the problem with making art that orients the individual toward a shared experience or collective past is that our history and traditions themselves are ghastly, things we would do well to deface, or at least transcend. Yet the problem with *that*, and here I do find myself more sympathetic to Cavell's position than Krenek's, is that transcending one's history, much less defacing it, is wholly impossible in practice. To his credit, Krenek comes close to acknowledging this point, with the cost of his attempt being paid for by the work in the form of the listener's incomprehension—to which, he holds, the composer must be indifferent. "It may be stated," he writes,

> that whatever occurs in this piece at any given point is premeditated and therefore technically predictable. However, while the preparation and the layout of the material as well as the operations performed therein are the consequence of serial premeditation, the audible results of these procedures were not visualized as the purpose of the procedures. Seen from this angle, the results are incidental.[32]

Krenek's colleague Charles Wuorinen, also writing in the pages of *Perspectives*, took this position to its logical end, severing the work—his own work—from every discursive function that music had historically played in Western culture. "It seems that in music which is brought into being by the working out of externally created *a priori* statements regarding order, the act of performance has little significance—what counts is the accurate realization of the abstract *structure*, free of the expressive inflection that is built into human execution and is desirable in other kinds of music."[33]

LYSAKER: The act of performance has little significance. The results are incidental. I take these statements to mean that one cannot hear the work in the work. It would be like looking for the answer to a math problem in the shadings of differently numbered pencils. I think Cavell is right to term this fraudulent. It looks like a musical work, but it isn't because the "sounding matter" doesn't matter as matter or even sound. But is it nihilistic? The meaning is not in what is shared, and what is shared is, as shared, meaningless. Moreover, a long tradition of trying to share meaning in and through the generation of novel sounds, notes and chords, phrases, and structures is being kicked to the curb, presented as outmoded, even complicit with mind-numbing atrocities. I think one could argue that this is nihilism, which is what I sense, even feel when it dawns on me not only that what I'm listening for is the wrong thing, but moreover that listening itself is off base from the get-go. Not that I am unable to appreciate the bind you portray regarding dreaded entanglements and complicities. But it is difficult if not impossible to find in works of total serialism a path, even crumbs, leading elsewhere.

Let's set ourselves in an auditorium, awaiting the beginning of a performance of works composed in a total, serialist manner. What will transpire? Schoenberg imagined he would fashion a new harmonic sensibility that would eventually fuel new intuitions, new inspirations. Is something generative lurking in Krenek and total serialism, something that might still require performances and recordings? If not, and it seems not, I am inclined to regard such performances and recordings as ironic death notices. Each announces, without nostalgia, with either mourning or melancholia, "that which you have come to hear has died." If this is right, one also could treat total serialism as skepticism unhinged, and in a manner that Cavell also theorizes. Recall Krenek's distrust of inspiration. It actually seems much stronger than simple distrust. Total serialism aims to drive inspiration from music altogether, and to deny audiences any opportunity to be inspired by what they hear. And this recalls me to what Cavell finds in Shakespearean tragedies, a kind of annihilating comportment inherent in skepticism, whose "'doubt' is motivated not by (not even where it is expressed as) a (misguided) intellectual scrupulousness but by a (displaced) denial, by a self-consuming disappointment that seeks a world-consuming revenge."[34]

Interestingly, and I'm still thinking with Cavell, Cage might fare a bit better in this theoretical context, which surprises me. In Cage's works, the activity of sounds is what manifests when one no longer tries to express or even intend anything except a general *Achtung!* directed toward sounds coming and going, whether from twelve radios or the concert hall itself. The work thus genuinely offers or presents what is on offer, and that is what those in attendance share with it. I suppose the next question becomes whether that is sufficient to generate shared meaning. I want to say "yes"— there remains something to process and discuss, from conceptual aspects of the work to what one hears. Beyond the displacement of a set of traditional expectations, one also shares a certain here and now dilated by the work, even if the "music" does not really help you navigate it, whether by exemplification or through the establishment of vibratory attunements, as one finds in the events of "Deep Listening" generated by the work of Pauline Oliveros, your teacher Stuart Dempster, and behind them La Monte Young.

Looking back to 1964, therefore, I don't think the choice is either Krenek's integral serialism or a look back to Schoenberg and Stravinsky. Other trends in *avant-garde* music were already afoot.

V. Reich's Alternative Path

KARNES: Among the things that stand out to me in Cavell's critique of Krenek—and this is something Krenek's words point to—is his mapping of technique onto perception, or even of the *idea* behind a technique giving rise to a music that we perceive in a given way. Total serialism, owing to its algorithmic genesis and subsequent unimpeded unfolding, yields music that resists comprehension as part of a historically conditioned Western canon. But as you suggest, the same post-war Euro-American culture that gave rise to those works and approaches Cavell rejected saw the emergence of alternatives beyond what he considered, even ways out of the dead end he foresaw. One such alternative was proposed by Steve Reich in such early works as *It's Gonna Rain* (1965). The raw sound material of *It's Gonna Rain* is a tape recording of Brother Walter, a Pentecostal preacher Reich recorded in San Francisco. To create the work, Reich made loops out of several tape copies of the recording (his equipment consisted of a pair of reel-to-reel decks), which he played back simultaneously at slightly varying speeds. When listening to Part I, you can hear two tape loops slowly fall out of sync with each other, reaching a point of maximum separation halfway through, and then slowly merging back together. Part II plays another clip from Brother Walter's sermon on four tape decks simultaneously, letting pairs of the decks fall out of sync with each other gradually, yielding a texture of remarkable complexity before fading at the end.

   Like Krenek, Reich was absolutely committed to a vision of the creative act confined to algorithmic design and the selection of initial inputs into the algorithm—the former, in his case, being the tape-looping system, the latter being the selection of recorded material to be manipulated. No less than Krenek, Reich celebrated the generation of the work, in both its temporal unfolding and its sounding details, as something in which he played no further role. *It's Gonna Rain*, he wrote,

   is a literal embodiment of this process. Two loops are lined up in unison and then gradually move completely out of phase with each other, and then back into unison. The experience of that musical process is, above all else, impersonal; *it* just goes *its* way. Another aspect is its precision; there is nothing left to chance whatsoever. Once the process has been set up it inexorably works itself out.[35]

And not just in this single work: three years later, in an essay titled "Music as a Gradual Process," Reich elaborated his commitment to account for the totality of his music composed to date. "While performing and listening to gradual musical processes," he wrote, "one can participate in a particular liberating and impersonal kind of ritual. Focusing on the musical process makes possible that shift of attention away from *he* and *she* and *you* and *me* outward toward *it*."[36] Here, it seems, was Reich's version of Krenek's effort to exorcise certain ghosts of tradition, experience, and subjective intervention. Hence, once again, elevation of the "impersonal." Reich's project was to set a process in motion. Once it was going, he, like Krenek, stood back and observed the results.

And yet, where Krenek resigned himself to having committed to a method that consigned his works to popular incomprehensibility, Reich, a philosophy major at Cornell with a thesis on Wittgenstein, insisted on designing algorithmic processes whose unfolding was immediately comprehensible to the listener. "I am interested in perceptible processes. I want to be able to hear the process happening throughout the sounding music," he wrote.[37] John Cage, he noted, "discovered that he could take his intentions out of a piece of music and open up a field for many interesting things to happen, and in that sense, I agree with him. But where he was willing to keep his musical sensibility out of his own music, I was not."[38] While committed to a mode of composition that denied him the ability to intervene in the moment-to-moment unfolding of the process, he held fast to his artist's prerogative to shape whatever he could within the bounds of the system he chose, namely, to design the algorithm and select the input such that the process was clearly audible in the output. What's more, he sought processes whose sounding outputs bore audible ties to tradition, whose unfolding yielded works plausibly heard in dialogue with others in the Western canon. The phase-shifting of tape loops in *It's Gonna Rain* he described as "an extension of the idea of infinite canon or round. Two or more identical melodies are played with one starting after the other, as in traditional rounds, but [...] the time interval between one melodic pattern and its imitations(s), instead of being fixed, is variable." He summarized: "Good new ideas generally turn out to be old."[39]

This is all to say that I don't think a composer's commitment to an algorithmic, process-driven approach to composition, even one designed to impede the composer's ability to intervene in a work's generation at a granular level, must necessarily yield an incomprehensible music, or one that refuses dialogue with tradition or a collective past. Starting from a similar place and working at the same time, Reich and Krenek made very different choices. Their musics bear those out.

LYSAKER: Reich seems like a great place to end, in part because his work opens the kind of futures that total serialism did not, futures employing elements already operative in *It's Gonna Rain* including pulse (absent in total serialism and Cage), pitch possibilities opened by the human voice, and the technique of allowing parallel sound lines to fall out of phase.

Looking back then, I think our discussion is evidence that Cavell's feel for art, even hope for art, still resonates. Artworks exemplify a kind of meaning-finding-and-making outside secure, normative orders, and so they expose something at the heart of the human condition. And when successful they can further and intensify our own meaning-making ventures. Music that one cannot really hear does seem fraudulent, therefore, and when it is offered as the present and future of music, it inclines toward nihilism. I am thus grateful that Cavell forcefully challenged an emerging musical orthodoxy, although he still seems to favor the agon of modernism when he claims: "What modern artists realize, rather, is that taste must be *defeated*, and indeed that this can be accomplished by nothing less powerful than art itself."[40] I think we'd both settle for transporting surprise, and that need not require something as dramatic as defeating (or in your word, defacing) what passes for taste. A kind of singularity is more than enough, something that can emerge in music in a manner radically disconnected from tradition and yet isn't a ruse, as with Reich's work. More generally, we both think it important to have music that grapples with over-determining forces and/ or exposes us to things like the activity of sounds, which may require us to listen into sound rather than listen for how it has been organized. And this seems to mark a site where we are farthest from Cavell. Experiments with the activity of sound can expand our feeling for what can be intended and for how much intention is dependent on what was never intended, and that seems to better exemplify the very effort to intend anything at all. The idea of a totally composed work, hearable or not, has lost its allure, and I don't see anything nihilistic in abandoning that dream of high modernity.

Notes

1 Stanley Cavell, "Music Discomposed," in *Must We Mean What We Say?: A Book of Essays* (Cambridge: Cambridge University Press, 2002 [1976]), 169.

2 Ibid.

3 "Cavell's 'Music Discomposed' at 40," ed. Brian Kane and Stephen Decatur Smith, *Journal of Music Theory*, vol. 54, no. 1 (2010): 1–144.

4 Cavell, "Music Discomposed," *Must We Mean What We Say?*, 167.

5 Ibid., 174.

6 Arnold Schoenberg, "Twelve-Tone Composition," in *Style and Idea*, ed. Leonard Stein, trans. Leo Black (Berkeley: University of California Press, 1975), 207–8.

7 Theodor Adorno, *Philosophy of New Music*, ed. and trans. Robert Hullot-Kentor (Minneapolis: University of Minnesota Press, 2006), 85.

8   Ibid.

9   Ernst Krenek, "Extents and Limits of Serial Techniques," *The Musical Quarterly*, vol. 46, no. 1 (1960): 228.

10   The recording was reissued on the WERGO label in 1994 as WER 6247-2.

11   Arthur Danto, "The Artworld," *Journal of Philosophy*, vol. 61, no. 19 (1964): 574.

12   Cavell, "Music Discomposed," *Must We Mean What We Say?*, 183.

13   Ibid.

14   Mark Evan Bonds, *Absolute Music: The History of an Idea* (Oxford: Oxford University Press, 2014).

15   E. T. A. Hoffmann, "Review of Beethoven's Fifth Symphony," in *E. T. A. Hoffmann's Musical Writings*, ed. David Charlton, trans. Martyn Clarke (Cambridge: Cambridge University Press, 2004).

16   A. B. Marx, "The Consecration of the Hero," in *Musical Form in the Age of Beethoven: Selected Writings on Theory and Method*, ed. and trans. Scott Burnham (Cambridge: Cambridge University Press, 1998).

17   Tia DeNora, *Music in Everyday Life* (Cambridge: Cambridge University Press, 2000).

18   Cavell, "Music Discomposed," *Must We Mean What We Say?*, 199.

19   Ibid., 175.

20   Ibid., 195.

21   Ornette Coleman, *Beauty is a Rare Thing: The Complete Recordings of Ornette Coleman.* Rhino Records (1993), 12.

22   Ibid., 40.

23   Krenek, "Extents and Limits of Serial Techniques," *The Musical Quarterly*, 232.

24   Paul Fromm, "Young Composers: Perspective and Prospect," in *Perspectives of New Music*, vol. 1, no. 1 (1962): 1.

25   See John T. Lysaker, *Brian Eno's Ambient 1: Music for Airports* (New York: Oxford University Press, 2019).

26   Ralph Waldo Emerson, *Essays and Lectures*, ed. Joel Porte (New York: Library of America, 1983), 579.

27   Cavell, "Music Discomposed," *Must We Mean What We Say?*, 175.

28   Ibid., 186–7.

29   Krenek, "Tradition in Perspective," *Perspectives of New Music*, vol. 1, no. 1 (1962): 35.

30   Richard Taruskin, *Music in the Late Twentieth Century: The Oxford History of Western Music*, vol. 5 (Oxford: Oxford University Press, 2009), 41–4.

31   Krenek, "Extents and Limits of Serial Techniques," *The Musical Quarterly*, 228; Cavell, "Music Discomposed," *Must We Mean What We Say?*, 180–1.

32 Krenek, "Extents and Limits of Serial Techniques," *The Musical Quarterly*, 221.

33 Charles Wuorinen, "The Outlook for Young Composers," *Perspectives of New Music*, vol. 1, no. 2 (1963): 58.

34 Stanley Cavell, *Disowning Knowledge in Seven Plays of Shakespeare*, updated ed. (Cambridge: Cambridge University Press, 2003 [1987]), 6.

35 Steve Reich, "It's Gonna Rain," in *Writings on Music 1965–2000*, ed. Paul Hillier (Oxford: Oxford University Press, 2002), 20.

36 Reich, "Music as a Gradual Process," *Writings on Music*, 36.

37 Ibid., 34.

38 Reich, "Excerpts from an Interview in *Art Forum*," *Writings on Music*, 33.

39 Reich, "It's Gonna Rain," *Writings on Music*, 20.

40 Cavell, "Music Discomposed," *Must We Mean What We Say?*, 191.

11

Cavell's Odd Couple

Schoenberg and Wittgenstein

ERAN GUTER

STANLEY CAVELL'S LECTURE, "PHILOSOPHY AND THE UNHEARD,"
which he gave in 1999 at a Harvard conference on Arnold Schoenberg's
chamber music in honor of his longtime friend music theorist, David Lewin,
was an occasion for him to dwell in a philosophical site structured as a set
of mutually reflecting panels.[1] In that lecture, Cavell revisited his younger
self as a music student at the University of California, Berkeley, studying the
great scores together with Lewin, tracking the work that art does, savoring
the rigor and the beauty one looks and listens for, as he pondered quite
candidly the scarcity of his own writings about music as a philosopher
over the ensuing decades. In this lecture, reflections and refractions abound
as Cavell attempts to come to terms with this omission, so very personal
to him, but also with a possibility for a new philosophy which would be
responsive to the reciprocities of music and language. The young and the
older Cavell, the aspirations of music and the vagaries of philosophy, and at
the center of it all: Schoenberg and Wittgenstein set to reflect one another
at the chasm of modernity, whose topography is the subject matter of so
much of Cavell's philosophical writing.

The usual problem with coupling Wittgenstein and Schoenberg is that
it involves not only patent suppression of Wittgenstein's well-documented,
and, I contend, also well-grounded, reasons for rejecting modern music as a
major premise in the attempt to adduce a proper Wittgensteinian response to
Schoenberg's notion of twelve-tone composition, but also some measure of
patronizing, which is manifest in the very thought that there must have been

some intellectual failure on Wittgenstein's part for not developing a taste for the *avant-garde* worthy of his advanced, revolutionary philosophical ideas. Such opinions are quite typical among writers on the topic: before Cavell's lecture, which was originally published in 2000 by Harvard University Department of Music as an epilogue to a collection of papers from the 1999 conference, and after, by those who also opt to mask these fallacies with a veritable splurge of superficial affinities between Wittgenstein and Schoenberg. However, Cavell is quite different in this respect.

The centerpiece of Cavell's lecture is not a run-of-the-mill smear of bold brush strokes, which, more often than not, yield very little further understanding of either Schoenberg or Wittgenstein, but rather a highly specific analogy between Schoenberg's idea of the twelve-tone row and Wittgenstein's idea of grammar, which is supposed to encapsulate an expansive, sweeping philosophical program—Cavell's own. Cavell takes his cue from David Lewin's contention that Schoenberg's twelve-tone row is not a concrete and specific musical subject or object to be presented once and for all as referential in sound and in time. Rather, the row is an abstraction that manifests itself everywhere in the musical work. For Cavell, this suggests the idea of representing and communicating the omnipresent *unrepresentable* in all its manifold potentialities. As such, the twelve-tone row enables Cavell to articulate a thoughtful upshot:

> My suggestion is that the Schoenbergian idea of the row with its unforeseen yet pervasive consequences is a serviceable image of the Wittgensteinian idea of grammar and its elaboration of criteria of judgment, which shadow our expressions and which reveal pervasive yet unforeseen conditions of our existence, specifically in its illumination of our finite standing as one in which there is no complete vision of the possibilities of our understanding—no total revelation as it were—but in which the assumption of each of our assertions and retractions, in its specific manifestations in time and place, is to be worked through, discovering, so to speak, for each case its unconscious row.[2]

It's important to underscore here a trivial fact, which I've pointed out elsewhere.[3] Coupling Wittgenstein and Schoenberg rests in a convenient contextual limbo, underplaying a total absence of evidence—of any kind, of any direct influence—of interaction or mutual interest between the two men. There is absolutely no reference to Arnold Schoenberg in Wittgenstein's entire *Nachlass*, in his lectures, or in any of his known correspondences. Similarly, and perhaps less surprisingly, there is absolutely no reference to Ludwig Wittgenstein in Schoenberg's entire literary estate. This impasse means that external philosophical grounding and impetus are called for here. Indeed, this impasse clearly sets Cavell apart.

The allegory of Wittgenstein's philosophical deed in his *Philosophical Investigations* through Schoenbergian practice is designed to be illuminating enough to encourage one "to reflect further on why [...] the philosophical subject of the *Investigations*, the modern ego entangled in its expressions of desire (Wittgenstein speaks both of our urge to understand as well as of our equally pressing urge to misunderstand), is specifically characterized by Wittgenstein in its moments of torment, sickness, strangeness, self-destructiveness, perversity, suffocation, and lostness."[4] Cavell contends that it is in the paths and grounding of Wittgenstein's *Investigations* that we can learn a new responsibility with such concepts. Be that as it may, even within the realm of an allegory, Wittgenstein and Schoenberg remain an odd couple. In the remainder of this chapter, I shall focus on the following two main issues concerning the oddity of this coupling.

First, it behooves us to inquire about Cavell's self-conscious suppression of Wittgenstein's explicit rejection of the language of modern music, which Wittgenstein himself attested that he did not understand.[5] Importantly, Wittgenstein's attitude toward modern music was actually more nuanced than it may seem at first glance, so the task of approximating a "Wittgensteinian response," as Cavell puts it, to the work of Schoenberg requires an attention to detail that Cavell does not provide. It remains an open question, indeed crucial here, how to delineate the analogy between Schoenberg and Wittgenstein. I argue that, at least from Wittgenstein's perspective, Cavell tipped the analogy beyond the point of a textually grounded delineation.

Second, the focal point of Cavell's allegory remains opaque. Clearly, Lewin's suggestion propels Cavell to couple Schoenberg and Wittgenstein in a certain way. For Cavell, it is as if music theory teaches philosophy, as if a philosophical deed is bound to harness the intricacies of a musical procedure. Yet the question remains whether the "Schoenbergian unheard" is well-suited for its purported Wittgensteinian counterpart. Cavell's allegory has both a music-theoretical facet and a philosophical facet that seem to require better calibration, since, as I contend, Schoenberg and Wittgenstein differ here profoundly. Ultimately, in this "tale of two unheards," Cavell invariably remains on the side of Wittgenstein.

Let us begin the discussion with the question concerning the relevance of Wittgenstein's attitude toward modern music. Cavell's justification for suppressing Wittgenstein's rejection of modern music in coupling Wittgenstein with Schoenberg is found not in "Philosophy and the Unheard," but rather in his much earlier response to Georg Henrik von Wright's view on Wittgenstein in relation to his times.[6] The matter at hand was the nature and the philosophical import of Wittgenstein's sympathetic outlook on Oswald Spengler's ideas in *The Decline of the West*. Wittgenstein read Spengler's *magnum opus* during the spring of 1930, commenting at the time that "much, perhaps most of it, is completely in touch with what I have often thought myself."[7] Spengler's ideas about the morphological study of cultures propelled (albeit by way of criticism) Wittgenstein's growing fascination with the possibility of philosophizing by means of making illuminating comparisons, and as Wittgenstein's lectures in Cambridge in the 1930s make evident, this exerted a particular influence on his conception of aesthetics.

The crux of the debate between Cavell and Von Wright concerned Wittgenstein's understanding of cultural decline, *pace* Spengler. Cavell and Von Wright agree that Wittgenstein's conception of philosophy is intimately allied to a way of viewing contemporary civilization; they also agree that this intimate connection is shown in the way in which *Philosophical Investigations* expresses a sense of its own time and that this is connected to Wittgenstein's reading of Spengler. According to Von Wright:

> Wittgenstein [...] thought that the problems with which he was struggling were somehow connected with "the way people live," that is, with features of our culture or civilization to which he and his pupils belonged. [...] His way of doing philosophy was not an attempt to tell us what philosophy, once and for all, *is* but expressed what for him, in the setting of the times, it had to be.[8]

Cavell concurred, describing the *Investigations* as "a depiction of our own times" and attributing to it "a Spenglerian valence."[9] Cavell writes: "what Wittgenstein means by speaking outside language games [...] is a kind of interpretation of, or a homologous form of, what Spengler means in picturing the decline of culture as a process of externalization."[10] Rendering cultural decline in terms of a loss of orientation and a loss of home, Cavell later underlines, in "Philosophy and the Unheard," Wittgenstein's allegiance to Spengler by saying (as cited earlier) that "the philosophical subject of the *Investigations*, the modern ego entangled in its expressions of desire [...] is specifically characterized by Wittgenstein in its moments of torment, sickness, strangeness, selfdestructiveness, perversity, suffocation, and lostness."[11] In the passage to the time of civilization (as opposed to culture), we lose a community, an inheritance, a shared sense of life, and natural (as opposed to artificial) forms of interaction and expression.

However, Cavell sharply disagreed with Von Wright about the character of Wittgenstein's emulation of Spengler's point of view on cultural decline, especially pertaining to the nature of Wittgenstein's philosophical project (according to Cavell). Whereas Von Wright opted to view cultural decline in terms of an abnormal cancerous condition that has invaded our ways of life, Cavell rejected this image of a cultural malignancy, underscoring the stubborn normalcy or everydayness of cultural decline, noting that "Spengler's 'decline' is about the normal, say the internal, death and life of cultures."[12] Cavell's point is that:

Wittgenstein in the *Investigations* diurnalizes Spengler's vision of the destiny toward exhausted forms, toward nomadism, toward the loss of culture, or say of home, or say community; he depicts our everyday encounters with philosophy, [...] wherein the ancient task of philosophy, to awaken us, or say bring us to our senses, takes the form of returning us to the everyday, the ordinary, every day, diurnally.[13]

Cavell offers here an intriguing portrayal of Wittgenstein as a reluctant modernist—intellectually receptive to, and at times even deeply appreciative of, the various cultural manifestations of his time, yet never at peace with any of them; highly proficient and fully immersed in philosophical dialogue, yet never at home in what he perceived as its profound misuses of language. For one can never be at home when home is lost. Such intellectual meanderings bespeak the deepening of a sense of pervasive cultural critique, which Wittgenstein decidedly carried over, early on, from Karl Kraus to what later emerged as his mode of philosophizing in the *Investigations*. Forever stranded within language he kept running against the invisible walls of his cage, drawing back with a bloody head only to go on—every day, diurnally. Cavell's unique take on Wittgenstein's diurnalized Spenglerian mode of philosophizing in the time of one's own civilization makes Cavell's suppression of Wittgenstein's dislike and rejection of the language of modern music (for the purpose of coupling Wittgenstein with Schoenberg) more compelling, in a sense even logical despite its apparent paradoxicality: Wittgenstein's rejection is an embrace—this is his philosophical revolt against cultural decline.

   Yet for this arrangement to make sense, Cavell needs to render Schoenberg's method for composing with twelve tones as a "natural" phenomenon in the annals of modern music, that is, as part and parcel of the normal, internal death of "high culture" music in the West. Importantly, what Cavell requires (and assumes without argument) is a historical-musicological sense in which Schoenberg's twelve-tone music could be considered as an epitome of a music appropriate to the time of civilization (namely, modernity in the West), merely reflecting the fatality inherent in a seamless exhaustion of forms, in Spengler's sense; or, in Wittgenstein's framework, speaking outside of language games. It is here, I contend, that Cavell unwittingly parts ways with Wittgenstein.

   Wittgenstein's taste in music was powered also by his philosophical reasoning, which was organic to his philosophical development, and his philosophical attitude toward modern music ultimately manifested a deeply felt gradation. In such ranking, there is a figure who supplies a direct link between Spengler's outlook on cultural decline and Wittgenstein's attitude toward modern music, namely, Austrian music theorist and critic, Heinrich Schenker, with whose work Wittgenstein was acquainted. Wittgenstein's exposure to Schenker's ideas was facilitated by conversations in the early 1930s with his nephew, the musicologist Felix Salzer, while the latter was studying with Schenker in Vienna.[14] Schenker's philosophical outlook on cultural decline, as well as his theoretic diagnosis of the ensuing disintegration of musical sensitivities and creativity, closely aligned with Spengler's view in various ways.[15] It is reasonable to assume that Cavell was unaware of this connection at the time of writing "Philosophy and the Unheard."

On this Spengler–Schenker axis we encounter one of Wittgenstein's most unique passages concerning what he deemed to be different kinds of absurd in modern music.[16] An important observation in this passage concerns the characterization of our experience of the disintegration of cultural cohesion in terms of a constraint—understood as an inability to conceptualize the transition to the modern. Wittgenstein's point is that there is something, for sure, to be grasped and expressed amid cultural decline, but we are not astute enough to conceptualize it. The kind of cleverness which, according to Wittgenstein, we seem to lack, is not a matter of mental capacity but rather a matter of education and tradition: we are missing an acquired ability to comprehend cultural codes. We have become constrained by the incommensurability between us and the past and so we run up against a paradox: even if we knew "the truth," says Wittgenstein, we probably wouldn't be able to comprehend it. This problematizes the very idea of music appropriate to the time of civilization.

Such observations rise to a distinction that Wittgenstein maintained between two kinds of absurdities in modern music. There is music that reflects a constraint on seeing *that* we do not comprehend and there is another sort of music that reflects a constraint on seeing *what* we do not comprehend—on seeing through. The first sort of modern music corresponds to the various nonsensical maxims which derive from the purported forms of progress. For Wittgenstein, such music is absurd in a superficially attractive sense and for that reason, he concludes, it is rubbish. The other kind of modern music consists in denouncing such nonsensical maxims and formulations, but it ends up being vacuous or vacant [*nichtssagend*]—absurd, to be sure, but this time because it can't pass *as* absurd in the other, "dressed-up" sense, which for all its faults, enjoys some sort of social recognition. Such vacuous modern music bespeaks our short-sightedness; it gropes for something which it cannot express.

Wittgenstein's distinction between nonsensical modern music and vacuous modern music corresponds to the distinction made by Schenker (and also by Spengler) between progressive romantics, on the one hand, and classicist epigones, on the other. According to Schenker, the artificial noisiness that characterizes the music of progressive romantic composers (Richard Strauss, in particular) is symptomatic of their inability to bind their empty sonorities together as elaborations of a single chord. Hence, Schenker maintained, they try to mask the primitive design of their music with heavy orchestration, with noise and polyphonic clatter, and also they often resort to vulgar, extra-musical narratives in order to solve problems of musical continuity.

Meanwhile, contemporary classicist epigones relay on a reproductive reworking of old forms: they quite simply come up with worn-out imitations of the music of Johannes Brahms. For Wittgenstein, "music came to a full stop with Brahms; and even in Brahms I can begin to hear the sound of machinery."[17] Wittgenstein thought that the opposition of vacuous modern composers to the predominant form of progress was commendable, but their inability to express what they themselves could no longer understand exacted a heavy social price: as modern, such music was bound to appear foolish. Composer Josef Labor, a protégé of the Wittgenstein family, and a close friend, is named as a prime example of such a lamentable outcome.

It is a striking historical–musicological fact—countering Cavell's intuition—that the Schoenberg of the twelve-tone period fits neither of these genuinely Spenglerian categories of musical decline as upheld by Wittgenstein. (The early Schoenberg of *Verklärte Nacht* fame fits perfectly with the category of the nonsensical absurd alongside Richard Strauss.) It is an even more striking and inconvenient textual fact that Wittgenstein looked up to Gustav Mahler, despite hating his music, as the composer who could have produced music appropriate to the time of civilization, yet failed miserably. Wittgenstein said, "you would need to know a good deal about music, its history and development, to understand [Mahler]."[18]

For Wittgenstein, Mahler is a limiting case, a *sui generis* philosophical absurd.[19] Wittgenstein portrayed Mahler's musical deviancy by suggesting a metaphor:

A picture of a complete apple tree, however accurate, is in a certain sense much less like the tree itself than is a little daisy. And in the same sense a symphony by Bruckner is infinitely closer to a symphony from the heroic period than is one by Mahler. If the latter is a work of art it is one of a *totally* different sort. (But this actually itself a Spenglerian observation.)"[20]

Mahler's music is like a *trompe l'oeil* picture: it invites us to engage in a completely different set of games of participation. Wittgenstein voices a "Spenglerian observation," as he puts it, that a Mahler symphony might be a work of art of a totally different sort, embodying an entirely different kind of spiritual enterprise for which our aesthetic measuring rods are inadequate. Thus, for Wittgenstein, it was not inconceivable that Mahler's music might belong to the kind of spiritual enterprise that embodies civilization in the modern period. Mahler ought to have been capable of ushering in a new kind of absurd: modern music that is truly appropriate for an age without culture. From Wittgenstein's perspective, this would have been the strikingly absurd possibility of an artistic afterimage of a wholesale rejection of the internal relations that hold together musical gesture and human life. Indeed, this would have been a musical embodiment of a loss of home. Wittgenstein's great frustration with Mahler, more specifically, was that the prodigious composer was inauthentic and not courageous enough to fulfill this mission. Not being able to distinguish the genuine from the false, Mahler was lying to himself about his own inauthenticity. It is important, particularly from a Cavellian perspective, that Wittgenstein's criticism of Mahler was also explicitly self-directed as he was trying to own a certain style of philosophizing in the time of civilization. "I am in the same danger [as Mahler]," he wrote.[21] Wittgenstein thought that one cannot see oneself from within an overview, and therefore one can always (mistakenly) render one's otherness as some sort of excellence. Ultimately, the problem afflicting Mahler as a composer, and Wittgenstein as a philosopher and writer, is a problem of incommensurability, which pertains to the cultural presuppositions for making value distinctions in the first place. "For if today's circumstances are so different, from what they once were, that you cannot compare your work with earlier works in respect of its *genre*, then you equally cannot compare its *value* with that of the other work."[22] Wittgenstein concluded on a personal note: "I myself am constantly making the mistake under discussion. Incorruptibility is everything."[23] For Wittgenstein, the question, as Yuval Lurie put it, remained "whether the spiritual progression of our culture is still continuing (and it is us who are being left behind), or whether the culture has disappeared (and we are the only ones left to notice it)."[24]

Yet we now see that Schoenberg of the twelve-tone period has no place in Wittgenstein's overall conceptual scheme of musical decline. Not only does Schoenberg not fit into Wittgenstein's distinction between the nonsensical and the vacuous absurd in modern music, but also Wittgenstein had already reserved the liminal designation of the authentic composer for the time without culture (complete with the inevitable comparison with the possibility of genuine philosophizing) for Gustav Mahler, albeit to no avail. From Wittgenstein's perspective, there may well be something invasive, unnatural, abnormal, and uninhabitable about the case of Schoenberg in the vein of Von Wright's original suggestion.

Turning now to the second issue in this chapter, we need to inquire about the philosophical reasons for Schoenberg's being a blind spot within Wittgenstein's philosophical outlook. This takes us to the heart of Cavell's allegory in "Philosophy and the Unheard." The most obvious reason, which inexplicably escaped Cavell, is this: the later, post-1923 Schoenberg was not a composer for the time of civilization (i.e., for that specious present of cultural decline), but a composer *for the future*. Schoenberg maintained that there was no escape from total chromaticism; for him, the genie of dissonance, once emancipated, could never be returned to the bottle. He argued that his "method for composing with twelve tones which are related only with one another" is a necessary step in the evolution of Western music, and he designed it for the sole purpose of replacing the structural differentiations formerly furnished by tonality, thus enacting a revolution that would ensure that German music would reign supreme for the next hundred years or more.

Yet, as a matter of fact, Wittgenstein had his own unique vision of the music of the future.[25] Wittgenstein envisioned the music of the future as consisting in one voice [*einstimmig*], not as a continuation of the currently predominant, culturally entrenched musical formats that embody myriad voices. Rather, the future of music in Wittgenstein's program would mark a new cultural epoch by being "simple, transparent. In a certain sense, naked." Once again, Wittgenstein shows an allegiance with Spengler, who maintained that when a culture enters its final phases, artists simply work with the hollow forms of the old culture without understanding their essence, whereas the future always transcends the current epoch by means of a return to the simplest, most basic expressions of life, which are bound to reveal their limitations and could constitute the praxeological grounds for setting up ideals as "measuring rods" for a culture—a *new* culture, perhaps.

I contend that there can be no sharper contrast than the one between Wittgenstein's vision of the music of the future and Schoenberg's.[26] This contrast obfuscates Cavell's attempted allegory in "Philosophy and the Unheard." Central to Cavell's allegory is the notion, borrowed from David Lewin, of Schoenberg's twelve-tone row as an exemplification of that which is "unheard" and yet *omnipresent* in the realization of the musical work, in the communicable gesture. Still, one needs to get clear about the nature of the "unheard" here and to see whether it is indeed illuminatingly comparable to Wittgenstein's notion of grammar.

In the context of Schoenberg's twelve-tone system, the "unheard" is nothing more than a set of potential pitch relations without any motivic content that, in a sense, is "logically prior" to the composition. When embodied in the actual musical details of a given composition, it determines the succession of pitches used in a piece, although it does not determine their registers or their durations, nor prescribe the textural layout of the music or its form. Schoenberg conceived the twelve-tone row as a pre-compositional, musically inert fund for motivic possibilities, whence springs its sense of (unheard) omnipresence in the realized composition. The twelve-tone system is an extraordinary attempt to derive, through a series of deliberate, calculated manipulations, a wealth of material, complex and varied, from such a musically inert initial pitch collection. These procedures are driven, as Schoenberg put it, by "the desire for a conscious control over the new means and forms," which requires the composer to "find, if not laws or rules, at least ways to justify the dissonant character of these harmonies and their successions."[27]

The contrived nature of twelve-tone composition gives the notion of comprehensibility primarily theoretical importance for Schoenberg, not just personal, as Cavell noted in his lecture. The twelve-tone method is designed to provide both coherence and variation in the musical material. For Schoenberg, coherence is a necessary condition for comprehensibility, which in turn ultimately amounts to the listener's ability to analyze quickly, to determine components and their coherence. Conditions for comprehensibility in dodecaphonic music are thus dependent upon the correct, conscious application of the kind of contrived rules that would ensure coherence. "Composition with twelve tones has no other aim than comprehensibility," declared Schoenberg.[28]

Such an emphasis on comprehensibility brings to mind the famous repartee by Karl Kraus, which Wittgenstein surely would have appreciated: "The most incomprehensible talk comes from people who have no other use for language than to make themselves understood."[29] Schoenberg perceived cultural decline as a license (ironically, Schoenberg sought its legitimacy in Kraus) to invent auxiliary means of expression in order to regain control over unruly atonality for the sake of posterity. Schoenberg contended that:

One may let oneself be carried by language, but it carries only the man who would be capable, if it did not exist, of inventing it himself. "Language, mother of thought," says Karl Kraus—as wrongly as if he had said the hen is there before the eggs. And as rightly.[30]

Along with Schoenberg's advice to his students—to go on composing using traditional gestures of dynamics, form, and performance practice— the above contention signifies Schoenberg's decisive transgression *beyond* Wittgenstein's scheme of musical decline by means of the twelve-tone system, creating "a homunculus in music,"[31] as Heinrich Schenker called it, indeed, as an image of an invasive, abnormal occurrence in the corpus of an otherwise exhausted culture as it turns into civilization.

The "Schoenbergian unheard," then, is not only patently contrived, but also designed to dislodge tonality and forcefully take over its status as "phenomenology, and therefore grammar,"[32] which for Wittgenstein is inseparable from our ways of life, from "the pervasive yet unforeseen conditions of our existence," as Cavell put it in his lecture.[33] For Wittgenstein, the language of tonality is inextricably, internally related to who we are as human beings who partake in a certain culture. "Could one reason be given at all for why the theory of harmony is the way it is?" asked Wittgenstein, "[a]nd, first and foremost, must such a reason be given? It is here and it is part of our entire life."[34]

Schenker contended that "the great proof against Schoenberg is the people."[35] Such a notion can be insightfully recast along Wittgensteinian lines. There is simply no reason for the rules of the twelve-tone method (which are designed to ensure coherence and comprehensibility for the realized composition) to be what they are, given the kind of beings we are, the purposes we have, our shared discriminatory capacities, and certain general features of the world we inhabit. The kind of musical distinctions called for by the mechanical manipulation of the "Schoenbergian unheard" in order to generate coherent and varied materials for dodecaphonic composing—for instance, identifying a certain passage as based on a certain transposition of the inverted retrograde form of the original twelve-tone row used in the given piece—are not just very difficult to make, they are simply not important in our everyday lives.

Thus, it's clearly not the case that the "Schoenbergian unheard" in all its transformations could have been what Wittgenstein had in mind as "a paradigm" of its sonic occurrences—and by "paradigm" Wittgenstein means "the rhythm of our language, of our thinking & feeling."

If I say [about a musical theme] e.g.: it's as if here a conclusion were being drawn, or, as if here something were being confirmed, or, as if *this* were a reply to what came earlier,—then the way I understand it clearly presupposes familiarity with conclusions, confirmations, replies, etc.[36]

Wittgenstein's point is that for music to be characterizable, for it to have a face that "wears an expression," that is, akin to a familiarly human face, it must be interrelated with a host of other language games in which corresponding moves are presupposed and ultimately linked to "the whole field of our language games."

Yet, the "Schoenbergian unheard" in and of itself remains patently inert with respect to "the whole field of our language games." In the realized dodecaphonic piece, if there is a sense in which "the theme interacts with language,"[37] it is due only to Schoenberg's contention that, whereas the materials need to be generated by means of the twelve-tone method, "you use the row and compose as you had done it previously. [...] Use the same kind of form and expression, the same themes, melodies, sounds, rhythms as you used before."[38] But this is precisely where we get a sense of Schenker's contention that Schoenberg was producing "a homunculus in music." And this is precisely where the philosophical contrast between the "Schoenbergian unheard" and its purported Wittgensteinian counterpart comes to a head. Whereas Schoenberg's music of the future inheres in comprehensibility, Wittgenstein's music of the future inheres in transparency. Both are kinds of understanding but the contrast between them could not be more striking, and as Cavell would insist, they are joined also by distinctly different urges to misunderstand.

Wittgenstein's notion of transparency is twofold. It pertains equally to cultural critique and to our knowledge of human beings. For Wittgenstein, an important aspect of cultural decline is the paradoxical obfuscation of the notion of transparency. Clarity becomes only a means to construct ever more complicated structures; it is no longer an end in itself. "For me,"

Wittgenstein wrote, "on the contrary clarity, transparency, is an end in itself. I am not interested in erecting a building but in having the foundations of possible buildings transparently before me."[39] Wittgenstein's sense of transparency as surveyability is diametrically opposed to what is prescribed by the form of progress that Schoenberg, by his own admission, epitomized in his composition and theory, and of which Wittgenstein became increasingly suspicious and hostile. From Wittgenstein's perspective, then, Schoenberg's notion of comprehensibility amounts to using transparency as a means to compulsive over-structuring of "a building" as well as a fragmentation into calculable objects that reduce human expression to a method and a mechanism. Wittgenstein's contrary vision of the music of the future as transparent, naked, in one voice, exemplifies a sense of "attunement" (to use Cavell's word).[40]

There are additional aspects of transparency that relate to Wittgenstein's notion of knowing other human beings [*Menschenkenntnis*]. His discussion of our knowledge of human beings occurs in the so-called second part of the *Investigations* and it is fundamental to Cavell's remarks on the idea of soul-blindness in *The Claim of Reason*. For Wittgenstein, this sort of knowledge is a *skill*, an accomplished sensitivity to human physiognomy, an instance of "knowing how" rather than "knowing that." Such a skill cannot be accounted for in strictly epistemic terms since it admits into our judgments what he called "imponderable evidence." In Wittgenstein's view, this situation deeply characterizes our human lives and our daily exchanges with one another and the world. Importantly, I maintain, musical experience afforded Wittgenstein a genuine locus—a myriad of natural, everyday, straightforwardly instructive occasions and exemplars—for this kind of knowledge of human beings.[41]

Becoming one who knows human beings does not involve acquiring a technique but rather correct judgments of particular instances. The imponderability of the kind of evidence that is brought in support of such correct judgments is significantly reflected in how we attempt to communicate our knowledge of human beings, and in how the success of our justifications is measured. If we are successful, then the other person displays a willingness to follow the rules of the game that we are playing; in other words, to use concepts based on imponderable evidence. This imponderable, non-reductive measure of success marks the aesthetic achievement of "getting it right," a notion that clearly separates Wittgenstein's account of transparency from Schoenberg's description of comprehensibility. The moment of "getting it right" consists in an interrelated move in a language game, which can only be understood within the context of correlate, logically prior moves in "the whole field of our language games," hence constituted indeterminately—*and* because it is internally related to the experience involved.

For Wittgenstein, a musical gesture is transparent in this sense because it is *already* given to us with a familiar physiognomy, which is internally related to the preconditions as well as the lived, embodied realities of musical intelligibility. That is, for Wittgenstein, there is no sense in which we can say that a musical gesture needs to be made comprehensible. The "Schoenbergian unheard" necessitates comprehensibility precisely because it is external to "the whole field of our language games." In such cases, the strict, conscious, technically correct application of the rules would be crucial. By contrast, according to Wittgenstein, a musical gesture (in the language of tonality) is not transparent by virtue of a mechanism for correct application of some postulated "rules of transparency." Rather, its transparency resides precisely in the absence of such rules, indeed in the vacuity of the very notion that they are part of the reactions by which, as Wittgenstein said, "people find one another."[42] Music is physiognomic, intransitively transparent to human life; it betokens our capacity to make increasingly nuanced comparisons between multiform human practices as we chart the unexpected topography of the resemblances that give unity to our ways of being in the world. Importantly, then, from Wittgenstein's perspective, the Schoenbergian idea of the row with its unforeseen yet pervasive consequences turns out to be tantamount to an idea of grammar for a music for the meaning-blind.

I conclude by addressing Cavell's final suggestion in "Philosophy and the Unheard," which he leaves undeveloped, that the allegory of Wittgenstein and Schoenberg may enable one to envision what a philosophy of music *should be*, one which is itself illuminated by musical procedure. The kind of musical procedure that is involved in an unfolding of the "Schoenbergian unheard," as I argued above, cannot be philosophically illuminating if the task of philosophy concerns, as Cavell insisted, a return to the everyday. Simply put, there is nothing about the manipulations of the twelve-tone row that could be brought back to our ordinary experience.

Furthermore, even concerning the era of common-practice music, when Wittgenstein discussed with Felix Salzer the music theory of Heinrich Schenker, which met with Wittgenstein's general approval, he is reported to have said to Salzer that Schenker's theory, with its distinct way of analyzing musical procedures by relating them to a musical prototype, needed to be "boiled down."[43] By this phrase he meant, I take it, that musical procedures cannot illuminate philosophy if they are to be taken as bypassing musical understanding that is ultimately interrelated with "the whole field of our language games." And musical understanding is not just one thing, but many. Wittgenstein argued that "considering the piece in Schenker's way," i.e., as a mere musical procedure, is only one possible criterion for understanding what the music means.[44] It is but one among many reactions which enable us to distinguish between someone who hears with understanding and someone who merely hears. Cavell sincerely opens his lecture by vouching for what he has always demanded from philosophy:

[A]n understanding precisely of what I had sought in music, and in the understanding of music, of what demanded that reclamation of experience, of the capacity for being moved, which called out for, and sustained, an accounting as lucid as the music I loved.[45]

For these reasons, Cavell's perspective connects with Wittgenstein's unique quest for thinking about language as music, for invoking the understanding of a musical theme as a guide to philosophical understanding. For Cavell, this notion holds out "the promise of an understanding without meanings, [...] a utopian glimpse of a new, or undiscovered, relation to language, to its sources in the world, to its means of expression."[46]

Yet to uphold Cavell's vision of philosophy requires, as Wittgenstein did, shunning the illusion that our ordinary way of separating language and music implies that the distinction is, or could ever be, underpinned theoretically. The resources for drawing a line between language and musical procedure, that is, language itself, may not be sufficient to describe the musical "side" of the line, which, as Wittgenstein pointed out, we inevitably experience transparently, that is, in ways language can neither fully circumscribe nor make intelligible to us. Let this finding serve as an important lesson to be learned from Cavell's odd couple—Schoenberg and Wittgenstein—one that I imagine Cavell would have agreed with: that philosophy, as it mattered most to him, has no business with music for the meaning-blind.

Notes

1   Stanley Cavell, "Philosophy and the Unheard," in *Here and There: Sites of Philosophy*, ed. Nancy Bauer, Alice Crary, and Sandra Laugier (Cambridge, MA: Harvard University Press, 2022), 260–8.

2   Ibid., 267.

3   See Eran Guter, "'A Surrogate for the Soul': Wittgenstein and Schoenberg," in *Interactive Wittgenstein: Essays in Memory of Georg Henrik von Wright*, Synthese Library, vol. 349, ed. Enzo De Pellegrin (New York: Springer, 2011), 109–52.

4   Cavell, "Philosophy and the Unheard," *Here and There*, 267.

5   Ludwig Wittgenstein, *Culture and Value*, rev. ed., ed. G. H. von Wright, with Heikki Nyman, rev. ed. by Alois Pichler, trans. Peter Winch (Oxford: Blackwell Publishing, 2006 [1998]), 8.

6   Georg Henrik von Wright, "Ludwig Wittgenstein in Relation to his Times," in *Wittgenstein and his Times*, ed. Brian F. McGuinness (Chicago: University of Chicago Press, 1982). Stanley Cavell, "Declining Decline," in *The Cavell Reader*, ed. Stephen Mulhall (Oxford: Blackwell, 1996).

7   Ludwig Wittgenstein, *Movements of Thought: Diaries, 1930–1932, 1936–1937*, ed. James C. Klagge and Alfred Nordmann (Lanham: Rowman & Littlefield, 2003), 25; see also Wittgenstein, *Culture and Value*, 16.

8   Von Wright, "Ludwig Wittgenstein in Relation to his Times," *Wittgenstein and his Times*, 118.

9   Cavell, "Declining Decline, " *The Cavell Reader*, 337.

10 Ibid., 344–5.

11 Cavell, "Philosophy and the Unheard," *Here and There*, 267.

12 Von Wright, "Ludwig Wittgenstein in Relation to his Times," *Wittgenstein and his Times*, 118. Cavell, "Declining Decline, " *The Cavell Reader*, 336.

13 Cavell, "Declining Decline, " *The Cavell Reader*, 345.

14 See Eran Guter, "'A Surrogate for the Soul,'" *Interactive Wittgenstein* and also "The Good, the Bad, and the Vacuous: Wittgenstein on Modern and Future Musics," *The Journal of Aesthetics and Art Criticism*, vol. 73, no. 4 (2015): 427–39.

15 See Byron Almén, "Prophets of the Decline: The Worldviews of Heinrich Schenker and Oswald Spengler," *Indiana Theory Review*, vol. 17 (1996): 1–24.

16 Wittgenstein, *Movements of Thought*, 67–9; see Guter, "The Good, the Bad, and the Vacuous," *The Journal of Aesthetics and Art Criticism*.

17 *Recollections of Wittgenstein*, ed. Rush Rhees (Oxford: Oxford University Press, 1984), 112.

18 Ibid., 71.

19 See Guter, "The Good, the Bad, and the Vacuous," *The Journal of Aesthetics and Art Criticism*.

20 Wittgenstein, *Culture and Value*, 17; italics in original.

21 Ludwig Wittgenstein, *Wittgenstein Source*, MS 120, 72v (2019), wittgensteinsource.org.

22 Wittgenstein, *Culture and Value*, 77; italics in original.

23 Ibid.

24 Yuval Lurie, *Wittgenstein on the Human Spirit* (Amsterdam: Rodopi, 2012), 150.

25 Wittgenstein, *Movements of Thought*, 49.

26 See Guter, "'A Surrogate for the Soul,'" *Interactive Wittgenstein*.

27 Arnold Schoenberg, *Style and Idea: Selected Writings*, ed. Leonard Stein, trans. Leo Black (Berkeley: University of California Press, 1975), 218.

28 Ibid., 215.

29 Karl Kraus, *Half-Truths and One-and-a-Half-Truths: Selected Aphorisms* (Chicago: University of Chicago Press 1990), 65.

30 Schoenberg, *Style and Idea*, 369.

31 Robert Snarrenberg, *Schenker's Interpretative Practice* (Cambridge: Cambridge University Press, 1997), 69.

32 Ludwig Wittgenstein, *Philosophical Remarks* (Chicago: University of Chicago Press, 1975), 53.

33 Cavell, "Philosophy and the Unheard," *Here and There*, 267.

34 Wittgenstein, *Wittgenstein Source*, 157a, 24–6; my translation.

35 Snarrenberg, *Schenker's Interpretative Practice*, 69.

36 Wittgenstein, *Culture and Value*, 59; italics added.

37 Ibid., 60.

38 Schoenberg, *Style and Idea*, 213.

39 Wittgenstein, *Culture and Value*, 9.

40 See Stanley Cavell, *The Claim of Reason: Wittgenstein, Skepticism, Morality, Tragedy* (Oxford: Oxford University Press, 1979), 32.

41 See Eran Guter, "Musicking as Knowing Human Beings," in *Intercultural Understanding after Wittgenstein*, ed. Carla Carmona, David Perez-Chico, and Chon Tejedor (London: Anthem, 2023), 77–91.

42 Ludwig Wittgenstein, *Remarks on the Philosophy of Psychology*, vol. 1 (Chicago: University of Chicago Press, 1980), §874.

43 See Guter, "The Good, the Bad, and the Vacuous," *The Journal of Aesthetics and Art Criticism*.

44 Wittgenstein, *Wittgenstein Source*, 153b, 60v–61r.

45 Cavell, "Philosophy and the Unheard," *Here and There*, 260.

46 Ibid., 261.

12

Words Sing

Wittgenstein, Cage, and Cavell on the Poetics of Language and Music

GORDON C. F. BEARN

IT'S HARD TO IMAGINE WITTGENSTEIN enjoying the musical compositions of John Cage, perhaps impossible. Nevertheless, I am open to that possibility because of a good encounter which Stanley Cavell, one of Wittgenstein's most sensitive and musically sophisticated readers, had with one of Cage's performances.[1] The mere fact of that encounter encourages me to follow a few lines of thought, strings of words, in which what Wittgenstein writes can seem to have made room for the music of John Cage. But what of Cavell's good encounter?

It occurred in 1988 while Cavell was attending Cage's Norton Lectures at Harvard.[2] The text of those lectures had a complicated genesis. Most of the text was randomized by a computerized *I Ching*, but it was randomized within specific constraints. Each of the texts of Cage's six lectures was an organized vertical arrangement of words and series of words taken from 487 existing source texts, which he selected, texts that included excerpts from Wittgenstein, some passages from Cage's own earlier writings as well as extracts from Cage's usual suspects: Henry David Thoreau, Marshall McLuhan, Buckminster Fuller, and more. Cage sorted those 487 source texts into fifteen files to which he gave names appropriate to various dimensions of his compositional practices, and those fifteen names, printed without spaces, become what Cage thinks of as the "actual title" of the Norton Lectures, namely:[3]

MethodStructureIntentionDisciplineNotationIndeterminacy
InterpenetrationImitationDevotionCircumstancesVariableStructure
NonunderstandingContingencyInconsistencyPerformance.

The fifteen names of those files, sometimes stuttering, repeat their way, in a single file of uppercase letters, down the middle of each page of each lecture. On either side of that single file of letters, Cage added the I Ching randomized words and strings of words from those fifteen files, while at the same time making sure that the letters in vertical single file contributed to the spellings of the horizontal words arranged on their either sides, thus producing what Norman O. Brown taught Cage to call a Mesostic.[4] Cage did this six times, and thus produced the texts for six lectures, numbered I–VI, each designed to be read aloud in more or less one hour. They are scores. Along the bottom of each page of the published version of the lectures is a partial transcription of seminars that Cage held immediately after each of the lectures. I have left out some of the rules of this process, but you can see that it is an idiosyncratic discomposing of those 487 source texts, making it difficult to recognize the different source texts in the final arrangement, sometimes even difficult to recognize any sentential meaning at all.

Cavell, listening that day to what he calls Cage's "clear, fluent, rather sing-song tenor voice," describes his good encounter, in one sentence, this way:

I found myself charmed, my overall mood as of hovering in a sort of active peacefulness, freed from the demands either of sense or of silence, punctuated from time to time by the wonder whether something intelligible had found its way to speech, and more rarely, but striking with the force of a revelation, by a completely pure, unmistakable sentence, after which I actively for a while held myself in readiness for another such incredible gift.[5]

At first I was surprised by Cavell's response, since I had rather figured there would be nothing in Cage that could possibly appeal to Cavell, and to check this feeling I went back to one of Cavell's essays from the mid-1960s where I had expected to find a brisk dismissal of Cage, only to be surprised again. There I found Cavell admitting that he found Cage's "theorizing [...] quite charming," again that word, and even wondering: "Why couldn't we allow Pop Art, say, or Cage's evenings, or Happenings, to be entertainments of some kind without troubling about art?"[6] I am impressed, as always, by Cavell's generosity, even though he also insists that we cannot do what he asks, that is, we cannot remain untroubled by the art-status of a Cage composition, because the work of Arnold Schoenberg and Anton Webern, what Cavell calls the "genuine article," "really does challenge the art of which it is the inheritor and the voice."[7] For Cavell, to accept a Cage composition as *music* would be to accept it not as a clean instance of a crisply defined category of musical art, but rather as a continuation of an open series of various genuine articles, the criteria for which we only approach in accepting each member as part of that series. This means that our enjoyment of Cage's composition cannot, according to Cavell, remain untroubled by its art-status, by its membership in that series of genuine articles of art.

Our responsibility in accepting any member of such a series of artworks is to respond both to the work before us and to what Cavell almost calls the spirit of the series it follows.[8] This is an instance of, or a function of, Cavell's sense that in general "to have a concept is to be able, so to speak, to keep up with the word."[9] Although it is, first of all, our responsibility to the *past use* of the word "art" that will make trouble for simply enjoying a Cage composition as music untroubled by whether or not it is art, it is our responsibility, second of all, to that *singular performance today*, which in principle opens us to that enjoyment, and may in fact have provided Cavell his good encounter with Cage's Norton Lectures. Was Cavell's good encounter troubled by the category of art or was it, against the suggestion of that earlier essay, a simply untroubled enjoying?

Cage's "Lecture on Nothing," from 1959, is a verbal score which he asks not to be read in an artificial manner but "with the *rubato* one uses in everyday speech."[10] Cage's score opens with this arrangement of words in a sentence distributed loosely across the page:

I am here   ,   and there is nothing to say .

And, still on this opening page, we find this sentential arrangement:

                                                    I have nothing to say
          and I am saying it   and that is
     poetry   as I need it   .[11]

"I have nothing to say and I am saying it." We might read the first half of this sentence simply as saying there is nothing I have to say, and yet in that case what is there for the "it" to point to in the second half of the sentence?[12] "I have *nothing to say* and I am saying *it*." So by means of that "it," perhaps Cage is, comically or ironically enough, invoking a more or less substantial notion of nothing, and I guess he would enjoy the intimation of Buddhism, or of Suzuki's Zen emptiness, that this "it" calls out—but I'd prefer to hold off on that thought. If there is a way back to that emptiness it would have to include the idea that Zen emptiness is not simply without content; rather, it is somehow filled, perhaps as filled as the (empty, white) spaces lengthening out between the words and even the punctuation marks in Cage's own "Lecture on Nothing." "Emptied full," as Ammons put it.[13]

Instead of immediately rushing to Cage's Zen figurations, try to think of "I have nothing to say and I am saying it" as Cage's insistence that he is *not saying* anything over and above the words he *is* saying, at that moment pronouncing with the rubato of everyday speech. Try not to think of his words as being governed by rules or freighted with meanings. Try not to think of his sentences as carrying on their backs some timeless propositional content or of his silences as inseminated with semantic force. Rather, try to think of those punctuated words simply as a series of things threaded on silence. Does Wittgenstein think that this approach is what music *is* or even what *language* is? Things threaded on silence?

This interpretive gambit, thinking of Cage's words as not freighted with meaning, will of course remind Wittgenstein's readers of the conclusion of the *Philosophical Investigations'* first section, in which he denies that meaning was in question, at all (i.e., in his description of a theatrical shopping trip). In the next pages, Wittgenstein tells us that the very idea of meaning [*Bedeutung*] surrounds the working of language with a haze.[14] And again, later in that book, in a passage that was important to the L=A=N=G=U=A=G=E poet and student of Cavell, Charles Bernstein, Wittgenstein says: "When I think in language [*Sprache*], I don't have 'meanings' ['*Bedeutungen*'] in my mind in addition to verbal expressions; rather language *itself* is the vehicle of thought."[15]

In this chapter, I will be trying to find seeds, as it were, in Wittgenstein's writing that open a path *from* the skills required to perform or play in a language game *to* the skills required to be able to feel the power of Gertrude Stein's provocative assimilation of understanding and enjoying. In 1934, responding to a radio interviewer's gruff insinuation that her opera *Four Saints In Three Acts* was incomprehensible, un-understandable, Stein distanced herself from the pragmatism of her teacher, William James, by answering the interviewer: "You mean by understanding that you can talk about it in the way you have a habit of talking [...], putting it in other words [...], but I mean by understanding enjoyment."[16] Although that is my target, I will take my first clue from a different text.

Music Expresses Itself

Perhaps we can find some help with the above questions and concerns in a passage from Wittgenstein's *The Brown Book*:

The same strange illusion which we are under when we seem to seek the something which a face expresses whereas, in reality, we are giving ourselves up to the features before us.[17]

I interrupt Wittgenstein here to explain that he is referring to an illusion he had introduced a few pages earlier, an illusion he tells us is occasioned by the difference between what he called transitive and intransitive uses of words like meaning or expressing.[18] When a face is said to be expressive or remarkably expressive, then we may be ready to go on to say *what it is* that the expressive face expresses, perhaps a kind of quiet contempt. Wittgenstein calls *transitive* these contexts in which we can go on to say what is being expressed. If, however, we were simply giving ourselves up to or were dumbstruck by an expressive face, then we might not be ready or even able to go on to say *what in particular* the expressive face expressed. Wittgenstein calls these second contexts *intransitive*. The illusion he speaks of derives from taking an intransitive characterization of an expressive face for a transitive characterization. In such circumstances we can fall under the illusion that there is something being expressed when there is not, and then, flailing about in our effort to name what seems ineffable, we give ourselves mental cramp. There is, in these pages of *The Brown Book* something that I think sounds a little too much like Rudolph Carnap exploding pseudoproblems, only transposed into Wittgenstein's increasingly favored key of the everyday. But let's pretend we didn't hear echoes of Carnap, and pick up where we left off.

As the passage in *The Brown Book* continues, Wittgenstein finds himself turning to music:

that same illusion possesses us even more strongly if repeating a tune to ourselves and letting it make its full impression on us, we say "This tune says *something*," and it is as though I had to find *what* it says. And yet I know that it doesn't say anything such that I might express in words or in pictures what it says.[19]

Where earlier "giving ourselves up to the features" of the expressive face had evaporated our ability to say what the expressive face was expressing, here it is "letting the tune make its full impression on us" which forecloses our chance to say what particular meaning that tune had been freighted: in both cases plunging into the waters of the face or the tune which makes us unable to say what the face expresses or the tune says.

Wittgenstein imagines that discovering this inability in ourselves will be disappointing, as if the incapacity to say *what* the tune meant would deprive the tune of meaning anything at all, even though our first response to the tune had been that it does say *something*. So the passage continues:

And if recognizing this [inability], I resign myself to saying "It just expresses a musical thought," this would mean no more than saying "It expresses itself."[20]

There. That was the sentence I was heading towards. I take "music expresses itself" to contrast with music expresses *something else*, like an emotion or a meaning, and so the expression seems a way of saying something like "the music is what it is," or perhaps with a less Zen formulation, simply "what powerful music!" And so you can perhaps see why I feel the attraction between this kind of Wittgensteinian remark—and this is not the only one—and my suggestion for how to read Cage's "I have nothing to say and I am saying it."[21] I would have preferred Wittgenstein's discussion of music to say *exactly* what I am still seeking the courage to insist upon, namely, that most basically, we might say *language expresses itself*, or even better that most essentially, language presents itself as things threaded on silence. But Wittgenstein's texts, while (almost) always provocative are not often *entirely* cooperative. This is perhaps the effect of his philosophical honesty.

For instance, in this very passage, he worries that if all we could say about the *feeling* that some music says *something* were to say that the music expresses itself, then it might not make sense to distinguish better and worse ways of playing a tune. For in that case, we would seem to have lost the *something the music expresses* which might be exhibited more or less powerfully in this or that performance of the music. So Wittgenstein imagines an interrupting voice followed by another interlocutor:

"But surely when you play it you don't play it *anyhow* [or as we might put it, *any way*], you play it in this particular way, making a crescendo here, a diminuendo there, a ceasura in this place, etc." [To which another voice answers the one interrupting]—Precisely, and that's all I can say about it, or it may be all that I can say about it.[22]

If there are better and worse ways of playing the musical tune, then it might seem as if there would have to be more to the tune saying something than simply being things threaded on silence. If it were only that, viz., things threaded on silence, then how could there be better and worse ways of threading those things on silence. We seem compelled to insist upon there being a paradigm of the *best* way of playing the tune, which various playings of the tune more or less approximate. But this same paragraph of *The Brown Book* ends in resistance to the thought that there is anything *more than the tune itself* being expressed *in* the tune itself.[23]

The paragraph resists the idea that there is a separable mental paradigm that is expressed in "the best way" of threading those sounds on silence. Wittgenstein supposes:

Here one may be inclined to ask: "What is it like to know the tempo in which a piece of music should be played?" And the idea suggests itself that there *must* be a paradigm somewhere in our mind, and that we have adjusted the tempo to conform to that paradigm. [Nevertheless Wittgenstein puts up resistance by adding:] But in most cases if someone asked me "How do you think this melody should be played?," I will, as an answer, just whistle it in a particular way, and nothing will have been present to my mind but the tune *actually whistled* (not an image of *that*).[24]

Wittgenstein insists that better ways of playing are not better *expressions* of some mental paradigm separable from the tune whistled. His answer to *how* the melody should be played is not by offering an instruction to play it with more of something meant to be expressed *in* the music, rather his answer is just to whistle it, or to play the tune itself on an instrument.

To think of a tune as "things threaded on silence" is not to reduce all playings of that tune, or even all tunes to one category, for there remain the different *relations* between actual tones, tempi, timbres, and so on. In the *Investigations*, Wittgenstein suggests that those different relations don't express anything other than themselves, and he considers what it would be to say that any musical theme simply "tells me itself [*sagt mir sich selbst*]."[25] This idea comes in a passage from the *Investigations* turning parenthetically to music after considering whether sentences are more like genre pictures or portraits, and Wittgenstein seems to be leaning toward genre pictures:

"A picture tells me itself" is what I'd like to say. That is, its telling me something consists in its own structure, in *its* own forms and colors. (What would it mean to say "A musical theme tells me itself"?)[26]

I would describe the idea that Wittgenstein here rejects—viz., the idea that there is or must be something somewhere that is expressed *in* any actual playing of a tune—as expressivism, or even as an expressivist essentialism. But it is *turning away* from that expressivism that opens the possibility of receiving music, and even language, as things threaded on silence.

Turning Away from Expressivist Essentialism

Before looking at the places where Wittgenstein comes close to saying that not only music, but also language, expresses (only) itself, I will take up Wittgenstein distancing himself from expressivist essentialism.

Even in the passage from *The Brown Book* that I have been reading, Wittgenstein directs his criticism of the expressivist picture strictly to its mentalistic version, rejecting the idea that "there *must* be a paradigm *somewhere in our mind*, and that we have adjusted the tempo to conform to that paradigm."[27] I will be generalizing his opposition to this expressivist picture beyond its mental version so that his opposition would take in *any* form of expressivist essentialism. I realize that this approach runs afoul of such a famous line as "essence is expressed by grammar," but I think that Wittgenstein's general reasons for turning away from expressivist essentialism cannot be restricted to its mental version.[28] If Wittgenstein ever really endorsed such a philosophical theory as Grammatical Essentialism, and he may not have, then perhaps we will have to turn away even from that lingering form of what he called a "general disease." If that is so, and it may not be, then I think expressivist essentialism is an even more "general disease" of thinking than Wittgenstein did. But however that question settles out, here is how Wittgenstein puts it in *The Brown Book*:

There is a kind of general disease of thinking which always looks for (and finds) what could be called a mental state from which all our acts spring as from a reservoir. Thus one says, "The fashion changes because the taste of people changes." The taste is the mental reservoir. But if a tailor today designs a cut of dress different from that which he designed a year ago, can't what is called his change of taste have consisted, partly or wholly, in doing just this?[29]

I think the key move here—against a mentalistic form of expressivist essentialism—is how such a disease of thinking "always looks for (and finds)" a reservoir from which our acts spring.[30] When our seeking is never frustrated, it becomes easy to think that we have simply invented something to satisfy what seemed to be our needs. Nietzsche might have described this as a genealogy of all metaphysical discovery.[31] (It is more or less precisely the genealogy of what Frege calls a thought.) All we ever have access to is the fact that tailors are now cutting clothing differently, and the reservoir of taste from which this change is supposedly drawn from is only added to provide the petina of explanation. For some reason, we are not content merely to accept the fact that tailors are cutting cloth differently, so we invent an aesthetic reservoir to explain it. And the procedure works perfectly. Of course it works perfectly, it is an *occult* invention doing the one thing we wanted done.[32] Another strategy, however, would be to accept tailors cutting a new way as enough, as not needing a reservoir to explain its existence. Learning to say "the cutting expresses itself" might be a first step in that direction.

An expressivist approach to *language*, namely, the idea that when we speak we are expressing ourselves, is so natural to us that it is hard even to understand expressivism as an *optional* approach to language. It just feels natural: the way language works. However, in broad strokes, which I apologize for abbreviating even further, Foucault insists that expressivism is a specific characteristic of what he calls "the modern," roughly Europe in and perhaps since the nineteenth century. Before that time, during what he calls "the classical age," language was so tied to representation that when Victor of Aveyron uttered something like "milk" in the excitement and desire prompted by the appearance of a bowl of white liquid, that utterance could not yet count as a sign: "milk" only became a *sign* when it appeared in representational propositions like "there's no more milk."[33] Foucault summarizes: "It is in fact the proposition that detaches the vocal sign from its immediate expressive values and establishes its supreme linguistic possibility. For Classical thought, language begins not with expression, but with discourse."[34] By contrast, he tells us, that during the 1800s, language had "an irreducible expressive value [...] for, if language expresses, it does so not in so far as it is an imitation and duplication of things, but in so far as it manifests and translates the fundamental will of those who speak it."[35] Whether it is the essence of a people (inclining to racism), the species-being of humans (oppositely inclined), or the power of a poem, a painting, or a musical performance as the expression of the artist or performer, we don't even notice the expressivist essentialism we presuppose in our everyday reactions and assumptions. In each case, we assume that something invisible, unknowable, or even ineffable, is expressed *in* what we can see or know—or say; it is the idea, or article of faith, which is at the root of our incurable obsession with personal authenticity. But this is precisely the picture that Wittgenstein rejects when refusing the idea of a mental paradigm laid up somewhere as a model for how to play a tune powerfully.

Wittgenstein was not always opposed to expressivist essentialism, it was alive and well in the *Tractatus*. I bring this up not once again to raise the tangled question of whether the author of that book was whistling or not, but simply to make a contrast with where we have just arrived in *The Brown Book*. The *Tractatus* tells us that "propositions can represent the whole of reality, but they cannot represent what they must have in common with reality in order to be able to represent it—logical form."[36] Nevertheless, he also insists that we can "in a certain sense" talk about internal logical properties of facts, they are "manifest" otherwise than by talking about them.[37] More or less transparently he writes: "The existence of an internal relation between possible situations expresses itself in language by means of an internal relation between the propositions representing them."[38]

When logical form expresses itself *in* language, there is indeed a paradigm, inexpressible otherwise though it may be, which is expressed in meaningful language, but not in nonsense. Tractarian logical form is thus another form of the kind of hidden "reservoir" or paradigm which, in its mental version, is rejected in the *The Brown Book*. But there is, in fact, nothing hidden. I take the disappearance of the "in," giving us simply music expresses itself, as a mark of Wittgenstein's having put the reservoir picture almost completely behind him in *The Brown Book*.

Understanding Sentences as Understanding Musical Themes

Approaching the end of his discussion in *The Brown Book* of music as "expressing itself," Wittgenstein turns to the way language expresses itself, suggesting that "in many cases" understanding a linguistic sentence and understanding a musical theme are similar.[39] I cite a very similar passage from the *Philosophical Investigations* which is no longer hedged "in many cases."

> Understanding a sentence in language is much more akin to understanding a theme in music than one may think. What I mean is that understanding a spoken sentence is closer than one thinks to what is ordinarily called understanding a musical theme. Why is just *this* the pattern of variation and intensity and tempo? One would like to say: "Because I know what it all means." But what does it mean? I'd not be able to say.[40]

When such a passage appears in *The Brown Book* we find Wittgenstein toying with the distinction between transitive and intransitive uses of words (a distinction absent from the *Investigations*), but finally saying what the tune meant simply by whistling the tune itself. With such an analogy in mind, I hope you can appreciate why he had been tempted to say: music expresses itself. That would have amounted to a denial that there were two things, the music and what it meant, instead there would just be the sounds, no added meanings (occult or otherwise), just the played notes themselves. A world of immanence. Things threaded on silence.

In one of his late essays on music, "Philosophy and the Unheard," one specifically addressed to Arnold Schoenberg, Cavell finds himself facing the passage from Wittgenstein just cited, and his concern is with understanding why the similarity between understanding (in) music and (in) language is so very hard for us to admit.[41] Cavell supposes that Wittgenstein takes us to imagine that sentences are meaningful, when they are or appear to be, because the meanings those sentences combine are meaningfully combined.[42] Perhaps therefore it is difficult to link understanding in music and language, because we think that to understand a musical phrase all you need to attend to is the played notes themselves, whereas, to understand a linguistic phrase you need to attend to something other than the words, something behind them, namely, their meanings. And so Cavell takes Wittgenstein's mature philosophy to announce the promise of "understanding without meaning[s]"—and that goes as much for music as for language.[43] Cavell feels Wittgenstein gives us "a utopian glimpse of a new, or undiscovered, relation to language, to its sources in the world, to its means of expression."[44]

How to understand why music, for Cavell, was "a figure for the mind in its most perfected relation to itself, or to its wishes for itself"?[45] This expression—"understanding without meaning[s]"—shows up in another of Cavell's late essays, "Impressions of Revolution" (discussed at length by William Day in chapter 2). Reading Walter Benjamin's *The Origins of German Tragic Drama* (1928) prompts Cavell to these reflections on his own assimilation of emptiness and inexpressiveness:

A direct way of coming at this idea is to say that music allows the achieving of understanding without meaning, that is to say, without the articulation of individual acts of reference on which intelligibility is classically thought to depend. That words have meanings by virtue of being the names of things is the theory of meaning that Wittgenstein's *Investigations* opens by sketching and continues by tracing its seemingly endless implications, in each case to self-extinction.[46]

Cavell's interpretation of what the professors call "nonsense" as inexpressiveness (emptiness, madness, or self-extinction) surfaces also in Cavell's *The Claim of Reason*,[47] and this may have helped to seed the unitary view of nonsense, namely, that nonsense is of only one kind (gibberish), which has played such an important role in the "resolute" interpretation of the *Tractatus*.[48] I am attracted not so much to the Frege–Wittgenstein reduction of nonsense-as-category-confusion to nonsense-as-gibberish as to the denial of the existence of gibberish altogether—or, as Gertrude Stein put it: "it is impossible to avoid meaning."[49]

Understanding without meaning(s): what I am stretching out to greet here in Cavell's words could be put in terms of two different trajectories of that expression, and I do not want to disavow either one, or any other trajectory of that expression. Along one trajectory, the phrase "understanding without meanings" takes us to the understanding embodied in skillful activity of any sort: algebraically, as *corporeal* algebras—from shucking oysters, to removing a spleen, to conducting an effective legal cross-examination. It's a domain some Heideggerians abbreviate as the workshop, or simply "the hammer." Along another trajectory, understanding without meanings takes us close to Gertrude Stein's equation of understanding and enjoying, and closer still to Kierkegaard's sense that just to learn from things is a joy, the joy of pausing our energetic calculations as we follow the lead of things.[50] It might require practices of becoming silent, spiritual practices even, so that we are (increasingly) open to the call of things. Things might thereby be discovered to be inklings, each animating another, that is, if we would only stop naming and begin listening.

The "utopian glimpse" was, first, of an undiscovered relation to the sources of language in a world, a world of things, and second, of the sense that although the expressive means of language can indeed be construed narrowly, those expressive means should, at the last, exclude nothing—as if the ideal of *meaning what we say* was becoming the ideal of writing or speaking in such a way that every aspect of one's writing or speaking would *express itself*, even the spittle of the clarinetist. I suspect that the utopian glimpse provided by musical understanding was something Cavell came to feel was missing from his early defenses of ordinary language philosophy, when he was more exclusively Austin's student than Wittgenstein's. In "The Touch of Words," he talks about this change in his thinking:

> I could imagine that if I had known the *Investigations*, I mean had even read it through once, before writing the material of the essay "Must We Mean What We Say?", I would have concentrated on, or at least wished to include, in justifying Austin's procedures—along with insisting upon, or instancing what it means to speak of my knowledge of my language—an equal insistence upon my attachment to my words, my experience of them in their significance to the world, hence their significance to me. This seems to bring out the stakes in philosophizing out of the ordinary.[51]

I hear Cavell as offering a lesson in the transcendentalist underwriting of philosophizing out of the ordinary. Not only will we learn such algebraic distinctions as that between "by mistake" and "by accident," between the transitive and intransitive uses of "expressing" and "meaning," we will also learn of our being reached out to, touched by words—sometimes inky things, often only inklings. Sometimes I think this touch of words is the force of what, while considering Thoreau's *Walden*, Cavell calls a "word's literality": "just these letters, just here, rather than any others."[52] Listening to, being touched by inklings nesting in words and sentences, is how I see Cavell's transcendentalist account of the appeal to the ordinary.

When Wittgenstein marks the kinship between understanding a sentence and understanding a musical theme, he introduces the notion of "the 'soul' of words."[53] The soul of a word is what makes it feel strange to replace a given word with an alternate. What is missing from such a substitution is the "utopian glimpse" of the boundless, expressive powers of things that are words. What is missing is part of what made Esperanto disgust Wittgenstein and attract Carnap.[54] What is missing might be named, after Cavell, each word's literality.

After introducing the notion of the soul of words, Wittgenstein says some provocative things about understanding in music and in language which I hope reminds you of Gertrude Stein reprimanding her radio interviewer: "you mean by understanding that you can talk about it in the way you have the habit of talking [...] putting it in other words [...] but I mean by understanding enjoyment."[55] Here is Wittgenstein:

> We speak of understanding a sentence in the sense in which it can be replaced by another which says the same; but also in the sense in which it cannot be replaced by any other. (Any more than one musical theme can be replaced by another.)
>
> In the one case, the thought in the sentence is what is common to different sentences; in the other, something that is expressed only by these words in these positions. (Understanding a poem.)[56]

I enjoy, after Stein, how Wittgenstein's "expressed only by the words in these positions" seems to be an instance of "language expresses itself" where understanding is enjoying; and also how it aligns with Cavell's take on literality: "just these letters, just here, rather than any others." But I fear Wittgenstein might be marking too sharply the distinction between poetry and prose. It may be true that we attend to numberless aspects of the words in a poem that we do not typically attend to in prose, but that doesn't mean we could not. There sometimes seems no end of important things we can either thoughtlessly ignore or more affectionately attend to. And so, for example, we might feel like saying that in some moods, or for some purposes, the same theme played on different instruments might present itself as *the same*, a situation unlike what Wittgenstein calls a poem, but more like prose. Yet in other moods, the so-called "same" musical theme played on different instruments, by different players, might present itself as *different*. It might even be provocative to alter the instrumentation of a string quartet such that a new woodwind quartet's performance of the "same" would be both the same and different from the string version. Sometimes we will especially enjoy the differences. Concert instrumentalists care even about singular instruments: thrilled anonymously to receive the gift of a Guarneri cello, they will say everything is different (from even an excellent alternative cello), especially in certain registers. Every single thing has algebraic aspects and inkling aspects. It's not true, as Wittgenstein comes near to implying, that music and pansies and poetry are one thing and prose is another.[57]

Cavell's comments on understanding in music, his comments on the utopian glimpse it provided, arrive in an essay he wrote for a volume on Schoenberg who, as it happens, was Cage's teacher.[58] Pressed up against

Schoenberg, the author of "The Availability of Wittgenstein's Later Philosophy," finds himself, parenthetically, feeling resonances between Schoenberg's serialism and Wittgenstein's own work on continuing a mathematical series.[59] Schoenberg resisted writing in a musical key, since he believed that when writing in a given key, composition, however free it might be, is scaffolded or constrained by a circular pattern of musical keys, each of which is "grammatically" related to its dominant, subdominant, and so on. When writing in his serial style of "emancipated dissonance," by contrast, Schoenberg began a piece by arranging all twelve tones that span what is called an octave into one series of twelve tones in a row. It is as if each piece were written in a key specific to itself, while the traditional grammatical scaffolding of keys went entirely missing. The question—then as now—is how, unscaffolded, to go on. With the force of received musical grammar considerably diminished, there is already a Wittgensteinian resonance. And then, more or less precisely as with what Cavell calls "keep[ing] up with the word," we have two responsibilities: one to the past continuation of the singular series and another to the moment—now—of its singular continuation.[60]

In the mathematical case, the continuation will seem more mechanical, but it is Wittgenstein's genius to reveal that, even here, we are not following rails to infinity.[61] In Schoenberg's case, the singular series of twelve notes that were serialized specifically for that particular piece need to be continued in ways that the series calls for, and this calling will not be algebraical. I enjoy thinking that Cage learned this from his teacher, Schoenberg, and not just that he needed a feel for harmony, but rather that Schoenberg's compositional practice begins a path (for Cage) from tonality to singularity, with the only restriction that, for Schoenberg, this singularity is a singularity of the twelve regimented tones of the equal temperament European piano. Cage took this further such that he didn't consider music to be made of the grammatical "relationships of the sounds" at all, instead:

> Let us take a premise which seems apparent and elementary: music is made of sound. Every one with ears may hear it. The music is made to be heard. [...] From this point of view, the one which I am proposing, music need not be understood, but rather it must be heard.[62]

Cage completely releases the power of sound to express itself—and not by understanding something grammatical, but instead by ... enjoying.

Wittgenstein and Cavell, by the profundity of their musical sympathies, both sense that there may be a dimension of the ordinary *beyond grammar*, a dimension accessible by a different grammar, a grammar of resistance to conformism, which could be a spiritual practice of affectionate attention, opening us to hear, to feel the touch of things reaching out to us, not in terms of either an organized workshop or a collection of tool-words, but in terms of nothing more than things.[63] The things that are words, can indeed code this and that, but they are each of them, always also, things expressing themselves. There are lots of ways to educate grown-ups, but Wittgenstein and Cavell sometimes found themselves drawn to sentences as things threaded on silence, thus opening the possibility of a pedagogy of things. I have nothing to say and I am saying it.

Notes

1 Stanley Cavell, "Crossing Paths," in *Cavell on Film*, ed. William Rothman (Albany: State University of New York Press, 2005), 370. I would not know of this good encounter had I not been told of it by William Day, who for that reason, and others, seeded this entire paper. See Day's contribution to this volume, chapter 2.

2 See John Cage, *I–VI*, *The Charles Eliot Norton Lectures, 1988–89*.

3 Ibid., 2.

4 Ibid., 1.

5 Cavell, "Crossing Paths," *Cavell on Film*, 370.

6 Stanley Cavell, "Music Discomposed" and "A Matter of Meaning It," in *Must We Mean What We Say?: A Book of Essays* (Cambridge: Cambridge University Press, 1976), 196, 219.

7 Cavell, "A Matter of Meaning It," *Must We Mean What We Say?*, 219.

8 Ibid. Cavell writes: "So the original questions 'Is this music?' and 'Is this art?' are not independent. The latter shows, we might say, the spirit in which the former is relevantly asked."

9 Stanley Cavell, *The Claim of Reason: Wittgenstein, Skepticism, Morality, and Tragedy* (New York: Oxford University Press, 1979), 78.

10 John Cage, *Silence* (Hanover: Wesleyan University Press, 1961), 109.

11 Ibid.

12 I find myself putting it this way in the wake of attending my colleague Filippo Casati's series of seminars in fall 2019 on Heidegger's "What is Metaphysics?" (1929).

13 A. R. Ammons, *A Coast of Trees* (New York: Norton, 1981), 1.

14 Ludwig Wittgenstein, *Philosophical Investigations*, 4th ed., revised by P. M. S. Hacker and Joachim Schulte (Malden: Wiley-Blackwell, 2009), §5.

15 Wittgenstein, *Philosophical Investigations*, §329. I learned of the importance of this passage for Charles Bernstein in a conversation with him at a celebration of the work of Arakawa and Gins.

16 Gertrude Stein, "A Radio Interview (1934)," *The Paris Review*, vol. 116 (1990): 89.

17 Ludwig Wittgenstein, *The Blue and Brown Books* (New York: Harper Perennial, 1965), 166.

18 Ibid., 158–61; my attention was drawn to the importance of this distinction by Avner Baz in a paper now available as "Aspect Perception and Philosophical Difficulty," in *The Oxford Handbook of Wittgenstein*, ed. Oskari Kuusela and Marie McGinn (Oxford: Oxford University Press, 2011), 697–713.

19 Wittgenstein, *The Blue and Brown Books*, 166.

20 Ibid.

21 Cage, *Silence*, 109.

22 Wittgenstein, *The Blue and Brown Books*, 166.

23 It may seem to conflict with my emphasis on "language expresses itself" that even in these pages Wittgenstein writes: "one might say 'Understanding a sentence means getting hold of its content; and the content is *in* the sentence'" (*The Blue and Brown Books*, 167; italics added). This *seems* to suggest, confoundingly, that content somehow separable *from* the sentence is *in* the sentence, but even in this place, Wittgenstein denies that the sentence is pointing "to a reality outside the sentence." So, by insisting rather that the content is "*in* the sentence," again with my italics, he almost puts the content in the sentence *itself* (Ibid.). As I've already pointed out, in the passage that appealed to Charles Bernstein (see n.16), Wittgenstein does write that "language is *itself* the vehicle of thought" (*Philosophical Investigations*, §329; italics added). Naturally, I realize here and throughout that I may be urging Wittgenstein further in the direction he was heading than he ever actually went.

24 Wittgenstein, *The Blue and Brown Books*, 166.

25 Wittgenstein, *Philosophical Investigations*, §523.

26 Ibid.

27 Wittgenstein, *The Blue and Brown Books*, 166.

28 Wittgenstein, *Philosophical Investigations*, §371.

29 Wittgenstein, *The Blue and Brown Books*, 143.

30 Ibid.

31 Friedrich Nietzsche, *Beyond Good and Evil* (Cambridge: Cambridge University Press, 2002), §2.

32 Wittgenstein sometimes used "occult" as a term of criticism: "(It was just the occult character of the mental process which you needed for your purposes.)" Wittgenstein, *The Blue and Brown Books*, 5.

33 We are in the neighborhood of the Frege's 1884 context principle which appears in Wittgenstein's *Tractatus Logico-Philosophicus*, trans. David Pears and Brian F. McGuinness (London: Routledge & Kegan Paul, 1961), §3.3. The idea that sentences are words threaded on silence is a denial that their power depends on being in a game, so Wittgenstein himself can lean away from language games doing any *explanatory* work. See Wittgenstein, *Philosophical Investigations*, §654.

34   Michel Foucault, *The Order of Things* (New York: Vintage Books, 1994), 92.

35   Ibid. 290.

36   Wittgenstein, *Tractatus*, §4.12.

37   Ibid., §4.122.

38   Ibid., §4.125. I would not have put "music expresses itself" together with the "expresses itself in" of the *Tractatus* had I not been drawn to the Tractarian connections made by William Day in his "The Aesthetic Dimension of Wittgenstein's Later Writing," in *Wittgenstein on Aesthetic Understanding*, ed. Garry L. Hagberg, (Cham, Switzerland: Palgrave Macmillan, 2017), 3–29.

39   Wittgenstein, *The Blue and Brown Books*, 167.

40   Wittgenstein, *Philosophical Investigations*, §527.

41   Stanley Cavell, "Philosophy and the Unheard," *Here and There: Sites of Philosophy*, ed. Nancy Bauer, Alice Crary, Sandra Laugier (Cambridge, MA: Harvard University Press, 2022), 261.

42   Ibid.

43   Cavell, "Impressions of Revolution," *Here and There*, 276.

44   Cavell, "Philosophy and the Unheard," *Here and There*, 261.

45   Ibid., 260–1.

46   Cavell, "Impressions of Revolution," *Here and There*, 276.

47   Cavell, *The Claim of Reason*, 84, 242, 336, 461.

48   See Cora Diamond, *The Realistic Spirit: Wittgenstein, Philosophy, and the Mind* (Cambridge, MA: MIT Press, 1991).

49   Gertrude Stein, *How to Write* (New York: Dover Publications, 1975), 71.

50   Søren Kierkegaard, *The Lily of the Field and The Bird of the Air (Three Godly Discourses)*, trans. Bruce Kirmmse (Princeton: Princeton University Press, 2016).

51   Stanley Cavell, "The Touch of Words," in *Seeing Wittgenstein Anew*, ed. William Day and Victor J. Krebs (Cambridge: Cambridge University Press, 2010), 85.

52   "That our meaning a word is our return to it and its return to us—our occurring to one another—is expressed by the word's literality, its being just these letters, just here, rather than any others." Stanley Cavell, *The Senses of Walden, an Expanded Edition* (San Francisco: North Point Press, 1981), 63.

53   Wittgenstein, *Philosophical Investigations*, §530; see also Part II §270.

54   Wittgenstein, *Culture and Value*, 60; and *The Philosophy of Rudolf Carnap*, ed. Paul A. Schlipp (Carbondale: Library of Living Philosophers, 1963), 25.

55   Stein, "A Radio Interview (1934)," 89.

56   Wittgenstein, *Philosophical Investigations*, §531.

57   Wittgenstein, *The Blue and Brown Books*, 178. "A friend and I once looked at beds of pansies. Each bed showed a different kind. We were impressed by each in turn. Speaking about them my friend said, 'What a variety of color patterns, and each says something.' And this was just what I myself wished to say. [...] If one had asked what the color pattern of the pansy said, the right answer would have seemed to be that it said itself." Hence we could have used an intransitive form of expression, as he does: "[e]ach of these color patterns impresses one."

58   Cage recalls: "Schoenberg was a magnificent teacher, who always gave the impression that he was putting us in touch with musical principles. I studied counterpoint at his home and attended all his classes at USC and later at UCLA when he moved there. I also took his course in harmony, for which I had no gift. Several times I tried to explain to Schoenberg that I had no feeling for harmony. He told me that without a feeling for harmony I would always encounter an obstacle, a wall through which I wouldn't be able to pass. My reply was that in that case I would devote my life to beating my head against that wall—and maybe that is what I've been doing ever since. John Cage, *Conversing with Cage*, 2nd ed., Richard Kostelanetz (New York: Routledge, 2003), 5.

59   Cavell, "Philosophy and the Unheard," *Here and There*, 261.

60   Cavell, *The Claim of Reason*, 78.

61   Wittgenstein, *Philosophical Investigations*, §218.

62   John Cage, *John Cage: Writer: Selected Texts*, ed. Richard Kostelanetz (New York: Cooper Square Press, 2000), 17.

63   In *How to Write*, Stein contrasts a "grammar in resistance" (86) with a "grammar in retrospect" (77).

CODA

Out Waltzed Stanley

CHARLES BERNSTEIN

But I go into the library once in a while, to look around, and last week I saw a book about Thoreau and Emerson by a man named Lipschitz [...]" "What of it? A name like that?" Allbee said this with great earnestness. "After all, it seems to me that people of such background simply couldn't understand [...].
—SAUL BELLOW, *The Victim* (1947)[1]

These doubts may usefully raise the question of the audience of philosophy, perhaps in the form of asking how philosophizing is to sound.
—STANLEY CAVELL, *The Senses of Walden* (1972)[2]

WHAT IS CAVELL'S LEGACY?, David LaRocca prompts. This collection offers manifold answers. But one legacy is surely that you don't need to stay in your lane; you can write about whatever you are able to say something substantial about. Genre and modes don't limit subject. I don't want to make Cavell into a literary critic, a film theorist, a musicologist, a Shakespearean, an Emerson scholar, an essayist, a memoirist. Of course, he is all of these, but under the sign of philosophy. He never moved away from philosophy but rather brought philosophy to bear on these several subjects.

We say literary theory but not philosophical theory, though I suppose that would be Logical Positivism and its legacy. Cavell, like the philosophers he champions, is against theory in favor of praxis.

FIGURE 2 *(Opposite) A fifteen-year-old Stanley Cavell leading the band, the McClatchey Melodiers, and playing alto saxophone at C. K. McClatchey High School, Sacramento, California, 1942.*

The meaning of Cavell's philosophy is not just in what he argues, but also in what motivates his arguments and what his work makes possible. This is why his autobiographical turn is defining. He offers a poetics not a logic. Intention and meaning exceed knowledge: as much as deductive reasoning, philosophy is a matter of finding by sounding and "finding as founding."[3] Cavell is adept at tracing unrecognized connections both within and across works and genres. We interpret not just literal but figurative meanings until the figurative comes to seem literal and the literal figurative: this is a basic tenet of Midrashic antinomianism.[4]

Fluency and ordinary language are vexed issues for both philosophers and second language speakers. Is difficulty a sign of disfluency or a kind of music? Or is it a mark that words must and do mean what we say? After noting his Yiddish-speaking father's talent for "improvisation," meaning doubletalk, or let's call it extravagant speech, Cavell says:

I mean also that it reminds me of the causes he had for hating me, for example, that my English was unaccented. Is that really a credible cause of hatred? Consider that it meant that my future, unlike his, was open. Of course, exactly this difference was also something he wanted. He was, for example, more ferocious in insisting on my practicing the piano every day than my pianist mother was.[5]

The Bar Mitzvah gift of a saxophone is both the instrument of Cavell's fluency and sign of his entering into a Midrashic relation to the law of the father—that is to say, language, the symbolic. The saxophone's voicings are neither in Yiddish nor English, much less Hebrew. Music is an Esperanto that binds father to son in a pledge of allegiance to the new world to come, *this new yet unapproachable America*, to cite Cavell's keynote echo of Emerson.[6]

"*After all, it seems to me that people of such background simply couldn't understand*," Bellow's antisemite says. But, as we know, those who say that are the ones who don't understand the gift of our shared American possibilities. Cavell hears Thoreau and Emerson's music—"he hears a different drummer. Let him step to the music which he hears, however measured or far away."[7]

I remember, as a student, Cavell sounding out this passage in his 1970 *Walden* improvisations, making the words his own and making them ours, too, as active listeners. This is Cavell's legacy, call it his philosophy: *step to the music you hear* and you will find the music you need. The danger is neither disfluency nor skepticism's fear of the bottomless. *Walden*: "Who that has heard a strain of music feared then lest he should speak extravagantly any more forever?"[8] *The Senses of Walden*: "We do not know what the bottom of a pond is if we do not know, e.g., what it is to sound the bottom, vaguely imagining that it is abysmally deep."[9]

CAVELL'S WRITING RESISTS (or better to say, wrestles with) the kind of aphoristic memes and jingles so popular in poets' epigraphs. However, Cavell did have an epigrammatic moment. In *Little Did I Know*, in the August 1, 2004 entry,[10] he offers a set of short remarks transcribed from a 1972 notebook. In contrast to Cavell, but perhaps echoing Thoreau, I can't resist aphorism and fractured clichés. What's a coda without a codicil— playing in, around, and outside Cavell's tunes?

Skepticism is the avoidance of love.
Remarriage is real marriage.
Moral perfectionism: we try harder.
The medium is the essence.
Intention is 9/10 of the flaw.
If you meant it, you mean it.
Intention without meaning is like lightning without a storm.
The view from nowhere isn't a view.
Discompose me, you sweet, embraceable you.
Think twice, it's all right.
Ethics without aesthetics is like a body without a soul.
Praise brings the world near.
Dasein precedes design, depending on what you have in mind.
Kant flipped sideways is better than Hegel erect.
Ordinary language has a lot to say.
Wittgenstein is as available as you are or, anyway, as you might be.
Walden Pond makes the sound of one hand clapping.
The limits of language are sublime: Don't sublime sublimity.
Whose on first is doing a pretty good job except when it comes to
  pitching.
Let the music play even if no one hears it; though maybe they do, but
  can't yet acknowledge it.
Music announces itself as we fall asleep and as we wake.
Tangles are not *cul-de-sacs*.
Intention has as much to do with the frame as the utterance.
"A name like that": Sometimes a thought needs to sound foreign
  before it can become familiar.
Music, in the sense of language's rhythms and pitches, is necessary
  but not sufficient for thought.
Music is thought's medium.
Extending Zukofsky on poetry: Philosophy has its "Lower limit
  speech/Upper limit music."[11]
Philosophy and poetry sound language in search of lost meanings.
If we say philosophy gives thought a hearing, can we say poetry
  gives music words? Or is it that philosophy finds its thoughts in

listening and poetry finds its musics in hearing (—*inhering*)? Then
is philosophy a rehearsal and poetry a recital?
The Senses of Walden: "But then you may find yourself conjecturing
whether one is quite sure one hears, or knows, the sound of one's
own voice."[12]
Cavell's music is the voicings he brings to his words.
It takes two to waltz but only one to carry a tune.

Notes

1   Josh Lambert discusses this passage in *The Literary Mafia: Jews, Publishing,
and Postwar American Literature* (New Haven: Yale University Press,
2022), 17.

2   Stanley Cavell, *The Senses of Walden, an Expanded Edition* (Chicago: The
University of Chicago Press, 1992), 152.

3   Stanley Cavell, *This New Yet Unapproachable America: Lectures after
Emerson after Wittgenstein* (Chicago: The University of Chicago Press, 2013
[1988]), 77.

4   See my "The Pataquerical Imagination: Midrashic Antinomianism and
the Promise of Bent Studies" in *Pitch of Poetry* (Chicago: The University
of Chicago Press, 2016); the book's title acknowledges Cavell's *A Pitch of
Philosophy* (1996).

5   Stanley Cavell, *Little Did I Know: Excerpts from Memory* (Stanford: Stanford
University Press, 2010), 10.

6   I discuss doubletalk and the Jewish origins of Esperanto in *Doubletalking
the Homophonic Sublime: Comedy, Appropriation, and the Sounds of One
Hand Clapping* (Barrytown, NY: Station Hill Press, 2021). My discussion
of doubletalk focuses on Sid Caesar. Like Cavell, Caesar, four years his
senior, came from a Yiddish-speaking family and the saxophone was his first
instrument, preceding his verbally pyrotechnic comedy routines.

7   Henry David Thoreau, *Walden, or Life in the Woods* (Boston: Houghton,
Mifflin, 1854), ch. 27, "Conclusion," 502.

8   Ibid.

9   Cavell, *The Senses of Walden*, 64.

10   Cavell, *Little Did I Know*, 481–7.

11   "A"-12 in *Louis Zukofsky: Selected Poems*, ed. Charles Bernstein (New York:
Library of America, 2006), 102.

12   Cavell, *The Senses of Walden*, 38.

ACKNOWLEDGMENTS

THE FIRST NOTE OF ANY TUNE commissioned to convey my gratitude on this occasion would be struck for the talented roster of players here joined variously in chorus and conversation, in virtuosic solos and collaborative chamber pieces. Orchestrating this event, I hoped such scholars—some of them accomplished musicians and composers in their own rights—would feel moved to join the session. Now with the final ledger locked, I am duly in their debts.

At Bloomsbury, Haaris Naqvi, Director of Scholarly and Student Publishing and Editorial Director of Literary Studies, continues to offer me essential orientation mixed with enduring amity. Throughout the book's development—from initial pitch to final proof—I've had, the book has had, the good fortune of placement on the Music and Sound Studies list under the guidance and expertise of Publisher, Leah Babb-Rosenfeld and Assistant Editor, Rachel Moore. I remain fortunate to collaborate with all of them and the wider, talented team at the press.

During the book's gestation, I found myself in dialogue with an esteemed scholar, one deeply familiar with Stanley Cavell's life and work—including what music meant to him. While trying to convey the spirit of the volume (along with other recent Bloomsbury titles devoted to Cavell and cinema, and an Exeter collection on Cavell and television), I said the aspiration was to make Cavell and music attractive, engaging, and necessary to the contemporary conversation operating in both realms, and especially where and when they overlap, or might. My interlocuter replied unironically with nonchalant confidence: "Oh, that shouldn't be hard." *Touché*, fine sir. And yet, *also* difficult because one wants to rise to the level of the subject of one's undertakings—and so, in this case, the bar is high, the desire to meet it daunting; in turn, the results of such efforts, one hopes will be worthy, if admittedly, even happily, provisional. There is always more work to be done. Needless to say, on this particular portfolio of reports, I have been aided and inspired in myriad ways by many admired others.

All of the contributors have, in their writing on Cavell and music (here and elsewhere), shaped the reception of the twinned topic: what we should be writing about, and how; what questions to ask and then after submitting initial replies, how to pursue still further findings. For attentive reflections on my work in this volume, I should like to thank especially Garrett Stewart, whose own body of work feels perpetually in conversation with Cavell's. Stewart here, in his fourth such outing under my editorial stewardship, along with our collaboration for Bloomsbury entitled *Attention Spans*, has had, as in many other such critical instances, immense and consequential input on this project—especially in the light of his path-making remarks on phonemic reading, the sound of prose, and the pertinence of Barbra Streisand. Another longtime collaborator, William Day, who, like Stewart, has featured in several of my previous edited collections, returns here with important late remarks on a subject so central to his own life as a musician who is also a philosopher. Hearty thanks to them both, then, for helping me get closer to what I mean to say—for careful annotations as well as for modeling fine scholarship. Not far behind, but in a wider orbit of conversation over the years at in-person conferences and during synchronous online forums, I thank Jean-Philippe Antoine, Jocelyn Benoist, Richard Eldridge, Garry L. Hagberg (another musician–philosopher), and Paul Standish. John T. Lysaker and I began discussing music two decades ago at an NEH Institute and I'm thrilled that for this project he magnanimously shared his pages with Kevin C. Karnes; together they make a captivating new duo. Eran Guter and Gordon C. F. Bearn round out our playlist with two companionable pieces, a felicitous duet to conclude the four movements of this composition.

As you can see, the indomitable and ever-eloquent Charles Bernstein has done double duty—tapping his baton upon the score to summon a rousing overture, and later, sending us off with a memorable coda. From paths crossed at the State University of New York at Buffalo to lucky connections on New York subways to memorial notes shared in the round at Harvard's Emerson Hall, I'm grateful anew for his generous support of this volume and honored by his fitting double presence in it.

John Harbison, who among this group knew Cavell the earliest, and thus the longest, accepted the unlooked for labor of recounting his memories of Stanley, of providing a sense of the scale of Cavell's enduring significance to the thought and study of music, the fulfillment of which we can all be grateful for. I know I am. As I am to John's amiable assistant, Sarah Schaffer.

Conversations, even brief ones, can have substantive effects on the shape and qualities of such a collective effort as this book. For me, decisive encounters—including remarks received, recommendations made—that proved transformative include those with Emily Apter, Nancy Bauer, J. M. Bernstein, Rex Butler, Cathleen Cavell, Alice Crary, Paul Cronin, Paul Deb, Hent de Vries, Juliet Floyd, Jeroen Gerrits, Lydia Goehr, Grégoire Halbout, Neil Hertz, Amir Khan, Victor Krebs, Sandra Laugier, Paola Marrati, John Opera, Lawrence Rhu, and another cherished collaborator, Oscar Jansson, devoted to the experience and expression of sound in the air—and on the page.

Lastly, because foremost, I underscore my abiding adoration of K. L. Evans, and our daughters, Ruby and Star, who make such endeavors possible and worthwhile. They bring much needed joy and intelligence, perspective and sense—for which I'm sincerely grateful. Attesting to Emerson's customary prudential clarity, my findings echo his own: "The domestic man, who loves no music so well as his kitchen clock and the airs which the logs sing to him as they burn on the hearth, has solaces which others never dream of."

CONTRIBUTORS

Jean-Philippe Antoine is Professor Emeritus of History and Theory of Contemporary Art at Université Paris 8 Vincennes-Saint Denis. His published research bears on modern and current redefinitions of art, the value of images, and the social construction of memory. After having examined the relationship between the medieval art of memory on late medieval and early Renaissance Italian painting, he has mostly written about the works of modern and contemporary artists, such as Marcel Broodthaers, Mike Kelley, and Joseph Beuys, sometimes with special emphasis on music and sound as well as on historians/theorists, such as George Kubler and Brian O'Doherty. He has also written on the transformation of sound sculpture into sound art, and Stanley Cavell's relationship to film and music. An artist, he works with painting, installations, soundworks, and lectures–performances. His latest published soundwork is *I who make a profession of dumb things*, an aural rendering of Nicolas Poussin's second series of *The Seven Sacraments* in the Scottish National Gallery in Edinburgh (CD, Firework Edition records, 2023).

Gordon C. F. Bearn is Stewardson Professor and Chair of Philosophy at Lehigh University. He is the author of *Waking to Wonder: Wittgenstein's Existential Investigations* (1997) and *Life Drawing: A Deleuzean Aesthetics of Existence* (2013), as well as "Staging Authenticity: A Critique of Cavell's Modernism" (in *Philosophy and Literature*), "Sounding Serious: Cavell and Derrida" (in *Representations*), and "Cavell, Wittgenstein, and Human Finitude" (in the Proceedings of the Eighth International Wittgenstein Symposium, Kirchberg am Wechsel). As Bearn notes: "Never officially Cavell's student, there is a realm of philosophy and swathes of movies and literature that I only read and enjoyed because he wrote about them. My musical life would have been richer had Cavell written more about music. Left to my own devices, however, I found John Cage performing early versions of *Empty Words*, and have myself performed works by Cage and Alvin Lucier, as well as the work of those in or adjacent to Fluxus such as La Monte Young, Ben Patterson, and Alison Knowles."

Jocelyn Benoist is Professor of Contemporary Philosophy and Theory of Knowledge at the Université of Paris 1 Panthéon-Sorbonne and author of, among numerous books, *Concepts, Les limites de l'intentionalité* (*The Bounds of Intentionality*, 2005), *Le bruit du sensible* (*The Noise of Sensible Things*, 2013), *Toward a Contextual Realism* (2021), and *Von der Phänomenologie zum Realismus* (Mohr 2022). Former Director of the Husserl Archive of Paris, he was a Fellow at the Wissenschaftskolleg of Berlin in 2013–14, received a Gay-Lussac Humboldt Prize in 2015, and the Silver Medal of the Centre national de la recherche scientifique (CNRS) in 2019. He runs the International Associated Laboratory RPRCT (Realism as a Philosophical Response to the Challenges of our Time, Bonn-Paris-Turin) with Markus Gabriel and Maurizio Ferraris.

Charles Bernstein was born in Manhattan in 1950. He is the author or editor of over fifty books, ranging from collections of poetry and essays to pamphlets, libretti, and collaborations, most recently *Topsy-Turvy* (2021) and *Pitch of Poetry* (2016). His work was the subject of *The Poetry of Idiomatic Insistences*, edited by Paul Bove for the fall 2021 issue of *boundary 2*. Other recent publications include *The Course*, a collaboration with Ted Greenwald; an annotated, facsimile edition of *L=A=N=G=U=A=G=E* magazine, a separate volume of related letters, and another containing the late 1970s collaborative poem *Legend*. He is the winner of the 2019 Bollingen Prize from Yale University for *Near/Miss* and lifetime achievement in poetry. He lives in Brooklyn and Kinderhook, New York. More info at http://writing.upenn.edu/epc.

William Day is Professor of Philosophy at Le Moyne College (Syracuse, New York). He is contributing coeditor with Victor J. Krebs of *Seeing Wittgenstein Anew: New Essays on Aspect Seeing* (2012), and has published numerous articles and book chapters on Wittgenstein, Cavell, and topics in aesthetics. These include examinations of the moral perfectionist structure of exemplary jazz improvisation, as well as readings of post-1940s films in light of Cavell's study of remarriage comedies (*Moonstruck, Eternal Sunshine of the Spotless Mind, Before Midnight*) and unknown woman melodramas (*Woman at War*). Among Day's writings addressing Cavell's thought directly are "A Soteriology of Reading: Cavell's Excerpts from Memory" (*Stanley Cavell: Philosophy, Literature, and Criticism*) and "*Zhenzhi* and Acknowledgment in Wang Yangming and Stanley Cavell" (*European and Chinese Philosophy: Origins and Intersections*), which one reviewer has called "the very best account of the notion of acknowledgement in any of the literature that I am aware of."

Richard Eldridge is Charles and Harriett Cox McDowell Professor Emeritus of Philosophy at Swarthmore College and Lecturer in Philosophy at the University of Tennessee, Knoxville. He is the editor of *Stanley Cavell* (2003), *Stanley Cavell and Literary Studies* (2011, with Bernard Rhie), and the series

Oxford Studies in Philosophy and Literature. He has published widely in the philosophies of art, literature, and music, as well as on Wittgenstein and German Idealism. His most recent book is *Werner Herzog: Filmmaker and Philosopher* (Bloomsbury, 2019).

Eran Guter is Senior Lecturer in Philosophy and Director of the Honors Program at the Max Stern Yezreel Valley College in Israel, having earned a Ph.D. in philosophy from Boston University. His study of the full array of Wittgenstein's remarks on music spans almost two decades, and he has published numerous articles that concern the historical aspects of these remarks, their importance for understanding the evolution of Wittgenstein's philosophy, and the challenge which they pose for contemporary analytic philosophy of music. He is the author of *Aesthetics A–Z* (2010) and *Wittgenstein on Music* (2024).

Garry L. Hagberg is James H. Ottaway Professor of Philosophy and Aesthetics at Bard College, and has also held a Chair in the School of Philosophy at the University of East Anglia. Author of numerous papers at the intersection of aesthetics and the philosophy of language, his books include *Meaning and Interpretation: Wittgenstein, Henry James, and Literary Knowledge* (1994); *Art as Language: Wittgenstein, Meaning, and Aesthetic Theory* (1995); and *Describing Ourselves: Wittgenstein and Autobiographical Consciousness* (2008). He is editor of *Art and Ethical Criticism* (2008) and *Fictional Characters, Real Problems: The Search for Ethical Content in Literature* (2016) as well as his seven edited volumes from Palgrave, *Wittgenstein on Aesthetic Understanding* (2017); *Stanley Cavell on Aesthetic Understanding* (2018); *Narrative and Self-Understanding* (2019); *Fictional Worlds and the Moral Imagination* (2021); *Fictional Worlds and Philosophical Reflection, Literature and Its Language: Philosophical Aspects* (2022), and *Fictional Worlds and the Political Imagination* (2024). Coeditor of *A Companion to the Philosophy of Literature* (2010) and editor of the journal *Philosophy and Literature*, Hagberg's most recent book is on the contribution literary experience makes to the formation of self and sensibility, *Living in Words: Literature, Autobiographical Language, and the Composition of Selfhood* (2023). He is presently completing three new books: *Consciousness Portrayed: Seven Case Studies in Philosophical Literature*; *Narratives of the Mind: Henry James, Philosophy, and the Writing of Modern Subjectivity*; and *Art and Meaning: On Artworks and Their Implications.*

John Harbison is Institute Professor Emeritus of Music at the Massachusetts Institute of Technology and a member of the American Academy of Arts and Letters. One of the dominant compositional voices of his generation, Harbison has authored a concert music catalog of more than three hundred works, anchored by three operas, six symphonies, six string quartets, twelve concerti, a ballet, an organ symphony, numerous song cycles and chamber works, a large body of sacred music, and innumerable jazz compositions and arrangements. He has received commissions from most of America's premiere musical institutions, including the Metropolitan Opera, Chicago Symphony, Boston Symphony, New York Philharmonic, and the Chamber Music Society of Lincoln Center. His abundant and estimable awards and honors include a MacArthur Fellowship and a Pulitzer Prize. He is author of the book, *What Do We Make of Bach?: Portraits, Essays, Notes* (2018). John and wife Rose Mary Harbison's lifelong friendship with Stanley Cavell began in September 1962, first in Princeton, then continuing in Cambridge, where they were part of a group of intellectuals engaged in spirited and congenial discourse on topics of philosophy, music, and social issues—meetings among many (he recalls in his contribution to the present volume) "whose thought, work, and sense of adventure still sounds with those long, excited days and evenings." They played music together, deeply connected through their love of jazz, and they were part of a Civil Rights group that worked at Tougaloo College, Mississippi in the summer of 1964. With Stanley Cavell, the Harbisons enjoyed a cherished friendship of deep admiration and respect.

Kevin C. Karnes is Professor of Music and Associate Dean for the Arts at Emory University. A musicologist who studies sounding expressions of identity, difference, and belonging in Eastern and Central Europe from the nineteenth century to the present, his work bridges archival research and ethnography, engaging projects in such fields as sound studies, philosophy, anthropology, and art history. He is the author of four books, most recently *Sounds Beyond: Arvo Pärt and the 1970s Soviet Underground* (2021), and the editor of seven volumes, including *Korngold and His World* (Princeton, 2019). He has served as editor-in-chief of the *Journal of the American Musicological Society* (2020–22) and founding series editor of the Oxford Keynotes Series (2014–20). His work has been funded by grants, fellowships, and awards from the ACLS, the NEH, the NEA, and the Association for the Advancement of Baltic Studies. He is currently writing a new book entitled *Electric Future: Berlin, Techno, the USSR, and the Dream of a New Europe.*

David LaRocca is the author or contributing editor of sixteen previous books, including *Emerson's English Traits and the Natural History of Metaphor* (2013). Recipient of a teaching commendation from Harvard Extension School, he served as Harvard University's Sinclair Traveling Fellow in the United Kingdom and has held visiting research or teaching positions in the United States at Binghamton, Cornell, Cortland, Harvard, Ithaca College, the New York Public Library, the School of Visual Arts, and Vanderbilt. Advised by Stanley Cavell during doctoral research, he later edited, annotated, and indexed Cavell's *Emerson's Transcendental Etudes*

(2003, published under his bachelor name, David Justin Hodge, as was *On Emerson*, also 2003) and worked as Cavell's research assistant during the time he was completing *Cities of Words: Pedagogical Letters on a Register of a Moral Life* (2004) and *Philosophy the Day after Tomorrow* (2005), and beginning *Little Did I Know: Excerpts from Memory* (2010). A recipient of the Distinguished Achievement Award from the Ralph Waldo Emerson Society, LaRocca has edited additional books featuring Cavell's work, including *Estimating Emerson: An Anthology of Criticism from Carlyle to Cavell* (2013), *The Bloomsbury Anthology of Transcendental Thought: From Antiquity to the Anthropocene* (2017), and *The Geschlecht Complex* (2022); and contributed chapters to *Stanley Cavell, Literature, and Film: The Idea of America* (2013), *Stanley Cavell and Aesthetic Understanding* (2018), and *Understanding Cavell, Understanding Modernism* (2024). LaRocca served as guest editor of a commemorative issue of *Conversations: The Journal of Cavellian Studies*, no. 7 (2019): *Acknowledging Stanley Cavell*, and edited *The Thought of Stanley Cavell and Cinema: Turning Anew to the Ontology of Film a Half-Century after* The World Viewed (2020), *Inheriting Stanley Cavell: Memories, Dreams, Reflections* (2020), *Movies with Stanley Cavell in Mind* (2021), and *Television with Stanley Cavell in Mind* (2023, coedited with Sandra Laugier). He is the editor of *The Philosophy of Documentary Film: Image, Sound, Fiction, Truth* (2017), and author of "Contemplating the Sounds of Contemplative Cinema: Stanley Cavell and Kelly Reichardt" (2021) and "From Lectiocentrism to Gramophonology: Listening to Cinema and Writing Sound Criticism" (2022). www.DavidLaRocca.org

John T. Lysaker is William R. Kenan Professor of Philosophy and Director of the Center for Ethics at Emory University. His work explores conditions for human flourishing and so moves across ethics, the philosophy of art, and philosophical psychology. Included among his various monographs and papers are several engagements with the work of Cavell including *Emerson & Self-Culture* (2008), *After Emerson* (2017), *Philosophy, Writing, & the Character of Thought* (2018), and *Hope, Trust, and Forgiveness: Essays in Finitude* (2023), which elaborates a conception of perfectionism in the context of improvisation. He is also the author of *Ambient 1: Brian Eno's Music for Airports* (2018), which situates that seminal album in the context of experimental music, including the theories and compositions of John Cage.

Paul Standish is Professor and Head of the Centre for Philosophy of Education at the University College London Institute of Education (UCLIOE). He has extensive teaching experience in schools, colleges, and universities, and his research reflects that range. He is the author or editor of some twenty books, with a sustained interest in Wittgenstein extending from his *Beyond the Self: Wittgenstein, Heidegger, and the Limits of Language* (1992) to *Wittgenstein* *and Education: On Not Sparing Others the Trouble of Thinking* (2023), coedited with Adrian Skilbeck. He is the author of many essays on Stanley Cavell, as well as coeditor with Naoko Saito of two books: *Stanley Cavell and the Education of Grownups* (2012) and *Stanley Cavell and Philosophy as Translation: The Truth is Translated* (2017). He is President of the Philosophy of Education Society of Great Britain and coeditor of the *Journal of Philosophy of Education.*

Garrett Stewart is James O. Freedman Professor of Letters at the University of Iowa, and since 2010, a member of the American Academy of Arts and Sciences. He contributed "The Avoidance of Stanley Cavell" to *Contending with Stanley Cavell* (2005); wrote about Cavell, Emerson, Poe, and Wittgenstein in *The Deed of Reading: Literature * Writing * Language * Philosophy* (2015; see especially chapter 4, "Imp-aired Words"); and addressed *The World Viewed* in "'Assertions in Technique': Tracking the Medial Thread in Cavell's Filmic Ontology" for *The Thought of Stanley Cavell and Cinema* (Bloomsbury, 2020, ed. David LaRocca). His most recent books include *The Metanarrative Hall of Mirrors* (Bloomsbury, 2022), *Streisand: The Mirror of Difference* (2023), and *Attention Spans: Garrett Stewart, a Reader* (Bloomsbury, 2024, ed. David LaRocca).

INDEX